Core Civil Procedure

Core Civil Procedure
Learning Through Multiple-Choice Questions

Ray Brescia

HON. HAROLD R. TYLER CHAIR IN LAW AND TECHNOLOGY
PROFESSOR OF LAW
ALBANY LAW SCHOOL

CAROLINA ACADEMIC PRESS
Durham, North Carolina

Library of Congress Cataloging-in-Publication Data

Names: Brescia, Ray, author.
Title: Core civil procedure : learning through multiple-choice questions /
Ray Brescia.
Description: Durham, North Carolina : Carolina Academic Press, LLC, [2023]
Identifiers: LCCN 2023000061 (print) | LCCN 2023000062 (ebook) | ISBN
9781531026110 (paperback) | ISBN 9781531026127 (epub)
Subjects: LCSH: Civil procedure--United States--Examinations, questions,
etc. | LCGFT: Study guides.
Classification: LCC KF8841 .B733 2023 (print) | LCC KF8841 (ebook) | DDC
347.73/5--dc23/eng/20230403
LC record available at https://lccn.loc.gov/2023000061
LC ebook record available at https://lccn.loc.gov/2023000062

CAROLINA ACADEMIC PRESS
700 Kent Street
Durham, North Carolina 27701
(919) 489-7486
www.cap-press.com

Printed in the United States of America

Contents

Introduction

Welcome and Overview

This guide is designed to supplement and build your knowledge around the topic of civil procedure. It does so through multiple-choice questions designed to test and deepen your understanding of the topic through the concept of *deliberate practice*, which is work toward an obtainable but far-off goal, with constant feedback. As you work through the material in this guide, you will slowly build your understanding of the core concepts of civil procedure and move on to the next topic area once you have done so. Use this guide to supplement a class on civil procedure and as preparation for the bar exam. While this guide focuses mostly on the specific rules relevant to civil procedure in the federal courts, and it certainly serves as an effective and useful complement to a course on federal civil procedure, the core concepts it covers are relevant to litigation in state courts as well. Because of its emphasis on the specific rules governing litigation in the federal courts in the United States, it is also useful for practitioners not used to the functioning of the federal courts who might want to develop a greater facility with and knowledge of their practices.

While many of the questions in this guide are a bit more complex and challenging than what one might find in a typical bar exam, their relative difficulty will prepare you well to spot the key issues, identify the knowledge a particular question is testing, and select the correct answer in the sometimes more straightforward questions you might typically see in a bar examination. Working with these questions will also facilitate your ability to read critically and effectively and train you to do so more quickly, which are all skills you will need in any examination.

In addition to the questions themselves, at the end of each chapter there is a Formative Assessment Quiz which helps you gauge your understanding of the material in that chapter. The answer key in Chapter 9 provides just the correct answer to each question in the book and Chapter 10 then provides an in-depth explanation for each answer. Those explanations contain not just the answer but also the sources for the answer, from the Federal Rules of Civil Procedure, statutory law, and case law. Use these explanations to not just understand the questions you got wrong and identify the concepts with which you may struggle but also to ensure you are understanding the things you got right. Think of them as a coach along the way. This coaching is a particularly important aspect of deliberate practice.

You can use the Formative Assessment Quiz when you have concluded your work in a given chapter. You can also wait to take the Formative Assessment Quiz until you have finished a few chapters and have it serve as a "midterm exam," to test your understanding of the issues at different points in the semester or during the course of your studies. Note that instead of a Formative Assessment Quiz, Chapter 8 contains a Summative Assessment Quiz. This is an excellent way to review the material contained in the entire guide and to prepare for a final examination as well as the bar exam.

This guide is structured by chapters devoted to different topics and sub-topics related to a particular chapter's broad subject matter. You can work through the material in each chapter and follow along with a course or bar review based on the topical sections in each chapter.

What This Guide Covers, and What It Does Not

This course is designed to introduce the reader to the issues that are typically covered in an introductory course on federal civil procedure, one taught in every law school in the United States. Because of that, there are comprehensive chapters on core concepts like personal jurisdiction, subject matter jurisdiction, and pleadings. There is also a chapter on joinder of claims and parties, which, in many ways, builds on the lessons of personal jurisdiction and subject matter jurisdiction. The chapters on discovery and trials and appeals are less comprehensive, partly because those subjects tend to be less of a focus of the introductory course and students can learn more on those topics in an upper-level course or courses. Similarly, this guide does not cover the topics that tend to be covered more in upper-level courses on federal jurisdiction, advanced civil procedure, or even constitutional law, like standing, class actions, interpleader, and other similar topics.

A Note to Students

This book is designed to be *modular*. You can follow along with whatever course plan or casebook your instructor may use, aligning your work in this guide with the structure and order of materials your instructor uses. Try to refrain from diving into material you have not yet learned in whatever course you are taking. The understanding and skills you will gain from working through this guide will occur through testing your knowledge of the information learned in a traditional course. It will also strengthen that learning. At the same time, it is no substitute for what you will learn in a traditional course.

First and foremost, you should use the information you learn from these exercises to deepen your understanding of the knowledge you are supposed to be developing. In addition, you can also use these exercises to gather information about *you*, how well you are absorbing the material, the effectiveness of your study strategies, etc. Use this second-order information to hone in on not only your strengths but also your weaknesses so you can build on the former and shore up the latter.

One more important note: given the format of the answers, it is very difficult to take these questions and then look for the answer after each question. You will invariably see the answer to the next question. At a minimum, it is recommended that you take the questions in a particular section before looking up the answers.

Taking Multiple-Choice Exams

Multiple-choice questions are challenging. It is easy to get lost in the weeds of the fact pattern: you may think it is taking you in one direction, and then you find the question is completely different from what you were anticipating. Once you start on that other direction, certain facts and issues will seem important to you, and when you get to the call of the question, you find that you might have to read the question all over again. I am sorry to report that this is often the express design of the questions you will face. Figuring out how to sort out the signal from the noise is a critical skill you will need to develop. In addition, having potential answers available to you might give you some degree of comfort, but those can be deceptive, and just because the wording of a potential answer might seem *familiar* to you does not mean that it is *correct*. The key question to ask with every multiple-choice question is "What knowledge is this question testing?" There can be many false paths, red herrings, and dead ends in a multiple-choice question (to mix my metaphors!). When trying to answer a multiple-choice question, you must identify the specific nugget of knowledge, regarding a very particular issue, that is the focus of the question. A question cannot cover every possible issue under the sun, and practically every question is trying to assess your understanding of a very discrete topic. In order to ensure you can focus on what knowledge a particular question is testing, use the following approach, one that I call, with a nod to popular culture, *using the F.O.R.C.E.*

F. *Find* the question:

Turn first to the call of the question to get a general sense of what the exam question is asking. It might require you to read the last sentence or two of the fact pattern if the question itself is opaque, such as when it says something like "Should the motion to dismiss be granted?" Finding the question first helps you avoid turning down a distracting and diverting path in the fact pattern.

O. *Observe*:

What are the facts of the fact pattern and how do they relate to the call of the question?

R. *Reorient*:

This is the most important step. Once you have read the call of the question and understand the facts, you now ask yourself, "What knowledge is this question testing?" Once you can focus in on that, it will likely make certain facts more salient and important than others. Then you can focus on the important ones and orient yourself toward the direction in which the question is truly going.

C. *Codify*:

Here, you are going to identify the applicable rule that addresses the question presented. It is the next logical step following Step 3; once you have re-oriented yourself to understand what knowledge the question is testing, you can then align the question, facts, and the appropriate rule that governs the situation. And when we say "rule" in the context of a federal civil procedure exam, sometimes it means a specific Federal Rule of Civil Procedure, and sometimes it means a rule that comes from a statute or case law. It can even come from the U.S. Constitution itself. For example, if the knowledge the question is testing is your knowledge of general personal jurisdiction (*see* Chapter 2), the "rule" to apply in that situation is derived, very loosely, from the U.S. Constitution but really is found in case law. Whatever the situation, apply the correct and appropriate "small r" rule to fact pattern and question presented.

E. *Execute*:

Finally, it is time to look at the potential answers offered to you. Here, you will choose the answer that best matches your identification of the knowledge tested in Step 3 and your codification of the answer in Step 4. Really try to figure out what the answer should be before you look at the potential answers. And be aware of "traps"—for example, you might see an answer that sounds familiar and want to choose it as a result, but the answer might only be familiar because it relates to a legitimate rule in the pantheon of civil procedure rules, not because it is actually the proper rule to apply in a given situation.

Once again, the most important step in this process is Step 3. Every multiple-choice question is testing specific knowledge. Once you can hone in on what specific knowledge a particular question is testing, the extraneous issues melt away, and the answer should become clear. It takes some practice to utilize this approach, and you can experiment with it without time constraints at first. Eventually, it will become habitual. You will find that it actually makes reading less time-consuming (with less time spent rereading the question), and your answering the question will go more quickly.

Using Multiple-Choice Questions to Deepen Your Learning and Prepare for Essay-Based Questions

First, while the questions in this guide stand on their own and can be utilized to develop your understanding of particular issues at face value, you can also use them creatively to further deepen your learning. First, you can take apart a particular question and manipulate the facts to determine whether a change in facts might change the outcome. For example, when it comes to the subject matter jurisdiction of the federal courts (*see* Chapter 3), diversity jurisdiction may be available based on the citizenship of a particular party given its state of incorporation, as presented in the fact pattern on a given question. What happens if that citizenship changes? What change will change the outcome? Which will not? You can play around with each of the fact patterns in each question to help you develop a deeper understanding of the application of the different rules in particular situations. This can also help prepare you for anything—any iteration of a range of general facts that dictate the results in a particular situation. Pull together a study group of your colleagues. Have each of you change the fact pattern of a few questions and then share those changed fact patterns within the group. (Study groups are highly recommended generally.)

On a related note, you will probably notice that for a small percentage of questions, the fact patterns appear very similar. That is by design. For a few questions, this guide uses this method to test your knowledge and understanding of the material by borrowing some facts from a previous question and changing them up a bit. The basic elements of the question may even come from a different chapter altogether. Do not be fooled into thinking the question is the same, and, as a result, the answer and outcome are the same as well. Sometimes the facts change, but it does not necessarily change the outcome. At other times, the facts will change, and it *will* change the outcome. If you develop an ability to identify these situations and determine what changes to the outcome, if any, may occur as a result of those changes, you are on the road to mastery.

Second, since many law school exams and bar examinations include essay questions, any one of the questions contained in this guide can be converted into an essay question. Just ignore the potential answers and ask yourself, "How would I answer this question if it were an essay?" You can elaborate on the given facts and expand the issues you want to address, but you can certainly use these fact patterns as prompts for an essay-based question and answer. Again, pull together a study group to help expand your capacity to do this by tackling a number of questions in this way.

A Note to Instructors

The chapters in this guide are presented in a particular order, one commonly used in an introductory federal civil procedure course. At the same time, as described above, the chapters and the sections found within them are modular. You can align them with your course syllabus and assign them by chapter and even section within specific chapters to correspond to the structure and order of your course. Students can use the Formative Assessment Quizzes that conclude each chapter as a way to chart their progress on a particular topic, or you could recommend that students use those quizzes together as a "midterm" of sorts. If, for example, after the first month or so of class, you have covered personal jurisdiction and subject matter jurisdiction, you can recommend that students take the Formative Assessment Quizzes at the ends of Chapters 2 and 3 together, as a way to assess their progress and understanding of the material. The Summative Assessment Quiz (Chapter 9) can also serve as a good review prior to your final exam. Once again, I do not see the materials in this guide as supplanting anything you are teaching, or as a substitute for it, but rather as a way to supplement the important work you are doing inside and outside the classroom.

Acknowledgments

I have long been interested in and intrigued by the subject of civil procedure since my first days at law school. Because of that interest, I have sought out and benefited from the mentorship of many wonderful teachers and colleagues who have taught me so much over the years. This interest in civil procedure probably started in my first class in law school, taught by the late Geoffrey Hazard. Working alongside Harold Hongju Koh and the late Michael Ratner on several cases was incredibly rewarding and edifying. Clerking for the Hon. Constance Baker Motley was a gift. I learned so much from all of these mentors. Fellow civil procedure instructors at Albany Law School have also taught me so much, including current colleagues Rosemary Queenan, Connie Mayer, and Nina Farnia. Former colleagues Donna Young and Dale Moore were so very patient, kind, and generous to me when I first started teaching in this area. Former colleague Joe Buffington also helped to sharpen my approach to writing multiple-choice questions. In addition, Polly Boyle, Alice Broussard, Noah Chase, Paige Gottorff, Danielle Piccone, and Taylor Yensan offered editorial assistance with this guide, and my intrepid colleague Sherri Meyer offers tireless assistance in all of my work. Finally, the fantastic team at Carolina Academic Press has been wonderful to work with, including Carol McGeehan, Ryland Bowman, Jennifer Hill, and Scott Sipe. More than anything, though, this guide is a product of countless conversations and mutual learning with students in my civil procedure class, who have taught me so much. This book is a small token of my appreciation of them.

Core Civil Procedure

Chapter 1

Personal Jurisdiction

This first substantive chapter covers personal jurisdiction and related issues like service of process, venue, and the doctrine of *forum non conveniens*. The concept of personal jurisdiction—the power of a court over the parties before it—is elemental. This chapter will address the core concepts related to personal jurisdiction, which center around notions of due process. When is it fair for a court to exercise power over a particular party? Until the middle of the twentieth century, the authority of courts to exercise this power was often limited to the territorial reach of those courts. A court located in Oregon, for example, was generally recognized as having the ability to exercise power over only those individuals and things physically located within the confines of that state. A party who was an out-of-state resident yet was served with legal process while in a particular state would be subject to the court's jurisdiction in that state. On the other hand, a party who was physically outside of the state was also considered outside the jurisdiction of the court of that state. In the landmark case of *International Shoe v. Washington*, 326 U.S. 310 (1945), the Supreme Court determined that an out-of-state defendant with certain contacts with the forum state could be subject to personal jurisdiction in that forum state, and, since that decision, courts have recognized the authority of courts to exercise personal jurisdiction over parties located outside the borders of the state, and even the country, where the court is located. This chapter will address the different issues related to personal jurisdiction. The first sections explore the different approaches to personal jurisdiction—that of specific personal jurisdiction and general personal jurisdiction. It then addresses some additional mechanisms for securing personal jurisdiction over parties and then tests your knowledge of these concepts in a section that covers each of these different ways of obtaining personal jurisdiction over a party. It then introduces the concept of venue—the location where a particular dispute will be resolved—as well as the doctrine of *forum non conveniens*: the notion that while there might be a forum in which a dispute could be heard, there are good reasons for resolving it in a different forum. As in all chapters, this one concludes with a Formative Assessment Quiz that tests your understanding of these concepts.

1.1 Specific Jurisdiction

The first category of personal jurisdiction discussed here is the notion of specific jurisdiction. This manner of obtaining personal jurisdiction over a party hinges on the extent to which a party could reasonably anticipate that their actions within a particular forum could lead to them being sued in court and the extent to which those actions were purposeful or intentional. If a party takes actions related to or directed at a particular forum, then if those actions cause harm in the forum, the exercise of personal jurisdiction in a lawsuit connected to those actions does not violate the due process rights of the party. This section poses a few questions on the basic contours of specific personal jurisdiction as an introduction. We will return in Section 1.5 to more challenging questions that cover the range of issues related to personal jurisdiction, including testing your ability to synthesize the different aspects of this form of personal jurisdiction and others.

1. SPI is a Japanese manufacturer of heavy-duty surveillance drones. They are sold and marketed throughout the world through a network of local dealers in each country in which SPI does business. Sales to residents of the United States are shipped from SPI's U.S. distributor, Drones-R-US, which is based in the state of Oregon. One of SPI's drones, what it calls the "Texas Longhorn," is specifically designed by SPI and built for cattle ranchers in Texas so that they can use a video camera mounted on the drone to monitor their herds of cattle over the large expanses of the Texas plains. The Texas Longhorn is marketed at trade shows in Texas by Drones-R-US representatives, with instructions by SPI to market it at such events. SPI has no other contact with the state of Texas. It is a Japanese company, incorporated under the laws of Japan and located in Osaka, Japan. Drones-R-US is incorporated in Delaware, with its principal place of business in Oregon. One day, as a rancher is using a drone purchased from Drones-R-US at one of these Texas trade shows to monitor her herds outside of Waco, Texas, the drone loses control

and kills one of the rancher's prize bulls, valued at $100,000. Rancher sues SPI and Drones-R-US in federal district court for the Western District of Texas, the site of the injury, invoking the court's diversity jurisdiction over her state tort claims.

Drones-R-US waives any objection to personal jurisdiction, but SPI challenges personal jurisdiction over it. Assume the Texas long-arm statute would vest the court with personal jurisdiction over SPI. Rancher is a resident and citizen of Texas.

Can the court exercise personal jurisdiction over SPI? If so, why? If not, why not?

A. The court cannot exercise personal jurisdiction over SPI because to do so would offend traditional notions of fair play and substantial justice.

B. The court can exercise personal jurisdiction over SPI because it purposefully availed itself of the protections of the state of Texas and could reasonably foresee being haled into court there.

C. The court cannot exercise personal jurisdiction over SPI because it did not purposefully avail itself of the protections of Texas and could not reasonably foresee being haled into court there.

D. The court can exercise personal jurisdiction over SPI because its contacts with the state of Texas are systematic and continuous so that it is essentially at home in the forum state.

2. In *World-Wide Volkswagen v. Woodson*, 444 U.S. 286 (1980), the court found that a court had to weigh several reasonableness factors to determine whether it could exercise personal jurisdiction over an out-of-state defendant.

Which of the following is NOT one of the *World-Wide Volkswagen* reasonableness factors?

A. The forum state's interest in adjudicating the dispute.

B. The interest in having the trial of a diversity case in a forum that is at home with the law that must govern the action.

C. The interstate judicial system's interest in obtaining the most efficient resolution of controversies.

D. The shared interest of the several states in furthering fundamental substantive social policies.

1.2 General Jurisdiction

This section explores the issue of general jurisdiction, a departure from the focus on the specific contacts a party has with a particular dispute to a focus on a party's potentially deeper connections to the subject forum.

3. Brighter-Mayer (BM), a large multinational corporation, manufactures and distributes Plarex, a medication that helps to reduce blurry vision in individuals recovering from cataract surgery. Plarex is manufactured in a BM processing plant in Bridgeport, Connecticut, which it constructed five years ago and which has been in operation there since. BM operates a total of seven medication processing plants that process other medications distributed by BM, but all of these other such plants are located in Massachusetts and New Hampshire. Sale of Plarex constitutes 5% of BM's total global medication sales. BM is incorporated in Delaware, with its principal place of business in New Jersey. Plaintiffs are several individuals who ingested Plarex and complain that the medication gave them intense migraines over an extended period of time, and long after they were prescribed and ingested the medication. Plaintiffs are all residents and citizens of Ohio and Pennsylvania. BM engaged in aggressive marketing of the medication in both states but distributes the medication only through a mail-order program ad-

ministered through a distribution center in the state of Virginia. Plaintiffs bring an action based on state tort law seeking $1 million in damages based on their legitimate pain and suffering. Please assume these claims satisfy the amount-in-controversy requirement. Plaintiffs wish to file their action in federal court and expect to claim that BM is subject to personal jurisdiction on a theory of general jurisdiction.

In which state or states would a court likely find that BM is subject to personal jurisdiction on a theory of general jurisdiction?

A. Connecticut only.

B. Delaware only.

C. Delaware and New Jersey, but not Connecticut.

D. Delaware, New Jersey, and Connecticut.

4. Plaintiff brings an action in federal district court in Louisiana alleging banking fraud under federal law against Panhandle Bank (Panhandle). Panhandle is charged with opening and closing fraudulent accounts on behalf of its customers without their asking the bank to do so, and it charged those customers millions of dollars in fees when it took those actions. Plaintiff is a citizen of Louisiana, and his home is located in New Orleans, Louisiana. Panhandle is incorporated in Delaware, with its principal place of business in Gainesville, Florida. Plaintiff alleges that Panhandle violated federal law when the bank took these actions with respect to the fraudulent accounts. There is no allegation that these fraudulent actions took place in Louisiana but rather were carried out by workers in a bank back office in Gainesville, Florida. Panhandle is a regional bank, with branches spread throughout the Gulf Coast, including in Florida, Mississippi, Alabama, and Louisiana. It has at least twenty-five branches in each state and has been in Louisiana, uninterrupted, with no fewer than twenty branches operating in the state, since 1975, when it first entered into the Louisiana market. Plaintiff sues Panhandle, seeking $10,000 in damages allowed under the applicable federal statute. Panhandle chooses not to file a pre-answer motion to dismiss and instead files an answer in federal court alleging, among other things, that the court does not have personal jurisdiction over Panhandle.

How should the court view Panhandle's defense of lack of personal jurisdiction?

A. The court should consider the defense a weak one because Panhandle's contacts with the forum state are so systematic and continuous that the court will deem it at home in the forum state.

B. It should consider it a weak one because Panhandle has insufficient property in the jurisdiction to warrant the grant of *quasi in rem* jurisdiction.

C. It should consider it a strong one because Panhandle's actions in this case are not connected to the subject forum, so the exercise of personal jurisdiction over Panhandle in this case would offend traditional notions of fair play and substantial justice.

D. The court should consider it a weak one because Panhandle's connection to the forum state is not so systematic and continuous that it is at home in the forum state.

5. Defendant International Blue (Blue) is a business-to-business wholesaler of solar panels that sells its panels exclusively to areas outside the United States. Unbeknownst to Blue, it shipped a defective solar panel from its Upstate New York manufacturing plant to Mexico City, Mexico, to SolarMex, which sells and installs solar panels throughout Mexico, using Blue as its main supplier of panels. Blue is incorporated in Delaware, with its principal place of business in New York. Blue has extensive dealings with its international clients through its offices in Miami Beach, Florida. In a lot outside its offices there, it has solar panel farms where it displays its models. From the Miami Beach offices, Blue negotiates all of its international contracts of sale, including the one with SolarMex that results in the shipment of the defective solar panel. The defective solar panel, which was designed in North Carolina and manufactured in New York, malfunctions, which results in a massive fire at a waste treatment facility, killing dozens of workers and making thousands of area residents seriously ill. Family members of those killed as well as many area residents injured by the fire file a lawsuit in federal district court in Texas against Blue alleging defective product design as the proximate cause of Plaintiffs' injuries. Plaintiffs have chosen Texas as the site of the lawsuit because of Blue's contacts with the forum state. For the last ten years, various parts of some of Blue's different solar panel designs have been manufactured, and continue to be manufactured, in Blue's state-of-the-art, $500 million, Austin, Texas, manufacturing plant. Blue also periodically runs installation seminars for Blue's customers that purchase Blue's solar panels. These two-

day training sessions take place on site in Blue's Austin, Texas, manufacturing facility. These sessions occur about once every month and have taken place there for the last three years. Parts for the defective panel were not manufactured in the Texas plant, however. In addition, Solar-Mex's workers were trained in Texas, but there is no allegation that the panels were defectively installed or that the workers received inadequate training.

If Blue, the only Defendant in the action, challenges the Texas court's personal jurisdiction over it, should the court grant the motion to dismiss? If so, why? If not, why not?

A. The motion should be denied because Blue's contacts with the forum state are systematic and continuous even though they are not connected to the underlying dispute.

B. The motion should be granted because Blue's contacts with the forum state are not systematic and continuous but are connected to the underlying dispute.

C. The motion should be granted because Blue's contacts with the forum state are unrelated to the underlying dispute and are not systematic and continuous.

D. The motion should be granted because Blue's contacts with the forum state are not connected to the underlying dispute.

1.3 Other Issues Related to Personal Jurisdiction: Tag Jurisdiction, "Consent" Jurisdiction, and Long-Arm Statutes

This section will cover other issues related to personal jurisdiction, including so-called "tag" jurisdiction and the application of state long-arm statutes.

6. Plaintiff sues Defendant in federal court for the Central District of California, the district encompassing the city of Los Angeles. California's long-arm statute provides that it permits a court in California to exercise personal jurisdiction over parties before it to the full extent of the Due Process Clause of the U.S. Constitution. Plaintiff has established residency and citizenship in California, having moved his domicile from Oregon to Los Angeles six months prior to the filing of the suit by Plaintiff, and he has an intent to remain there indefinitely. Plaintiff's suit against Defendant is based on state law claims under Oregon law and pertains to Defendant's alleged breach of a contract between the parties. Plaintiff claims that Defendant failed to design a parking garage in Portland, Oregon, according to Plaintiff's specifications. Plaintiff argues that, according to the original designs he supplied to Defendant, Plaintiff was supposed to earn an additional $10,000 per month in parking fees, but Defendant's failure to design the garage according to Plaintiff's directions meant that the garage had fewer spaces than the original plans provided. The garage has been operating for a year now. Plaintiff seeks $120,000 in damages on the contract claim and future damages for the lost fees moving forward, unless and until the garage is redesigned to accommodate more cars. The contract between the parties was negotiated in Oregon prior to Plaintiff relocating to California, and all work done on the contract was performed by Defendant in Oregon. Defendant is a resident and citizen of Oregon. Unrelated to her contract with Plaintiff, Defendant was hired by a company in Los Angeles, California, to work as an engineering consultant in the effort to design a "Hyperloop," a rapid transit system that will operate between Los Angeles and San Francisco, California. In performing work on this other contract, Defendant travels to Los Angeles, California, as much as twice a month, for meetings that last up to three hours at a time. Defendant has been working in this capacity only for the three months immediately preceding Plaintiff's commencement of the suit between the parties.

Defendant has no contacts with the state of California other than those specified and did no work on Plaintiff's project while in California. Defendant is served, personally, in Los Angeles, on one of these business trips to work on the Hyperloop project.

If Defendant files a motion to dismiss Plaintiff's action by challenging the federal court in California's exercise of personal jurisdiction over her, will the court grant the motion? If so, why? If not, why not?

A. The court will grant the motion because Defendant's contacts with the forum state are unrelated to Plaintiff's claims against her and they are not so systematic and continuous to render her essentially at home in the forum state.

B. The court will deny the motion because the Defendant's contacts with the forum state are systematic and continuous such that she is essentially at home in the forum state.

C. The court will deny the motion because Defendant was served personally within the state of California.

D. The court will grant the motion because, although the Defendant was served personally in California, her presence in the state at the time of service was unrelated to Plaintiff's action.

7. Which of the following was NOT one of the reasons given by the different judicial opinions concurring in the judgment in *Burnham v. Superior Court*, 495 U.S. 604 (1990), as to why the exercise of personal jurisdiction was appropriate over an out-of-state defendant who was found physically within the forum state when he was served with process?

A. Service of process on an otherwise out-of-state defendant while he or she is physically within the forum state (so-called "tag" or transient jurisdiction) is a traditional method by which personal jurisdiction can be obtained over an otherwise out-of-state defendant, and thus it does not violate the Due Process Clause of the Fourteenth Amendment.

B. One who is physically present in a forum state has consented to the jurisdiction of the courts there.

C. An out-of-state defendant's presence in the forum state establishes the court's *quasi in rem* jurisdiction over the defendant sufficient for the court to exercise personal jurisdiction over the individual.

D. When visiting a state, an otherwise out-of-state defendant benefits from police and fire services and other protections when in that state, and thus he or she should be subject to the jurisdiction of the courts when there.

8. Plaintiffs are several tourists who were injured in a bus crash in Rome, Italy. One of the main reasons for the crash was a defect in both the design and the manufacturing of the bus's steering column. Because of the design flaw, substandard parts used in the manufacturing of the column gave way and caused the steering column to crack. As a result, the driver lost control of the steering, which ultimately led to the accident. The bus involved in the crash was a bus sold by General Motors (GM). It was assembled in a GM assembly plant in Michigan, with parts supplied by a Japanese company, Tokyo Manufacturing (Tokyo), and a Chinese one, Beijing Industries (Beijing). Beijing supplies its parts to companies throughout the world, including the United States, and it is aware that many of the vehicles in which its parts are placed ultimately make their way into the U.S. and European markets. The steering column in the bus involved in the accident was designed by GM in Detroit, Michigan. GM is based in Detroit, Michigan, where it has its principal place of business and where it is incorporated. Tokyo is incorporated in Japan, with its principal place of business in the city of Tokyo in that country. Tokyo also has a small plant in Tennessee where it manufactures steering columns for buses, including the steering column that ultimately made its way into the bus that caused the crash at the center of Plaintiffs' lawsuit. Beijing is incorporated in China, with its principal place of business in the city of Beijing in that country. Beijing's defective steering column parts were mailed directly from Beijing's plant in China to Tokyo's Tennessee plant, where they were incorporated into the defective steering column. The Plaintiffs are residents and citizens of North Carolina. They bring an action against GM, Tokyo, and Beijing in federal court in Tennessee, raising state law claims and seeking $20 million in damages. GM does not contest personal jurisdiction. Assume that neither Tokyo nor Beijing satisfies the long-arm statute of Tennessee.

Which of the following statements most accurately reflects the extent to which the court in Tennessee has or does not have personal jurisdiction over the defendants Tokyo and Beijing?

A. The court has personal jurisdiction over both Tokyo and Beijing.

B. The court has personal jurisdiction over Tokyo but not Beijing.

C. The court has personal jurisdiction over Beijing but not Tokyo.

D. The court has personal jurisdiction over neither Tokyo nor Beijing.

1.4 Service of Process and Waiver of Service of Process

This section deals with issues related to service of process—the mechanism for starting a lawsuit—as well as the procedures related to waiving formal service of process.

9. Arya wishes to bring an action against Bran claiming he engaged in fraudulent transactions involving his maintenance of her stock portfolio. Bran is Arya's stockbroker. Bran claimed that he was engaged in transactions on Arya's behalf, when, in reality, he was stealing money from Arya's portfolio while claiming that the losses were due to standard market fluctuations and not his malfeasance. Arya's portfolio was rather large, amounting to roughly $10 million, and Arya claims Bran stole at least $1 million from her. At the time of his servicing of Arya's account, Bran was a resident and citizen of New York. Arya is a resident and citizen of Connecticut. According to state law, as a stockbroker registered in New York, Bran must register with the state Department of Financial Services (DFS) and provide all customers with a post office box in the state of New York where he can receive mail. He must display this post office address prominently on all communications with those customers. Once Arya learns of Bran's deception, and Bran learns that Arya knows he has been stealing from her, Bran flees the state and no one knows his current whereabouts. Arya wants to bring an action based on violations of federal and state law against Bran seeking over $1 million in damages. She wishes to commence the action in federal court in New York where the deceptive practices are believed to have occurred. Arya's counsel communicates with the post office where Bran had registered his mailing address with DFS, and the postal clerk says that Bran recently cancelled the post office box and left no forwarding address. The postal clerk states that any mail sent to such a cancelled box will be returned to the sender of any mail directed to that box. Assume that New York law provides that when commencing an action in the state, a plaintiff may serve the defendant with a copy of the summons and complaint by first-class mail at the last known mailing address of the defendant and a post office box qualifies as a mailing address under the law. Arya's counsel, not knowing any other way of serving Bran with a copy of the summons and complaint, mails both documents to the post office box in New York that Bran had registered with DFS. Bran's counsel learns of the action by monitoring court filings and will appear in the action to contest service. Bran's counsel makes a pre-answer motion to dismiss, objecting to service of process and challenging the manner of service as insufficient.

Should Bran's counsel challenge the adequacy of the method of service utilized by Arya's counsel, will that effort succeed? If so, why? If not, why not?

A. Yes, because the failure to serve Bran personally when he was physically within the jurisdiction means the court cannot obtain personal jurisdiction over Bran.

B. Yes, because the manner of service utilized by Arya's counsel was not contemplated by the Federal Rules of Civil Procedure.

C. Yes, because the manner of service was not reasonably calculated to actually reach Bran.

D. No, because the fact that Bran was served personally within the forum, even if by mail, means the court can obtain personal jurisdiction over Bran.

10.   Plaintiff brings an action against Defendant for breach of contract. Plaintiff seeks over $100,000 for the claim, which is based on state law. Plaintiff, an individual, is a resident and citizen of New York. Defendant, also an individual, is a resident and citizen of Massachusetts. Defendant contracted to supply containers of sodas and carbonated water to Plaintiff's ice cream store at a set price and on a regular schedule. During a heat wave, and when Plaintiff's business was particularly busy, Defendant failed to supply the soda they were obligated to provide according to the schedule, and Plaintiff lost a substantial amount of business when they ran out of soda. New York law provides that a lawsuit can be commenced in the state against a defendant by serving that defendant with copies of the summons and complaint in the action by regular, first-class mail to the defendant's last known mailing address. Plaintiff's lawyer commences the action in federal district court for the Northern District of New York against Defendant and mails copies of the summons and complaint by regular, first-class mail to Defendant's last known address in Massachusetts. The address that Plaintiff's lawyer used was correct, and Defendant admits that they received these documents. Defendant will contest this manner of service when they submit the answer to Plaintiff's complaint.

Was service on Defendant in the manner in which it was carried out in Plaintiff's federal action authorized under the Federal Rules of Civil Procedure? If so, why? If not, why not?

A. No, the manner of service utilized by Plaintiff's counsel was not consistent with any manner of service permitted under the Federal Rules of Civil Procedure.

B. Yes, because the manner of service was consistent with the New York statute, it was authorized under the Federal Rules of Civil Procedure.

C. Yes, because Defendant admits they received the summons and complaint.

D. No, because the manner of service was not reasonably calculated to apprise the Defendant of the pendency of the action and afford Defendant an opportunity to present any objections to the suit.

11.   Manny is an adult, full-time, live-in domestic worker who cares for the young children of Jo and Kris, a married couple of prominent lawyers who practice in Albany County, New York, yet reside just over the border in the state of Massachusetts, in the town of Egremont. Manny, Jo, and Kris are all citizens of Massachusetts for personal jurisdiction purposes. Jo is the subject of a legal malpractice action alleging that Jo failed to file a massive personal injury action on behalf of a small group of plaintiffs who were injured by a release of toxic gas resulting from a train car explosion in the Port of Albany, in New York State. It is alleged that Jo failed to file the complaint in the action in a timely fashion, meaning it was barred by the applicable statute of limitations. The legal malpractice suit arises under state law and seeks $2 million in damages (which plaintiffs can easily show). Plaintiffs are all U.S. citizens who reside permanently in New York State. Plaintiffs commence their action against Jo in federal district court in the Northern District of New York, where they reside and where they claim the legal malpractice occurred (i.e., in Jo's office, where they had met with Jo and where the bulk of his actions and inactions on their behalf took place). Plaintiffs' counsel attempts to have a process server serve Jo with a copy of the summons and complaint in the action at his principal place of business, but the process server is unsuccessful at doing so there. Under a great deal of stress due to the bad press Jo is receiving from the alleged malpractice, Jo and Kris leave town for a long weekend at a spa in the Berkshires, leaving their children with Manny. The process server visits the home while Jo is not there, and Manny answers the

door after the process server rings the bell. The process server leaves a copy of the summons and complaint with Manny, asking that he give the documents to Jo.

Given these facts, has the process server properly effectuated service upon Jo under Rule 4 of the Federal Rules of Civil Procedure? If so, why? If not, why not?

A. Yes, because Jo was not home when the process server attempted to effectuate service upon Jo, the process server can leave a copy of the summons and complaint with anyone she finds at the home.

B. No, because Manny is not an immediate member of Jo's family.

C. Yes, because Manny is a person of suitable age and discretion who resides at Jo's usual place of abode.

D. No, because Manny is not a person of suitable age and discretion who resides at Jo's usual place of abode.

12. Dan Smith runs a restaurant. His 22-year-old son, Dan Jr., who is still looking for more lucrative work after recently graduating college, is one of the waiters at the restaurant. After graduation, the son moved back in to live with his parents in their home. Dan is being sued by a former business associate, Peter, in a separate business venture: a small, internet-based company that produces content for a mobile food application that helps consumers find stores that sell locally sourced food products. Dan had contracted with Peter to supply some content for the site: recipes for how to use the products the application helped its customers find. Dan was employed as an independent contractor by Peter, in his personal capacity (that is, the contract was with him individually, and not his restaurant). Because business at his restaurant was busy, and Dan was having second thoughts about revealing some of the secrets behind his famous recipes, he had dragged his feet on supplying content for the site and was in material breach of his contract with Peter. Peter was suing Dan to produce as promised under the contract, or, in the alternative, for a refund of some of the payments made to Dan under the contract because he had failed to deliver on his commitments. Peter commences the action in federal district court for the Northern District of New York, in Albany. Peter is a resident of Massachusetts and Dan is a resident of New York. The contract between Dan and Peter was executed in Massachusetts. Peter has sued Dan for $100,000, which represents the last six months of payments made to Dan, a period during which Dan did not satisfy his obligations under the contract. Soon after the suit is commenced, Peter's attor-

ney has a paralegal in her office attempt to serve Dan with the summons and complaint in the lawsuit. Because Dan works long hours, he is rarely home. After repeated attempts to serve him at his home, the process server goes to the restaurant with the summons and complaint. She appears at the restaurant at a time when business is slow: 4 p.m. on a Wednesday. She asks the person she meets at the waiter's station where she can find Dan Smith. The person she is speaking to is Dan Jr. He responds, "I'm Dan Smith." She hands him an envelope with the summons and complaint inside and says to him: "You've been served." Assume that the relevant state law on service of process is identical to the Federal Rules of Civil Procedure provisions and offers no alternate means of service in this situation. Assume, also, that Dan Jr. is not otherwise authorized to accept service for Dan Sr.

Without regard to any issues related to the merits of the action or whether the federal court would have subject matter jurisdiction over it, was the process server's effort to serve Dan Smith Sr. consistent with Rule 4 of the Federal Rules of Civil Procedure? If so, why? If not, why not?

A. Service was appropriate because service on a child of a named defendant is lawful under the Federal Rules of Civil Procedure.

B. Service was appropriate because Dan Jr. is a person of suitable age of discretion who resides with Dan Sr. at Dan Sr.'s dwelling.

C. Service was inappropriate because service was not effectuated on Dan Jr. at Dan Smith Sr.'s dwelling or usual place of abode.

D. Service was inappropriate because the party served is not a person of suitable age and discretion.

13. Plaintiff wants to bring an action against Defendant in federal court in the Northern District of New York alleging that Defendant engaged in unfair business practices. Plaintiff seeks over $100,000 for the claim, which is based on state law. Plaintiff, an individual, is a resident and citizen of New York. Defendant, also an individual, is a resident and citizen of Massachusetts. Most of the acts that form the basis of Plaintiff's claims occurred in New York, where Plaintiff operates her business. Defendant runs a rival gas station chain, and Plaintiff alleges that Defendant's agents engaged in intimidating tactics at and around Plaintiff's gas stations, all located in New York, to discourage Plaintiff's suppliers from doing business with Plaintiff. New York state law provides that a lawsuit can be commenced against an out-of-state defendant who engages in tortious acts within the state by serving that defendant with copies of the summons and complaint in the action if those documents are sent by regular, first-class mail to the defendant's last known mailing address. This manner of service is also consistent with Massachusetts law. Plaintiff's lawyer follows New York state law when she commences the action against Defendant and mails copies of the summons and complaint by regular, first-class mail to Defendant's last known address. The address that Plaintiff's lawyer used was correct and Defendant admits that he received the mailing. Nevertheless, Defendant wishes to contest this manner of service when he submits his answer to Plaintiff's complaint.

Was service on Defendant in the manner in which it was carried out in Plaintiff's federal action consistent with a manner of service authorized under the Federal Rules of Civil Procedure? If so, why? If not, why not?

A. No, the manner of service utilized by Plaintiff's counsel was not authorized under the FRCP because the Federal Rules of Civil Procedure does not expressly contemplate service by regular first-class mail to a person's last known address.

B. Yes, because the manner of service was consistent with the applicable state statute and thus authorized under the Federal Rules of Civil Procedure.

C. Yes, because Defendant admits he received the summons and complaint.

D. No, because the manner of service was not reasonably calculated to apprise the Defendant of the pendency of the action and afford Defendant an opportunity to present any objections to the suit.

14. MeBay is a popular online auction website that is embroiled in a controversy over certain auctions of supposedly pristine Buzz Lightyear figures which were held on its site at the time of the release of Toy Story Seven. MeBay is based in California and has a choice-of-forum clause in all of its Terms of Service agreements that requires that any dispute arising through its services must be resolved in federal court in California. It also requires that anyone active on the site—buyer or seller—must have a valid email account through which MeBay may communicate with him or her. It does not generally maintain mailing addresses for those who use its site. Knowing that many of the companies that pay taxes to the state are dependent on internet commerce, the state legislature in California recently passed legislation that authorizes litigants bringing actions in state court that involve internet commerce affecting the state to commence an action by using the most current and known email address of the defendant to effectuate service. The "Service-by-Email" statute, as it has come to be known, provides that the plaintiff cannot resort to service by email if the plaintiff has knowledge that a particular email account is no longer valid for the intended recipient (including if the plaintiff receives an error message when he or she attempts to use a particular email address that the email address is no longer valid or does not exist). When the Buzz Lightyear debacle occurs (it turns out that the Seller of the figures misrepresented the quality of the figures), MeBay wishes to sue the Seller in federal court on state fraud and contract claims. The Seller is a resident and citizen of Nevada. MeBay is incorporated in Delaware, with its principal place of business in California. MeBay commences suit in federal court in California and, because the case affects internet commerce, utilizes the California Service-by-Email law to effectuate service upon the Seller. Seller does not challenge the court's subject matter jurisdiction over the action, nor does he deny that he received the email containing the summons and complaint in the action. Seller will, nevertheless, challenge the constitutionality of the Service-by-Email statute and move to dismiss the action.

Will the court grant Seller's motion to dismiss based on the argument that the Service-by-Email statute is unconstitutional? If so, why? If not, why not?

A. No. The court will deny the motion because Seller actually received a copy of the summons and complaint.

B. Yes. The court will grant the motion because the manner of service used was not reasonably calculated under the circumstances to apprise the Seller of the pendency of the action.

C. No. The court will deny the motion if it finds that the manner of service used was reasonably calculated under the circumstances to apprise the Seller of the pendency of the action.

D. Yes. The court will grant the motion because MeBay failed to follow the Federal Rules of Civil Procedure in effectuating service on the Seller.

15. Laura is a lawyer representing a plaintiff in a civil action filed in federal court in the Southern District of New York. The action seeks damages under federal labor laws for unpaid wages under the Fair Labor Standards Act (FLSA). In a manner that complies with the requirements of Federal Rule of Civil Procedure (FRCP) 4(d) in all respects, Laura's counsel has sent a copy of the complaint in the action by regular mail to her client's employer, the defendant in the suit, requesting that the employer waive service of process of the summons. The employer is a corporation incorporated in New York State, with its principal place of business in New York State, and it is the address of that principal place of business where the request to waive service of the summons is mailed to an agent authorized to accept service on behalf of the corporation.

If the employer chooses not to waive service of process and has no good cause for refusing to waive service, which of the following does *not* describe the employer's position at this time?

A. The employer will have waived its right to contest personal jurisdiction.

B. The court will require that the employer pay the expenses incurred by Laura in ultimately effectuating service and the costs of making a motion to seek compensation for such expenses.

C. The employer will have to respond to the complaint within 21 days of ultimate receipt of the summons and complaint once it is formally served.

D. The employer will have to assert a defense based on a lack of personal jurisdiction, if it has one, in either its pre-answer motion to dismiss or in its answer.

16. Plaintiff, an individual who resides in New York State, files an action in federal court against Defendant, who is also a resident of New York State. Plaintiff seeks to have the Defendant waive initial service of the summons and complaint. Plaintiff mails the requisite forms under Rule 4 of the Federal Rules of Civil Procedure to request that Defendant waive such formal service. Defendant chooses to ignore the request to waive formal service of process, insisting that the Plaintiff follow the requirements for formal service of process upon them.

Which of the following is *not* a consequence of the Defendant refusing to waive formal service of process?

A. Defendant will be responsible for the cost incurred by the Plaintiff in formally serving the Defendant.

B. Defendant will be responsible for the reasonable expenses incurred in proving formal service of process upon Defendant.

C. Defendant will have waived any potential objection to venue.

D. Defendant will have to answer the complaint within twenty-one days of formal service of the summons and complaint.

1.5 "Mixed" Questions

This section will test your ability to apply your knowledge of the topics covered in previous sections.

17.   A group of plaintiffs brings a personal injury action against Defendant, the producer of Purple Cow, an energy drink, alleging the product resulted in an extreme allergic reaction in Plaintiffs. The four plaintiffs will each seek $100,000 in damages on state tort claims against Defendant, seeking a total of $400,000 in their action. Plaintiffs are all residents and citizens of California (the "California Plaintiffs"). The California Plaintiffs understand that Defendant is being sued in federal court in Nevada by residents and citizens of Nevada (the "Nevada Plaintiffs") for claims about the same product that the California Plaintiffs allege harmed them. The California Plaintiffs file their claims based on California and Nevada state law in federal court in Nevada, the same federal court where the action was filed by the Nevada Plaintiffs. Defendant does market and sell Purple Cow in Nevada to Nevada residents. Defendant also explicitly markets the product in Nevada to residents of other states, with billboards in and around the Las Vegas casinos that say things like "Ride Purple Cow All the Way Home to Los Angeles," and "Purple Cow: What Visitors from San Diego Crave When They're Up All Night." The California Plaintiffs allege that they saw these and other similar advertisements while visiting Nevada casinos and purchased and ingested the product in that state as a result. Defendant is incorporated in Delaware, with its principal place of business in New York. It does roughly 5% of its overall business in the state of Nevada. The Purple Cow product is itself manufactured in South Dakota, at Defendant's processing plant there. Assume that Nevada's long-arm statute provides that it permits a court in the state to exercise personal jurisdiction in any manner consistent with the Due Process Clause of the U.S. Constitution. Defendant does not challenge personal jurisdiction in the action brought by the Nevada Plaintiffs. In the action brought by the California Plaintiffs, however, Defendant will argue that the exercise of personal jurisdiction over Defendant in a Nevada federal court in that action violates the Due Process Clause of the Fifth and Fourteenth Amendments to the U.S. Constitution and moves to dismiss the California Plaintiffs' actions on that ground.

Will the court grant Defendant's motion to dismiss the case filed by the California Plaintiffs in the federal court in Nevada? If so, why? If not, why not?

A.   No, because the injuries suffered by the California Plaintiffs are connected to Defendant's actions in Nevada.

B.   No, because Defendant's connections to Nevada are so systematic and continuous that Defendant is essentially at home in that forum.

C.   No, since Defendant has consented to the jurisdiction of the federal court over litigation involving the Nevada Plaintiffs, Defendant has consented to the exercise of personal jurisdiction in any similar action filed in that same district.

D. Yes, but only if the court finds Defendant's connections to the jurisdiction are not so systematic and continuous that they are essentially at home in the forum.

18. Defendant is the head of a publicly traded company that has invested heavily in a cryptocurrency, CatCoin. Defendant has a personal share of CatCoin that is significant, equaling tens of millions of dollars based on the current valuation of the coin. Defendant has gained some notoriety as a public figure and is even invited to host a television comedy show, Friday Night Live. While Defendant is giving her opening monologue on the show, which all guest hosts give, she expresses her support for cryptocurrencies as the "wave of the future" and expressly mentions CatCoin. She also says, "Don't mess around with those other cryptos, like BritCoin, they're a scam." Plaintiff is an investor in the rival cryptocurrency BritCoin. After Defendant's statement on national television, the value of CatCoin skyrockets and that of BritCoin drops considerably, causing Plaintiff a financial loss of tens of millions of dollars. Defendant, a recent immigrant to the United States who has permanent residency status in the United States, has only visited New York City and New York State once, the day she hosted Friday Night Live. The show concluded recording at 11:00 p.m. on the evening the show aired. Defendant was on her private jet by 1 a.m. the next morning and did not sleep even one night in New York State. Plaintiff's lawyer commences suit in federal district court in New York alleging several federal law theories of recovery all based on Defendant's statements criticizing BritCoin during her monologue on Friday Night Live. That monologue was given at the Friday Night Live studio in Manhattan, New York. Defendant is a resident of Florida. Plaintiff's lawyer serves Defendant personally with a copy of the summons and complaint at their Florida

home. Defendant will seek to dismiss the complaint for the New York court's lack of personal jurisdiction over them.

Will the court grant Defendant's motion to dismiss the case for lack of personal jurisdiction? If so, why? If not, why not?

A. No, because Defendant was served personally at her home.

B. Yes, because Defendant does not have sufficient contacts with the forum.

C. No, because Defendant has sufficient contacts with the forum.

D. Yes, because Defendant is not at home in the forum.

19.   Northland Granite (Northland) is a corporation incorporated in Delaware, with its principal place of business in New Hampshire. Northland supplies granite to building contractors throughout the United States. It extracts all of its granite from quarries located in Rhode Island. It has operated as a business continuously since 1901 and has mined granite from the Rhode Island quarries since that time. Trucks owned by Northland pick up the granite from the quarries in Rhode Island and drive through Massachusetts to bring the granite to Northland's plants in New Hampshire. The granite is then shipped out from those plants directly to the contractors who use the granite. Northland is currently supplying granite to an educational institution in the City of Albany in New York State. A Northland truck driving through Vermont on its way to Albany strikes a cyclist, leaving him paralyzed. The cyclist is a resident of New Jersey who was in Vermont on vacation at the time of the accident. The cyclist commences an action against Northland in federal court on state tort law theories of recovery seeking over $3 million in damages and asserting diversity jurisdiction. For the purposes of this question, please assume that all states listed below have a long-arm statute that permits courts in the state to exercise jurisdiction over any party in a manner that is consistent with the full reach of the Due Process Clause of the U.S. Constitution.

Federal courts in which of the following groupings of states will have personal jurisdiction over Northland in an action filed by the cyclist?

A. New Jersey and New York.

B. Vermont, Rhode Island, and Massachusetts.

C. Vermont, Delaware, and New Hampshire.

D. New Hampshire and New Jersey.

20. Defendant, pharmaceutical company Sackville-Baggins (S-B), has been charged with an illegal scheme to promote opioid use that, it is alleged, has led to addiction, disease, and death among those who have had S-B's medication prescribed to them in a reckless manner. S-B is incorporated in Delaware, with its principal place of business in New York. Defendant faces multiple lawsuits regarding this alleged practice. In one case, filed by New York residents in federal court in the Northern District of New York asserting federal and state claims, S-B is alleged to have engaged in the fraudulent scheme by promoting its product extensively within New York State. The plaintiffs in this action are all residents of New York State who had the product marketed to them within the state and prescribed to them in the state. They also ingested the product in the state. A second group of plaintiffs are residents of Connecticut. They advance similar legal claims as those raised in the action by the New York Plaintiffs, but their state law claims are based in Connecticut law. Unlike the New York Plaintiffs, S-B marketed to these Connecticut Plaintiffs in Connecticut, where they were prescribed the medication and ingested it. The Connecticut residents wish to commence an action against S-B, also in federal court. S-B will likely raise the defense of lack of personal jurisdiction to any claim filed by the Connecticut Plaintiffs unless the action is filed in a federal court in Connecticut. Assume that in all jurisdictions listed below, the relevant long-arm statute allows courts to exercise personal jurisdiction to the full extent permitted under the U.S. Constitution's Due Process Clause.

In addition to the federal courts in Connecticut, in the federal courts of what other states, if any, can the Connecticut Plaintiffs commence their action against S-B such that the court will certainly have personal jurisdiction over S-B?

A. New York only.

B. New York and Delaware.

C. Any state in which S-B purposefully availed itself of the benefits of the forum when marketing its medications to the citizens of that state.

D. In no states other than Connecticut.

21. Plaintiff sues the Baja Surfboard Company (Baja), the largest and most popular surfboard company in the world, alleging personal injuries based on product defects in violation of California state tort law. Baja is incorporated in Mexico, with its principal place of business in Rosarito Beach, in northwest Mexico. Baja does not need to market its products because it is generally recognized as manufacturing the world's best surfboards. It sells all of its products out of its lone surf shop located in Rosarito Beach or out of its warehouse located in the border town of Tecate, Mexico. Plaintiff is a resident and citizen of California who surfs off the coast of Santa Cruz, California. Plaintiff is injured off the coast of California when the Baja surfboard she is using malfunctions, splitting in two and casting her against the rocks. She suffers extensive physical injuries and is mentally scarred. Plaintiff sues Baja in federal court for the Northern District of California, seeking $2 million in damages under state tort theories of recovery. Baja sells roughly 10% of its global sales through wholesale and retail sales to Californians, which it has done consistently for the sixty years of the company's existence. Because the boards are so delicate, Baja refuses to ship them to purchasers. Instead, individuals who wish to purchase Baja boards directly from Baja and companies that sell Baja surfboards to their own customers can only purchase Baja boards by physically visiting Baja's own surf shop in Rosarito Beach or its warehouse in Tecate. Plaintiff purchased her Baja board from a local surf shop in Santa Cruz, California. This shop operates completely independently from Baja. The owner of that surf shop, like other surf shops, purchased all of its

Baja boards directly from the Baja warehouse in Mexico by going there in person. Baja will challenge the court's ability to exercise personal jurisdiction over it in a California court. Plaintiff will argue that the court has both specific and general jurisdiction over Baja. Assume that California's long-arm statute allows a court to exercise personal jurisdiction over an out-of-state defendant in any manner consistent with the Due Process Clause of the U.S. Constitution.

Which statement accurately reflects the California federal court's ability to exercise personal jurisdiction over Baja in a manner that is consistent with the Due Process Clause of the U.S. Constitution?

A. The court has specific but not general jurisdiction over Baja.

B. The court has general but not specific jurisdiction over Baja.

C. The court has both general and specific jurisdiction over Baja.

D. The court has neither general nor specific jurisdiction over Baja.

22. A small group of plaintiffs brings a personal injury action against Defendant, a pharmaceutical company, alleging a medicine produced and sold by Defendant worsened their symptoms. The four plaintiffs each seek $100,000 in damages on state tort claims against Defendant, seeking a total of $400,000 in their action. Plaintiffs are all residents and citizens of California (the "California Plaintiffs"). The California Plaintiffs understand Defendant is also being sued in federal court in Nevada by residents of Nevada (the "Nevada Plaintiffs") for claims concerning the same medicine that the California Plaintiffs allege harmed them. For the convenience of their lawyers who are also based in Nevada and the perceived convenience of Defendant, the California Plaintiffs file their claims based on California state law in the same federal court as the action filed by the Nevada Plaintiffs. Defendant has extensive contacts with the state of Nevada regarding the sale and distribution of the medication that is at the center of the separate complaints filed on behalf of both the California and Nevada Plaintiffs. Defendant does market and sell this medication in Nevada to Nevada residents, but there is no allegation that any California Plaintiff purchased or ingested it in Nevada. At the same time, there are also no allegations that the medication that was ingested by the California Plaintiffs was manufactured in Nevada. Furthermore, the California Plaintiffs do not allege that Defendant marketed the medication from Nevada to the California Plaintiffs, or even that the California Plaintiffs were marketed the medication when they were present in Nevada, which they visited with some frequency. Defendant is incorporated in Delaware, with its principal place of business in New York. Assume that Nevada's long-arm statute provides that it permits a court in the state to exercise personal jurisdiction in any manner consistent with the Due Process Clause of the U.S. Constitution. Defendant does not challenge personal jurisdiction in the action brought by the Nevada Plaintiffs but nevertheless argues that the exercise of personal jurisdiction over Defendant in a Nevada federal court in an action brought by the California Plaintiffs violates the Due Process Clause of the Fourteenth Amendment to the U.S. Constitution and moves to dismiss the California plaintiffs' actions on that ground.

Will the court grant the motion to dismiss the case filed by the California Plaintiffs in the federal court in Nevada? If so, why? If not, why not?

A. Yes, because the injuries suffered by the California Plaintiffs are not connected to Defendant's actions in Nevada.

B. No, because Defendant's connections to Nevada are so systematic and continuous that Defendant is essentially at home in that forum.

C. No, since Defendant has consented to the jurisdiction of the federal court over litigation involving the same medication that injured the California Plaintiffs in the action filed by the Nevada Plaintiffs in federal court in Nevada, Defendant has consented to the exercise of personal jurisdiction in any similar action filed in that court.

D. Yes, but only if the court finds Defendant's connections to the jurisdiction are not so systematic and continuous that they are essentially at home in the forum.

23.   In the town of Godric's Hollow, Massachusetts, located near the New York-Massachusetts border, is a popular gas station owned and operated by Bess Oil. Because the state tax on gasoline is lower in Massachusetts, customers of Bess Oil pay far less per gallon for gasoline in that state than in the states of Connecticut and New York. Bess Oil is a company incorporated in Delaware, with its principal place of business in Houston, Texas. This particular Bess Oil station is quite popular, not just because residents from New York State travel to it to purchase gas but also because it is the only gas station for miles around. Massachusetts and even Connecticut residents patronize this station with great frequency. What these customers of the Bess Oil station did not know at the time they purchased fuel from Bess Oil was that the gas tanks holding the gasoline they purchased were contaminated; any gas pumped from them corroded the machinery in their cars, causing significant damage to the vehicles. The contaminants, when emitted through a vehicle's emissions system, also released incredibly harmful greenhouse gasses into the atmosphere. The damage to the vehicles requires complete replacement of major components of the fuel injection systems at a cost of nearly $5,000 per repair. In addition, the harm to the environment is considerable. Plaintiffs bring damages claims for the cost of the repairs, claims based on state laws that prohibit unfair and deceptive practices, and claims alleging the release of these contaminating gasses created a nuisance. Three groups of plaintiffs, made up of citizens of Massachusetts, Connecticut, and New York, respectively, commence separate actions against Bess Oil in state court

in Massachusetts. They seek well over $50 million in actual and punitive damages in each case because Plaintiffs allege Bess Oil knew of these likely harms from the contamination.

Each of these groups of plaintiffs can show that Bess Oil's actions bring it within the applicable long-arm statute of the State of Massachusetts, but Bess Oil seeks to dismiss the actions brought by the Connecticut and New York residents on personal jurisdiction grounds. Plaintiffs are not asserting jurisdiction over Bess Oil on a theory of general jurisdiction but instead are alleging that there is personal jurisdiction based on the theory of specific jurisdiction. Please assume the long-arm statute of Massachusetts is satisfied with respect to Plaintiffs' claims in each case.

Which of the following factors will the Massachusetts court take into account when considering whether there is personal jurisdiction over Bess Oil in a Massachusetts court under a theory of specific jurisdiction with respect to the actions brought by the Connecticut and New York Plaintiffs?

A. The ability to compel the testimony of witnesses in a Massachusetts court.

B. Whether New York and Connecticut courts might have an interest in adjudicating the dispute.

C. Whether Bess Oil is, for all intents and purposes, at home in the forum state.

D. Whether Plaintiffs can satisfy the amount-in-controversy requirement.

24. Plaintiff is injured when the automobile she is driving in "autonomous" mode fails to recognize that a car in an adjacent lane on a highway is intending to merge into the lane in which plaintiff's car is operating. Plaintiff suffers extensive injuries as a result of the ensuing car crash. Plaintiff will seek $1 million in damages on state tort theories of recovery from two defendants: the company that manufactured the car and the company that designed and installed the computer software that allegedly failed and resulted in the accident. Plaintiff is a resident and citizen of Maine. Defendant Manufacturer is incorporated in Delaware, with its principal place of business in Michigan. Plaintiff purchased her car from one of Defendant Manufacturer's dealerships in Maine. The accident occurred in California when Plaintiff was on a cross-country trip. The computer system in Plaintiff's car that Plaintiff alleges was defectively designed and allegedly caused the accident was installed in only a small number of Defendant Manufacturer's cars as part of a pilot program initiated by Defendant Manufacturer. This special fleet was marketed and sold only in the New England states. The computer system was designed by the second defendant named in Plaintiff's case: Hessla. Hessla is a foreign corporation, incorporated and with its principal place of business in Frankfurt, Germany. Hessla operates a small office in Boston, Massachusetts, so that it might coordinate its efforts deploying the computer system in defendant's New England fleet. Hessla does not market its automobile guidance systems in the United States. Rather, it markets these systems only at automobile trade shows in countries outside the United States. Hessla reached a deal to install in Frankfurt the Hessla autonomous guidance software into the New England fleet of Defendant Manufacturer's vehicles. Hessla has its computer technicians install its autonomous guidance software in Defendant Manufacturer's cars destined for New England in Defendant Manufacturer's main plant in South Carolina. However, Hessla has contacts with California because other software it creates was installed there one year ago and is presently operating in several power plants in the state, but such software is very different from the software installed in Defendant's New England fleet that allegedly is responsible for Plaintiff's injuries. Plaintiff brings its tort action in state court in California. Defendant Manufacturer does not challenge personal jurisdiction. Hessla, however, will challenge the California court's exercise of personal jurisdiction over it as violating the U.S. Constitution, arguing that the court has neither general nor specific personal jurisdiction over it.

Does the court have specific and/or general personal jurisdiction over Hessla?

A. The court does not have general personal jurisdiction over Hessla but does have specific personal jurisdiction over it.

B. The court has general personal jurisdiction over Hessla but does not have specific personal jurisdiction over it.

C. The court has neither general nor specific personal jurisdiction over Hessla.

D. The court has both general and specific personal jurisdiction over Hessla.

25.   MexiChem is a chemical manufacturer that supplied defoliation chemicals to the government of Guatarica, a small, Central American country that used such chemicals in its effort to suppress a rebel uprising there in the early 2000s. Civilians who fled the war-torn country want to file a suit in federal district court against MexiChem for the distribution of chemicals that, Plaintiffs allege, MexiChem knew were being used essentially as chemical weapons. Victims exposed to the chemicals in Guatarica suffered severe illnesses, and the children of women exposed to the chemicals during pregnancy suffer from severe birth defects. Plaintiffs seek $100 million in damages from MexiChem, alleging a variety of state and federal claims. MexiChem is incorporated in Mexico, with its principal place of business in Mexico City, Mexico. Plaintiffs, now lawful permanent residents of the United States residing in California, allege that the chemicals used by the Guatarican government that harmed them were manufactured in a plant in New Mexico in the United States. MexiChem is a sprawling multi-national corporation with distributors throughout North and Central America. In the United States, these distribution centers are located in New Mexico, Oregon, and Washington State. It does an equal amount of business out of each of the distribution centers listed above, although its overall sales in the United States generally represent just 10% of its total sales throughout the world. All of the sales of the chemicals to the Guatarican military took place from a distribution center in Mexico City, Mexico. Assume that the long-arm statutes of New Mexico and Washington State authorize courts operating in those states to exer-

cise personal jurisdiction to the full extent permitted by the U.S. Constitution's Due Process Clause. Plaintiffs want to pursue a federal suit against MexiChem in either federal court in New Mexico or Washington State.

If plaintiffs seek to file a federal complaint against MexiChem, which court or courts, if any, are likely to have personal jurisdiction over MexiChem?

A. The federal court in New Mexico will not have personal jurisdiction over MexiChem, but the court in Washington State will have such jurisdiction.

B. The federal court in New Mexico will have personal jurisdiction over MexiChem, but the federal court in Washington State will not.

C. Neither federal court will have personal jurisdiction over MexiChem.

D. Both federal courts will have personal jurisdiction over MexiChem.

26. Paula travels from Southern Vermont to her sculpting studio in Hudson, New York, three days a week. Hudson is located within the jurisdiction of the federal court for the Northern District of New York. During one of her commutes on a Friday afternoon on her way home from work, she is rear-ended by Dan and suffers serious injuries as a result. Dan was on his way to his weekend home in Massachusetts, which is located just across the border from New York, outside of Hudson. The accident occurs just outside the center of the City of Hudson, but within city limits. Dan has no other contacts in the Northern District of New York. His car is regularly serviced in Great Barrington, Massachusetts. In conversations with Dan's insurance company before the action is filed, Paula's lawyer learns that Dan's car was recently serviced at GB Auto Repair (GB) in Great Barrington, and the insurance company claims it was GB's failure to adequately service the brakes on Dan's car that resulted in the accident. When the complaint is filed, Paula's attorney names GB as a co-defendant in the action. Dan is a citizen of New Jersey with his primary residence in Newark, New Jersey, which is located in the U.S. District Court for the District of New Jersey. GB is incorporated in Delaware, with its principal place of business in Great Barrington, Massachusetts. GB does not advertise in New York; it only advertises locally, in the Massachusetts market, although GB's management knows that some of the cars it services come from New York because GB offers better prices than New York service stations. Paula is a resident and citizen of Vermont. Paula sues Dan and GB in federal district court in the Northern District of New York, alleging state tort claims. She alleges over $200,000 in damages for the serious injuries she sustained in the accident. Both defendants want to challenge the court's personal jurisdiction over them. Assume both satisfy the New York long-arm statute.

If Dan and GB both challenge the court's personal jurisdiction, what is the likely result of their respective motions?

A. Dan's motion will be granted and GB's will be denied.

B. Dan's motion will be denied and GB's will be granted.

C. Both motions will be granted.

D. Both motions will be denied.

27. Danco produces parts for wind turbines throughout the United States. It is incorporated in Delaware, with its principal place of business in Pennsylvania. Danco has secured a large contract with TurbineNY, a large public-private partnership located in New York State that is creating a wind farm on the outskirts of the Adirondacks in New York State. Since securing the contract, Danco has hired two employees who are independent contractors as technicians on site with TurbineNY in New York State. Those workers consult with TurbineNY as it sets up the wind farm using Danco's turbines. The current plan is for the Danco contractors to consult with TurbineNY on site throughout the life of the wind turbine project, which could last at least two years. However, the independent contractors' work is sporadic. They only work an average of ten hours each per week, though sometimes they might work on the turbines for as few as two hours a week, while other times they might work as many as twenty hours per week.

New York's long-arm statute reads in relevant part that a corporation that "regularly conducts business in the state" is subject to personal jurisdiction for all harm that occurs to individuals in the state, whether that harm is caused in the state or outside of it.

Danco begins to fall on hard times; its investments in renewable energy are not paying off because of the drop in the price of fuel oil. Danco fails to pay the independent contractors it has hired to administer the TurbineNY contract. The independent contractors sue TurbineNY in federal court in New York for violations of the Federal Labor Standards

Act (FLSA). They allege that when they were paid, their payment did not satisfy the federal minimum wage laws. Despite Plaintiffs' being considered independent contractors, they are covered under FLSA's protections as employees. Plaintiffs are all residents and citizens of New York State. Their suit seeks over $10,000 in damages, $5,000 for each Plaintiff. Danco asserts that the "harm" allegedly suffered by plaintiffs flows from Danco's failure to pay them under their contract, and such lack of payment, if any, occurred out of its offices in Pennsylvania. It has no other contracts with New York entities and conducts no other business in New York State.

Assume that the court rules that Danco's conduct in New York State brings it within the reach of the state's long-arm statute. A court determining whether the exercise of personal jurisdiction over Danco is consistent with the Due Process Clause of the U.S. Constitution is likely to find which of the following?

A. That the exercise of personal jurisdiction over Danco is consistent with the Due Process Clause because Danco's conduct and presence in the forum state is systematic and continuous, even though it is not connected to the controversy with Plaintiffs.

B. That the exercise of personal jurisdiction over Danco is consistent with the Due Process Clause because, at a minimum, Danco's contacts are tied specifically to the conduct that caused injury to Plaintiffs.

C. That the exercise of personal jurisdiction over Danco is inconsistent with the Due Process Clause because Danco's connection to the forum state has not been systematic and continuous and is not related to the dispute with the Plaintiffs.

D. That the exercise of personal jurisdiction over Danco is consistent with the Due Process Clause because the long-arm statute is satisfied with respect to Danco's conduct.

28. Plaintiff works at Jersey Furniture (Jersey) in Mahwah, New Jersey. She is a resident of Staten Island, New York, and commutes from Staten Island to Mahwah each day. Jersey is incorporated in Delaware, with its principal place of business in Mahwah. Plaintiff is injured when a large circular saw malfunctions and her arm is significantly damaged. The saw was manufactured in Bristol, England, at Bristol Saw. Plaintiff cannot sue Jersey because Jersey is protected by New Jersey's worker's compensation system.

Bristol sells saws in the United States through its main distributor, Chinatown Furniture Supply (Chinatown). On occasion, Bristol sends sales representatives to various furniture trade shows throughout the United States, including the main trade association show in the Jacob Javits Center in New York City, New York. It has marketed many of its lines of saws in the United States through these sales representatives and through Chinatown, but not the saw in question that injured Plaintiff, and not specifically to the New Jersey market. The saw that injured Plaintiff was a specialized saw made for a particular type of circular saw that is only available in the European market, which Jersey's owner purchased on a business trip to England. Chinatown is incorporated in Delaware, with its principal place of business in New York City. It routinely sends its sales agents to New Jersey and Connecticut to sell various types of furniture manufacturing equipment throughout both states. Chinatown does have a small showroom in Newark, New Jersey, where it displays some samples of the equipment it sells, including several of Bristol's models. This showroom was opened three years ago and has been open since. The saw that injured Plaintiff was never on display in the Newark showroom, however. Bristol is incorporated in England with its principal place of business in that nation. Plaintiff brings an action against Chinatown and Bristol in state court in New Jersey, in an action based in tort for products liability and defective product design. The action is consistent with the state's long-arm statute. Both Chinatown and Bristol challenge the court's personal jurisdiction over them.

Which of the following statements most accurately reflects the extent to which the state court in New Jersey has or does not have personal jurisdiction over the defendants Bristol and Chinatown?

A. The court has jurisdiction over neither Chinatown nor Bristol.

B. The court has jurisdiction over Chinatown but not Bristol.

C. The court has jurisdiction over Bristol but not Chinatown.

D. The court has jurisdiction over both Bristol and Chinatown.

29.   Plaintiff is a retired musician who had a big hit in the 1980s: "Nothing Compares 2 My Cruel Summer." She lived in SoHo in Manhattan for much of her adult life, reveling in the club scene and being the toast of the town, at least for a few months. She continues to get royalties from the various "Hits of the 80s" compilation albums on which her hit single appears. Barrister Records, the premiere record company for music from the 80s, pumps out a new compilation album every year, in which they just repackage the same songs. The records continue to sell and Plaintiff earns a decent living from these royalties. Finally getting bored with life in Manhattan, she decides to move south to a warmer climate. She does not want her small set of devoted followers to know that she has left the big city, though, so she sets up a post office box in New York and has an assistant collect her mail and forward it to her in South Carolina. Barrister Records continues to send Plaintiff's royalty checks once a month to her P.O. Box in New York, and then Plaintiff's assistant forwards them to South Carolina together with the fan mail.

Barrister markets its products on late-night TV shows in select markets, but not South Carolina's. After Plaintiff changes her domicile, Barrister begins to rethink its business model and starts to package compilation albums from grunge bands of the 1990s. Despite the fact that Barrister is still selling albums on which Plaintiff's song appears, it stops sending royalty checks to Plaintiff. Plaintiff commences a contract action against Barrister seeking $100,000 in unpaid royalties.

Barrister is incorporated in Delaware, with its principal place of business in New York State. Plaintiff sues Barrister in federal district court in South Carolina. Plaintiff's domicile is South Carolina. Barrister challenges the court's personal jurisdiction over it in South Carolina. Assume the exercise of jurisdiction by the court is consistent with the applicable South Carolina long-arm statute.

Can the federal district court in South Carolina exercise personal jurisdiction over Barrister? If so, why? If not, why not?

A. No. The fact that Plaintiff moved to South Carolina does not give rise to the legitimate exercise of personal jurisdiction over Barrister in South Carolina.

B. Yes. Given the way it has marketed its products, Barrister is subject to personal jurisdiction in South Carolina.

C. Yes. Since Barrister is incorporated in Delaware, with its principal place of business in New York, there is complete diversity between it and Plaintiff, and the South Carolina court can exercise jurisdiction over it in this action.

D. Yes. By sending Plaintiff royalty checks even after she moved to South Carolina, Barrister has sufficient minimum contacts with the forum state to warrant the exercise of personal jurisdiction over it by the district court of that forum.

30. Plaintiff is a lawyer based in Albany, New York, who has handled an estate matter for Darlene in New York State. Darlene is a resident of Los Angeles, California, who has never before set foot in New York. Darlene's great aunt, Annie, who was her favorite aunt, used to reside in Sacramento, California, where Darlene would spend many summer months during her childhood. After Darlene grew into adulthood, Annie moved to the Albany area, where she joined the faculty at State Law School. Because Darlene was a very busy actor, she rarely got to see Annie, even when Annie grew ill. Since Annie was childless and a widow, Darlene was one of her only living relatives. When Annie died, Darlene learned that Annie had left her a significant amount of money in her will as well as a significant bequest to State Law School. Darlene contacted a business associate in the Albany area who referred her to Plaintiff. As it so happened, Plaintiff was traveling to Los Angeles on some business, and the two met at a local restaurant where Darlene agreed to hire Plaintiff, executing a contract for Plaintiff's services. Plaintiff represented Darlene in settling the estate under New York law, in New York. After resolving a few time-consuming matters with the estate and securing payment for Darlene from the proceeds of the liquidation of the estate, Plaintiff ensured Darlene received payment and then sent Darlene a bill for services rendered in the amount of $15,000, a reasonable fee given the sizable estate and the amount of work that went into the estate's resolution. Darlene refused to pay the fee, saying it was exorbitant. Plaintiff brought an action in state court in New York for the failure on the part of Darlene to honor her obligations under the contract she signed in Los Angeles when she hired Plaintiff. Plaintiff learned that Darlene was coming to Albany for a memorial service at State Law School, at which the school would dedicate a new classroom in honor of Annie's long years of service to the school and her substantial bequest to it. When Darlene arrived at the law school, Plaintiff ensured that her process server was there to greet her. At a quiet moment away from the ceremony, the process server handed Darlene a summons and complaint in federal court in New York for the unpaid legal fees. Darlene hires another attorney in New York who files a special appearance in which the attorney challenges the personal jurisdiction of the New York court over Darlene. Assume that the state's long-arm statute is satisfied by these facts.

Does the federal court in New York have personal jurisdiction over Darlene in the action for the unpaid legal bills? If so, why? If not, why not?

A. Yes. Service of process upon Darlene in the forum state established the court's personal jurisdiction over Darlene.

B. Yes. Darlene's connection to the forum state by the use of Plaintiff's services to secure Annie's bequest to her represents a systematic and continuous presence in the forum state to such an extent that the court has personal jurisdiction over her in a manner consistent with the Due Process Clause of the Fourteenth Amendment to the U.S. Constitution.

C. No. Darlene's mere temporary presence in the state and lack of minimum contacts with the state mean the court cannot obtain personal jurisdiction over Darlene.

D. No. Service of process upon Darlene when she was attending a memorial service was not an appropriate means of securing personal jurisdiction over her.

1.6 Venue

This section will cover the issue of venue: where a particular case can and/or should be adjudicated. Embedded in the venue determination are sometimes issues related to personal jurisdiction.

31. Plaintiff is injured in a car accident that occurs in the state of Massachusetts. Plaintiff is a resident and citizen of New York. Plaintiff was rear-ended by the car driven by Cam, who is a resident and citizen of Connecticut. Cam only hit Plaintiff because Cam's car was rear-ended by Randi, a resident and citizen of Rhode Island. Plaintiff commences an action against Cam and Randi in the federal district court in Massachusetts. Assume that there is subject matter jurisdiction in federal court over the matter.

Is venue over Plaintiff's action appropriate in the federal district court in Massachusetts? If so, why? If not, why not?

A. No, because venue is only appropriate in federal court when all defendants are from the same state.

B. No, because venue is only appropriate in a state in which at least one defendant is a resident and citizen.

C. Yes, because a substantial part of the events giving rise to the liability in Plaintiff's case occurred in Massachusetts.

D. Yes, because the defendants are both subject to personal jurisdiction in Massachusetts.

32. Plaintiffs purchase plane tickets over the internet to travel on American Airways (Airways). The trip has Plaintiffs flying out of New York City's John F. Kennedy (JFK) airport to Charles de Gaulle (CDG) airport in Paris, France, on an Airways flight. JFK has been one of Airways's major hubs for over thirty years, with dozens of its planes flying out of the airport every day. Plaintiffs are U.S. citizens and residents of New York State. Airways is incorporated in Illinois, with its principal place of business in Chicago, Illinois. Plaintiffs are injured as their plane flies over international waters when turbulence causes a drink cart to crash into them. They bring a tort action based in state law in federal court in New York State for the Eastern District of New York (the site of JFK airport) seeking compensation from Airways for their injuries, which are extensive, meaning that they meet the amount-in-controversy requirement.

If Defendant seeks to transfer venue to the federal court for the Northern District of Illinois, should the court grant Defendant's request?

A. The motion should be granted. The Defendant is not subject to personal jurisdiction in New York.

B. The motion should be granted. The Defendant is at home in the Chicago forum and an out-of-state Defendant should not be burdened with litigating in a domestic venue that is neither located in its state of incorporation nor where it maintains its principal place of business.

C. The motion should be denied. An Illinois jury should not be burdened with a case where it is not familiar with the applicable law.

D. The motion should be denied. The Defendant may be deemed to reside in the Eastern District of New York for the purposes of determining venue.

33. Plaintiff RuntheRunway (RTR) is a darling of Silicon Valley, having created a service providing what it calls "Uber for Jets," in which it organizes private flights for billionaires. The U.S. Department of Justice has begun to investigate whether RTR is engaged in illegal price gouging because it raises its prices whenever there is a surge in demand for its services. RTR is incorporated in Delaware and has its principal place of business in San Francisco, California (which is within the Northern District of California). Plaintiff wants to file an action alleging that the federal government is engaged in malicious prosecution of RTR in violation of RTR's constitutional rights. RTR wants to bring an action in federal court against the U.S. Attorney General, in her official capacity, who resides in Alexandria, Virginia (in the Eastern District of Virginia). Plaintiff alleges that the local office of the Department of Justice, in San Francisco, in constant communication with the Attorney General in the Department of Justice's main offices in Washington, DC, is where the decision to investigate and pursue RTR was made. No real property is involved in the action.

Putting aside the question of which court would be the most appropriate court for venue purposes, where will venue certainly NOT lie in RTR's action?

A. The District of Delaware.

B. The District Court for Washington, DC.

C. The Eastern District of Virginia.

D. The Northern District of California.

34. Plaintiffs purchase plane tickets over the internet to travel on Eagle Flight Airlines (Eagle). Eagle is a subsidiary of American Airways (Airways). The trip has Plaintiffs flying out of New York City's John F. Kennedy (JFK) airport to Charles de Gaulle (CDG) airport in Paris, France, on an Eagle flight. Plaintiffs are U.S. citizens and residents of New York State. Eagle is incorporated in Delaware, with its principal place of business in New Jersey. American is incorporated in Illinois, with its principal place of business in Chicago, Illinois. The "fine print" in the terms of the contract that Plaintiffs accepted when they agreed to purchase the plane tickets included a choice of law clause stating that all litigation between the parties to the contract related to the tickets should be decided under Illinois law. Plaintiffs are injured as their plane flies over international waters when turbulence causes a drink cart to crash into them. They bring a tort action in federal court in New York State for the Eastern District of New York (the site of JKF airport) seeking compensation for their injuries, which are extensive, meaning that they meet the amount-in-controversy requirement. They sue both Eagle, the subsidiary, and Airways, the parent company. Despite the action being founded in tort, it is correctly argued that the applicable law governing the dispute is Illinois law, based on the choice of law clause in the ticket contract. Defendants seek to transfer venue to the federal court for the Northern District of Illinois, where Chicago is located. Airways has an airport hub in JFK, and 20% of its hundreds of flights pass through that airport on a daily basis. JFK airport is a major hub for Eagle, and 50% of its flights pass through, start, or commence at that airport. Plaintiffs have no connection to the state of Illinois other than the choice of law clause contained in the contract.

Should the court grant the Defendants' request to transfer venue?

A. The motion should be granted. The choice of law clause determines that venue is appropriate in a court in Illinois.

B. The motion should be granted. Defendant Airways is at home in the Chicago forum and that is the only forum where it is subject to jurisdiction.

C. The motion should be denied. The choice of law clause should not determine the venue of the action, and venue is proper in Plaintiffs' chosen forum.

D. The motion should be denied. Airways is not subject to jurisdiction in the Eastern District of New York.

35. Plaintiff Paul brings an action against several corporations for what he believes are anti-competitive actions. Paul operates a small software company that has developed a smart phone application that can determine the best time of day to go surfing off of California's coast. He wishes to market the application through several operating systems, but he cannot seem to convince any technology company to allow his application to run on its operating system. Paul believes these companies are conspiring against him to drive down the cost of his application. All three of the companies are incorporated in Delaware. Two of the companies have their principal place of business in San Jose, California, located in the Northern District of California, and a third has its principal place of business in Las Vegas, Nevada, in the territorial jurisdiction of the federal district court for the District of Nevada. Paul resides in San Francisco, California. Paul's case is based on his allegation that a meeting was held between the three defendant companies in San Francisco in which representatives of these companies conspired to each offer him a low compensation package for his application. He receives information from a corporate whistleblower from within one of these companies about this meeting and the communications had within it. He has no evidence of any other actions taken by these companies against his product. Nevertheless, Paul's lawyer believes the actions of these companies to conspire together at this one meeting to lower the asking price for Paul's product give him a strong case of anti-competitive behavior on the part of these technology companies.

San Francisco is located in the federal district court for the Northern District of California. Paul files his suit in federal court in San Francisco, alleging violations of federal antitrust laws. Defendants challenge venue.

Is venue appropriate in the Northern District of California?

A. Yes. The events that gave rise to defendants' alleged liability all took place in the Northern District of California.

B. No. Not all of the defendants reside in the Northern District of California and thus venue is inappropriate there.

C. Yes. Plaintiff resides in the Northern District of California and, since not all of Defendants reside in the same district, Plaintiff's residence determines venue.

D. Yes. Venue will lie in the district in which any defendant is deemed to reside.

36. Mayor Cathy Meehan of the City of Oshkosh, Wisconsin, has surprised everyone by rising to the top of the crowded field of primary candidates in her party in the Iowa Caucuses. One day while on the campaign trail, her campaign bus is side-swiped while driving through the heart of Sioux City, Iowa, by a pickup truck that is in the fleet of Sioux City Construction. It is alleged that the pickup truck's steering column malfunctioned due to a design defect. The company that designed and manufactured the steering column is a Canadian company, Canada Steering Company (Canada Steering), which is incorporated and has its principal place of business in Ontario, Canada. With respect to the Iowa market for steering columns, Canada Steering markets its products only to locations found in the jurisdiction of the federal court for the Southern District of Iowa. Sioux City Construction is based in Sioux City, Iowa, which is located in the jurisdiction of the federal court for the Northern District of Iowa. Three of Meehan's campaign workers, all residents and citizens of Wisconsin, are injured in the accident. Meehan's Iowa office is located in the city of Des Moines, which is located in the jurisdiction of the Southern District of Iowa. Sioux City Construction operates only in Sioux City and does not market its services or provide those services outside the jurisdiction of the Northern District of Iowa. Sioux City Construction is incorporated in Iowa, with its principal place of business in Sioux City, Iowa. Thinking it will be more convenient to bring their action in Des Moines, where their temporary office is located, the three injured campaign workers file their action in the federal court for the Southern District of

Iowa, which encompasses Des Moines, suing both Sioux City Construction and Canada Steering. Plaintiffs seek $1.2 million in damages, $400,000 each, under state law theories of recovery. Sioux City Construction will seek to transfer venue to the Northern District of Iowa.

Will the court grant the motion to transfer venue? If so, why? If not, why not?

A. The court will grant the motion unless Canada Steering does not consent to the transfer of venue.

B. The court will grant the motion despite Canada Steering's lack of contacts with the Northern District of Iowa because of Sioux City's connection to the Northern District of Iowa and its lack of connection to the Southern District of Iowa.

C. The court will deny the motion because of Canada Steering's contacts with the Southern District of Iowa.

D. The court will deny the motion because both Sioux City Construction and Canada Steering have minimum contacts with the Southern District of Iowa.

37.   Plaintiff brings an action in federal court against several defendants: Paris-America Bank, NA (PAB); PAB's parent corporation, France Bank (FB); and an individual who conducted real estate appraisals for PAB. PAB is incorporated in Delaware, with its principal place of business in South Dakota. FB is incorporated in France, with its principal place of business in Paris in that country. The appraiser is an individual who resides in and is a citizen of New Jersey. Plaintiff alleges that PAB, FB, and the appraiser are engaged in a fraudulent scheme to artificially inflate the costs of mortgages through faulty appraisals. Plaintiff, an individual, is a real estate developer in Upstate New York and alleges the defendants' scheme has made the cost of financing her developments more expensive. Plaintiff is a resident and citizen of New York. Plaintiff alleges that PAB, operating out of an office in Rutland, Vermont, hired the appraiser to carry out these fraudulent appraisals on a series of properties all located in Troy, New York. Plaintiff brings an action in federal court in the Northern District of New York, the district that encompasses Troy, New York, alleging state law fraud claims and seeking $1 million in damages from the three defendants. Plaintiff alleges that PAB and the appraiser were operating under the direction of FB. Plaintiff also alleges that FB was aware of the fraudulent actions of PAB employees working in conjunction with the appraiser and who were physically on site at the properties when the allegedly fraudulent appraisals were carried out by the appraiser. While none of the defendants challenges the court's exercise of personal jurisdiction over them, PAB, FB, and the appraiser challenge the venue of the action in the Northern District of

New York and seek transfer to the U.S. District Court for the District of Vermont.

Is venue proper over this action in the Northern District of New York? If so, why? If not, why not?

A. Yes, because the court may find that venue is proper over the foreign defendant, FB, because a foreign defendant can be sued in any district where there is personal jurisdiction, and once it has venue with respect to one defendant, the court will have venue over the entire action.

B. No, because the defendants do not have minimum contacts with the forum.

C. No, because a substantial number of the events giving rise to Plaintiff's claims did not occur in the forum.

D. Yes, because a substantial number of the events giving rise to Plaintiff's claims occurred in the forum.

38. Plaintiffs are farmworkers employed to pick grapes in the Yakima Valley in Eastern Washington State, which is located in the jurisdiction of the federal district court for the Eastern District of Washington State, and all Plaintiffs also reside in that district. The farmworkers allege that their employer, Yakima Valley Wines (YVW), has failed to pay them in accordance with federal and state wage and hour laws. The allegations flow from the same facts, i.e., that they worked many more hours than those for which they were paid, that YVW did not make mandated overtime payments, and that YVW often paid them less than the minimum wage required by state and federal law. The different bodies of law—state and federal—bring with them different remedies and penalties that will be imposed on the employers if they are found guilty of violating such laws based on these facts. The federal and state courts have concurrent jurisdiction over these types of claims. The farmworkers are represented by lawyers at the law firm of Smith & Jones, a prominent Seattle-based firm. These lawyers are handling the representation of the farmworkers on a volunteer/pro bono basis and are not charging the workers for their services. For their own convenience, the lawyers at Smith & Jones who are representing the farmworkers want to file the action in the federal district court in Seattle, which is located in the Western District of Washington State. YVW is incorporated in the Delaware, with its principal place of business in Spokane, which is located within the jurisdiction of the federal district court for the Eastern District of Washington State. All of the work performed by the workers and which forms the basis of their wage and hour claims took place in YVW's orchards in the Eastern District of Washington State. YVW does not market its products, high-end wines, anywhere. It only sells wholesale to wine distributors. It does not sell direct to wine consumers because it does not have a license to do so. It does no marketing because it does not have to; YVW is one of the oldest wineries in the country, and wine distributors come to its warehouse in Spokane to purchase YVW's product, which is generally recognized as among the finest wines sold in the United States. Once Plaintiffs' action is filed in federal court in Seattle, YVW will file a motion pursuant to 28 U.S.C. §1406 arguing that venue is improper in the Western District of Washington and that in the interests of justice, the matter should be transferred to the federal court for the Eastern District of Washington.

Will the court grant YVW's motion to transfer venue? If so, why? If not, why not?

A. The court will deny the motion because there is only one defendant in the action, YVW is at home in the state of Washington, and it is subject to personal jurisdiction in any court in the state.

B. The court will grant the motion because YVW's contacts for venue purposes are solely with the Eastern District of Washington.

C. The court will deny the motion because it is more convenient for the farmworkers' lawyers to litigate the dispute in the Western District of Washington.

D. The court will grant the motion because Plaintiffs are all residents of the Eastern District of Washington.

39.   Frank is the CEO of Novelties, Inc. (Novelties), a company incorporated in Pennsylvania, with its principal place of business in Pittsburgh, Pennsylvania. Novelties enters into a franchise agreement with Kurver Kreme, a chain of fast-food restaurants based in New York. Novelties wishes to set up a Kurver Kreme facility in Pennsylvania. Before doing so, employees of Novelties, including Frank, must receive training in Kurver Kreme policies. Frank, on behalf of Novelties, attends one training session in Rochester, New York; one in Manhattan, New York; and one in Riverhead, New York. Each of these training sessions lasts just one day. After Frank attends these three training sessions, he travels to Albany, New York, where Kurver Kreme has its corporate offices, to negotiate the final franchise agreement. The negotiations are somewhat protracted, and, after three days of discussions in the offices of Kurver Kreme's lawyers in Albany, Frank signs a contract on behalf of Novelties. Novelties opens its Kurver Kreme franchise in Pittsburgh. After several years, the site sees a decline in business and stops sending payments under the franchise agreement to Kurver Kreme in Albany. Novelties owes over $200,000 in payments to Kurver Kreme. Rochester is located in the jurisdiction of the U.S. District Court for the Western District of New York, Albany in the Northern District, Manhattan in the Southern District, and Riverhead in the Eastern District.

If Kurver Kreme brings an action in federal court seeking payment on the franchise agreement between Kurver Kreme and Novelties, which district court will most likely have venue over the action, and what is the reason that district court will have venue?

A. The Northern District of New York because this is the district with which Novelties appears to have the most significant contacts.

B. The Northern District of New York because this is the district where Kurver Kreme has its principal place of business.

C. The Northern District of New York because this is where Kurver Kreme has the most significant contacts.

D. There is no district court in New York State where venue is appropriate.

40.   Plaintiff, a lawyer who resides in and is a citizen of New York State, purchases an airline ticket over the internet from Northwest Airlines (NW), which is incorporated in Delaware and has its principal place of business in Athens, Georgia. Plaintiff reviews and accepts the terms of service contained in the contract for the e-ticket, which include the following: NW reserves the right to cancel the ticket at any time and any disputes related to the purchase and use of the ticket must be resolved in federal court for the federal district court that encompasses Athens, Georgia (which is found in the Middle District of Georgia). When Plaintiff goes to use his ticket, he is informed by the flight crew in Albany, New York, where the flight originates, that because the flight is overbooked, Plaintiff's ticket has been cancelled in accordance with the terms of service contained in the contract for the e-ticket. Plaintiff misses an important meeting with a prospective client due to losing his seat on the flight and, as a result, loses out on a new client contract valued at over $1 million. The contract instead goes to a different lawyer, all because Plaintiff missed the meeting with that prospective client when he could not get on the flight as planned. Plaintiff sues in federal district court in the Northern District of New York, which encompasses Albany International Airport, for breach of contract under state law theories of recovery against NW, alleging $1 million in damages. Plaintiff has no other contacts with the Georgia forum, and it would be difficult for him to have to litigate the case in that forum.

If NW moves to transfer venue to the Middle District of Georgia, how will the

court rule on the motion, and what will be its basis for doing so?

A. The court will grant the motion for the convenience of the parties.

B. The court will deny the motion because it will be inconvenient for the Plaintiff to sue NW in Georgia.

C. The court will deny the motion because the forum selection clause is unenforceable on the facts given and cannot serve as an appropriate basis for the transfer of venue.

D. The court will grant the motion because the forum selection clause is enforceable on the facts given and serves as an appropriate basis for the transfer of venue.

41.   Paula is a resident and citizen of New Hampshire. Paula is injured while riding a motorcycle when the tire ruptures, resulting in a crash. She purchased the Bucati motorcycle on which she was riding in New York from Moto Cycles (Moto), a New York-based distributor of Bucati motorcycles. These motorcycles are manufactured in Italy by Bucati Cycles (Bucati), an Italian corporation. Moto representatives travel regularly to Milan, Italy, where Bucati has its principal place of business, to meet with Bucati executives to purchase the cycles from the manufacturer. Moto is organized under New York law, with its principal place of business in New York. While Moto might sell to out-of-state purchasers like Paula, it does not market to or target customers outside of New York State. Bucati has no distributors in New Hampshire and otherwise does not target the tiny New Hampshire market. Paula purchased the Bucati on which she was riding at the time of the accident from Moto's main showroom in Colonie, New York, while she was traveling in the state on business. The tire that ruptured was supplied to Bucati by the Italian company Ruoto, a company organized under the laws of Italy and based in Rome, Italy. Ruoto does not conduct direct business with the U.S. market but rather sells exclusively to motorcycle and automobile manufacturers in Europe. Paula alleges that the tire was designed defectively and negligently installed in the motorcycle on which she was riding, implicating both Bucati and Ruoto in the accident. Moto is charged with selling her a defective product. Paula commences a damages suit based on state tort law in federal court for the District of New Hampshire, in the state of New Hampshire, against Moto,

Bucati, and Ruoto, seeking over $500,000 in damages for the extensive physical injuries she sustained as a result of the accident, which occurred on a back country road in Connecticut.

If Moto files a motion to dismiss the case against it on the grounds that venue is improper in the district court of New Hampshire with respect to Moto, will the court grant the motion? If so, why? If not, why not?

A. The court will deny the motion because a foreign corporation can be sued in any district, and once venue is proper with respect to at least one defendant, the U.S.-based defendant must face suit in the Plaintiff's choice of district.

B. The court will deny the motion because New Hampshire is an appropriate district for venue because it is the state of Plaintiff's domicile.

C. The court will grant the motion solely because not all of the defendants are deemed to reside within the District of New Hampshire.

D. The court will grant the motion because there is no basis for a finding that venue is proper in the New Hampshire court with respect to Moto.

1.7 The Doctrine of *Forum Non Conveniens*

The final issue covered in this chapter is the doctrine of *forum non conveniens*. Apart from the statutory considerations related to venue, this doctrine enables a court to determine that the forum is so inconvenient for the parties that it is unfair for the matter to be adjudicated in that forum.

42. Plaintiff, a U.S. citizen, brings an action in federal court in New York based on diversity jurisdiction against a foreign defendant. The action claims that Defendant injured her in a traffic accident that occurred while Plaintiff was travelling in Rome, Italy. Defendant, an Italian corporation with an office in New York City, will move to dismiss the action based on *forum non conveniens* grounds.

Which of the following factors should the court take into account when ruling on Defendant's motion?

A. Whether the defendant has minimum contacts with the forum state.

B. Whether any problems will arise regarding the application of foreign law in the domestic court.

C. Whether Plaintiff's ability to recover on her claims will be diminished in any way in a foreign forum.

D. Whether Defendant has such systematic and continuous contact with the forum state that it can be considered at home in it.

43. Plaintiff is a human rights activist who has worked in the South American nation of Guyamala over the last several years advocating for indigenous tribes located in the rainforest in that country. Those tribes are slowly being driven from their lands by exotic animal poachers and government agents seeking to claim more land for deforestation. Plaintiff is attacked one night by Guyamalan government troops and tortured. The soldiers tell Plaintiff to flee the country immediately or else the next time those soldiers come around, they will not just torture the Plaintiff, but the Plaintiff will be "swallowed up by the jungle, never to be seen again." The soldiers tell Plaintiff that President Bolsinoso, the head of the government of Guyamala, sent them. Plaintiff flees the country and returns to his home in the United States. Several months later, on a diplomatic trip, President Bolsinoso visits the United Nations' headquarters in New York City, and Plaintiff files a personal injury action in federal court in New York against Bolsinoso, alleging violations of generally recognized international law prohibitions against torture. Bolsinoso's lawyers appear in the action on Bolsinoso's behalf and seek to dismiss the action on *forum non conveniens* grounds. The lawyers allege, among other things, that all the evidence and witnesses related to the alleged interaction with Bolsinoso's soldiers are in Guyamala, that Guyamalan law will govern the action, and that the trier of fact will likely want to visit the site of the alleged interactions with the Guyamalan soldiers. Plaintiff correctly asserts that if the defendant's motion is granted and he is forced to commence an action in Guyamala (which is what Bolsinoso's lawyers are arguing), both Plaintiff and their lawyers are likely to be in physical danger, as human rights activists are routinely threatened and subject to physical abuse in Guyamala.

Will Bolsinoso's motion to dismiss the action on *forum non conveniens* grounds succeed?

A. Yes, the public interest and private interest factors appear to all tip in favor of dismissal.

B. No, the public interest and private interest factors do not appear to all tip decidedly in favor of dismissal.

C. No, the Guyamalan forum is not a viable forum for Plaintiff's action and thus dismissal on *forum non conveniens* grounds is improper.

D. Yes, the allegations about whether the Guyamalan forum is a viable forum are highly speculative.

44. Plaintiffs are the families of Peruvian miners killed in a mine disaster in the Andean highlands in Peru. MineCo is a large multi-national company that operates mines throughout South America and Africa, including the Peruvian mine where the workers were injured. MineCo is based in New York State and is incorporated in New York State. Plaintiffs' families argue that the faulty design of the mine caused it to collapse, resulting in the deaths of their loved ones. Plaintiffs have sued MineCo in federal court for the Southern District of New York in Manhattan, seeking recovery in tort for wrongful death. Their claims arise under New York state law and Peruvian law. MineCo has moved for dismissal of the action based on *forum non conveniens* grounds. MineCo argues that although the mine was designed in MineCo's offices in New York, all of the evidence of the disaster and many of the witnesses are located in Peru. Miners who worked in the mine but survived as well as Peruvian government workers who inspected the mine prior to the collapse are likely witnesses, and they all reside in Peru. MineCo's defense is that construction and blasting being performed by another mining company in a nearby area was the reason for the collapse. The deceased were all Peruvian citizens who resided in Peru. Their next-of-kin, the plaintiffs, are also all Peruvian citizens and residents, and they claim that any recovery in Peru will be limited by the Peruvian equivalent of worker's compensation: i.e., they can only recover the equivalent of six months' wages, which amounts to $3,000 USD, for the loss of each worker. No matter where the trial takes place, some claims will arise under Peruvian law and others under New York law.

What facts should the court NOT consider when determining whether to grant the motion for dismissal based on *forum non conveniens***?**

A. That there is a cap on damages should Plaintiffs have to litigate their action in a Peruvian court.

B. That a significant number of witnesses are located in Peru.

C. That the design of the mine took place in New York City.

D. That it might be advantageous to have the jury inspect the mine site.

45. Plaintiff, an American citizen, is injured while working in a gold mine in the Peruvian Andes, outside of Cuzco, Peru. Plaintiff alleges that she was injured when the mine caved in, trapping her and twelve co-workers in the mine for ten days. She bears the scars of significant psychological trauma from the experience and seeks to bring an action against her employer, MinorCoPeru, for the injuries she has sustained by bringing an action in the U.S. district court in Florida, in the United States, her home state of residence and citizenship there. Plaintiff says she does not want to litigate her case in Peru because Peruvian law imposes a cap on damages when suing a state-owned company in the courts of that country, and that cap will limit her recovery to $100,000. Because of her extensive injuries, she could seek roughly $2,000,000 for her pain and suffering in a U.S. court, but she claims that her action will be significantly and substantially hindered in Peru because of the cap on damages that would apply in a suit involving MinorCoPeru. Her lawyers tell her that she will not face similar problems in a U.S. court. Peruvian law will apply to the suit, all of the witnesses are located in Peru, all of the evidence in the suit is located in Peru, and the site of the accident is in Peru. At the same time, the court in Florida is capable of resolving claims arising under Peruvian law, and a local jury in Florida would want to resolve the matter to address injuries sustained by a Florida citizen. Defendant MinorCoPeru, which is organized under the laws of the nation of Peru, with its principal place of business in Lima, Peru, appears in federal court seeking to dismiss the case on *forum non conveniens* grounds. The

trial court grants the motion. On appeal, Plaintiff seeks to overturn this ruling.

Should the appeals court reverse the district court's ruling on the motion to dismiss on *forum non conveniens* grounds? If so, why? If not, why not?

A. The decision should be reversed because the court should not give Plaintiff an unfair advantage in one court over another, and because it should ensure that Defendant is treated the same in a U.S. court as it would be in a Peruvian court.

B. The decision should be reversed because not all of the factors to be weighed in a *forum non conveniens* inquiry point in favor of dismissal based on *forum non conveniens* grounds.

C. The decision should be affirmed because it was not an abuse of discretion to find that the private and public interest factors appear to favor trial in a Peruvian court.

D. The decision should be affirmed because the inconvenience to Defendant of having to litigate in Florida is outweighed by the inconvenience to Plaintiff of having to litigate in Peru.

1.8 Formative Assessment Quiz

Take this formative evaluation quiz to test your knowledge of this chapter's materials.

46. Plaintiff sues Defendant in federal court for the Central District of California, the district encompassing the city of Los Angeles. California's long-arm statute provides that it permits a court in California to exercise personal jurisdiction over parties before it to the full extent of the Due Process Clause of the U.S. Constitution. Plaintiff has established residency and citizenship in California, having moved his domicile from Oregon to Los Angeles six months prior to the filing of the suit by Plaintiff, and he has an intent to remain there indefinitely. Plaintiff's suit against Defendant, based on state law claims under Oregon law, pertains to Defendant's alleged breach of a contract between the parties. Plaintiff claims that Defendant failed to design a parking garage in Portland, Oregon, according to Plaintiff's specifications. Plaintiff argues that, according to the original designs he supplied to Defendant, Plaintiff was supposed to earn an additional $10,000 per month in parking fees, but Defendant's failure to design the garage according to Plaintiff's directions meant that the garage had fewer spaces than the original plans provided. The garage has been operating for a year now. Plaintiff seeks $120,000 in damages on the contract claim and future damages for the lost fees moving forward, unless and until the garage is redesigned to accommodate more cars. The contract between the parties was negotiated in Oregon prior to Plaintiff relocating to California, and all work done on the contract was performed by Defendant in Oregon.

Defendant is a resident and citizen of Oregon. Unrelated to her contract with Plaintiff, Defendant was hired by a company in Los Angeles, California, to work as an engineering consultant in the effort to design a "Hyperloop," a rapid transit system that will operate between Los Angeles and San Francisco, California. In performing work on this other contract, Defendant travels to Los Angeles as much as twice a month, for meetings that last up to three hours at a time. Defendant has been working in this capacity only for the three months immediately preceding Plaintiff's commencement of the suit between the parties. Defendant has no contacts with the state of California other than those specified and is served, personally, at her place of residence in Oregon.

If Defendant should file a motion to dismiss Plaintiff's action, challenging the federal court in California's exercise of personal jurisdiction over her in the case brought by Plaintiff, will the court grant the motion? If so, why? If not, why not?

A. The court will deny the motion because Defendant was served personally at her normal place of abode and Defendant had a contractual relationship with a resident of California.

B. The court will grant the motion because the California long-arm statute overrides the Due Process Clause.

C. The court will grant the motion because Defendant's contacts with the forum state are unrelated to Plaintiff's claims against her and they are not so systematic and continuous to render her essentially at home in the forum state.

D. The court will deny the motion because the Defendant's contacts with the forum state are systematic and continuous such that she is essentially at home in the forum state.

47. Peter works for twenty years at the main offices of International Shoe, Inc., which is incorporated and has its principal place of business in St. Louis, Missouri. His employment contract contains a non-competition agreement, which requires that he refrain from selling shoes anywhere in the United States for a period of two years after he leaves the employment of International Shoe or is terminated. The employment contract also contains a choice-of-law clause that says that disputes under the contract are to be resolved under Missouri state law. Peter decides to leave International Shoe and moves to nearby Little Rock, Arkansas, where he is offered a job working in a local shoe retailer; however, he cannot accept this job because of the non-competition agreement in his employment contract with International Shoe. Peter, now a resident of Arkansas, brings an action in federal court in Little Rock under diversity jurisdiction, alleging $100,000 in damages for his inability to engage in the work for which he is most qualified: retail shoe sales. International Shoe has several stores in Arkansas, so the exercise of personal jurisdiction over it in that state is consistent with the Due Process Clause of the U.S. Constitution and the long-arm statute of the State of Arkansas. Nevertheless, International Shoe requests, in a timely manner, that the court transfer venue to the federal court in St. Louis, Missouri.

Which of the following is the factor that the court is LEAST likely to take into account in making its determination on the request to change venue?

A. That there is a choice-of-law clause in the employment contract that forms the basis of the complaint.

B. The convenience of the parties.

C. That International Shoe is subject to personal jurisdiction in Arkansas.

D. Whether the parties consent to the transfer of venue.

48. Brighter-Mayer (BM), a large multi-national corporation, manufactures and distributes Plarex, a medication that helps to reduce blurry vision in individuals recovering from cataract surgery. Plarex is manufactured in a BM processing plant in Bridgeport, Connecticut, which it constructed five years ago and which has been in operation there since. BM operates a total of seven additional medication processing plants that process other medications distributed by BM, but all of these other such plants are located in Massachusetts and New Hampshire. Sale of Plarex constitutes 5% of BM's total global medication sales. BM is incorporated in Delaware, with its principal place of business in New Jersey. Plaintiffs are several individuals who ingested Plarex and complain that the medication gave them intense migraines over an extended period of time, and long after they were prescribed and ingested the medication. Plaintiffs are organized into two different groups based on their respective state of citizenship. One group of plaintiffs consists of residents and citizens of Ohio. The second group of plaintiffs consists of residents and citizens of Pennsylvania. BM engaged in aggressive marketing of the medication in both Ohio and Pennsylvania but distributes the medication only through a mail-order program administered through a distribution center in the State of Virginia. The plaintiffs who reside in Ohio want to bring an action based on state tort law seeking $100 million in damages for their legitimate pain and suffering. The purchase of the medication by the Ohio Plaintiffs is not in any way related to the medication's sale in Pennsylvania, despite the fact that the medication is widely distributed there and BM advertises the medication throughout that state. Please assume these claims satisfy the amount-in-controversy requirement. The Ohio Plaintiffs wish to file their action in federal court and expect to claim that BM is subject to personal jurisdiction on a theory of specific jurisdiction.

In which state or states would a court likely find that BM is subject to personal jurisdiction in the case over Plarex brought by the Ohio Plaintiffs on a theory of specific jurisdiction?

A. Connecticut only.

B. Only Virginia and Connecticut.

C. Only Ohio, Connecticut, and Virginia.

D. Connecticut, Virginia, Ohio, and Pennsylvania.

49. Pam is a resident and citizen of Massachusetts who travelled to Brattleboro, Vermont, to purchase pottery from the Brattleboro Pottery Company (Pottery). Pottery is incorporated in Delaware, with its principal place of business in Vermont. Pottery sells its products and markets them exclusively throughout the New England states, including Massachusetts. All of Pottery's products are manufactured in Vermont from locally sourced products, and it uses local artisans to hand-paint the pottery. Pam purchases some pottery from Pottery and asks the clerk at the Pottery store to gift wrap the pottery because Pam intends to send it to her relative, Moz, who resides in Michigan, in honor of Moz's 50th birthday. The clerk wraps the package and gives it to Pam, who asks directions from the clerk to the nearest post office. The clerk points out the location of a nearby post office, which is just a few doors down from the Pottery store. Pam tells the clerk that she is excited to send the package to her friend, who is going to be jealous that New England has such excellent pottery. The owner of Pottery overhears the conversations and asks Pam to let her friend know that Pottery often gets customers traveling through New England, including from Michigan, who stop in their store. The owner asks Pam to tell her friend to "spread the word" about Brattleboro Pottery. Pam goes to the nearby post office to which the Pottery clerk had directed her and mails the package to Moz. Soon after receiving the pottery (a set of coffee mugs), Moz and his child get sick from chemical poisoning, which can be traced to the defective glaze that Pottery's workers applied to the mugs. Moz and his child are both residents and citizens of Michigan. Moz wants to bring an action against Pottery in federal court under state tort law theories of recovery seeking $400,000 in damages due to the severe illnesses Moz and his child suffered as a result of the poisoning. For the purposes of this question, please assume that each of the states listed below has a long-arm statute that permits courts in the state to exercise jurisdiction over any party in a manner that is consistent with the full reach of the Due Process Clause of the U.S. Constitution.

Should Moz seek to file a case in federal court, which of the following statements is accurate?

A. A court in Michigan will have personal jurisdiction over Pottery because its product was shipped to a resident there and harmed that resident in that state.

B. A court in Vermont will have personal jurisdiction over Pottery because Pottery is at home in that state.

C. A court in Vermont will not have personal jurisdiction over Pottery because Pottery is an in-state defendant and the federal court will not have personal jurisdiction over it in a diversity action.

D. A court in Massachusetts will have personal jurisdiction over Pottery because Pottery is at home in that state due to its marketing of its products there.

50.   Plaintiff files a case based on alleged federal banking law violations by a mortgage bank, Pocket Mortgage; an online mortgage bank; and a network of mortgage brokers. State courts have concurrent jurisdiction over such claims. Plaintiff's case is filed in the first instance in state court in California. The Defendants believe the most convenient place for the case to be litigated is New York because many of the witnesses and the evidence regarding Plaintiff's claims are located in the State of New York, specifically in and around the City of Albany, where the bank and the network of mortgage brokers are located and where each has its respective principal place of business. Defendants all agree that they would like the case adjudicated in the federal court for the Northern District of New York, the district encompassing the City of Albany.

What is the most appropriate way for Defendants to achieve the outcome of having the Northern District of New York adjudicate the dispute?

A. Remove the case to the Northern District of New York directly from the state court in California.

B. Remove the case to federal court in the Northern District of California, as that is the location of the state court in which the action has been filed, and then seek to transfer the case to the Northern District of New York.

C. Move for dismissal based on *forum non conveniens* grounds.

D. Move to transfer the case from the state court in California directly to the Northern District of New York.

51. Plaintiff is injured during a train ride between London, United Kingdom, and Paris, France. Plaintiff is a resident of Manhattan, New York. She is injured when a drink and snack cart operated by an employee of Sedexa, a food service company, bumps into her while being pushed down the aisle of the train compartment. Extremely hot coffee spills on Plaintiff as a result of the incident, causing her significant burns and serious injuries. Sedexa offers food services internationally to several companies that provide transportation, including several airlines that operate in the United States. Several routes that Sedexa services travel through John F. Kennedy airport, located in the Eastern District of New York. The incident in which Plaintiff was injured took place on the French side of the train trip, just outside of Paris. The train was travelling at an unsafe speed around a particularly sharp turn when the cart went out of control. Unfortunately, at the time the train was taking this sharp turn, the wheel gave out on the cart as it hit a snag in the carpeting in the aisle of the train. That snag was there due to poor maintenance on the part of the train operator's maintenance crews. Plaintiff alleges that this confluence of events led to her injuries, which would implicate both Sedexa and the company operating the train on which the accident occurred. The cart itself and the train car in which the incident occurred are both being stored in a lot outside of the main train station in Paris because of their involvement in the incident that injured Plaintiff. Plaintiff's lawyer reviews French law and realizes that there is a cap on damages for injuries that occur on trains operating in and through France such that Plaintiff will be limited to seeking no more than 1,000 €, or about $1,200 USD, in damages. Plaintiff would face no such limit on recovery in a U.S. court. Plaintiff files a diversity action in federal court for the Eastern District of New York, where Plaintiff resides, naming both Sedexa and EuroRail, the operator of the train. French law will likely govern the dispute because the incident took place on French soil. EuroRail is a British-French partnership incorporated under the laws of the United Kingdom, with its principal place of business in London. EuroRail has operated a ticket sales office in downtown Brooklyn, located in the Eastern District of New York, for the last twenty-five years. It is here where Plaintiff purchased her train ticket for this fateful trip. The terms of service printed on the ticket provide that any legal dispute involving Plaintiff's use of the ticket, even one alleging personal injury, must be resolved in a French court. Sedexa is also a company incorporated in the United Kingdom, with its principal place of business in Edinburgh, Scotland.

If Defendants seek to dismiss the case on *forum non conveniens* grounds, will the court grant the motion? If so, why? If not, why not?

A. The court will grant the motion because of the forum selection clause in the ticket's terms of service.

B. The court will deny the motion because Defendants' general connections to the forum are so systematic and continuous that they render Defendant at home in the jurisdiction.

C. The court will deny the motion because of the possibility of a less favorable remedy in a French court.

D. The court will grant the motion because Defendants' contacts with the
forum are not related to the dispute
between the parties.

52.   Defendant International Blue (Blue)
is a business-to-business wholesaler of
solar panels that sells its panels exclusively to areas outside the United States.
Unbeknownst to Blue, it shipped a defective solar panel from its Upstate New
York manufacturing plant to Mexico City,
Mexico, to SolarMex, which sells and installs solar panels throughout Mexico,
using Blue as its main supplier of panels.
Blue is incorporated in Delaware, with its
principal place of business in New York.
Blue has extensive dealings with its international clients through its offices in
Miami Beach, Florida. In a lot outside
its offices there, it has solar panel farms
where it displays its models. From the Miami Beach offices, Blue negotiates all of its
international contracts of sale, including
the one with SolarMex that results in the
shipment of the defective solar panel. The
defective solar panel, which was designed
in North Carolina and manufactured in
New York, malfunctions, which results in
a massive fire at a waste treatment facility, killing dozens of workers and making
thousands of area residents seriously ill.
Family members of those killed as well
as many area residents injured by the
fire file a lawsuit in federal district court
in Texas against Blue alleging defective
product design as the proximate cause of
Plaintiffs' injuries. Plaintiffs have chosen
Texas as the site of the lawsuit because of
Blue's contacts with the forum state. Various parts of some of Blue's different solar
panel designs are manufactured in an
Austin, Texas, manufacturing plant. Blue
also periodically runs installation sem-
inars for Blue's customers that purchase
Blue's solar panels for resale and installation. These two-day training sessions take
place in different cities in Texas about

once every twelve months and have taken place there for the last three years. Parts for the defective panel were not manufactured in the Texas plant, however. In addition, SolarMex's workers were trained in Texas, but there is no allegation that the panels were defectively installed or that the workers received inadequate training. Blue, the only defendant, challenges the Texas court's personal jurisdiction over it. Blue moves to dismiss the action for lack of personal jurisdiction.

Should the court grant the motion to dismiss? If so, why? If not, why not?

A. The motion should be denied because Blue's contacts with the forum state are systematic and continuous, meaning that the court has personal jurisdiction over Blue.

B. The motion should be granted because Blue's contacts with the forum state are not systematic and continuous but are connected to the underlying dispute.

C. The motion should be granted because Blue's contacts with the forum state are unrelated to the underlying dispute and are not systematic and continuous.

D. The motion should be granted because Blue's contacts with the forum state are not connected to the underlying dispute, although they are systematic and continuous.

53. Plaintiff is injured while on a motorcycle trip in the Peruvian Andes, outside of Cuzco, Peru. Plaintiff alleges that the accelerator on her motorcycle accelerated on its own, causing her to veer off the side of the road and into a ravine where she sustained serious injuries. She had rented the motorcycle from Cycle Machu Picchu (Cycle) in Cuzco. Cycle is a Peruvian company. Cycle purchases all of its motorcycles from Nippon Cycles (Nippon), a Japanese company with showrooms in Lima, the capital city of Peru. Cycle alleges that it purchased the motorcycle that injured plaintiff from Nippon in Lima. Nippon alleges that the motorcycle was designed and manufactured in Japan for the Peruvian market. It says its accelerators were designed especially for high altitude riding, particularly in the Peruvian Andes where there are sharp inclines and sharp declines. It is alleged that the accelerator malfunctioned due to a significant rise in altitude on the mountain road on which Plaintiff was riding. The damaged motorcycle is being held in a garage in Cuzco, under the custody of the local insurance company that insures Nippon. Plaintiff wishes to bring an action against Nippon and Cycle in the U.S. District Court in her home state of Florida, in the United States. Plaintiff says she does not want to litigate her case in Peru where there is a statutory cap on damages in actions brought by foreign plaintiffs. Despite her extensive injuries—in a U.S. court she could seek roughly $200,000 for her pain and suffering—Plaintiff would only be able to seek the equivalent of $2,000 in a Peruvian court. Defendants Nippon and Cycle appear in federal court seeking to dismiss the case on *forum non conveniens* grounds. The court denies the

motion, stating that the statutory cap on damages in the Peruvian court means that the Plaintiff will be effectively denied justice there: that is, in the court's opinion, she will have no effective recourse in a Peruvian court. Defendants file a request to appeal the court's ruling immediately, and the trial court grants the request.

On appeal, will the appellate court reverse the trial court? If so, why? If not, why not?

A. The appellate court will reverse the trial court because it should not have considered the statutory cap on damages as foreclosing Plaintiff's recourse in the Peruvian courts.

B. The appellate court will affirm the trial court's ruling because Plaintiff will be denied her day in court should the court dismiss the action on *forum non conveniens* grounds.

C. The appellate court will reverse the trial court because the trial court failed to recognize that the public and private interest factors weigh in favor of dismissing the case on *forum non conveniens* grounds.

D. The appellate court will affirm the trial court because the trial court correctly concluded that the public and private interest factors weigh against dismissing the case on *forum non conveniens* grounds.

54.   Defendant Iceland Batteries (Iceland) is a company that is incorporated in Iceland and has its principal place of business there. Iceland manufactures lithium batteries for electric cars manufactured by Tessie Motors. Tessie's principal place of business is in California, and it is incorporated in Delaware. Defendant Iceland makes lithium batteries for many products, including things like lawnmowers, cell phones, and computers. Its products are found everywhere in the world, in literally hundreds of millions of products. Plaintiff is involved in an accident driving one of Tessie's vehicles in New York. The accident is caused by the malfunctioning of the vehicle's Iceland battery. Iceland batteries are found in roughly 1% of the consumer products in the State of New York generally, and Iceland receives roughly 1% of its global sales revenue from the sale of lithium car batteries by Tessie to consumers in New York, a number that has remained steady over the last ten years of Iceland's global sales. Iceland does no marketing of its automobile batteries to the New York market because there are no electric vehicle manufacturers in New York, and it sells no automobile batteries directly to consumers there. Iceland only markets its automobile batteries to automobile manufacturers in California, where Plaintiff's Tessie vehicle was manufactured and where the Iceland battery was purchased by Tessie and installed by Tessie in Plaintiff's vehicle. At the same time, Iceland operates a manufacturing plant for fuel cells for solar panels in Rochester, New York, which it has operated in that city for ten years. Roughly 5% of Iceland's global revenue comes from the fuel cells manufactured in its Rochester plant. Plaintiff

commences a personal injury action in federal court in New York against Tessie and Iceland alleging diversity jurisdiction as the basis of jurisdiction and seeking $1 million in damages. Plaintiff is a resident and citizen of New York State. Tessie does not contest the court's ability to exercise personal jurisdiction over it. Iceland, however, despite the fact that the exercise of personal jurisdiction over it is consistent with the applicable long-arm statute, will move to dismiss the action for want of personal jurisdiction over it in federal court in New York.

Is Defendant Iceland subject to personal jurisdiction in New York in this action? If so, why? If not, why not?

A. Yes, because of Iceland's extensive contacts with the forum state, Iceland is effectively at home in that forum.

B. Yes, because of Iceland's extensive contacts with the forum state with respect to the sale of its lithium batteries, the exercise of jurisdiction over it is consistent with traditional notions of fair play and substantial justice and is not unreasonable.

C. No, because Iceland does not have sufficient contacts with the forum state to justify the exercise of personal jurisdiction over it in this action.

D. No, but only because Iceland was not served personally with the summons and complaint within the State of New York.

55.   SolarCo is a corporation incorporated in Delaware, with its principal place of business in Youngstown, Ohio. SolarCo manufactures solar panels. Because SolarCo's solar panels are particularly durable and can withstand extreme weather, its solar panels are purchased in communities with colder climates. For this reason, SolarCo's products are the solar panel of choice in Western New York. In fact, roughly 10% of all of SolarCo's global sales are to businesses and homeowners in the area around Buffalo, New York, which is located in the jurisdiction of the federal court in the Western District of New York. One day, a salesperson for SolarCo travels by plane from Youngstown to Albany, New York, to negotiate a contract of sale for roughly $10 million in solar panels that will be installed in a baseball stadium in Buffalo, New York, that houses a minor league baseball team, the Wildings, owned by WinCo. The contract for the sale is negotiated in Albany, New York, at WinCo's offices. At SolarCo's request, the contract contains a forum selection clause stating that any disputes related to the contract shall be adjudicated in the federal court in the Western District of New York. WinCo is incorporated in New York, with its principal place of business in Albany, New York. After the contract is finalized, the solar panels are delivered to the stadium by employees of SolarCo who reside in hotels in the Buffalo area for the three weeks it takes to install the solar panels at the stadium. SolarCo also contracts with local contractors to help its team install the panels. After the solar panels are installed, it is clear that they are not functioning correctly. WinCo wants to bring suit against SolarCo, seeking removal of the solar panels and for reim-

bursement for the cost of their purchase. The action will be filed under state tort and contract theories of recovery and seek over $10 million in damages. The case is filed in the federal district court for the Northern District of New York, where WinCo's offices are located. SolarCo will move to dismiss the case for lack of personal jurisdiction and for a transfer of venue to the federal district court for the Western District of New York. Assume that the court is willing to entertain both motions simultaneously and rule on both. Assume also that the applicable long-arm statute allows the relevant court to exercise personal jurisdiction to the full extent permitted by the Due Process Clause of the U.S. Constitution.

What is the most likely outcome with respect to these two the motions?

A. The motion with respect to transfer will be granted, but the motion with respect to personal jurisdiction will be denied.

B. The motion with respect to transfer will be denied, but the motion with respect to personal jurisdiction will be granted.

C. Both motions will be granted.

D. Both motions will be denied.

Chapter 2

Subject Matter Jurisdiction

The last chapter covered the issue of personal jurisdiction—the power of a court over a party. This chapter focuses on subject matter jurisdiction—the power of the courts to adjudicate the dispute based on the claim or claims involved in the suit. While state courts are considered courts of general jurisdiction—that is, they can hear most cases unless there is some barrier to them doing so, federal courts are courts of limited jurisdiction: they can only hear the cases they are empowered to by the U.S. Constitution and the governing statutes providing for such jurisdiction. This chapter will focus on the scope and contours of subject matter jurisdiction over the federal courts.

2.1 Federal Question

One of the most common grounds upon which a federal court has subject matter jurisdiction is what is known as "federal question" jurisdiction: when a court is asked to rule on an issue arising under federal law. These first questions help you understand how courts look at the issue of such federal question/"arising under" jurisdiction.

1. Plaintiff brings an action in federal district court in Florida alleging mortgage fraud against Delta Bank (Delta). Plaintiff is a citizen of Florida, and his home is located in Fort Lauderdale, Florida. Delta bank is incorporated in Delaware, with its principal place of business in Gainesville, Florida. Plaintiff alleges that Delta violated state unfair trade practices laws when it made certain disclosures with respect to his mortgage loan, and he sues Delta, seeking $100,000 in damages allowed under the applicable state statute. Plaintiff anticipates that Delta will argue that it complied with the federal Truth In Lending Act (TILA) when it made the disclosure. Plaintiff will argue that, despite the federal defense based on TILA, the state unfair trade practices law goes further than the federal law and mandates additional disclosures that Delta failed to follow when it entered into the mortgage agreement. Plaintiff believes, and states in his complaint, that the federal defense Delta will raise regarding TILA implicates important issues of federal law, even though TILA was not violated. Plaintiff wants the federal court to resolve the important federal questions while also ruling on Plaintiff's state unfair trade practices claim, which necessarily arises out of the same set of facts giving rise to the TILA defense.

If Delta files a motion to dismiss alleging that the court does not have subject matter jurisdiction over Plaintiff's case, how should the court rule on the motion, and why?

A. It should deny the motion. The federal question regarding TILA appears on the four corners of the complaint.

B. It should grant the motion. The federal question regarding TILA does not appear on the face of the well-pleaded complaint, and there are no other grounds for federal jurisdiction.

C. It should grant the motion. The parties are not diverse, and the Plaintiff fails to meet the amount-in-controversy requirement.

D. It should deny the motion. The Plaintiff can establish federal jurisdiction over the action.

2. Plaintiff brings a claim under federal fair housing legislation that bans discrimination in housing accommodations, alleging discrimination in mortgage lending based on race. Plaintiff alleges that he was seeking a mortgage for a weekend home in Simsbury, Connecticut, and was denied a mortgage because he is Asian-American. He seeks $150,000 in damages, the amount he will have to pay on the higher-priced mortgage he entered into when his mortgage bank turned him down based on his race. There is not exclusive federal jurisdiction over the anti-discrimination claim, and Plaintiff chooses to file his action in federal court in the State of Connecticut. Plaintiff is a resident and citizen of New York. Defendant is Hartford Mortgage Bank (HMB), which is incorporated in Delaware, with its principal place of business in Connecticut. After the action is filed in state court in Connecticut, HMB seeks to dismiss the case, claiming that it should not have been brought in federal court because there is not exclusive federal jurisdiction over the claim.

Will HMB be successful in dismissing Plaintiff's action for lack of subject matter jurisdiction? If so, why? If not, why not?

A. Defendant will succeed in dismissing the case because the federal court does not have exclusive subject matter jurisdiction over the proceeding.

B. Defendant will not succeed in dismissing the case because an in-state defendant is not able to claim a lack of subject matter jurisdiction.

C. Defendant will succeed in dismissing the case because the parties are not from the same state.

D. Defendant will not succeed in dismissing the case because the action raises a claim under federal law.

2.2 Diversity Jurisdiction

After federal question jurisdiction, the second most frequent basis for federal jurisdiction is what is known as diversity jurisdiction, which includes cases where the parties are from different states. This section explores this important basis of federal subject matter jurisdiction.

3. Plaintiff wants to bring an action against Defendant alleging violation of New Jersey state labor laws. Plaintiff is a resident and citizen of New Jersey and works in Defendant's factory on the outskirts of Hoboken, New Jersey. Defendant produces high-end pasta that it sells to restaurants, primarily in New York City. All of Defendant's products are made in the Hoboken site, its only factory. Defendant is incorporated in Delaware, with its principal place of business in Brooklyn, New York. Defendant's Chief Executive Officer and other members of the company's leadership team, four employees altogether, work out of Defendant's Brooklyn office. The Hoboken factory is where the remainder of the defendant's 250 employees work. Plaintiff files her action in federal court in New Jersey seeking $78,000 in damages, which represents the back pay she says she is owed for working for several years at the Hoboken factory earning less than the state-mandated minimum wage. Defendant will move to dismiss the action for lack of subject matter jurisdiction.

Will Defendant succeed in dismissing the federal action for lack of subject matter jurisdiction?

A. Yes, because Plaintiff is seeking only state law claims and there is no other basis for federal jurisdiction.

B. No, because Plaintiff satisfies the amount-in-controversy requirement and, had she filed a well-pleaded complaint, she would have alleged additional federal claims.

C. Yes, because Defendant's connection to the forum is systematic and continuous such that it is at home in the forum state, and thus there is no diversity between the parties.

D. No, because there is complete diversity between the parties and the plaintiff satisfies the amount-in-controversy requirement.

4.   Plaintiff brings an action alleging that she was injured while operating a crane to remove some damaged underground pipe. While working on the pipes, she inadvertently strikes a buried power line that was unmarked. She is burned and suffers serious injuries when the pierced power line sparks a fire. She cannot bring an action against her employer because of the protections of the worker's compensation system. Instead, she brings an action against the company that buried the lines (PowerInc) as well as the company that supplied the insulation that was supposed to prevent the lines from catching fire if pierced (SafeSeal). Plaintiff is a resident and citizen of New York State. She brings an action against PowerInc and SafeSeal in federal court in Albany, New York, in the Northern District of New York, under state tort law theories, seeking $500,000 in damages. PowerInc is incorporated in Delaware, with its principal place of business in New York. SafeSeal is also incorporated in Delaware, but with its principal place of business in Connecticut. Assume that both parties are joint and severally liable for Defendants' actions.

If Defendants both seek to dismiss the case for lack of subject matter jurisdiction, what is the most likely outcome of these motions?

A. The case will be dismissed as against both Defendants.

B. The case will be dismissed as against PowerInc only but will proceed against SafeSeal.

C. The case will be dismissed as against SafeSeal only but will proceed against PowerInc.

D. The case will proceed against both Defendants and both motions will be denied.

5. Big Bank enters into an agreement on a second mortgage with Harry, lending him money to finance some repairs to his home. Harry has not made the payments on this second mortgage for well over a year, and the outstanding principal on it is $70,000. Harry consults with an attorney and learns that Big Bank may have failed to follow the federal Truth in Lending Act (TILA) when it processed Harry's mortgage. Based on the particular violation of TILA alleged by Harry, Harry may be relieved of the obligation to pay his mortgage. Harry files an action in federal court alleging a violation of TILA. Big Bank wants to interpose a defense that Harry has failed to comply with his obligations under the mortgage, a defense arising under state law. The bank wants to move to dismiss the complaint for an alleged lack of federal jurisdiction over the case. Big Bank is incorporated in Delaware and has its principal place of business in New York. Harry is a resident of Rensselaer County, New York. The amount in controversy is $70,000.

Will Big Bank succeed in its motion to dismiss Harry's case based on an alleged lack of subject matter jurisdiction? If so, why? If not, why not?

A. No, the basis for federal jurisdiction appears on the face of Harry's complaint.

B. No, Big Bank's state of incorporation means there is complete diversity between the parties, giving rise to federal subject matter jurisdiction.

C. Yes, Big Bank's state law defense does not give rise to federal subject matter jurisdiction.

D. Yes, the claims do not satisfy the amount-in-controversy requirement.

6. Ned is a resident of New York State. Ned is out driving and is forced to slam on his brakes when a deer runs across the road in front of him. He is then rear-ended by Carla, who was following in her car close to Ned. Carla is a citizen of Italy as well as a lawful permanent resident of the United States. She resides in New York State. Ned files a case against Carla in federal district court in the Northern District of New York where the accident took place and where Carla resides. He brings only state law claims and seeks $75,000 in damages. He seeks no damages for personal injuries because he was not physically injured, but he wants Carla to reimburse him for the extensive damage to his AMC Gremlin, which he claims is a "classic." Carla's attorney researches the matter and determines that the maximum replacement cost of an AMC Gremlin, even one in the exact same condition as Ned's, is certainly less than the amount sought by Ned. While it is, in fact, a rare car with a small but devoted circle of owners and aficionados of the novelty cars of the 1970s, the absolute maximum price of the car for resale on the open market is only $50,000. Ned's attorney reviews the research conducted by Carla's attorney on the price of the replacement Gremlin and agrees that her findings are accurate.

Does the federal court have subject matter jurisdiction over this case? If so, why? If not, why not?

A. The court has subject matter jurisdiction over the case through diversity jurisdiction because the parties are diverse and the plaintiff's complaint satisfies the amount-in-controversy requirement.

B. There is subject matter jurisdiction over the case despite its appearing that the plaintiff cannot satisfy the amount-in-controversy requirement.

C. There is no subject matter jurisdiction over the case because the parties are not diverse, even though the plaintiff can satisfy the amount-in-controversy requirement.

D. There is no subject matter jurisdiction over the case for two reasons: the parties are not diverse and the plaintiff does not satisfy the amount-in-controversy requirement.

7.   Peter brings an action against Dalia alleging that she failed to pay him for painting her portrait. Peter is an internationally renowned portrait artist, and he charges $200,000 for each portrait he paints. Dalia claims that Peter did not follow the instructions for the portrait laid out in the contract they signed, and she thinks he violated the terms of the contract with the finished portrait. Dalia says that the portrait makes her look like a cube. Peter says he is a "neo-cubist" and she knew what she was getting into when she signed the contract. Dalia is wealthy and splits her time between Cos Cob, Connecticut, and Geneva, Switzerland. She is a citizen of the United States and a resident of Connecticut. Peter recently moved to Paris, France, having fled his hometown of Williamsburg, Brooklyn, New York, because he couldn't stand all the "flannel and beards." Peter brings an action against Dalia in federal district court for the District of Connecticut, alleging state law claims of breach of contract and seeking $200,000 in damages. Peter's complaint describes him simply as a "resident of France."

If the defendant moves to dismiss the case for lack of subject matter jurisdiction, what is the court likely to do in response, and why?

A. Dismiss the case with prejudice. Peter has failed to establish subject matter jurisdiction over the case.

B. Dismiss the case without prejudice because Peter has failed to establish subject matter jurisdiction over the case, but permit Peter to refile if he can establish subject matter jurisdiction.

C. Deny the motion to dismiss. Peter's case fits squarely within the subject matter jurisdiction of the federal courts because there is complete diversity between the parties.

D. Deny the motion to dismiss. Peter's case fits squarely within the subject matter jurisdiction of the federal courts because he satisfies the amount-in-controversy requirement.

8. Paul brings an action against Dalia alleging that she failed to pay him for painting her portrait. Paul is an internationally renowned portrait artist, and he charges $200,000 for each portrait he paints. Dalia claims that Paul did not follow the instructions for the portrait laid out in the contract they signed, and she thinks he violated the terms of the contract with the finished portrait. Dalia says that the portrait makes her look like a cube. Paul says he is a "neo-cubist" and she knew what she was getting into when she signed the contract. Dalia is wealthy and splits her time between Cos Cob, Connecticut, and Geneva, Switzerland. She is a citizen of the United States and a resident of Connecticut. Paul is a resident and citizen of Brooklyn, New York. He brings an action against Dalia in U.S. District Court for the District of Connecticut, alleging state law claims of breach of contract and seeking $200,000 in damages.

If the defendant moves to dismiss the case for lack of subject matter jurisdiction, what is the court likely to do in response, and why?

A. Dismiss the case with prejudice. Paul has failed to establish subject matter jurisdiction over the case.

B. Dismiss the case without prejudice. Paul has failed to establish subject matter jurisdiction over the case.

C. Deny the motion to dismiss. Paul's case fits squarely within the subject matter jurisdiction of the federal courts based on diversity.

D. Deny the motion to dismiss. Paul's case fits squarely within the subject matter jurisdiction of the federal courts because his complaint raises federal questions.

2.3 Supplemental Jurisdiction

In addition to the two jurisdictional bases described above which enable a party to get into federal court in the first instance, there are times when parties have additional claims not based on federal law that can be interposed in an action when those claims are related to claims already in the case. This section explores such instances.

9.   Plaintiff brings an action against Defendant alleging violations of federal anti-discrimination laws. Plaintiff resides in Hoboken, New Jersey, and works at Defendant's restaurant in Lower Manhattan in the State of New York. Defendant Restaurant is a corporation incorporated in New York State, with its principal place of business in that state. Plaintiff alleges that Defendant terminated her employment based on her race and gender in violation of federal employment law. She also seeks to file additional claims based on federal law and New York state law regarding the hourly wages she was paid. She alleges in her complaint that the restaurant failed to pay her in accordance with the requirements of federal and New York state law regarding the overtime she worked. These claims relate to the hours she worked and the pay she received for those hours, and if her allegations are true, the Defendant failed to pay her the overtime pay she earned under both federal and state law. She does not allege that the failure to follow the overtime requirements of these laws was based on her gender or race because she knows other individuals with a range of demographic backgrounds also experienced this alleged failure on the part of her employer to follow state and federal law, so she cannot trace that alleged violation of the law to her gender or race. She seeks to combine all of these claims in a single case to be filed in federal district court for the Southern District of New York, the court that encompasses the location of the restaurant. The Defendant will move to dismiss the Plaintiff's claims, arguing that the court does not have subject matter jurisdiction over it. Plaintiff seeks $15,000 on the discrimination claim and $10,000 for each violation of the federal and state overtime laws, amounting to $35,000 in total.

Will the Defendant succeed in dismissing any or all of Plaintiff's claims? If so, why? If not, why not?

A. Defendant will succeed in dismissing all of the claims related to alleged overtime violations because they do not arise under a common nucleus of operative facts as the federal discrimination claim.

B. Defendant will succeed in dismissing only the state overtime claim because it does not arise from a common nucleus of operative facts as the federal discrimination claim.

C. Defendant will succeed in dismissing all of the claims because they do not satisfy the relevant amount-in-controversy requirement.

D. Defendant will not succeed in dismissing any of the claims because the court has subject matter jurisdiction over all of the federal claims and the state overtime claim arises out of the same common nucleus of operative facts as the related federal overtime claim.

10. Plaintiff brings an action alleging violation of federal and state minimum wage laws. Most of Plaintiff's claims center around issues involving violation of federal law, and the overwhelming majority of the remedies are based on the federal laws governing the employer-employee relationship. Plaintiff is a resident and citizen of New York State. Defendant is incorporated in Delaware, with its principal place of business in New York. Plaintiff seeks $150,000 on his federal claims and $5,000 on a related state law claim. Plaintiff's state law claim involves the calculation of overtime wages, which differs slightly from the way federal law treats the issue. Assume that the Plaintiff's state law claim arises out of the same nucleus of operative facts as the federal claims, that is, the pay the employee received for his work. Defendant will make a motion asking the district court to dismiss the state law claim, alleging the court does not have subject matter jurisdiction over it.

Will the court grant Defendant's motion? If so, why? If not, why not?

A. Yes, because the Plaintiff's state law claim does not satisfy the amount-in-controversy requirement.

B. Yes, because the parties are not diverse.

C. No, because the state law claim arises from the same nucleus of operative facts as the federal claims.

D. No, because the Plaintiff has interposed a plausible claim for relief.

11. Plaintiff, a tenant, sues Defendant, a landlord, in federal court, alleging that Defendant discriminated against Plaintiff based on Plaintiff's ethnicity when Plaintiff was denied a rental apartment in one of Defendant's residential buildings. Plaintiff, a legal permanent resident residing in New York who is of Bosnian descent, alleges that he was discriminated against by Defendant, also a lawful permanent resident residing in New York but who is of Serbian descent. Such discrimination, if proven, would violate federal housing discrimination laws. Plaintiff seeks $50,000 in damages under this claim. Plaintiff seeks to add a state law claim that he was also discriminated against when his application was denied based on information found in his credit history that was supplied by a commercial credit reporting agency. Assume that after an inquiry by the New York State legislature into the unreliability of commercial credit reports in the completion of background checks, particularly those that mine an individual's social media history in creating such reports, the New York legislature had recently passed legislation making it illegal to make decisions to deny rental housing to a tenant based on those commercial credit histories that use information from an individual's social media activity as part of the credit-reporting process. Plaintiff alleges that the decision to reject his rental application was based, in part, on Defendant's review of Plaintiff's commercial credit report, which revealed not only his ethnicity but also his pro-Bosnian political stances, evident from his social media posts. Plaintiff believes the decision to reject his application was based on both the ethnic discrimination and the contents

of the commercial credit report containing the information from social media, in violation of the new state law on the topic. Plaintiff seeks $20,000 in damages based on this new state law. Defendant plans to challenge the constitutionality of the credit report law, stating that it violates his free speech rights under the New York State Constitution, which, Defendant argues, offers greater protections than the U.S. Constitution. Defendant also argues that these greater protections under the New York Constitution protect his communications with the credit reporting agency about Plaintiff's tenancy. This would be the first such case testing the constitutionality of the law under the New York State Constitution.

If Defendant wants to argue that the court may exercise its discretion to decline supplemental jurisdiction over the state law claim, which is the strongest argument in Defendant's favor on this point given the facts as presented?

A. The state law claim predominates over the federal claim.

B. The claim raises novel or complex issues of state law.

C. There are exceptional circumstances warranting dismissal of the state claim.

D. The court does not have subject matter jurisdiction over either the federal or state claims.

12.   Plaintiff, a resident and citizen of Maryland, travels into Delaware every day of the work week, where she works for a credit card company, BMNA. BMNA is incorporated in Delaware, with its principal place of business in New York City, New York. Plaintiff works in a BMNA call center where she handles customer service complaints and troubleshoots customer issues, like questions that arise involving alleged identity theft. One day, Plaintiff is told she is being fired because she allegedly assisted some hackers in getting information from the BMNA database for the purpose of engaging in the identify theft of BMNA's customers. Plaintiff denies this. Actually, Plaintiff is the one who identified the breach and brought it to the attention of BMNA officials as soon as she discovered it. She alleges that, by firing her, BMNA is singling her out for this treatment because of her ethnicity, a violation of federal employment discrimination law. She says that she is one of over one hundred individuals who had access to the BMNA data base who could have assisted the hackers, but she is the only employee out of this group of her ethnic background, and she is the only employee fired. Furthermore, she says that BMNA actually has evidence that other employees in the company were involved in the security breach, but those officials are high up in the company and it would be embarrassing to admit their involvement. Instead, Plaintiff alleges, BMNA is using her as a scapegoat. She files an action in federal court in Delaware, alleging that her termination violates federal civil rights statutes barring discrimination in employment. She seeks $50,000 on her federal claim, the wages she would have earned

had she not been terminated. Additionally, she alleges under well-established state law claims which prohibit discrimination based on ethnicity that her termination in this instance and in this way violates state law. Her complaint seeks to include both the federal and state law claims. She seeks an additional $10,000 in damages on the state claim alone. BMNA receives Plaintiff's complaint and seeks to dismiss the state law claim based on a lack of federal subject matter jurisdiction.

Should the court grant BMNA's motion to dismiss the state law claim for lack of subject matter jurisdiction over it? If so, why? If not, why not?

A. The motion should be granted because novel issues of state law predominate in Plaintiff's case.

B. The motion should be granted because the facts underlying the state law claim do not arise out of the same nucleus of operative facts as the underlying federal law claim, and there is thus no independent basis of jurisdiction over that claim.

C. The motion should be denied because the federal and state law claims are so related that they arise out of the same nucleus of operative facts.

D. The motion should be denied because the parties are diverse even though Plaintiff cannot satisfy the amount-in-controversy requirement.

13. Plaintiff sues her employer under federal civil rights statutes, alleging unlawful discrimination in employment based on her gender. She claims she was the victim of a hostile work environment. The environment was such that co-workers made sexual advances and would routinely walk up behind Plaintiff and rub her shoulders, despite her repeated protests that she did not appreciate such treatment. No male co-workers were subject to this treatment. Allegations regarding this offensive touching are included in the allegations Plaintiff says created a hostile work environment based on gender. Plaintiff also seeks to include a claim based on state labor law against her employer alleging that she along with several of her co-workers (all of them male) were not paid the overtime pay to which they were entitled. The employer is incorporated in New York, with its principal place of business in that state. Plaintiff, a restaurant worker, is a resident and citizen of New Jersey. She sues for $50,000 in damages in total: $25,000 under the federal claims and $25,000 under the state law tort claim.

Can Plaintiff include the state law claim in her federal lawsuit in federal court?

A. Yes. The parties are diverse.

B. Yes. The state law claim arises out of the same nucleus of operative facts as the federal claim.

C. No. The amount-in-controversy requirement is not satisfied for any of the claims.

D. No. The claims do not arise out of the same nucleus of operative facts.

14. Plaintiff is an accountant at Big Three Accounting (Big Three). She is working for one of the firm's clients, EnCon, conducting its annual audit. Plaintiff notices some serious deficiencies in the books maintained by EnCon. She knows that EnCon recently held a sale of corporate securities and Plaintiff believes the public documents released in support of that sale were willfully manipulated. If true, such conduct is illegal under federal securities law. Plaintiff brings the issue to her supervisors at Big Three, who tell her she should not raise the issue with the client because to do so could make the client fire Big Three as its accountant, and it could lead to EnCon being held liable for violations of federal securities law. They also tell her she should just "go along to get along" like she is "one of the boys," and not raise a stink about EnCon's "fuzzy math." None of this sits well with Plaintiff. She believes that she has a duty under federal law to report EnCon's fraudulent securities disclosures. She follows what she believes is her duty under federal law and reports the matter of EnCon's faulty disclosures to the local U.S. Attorney's Office. EnCon's President and CEO is brought up on federal securities law violations and EnCon is slapped with a multi-million dollar fine. Plaintiff is subsequently fired by Big Three. Plaintiff brings a federal anti-discrimination suit against Big Three alleging that she was treated differently because she is a woman. Her allegation that she was told to be "one of the boys" could lead a jury to conclude that she was discriminated against based on her gender, a violation of federal and state law. She also seeks to bring a supplemental state law claim alleging that she was discriminated against because of her gender on these same allegations. She seeks $100,000 in damages under each claim for a total of $200,000 in damages. Plaintiff is a citizen of New York and a resident of Albany, New York. Big Three is incorporated in Delaware, with its principal place of business in New York State. Big Three moves to dismiss the state law claim.

Should the court dismiss the state law claim? If so, why? If not, why not?

A. The state law claim should be allowed to remain in the suit because it arises out of the same nucleus of operative facts as the federal claim.

B. The state law claim should be dismissed because it does not arise out of the same nucleus of operative facts as the federal claim.

C. The state law claims should be dismissed because novel issues of state law predominate in the action.

D. The court should not dismiss the state law claim because the court has jurisdiction over it based on diversity jurisdiction.

15. Plaintiff, a resident and citizen of Maryland, travels into Delaware every day, where she works for a credit card company, BMNA. BMNA is incorporated in Delaware, with its principal place of business in New York City. Plaintiff works in a BMNA call center where she handles customer service complaints and troubleshoots customer issues, like questions that arise involving alleged identity theft. One day, Plaintiff is told she is being fired because she allegedly assisted some hackers in getting information from the BMNA database for the purpose of engaging in the identify theft of BMNA's customers. Plaintiff denies this. Actually, Plaintiff is the one who identified the breach and brought it to the attention of BMNA officials as soon as she discovered it. She alleges that, by firing her, BMNA is singling her out for this treatment because she is Latina, a violation of federal employment discrimination law. She says that she is one of over one hundred individuals who had access to the BMNA database who could have assisted the hackers, but she is the only employee out of this group of Hispanic descent. Furthermore, she says that BMNA actually has evidence that other employees in the company were involved in the security breach, but those officials are high up in the company and it would be embarrassing to admit their involvement. Instead, Plaintiff alleges, BMNA is using her as a scapegoat. She files an action in federal court in Delaware, alleging that her termination violated federal civil rights statutes barring discrimination in employment. She seeks $50,000 on her federal claim, the wages she would have earned had she not been terminated. She also alleges under state contract law that she was not paid in accordance with her employment contract with BMNA. Although her employment contract said she was entitled to overtime pay, she was routinely asked to work more than the 40 hours per week specified in the contract. Her complaint seeks to join a claim based on state contract law. Plaintiff will argue that while she was employed, she was underpaid each week by hundreds of dollars, and she will seek $10,000 in damages on the state claim alone. BMNA receives Plaintiff's complaint and seeks to dismiss the state contract law claim based on a lack of federal subject matter jurisdiction.

Should the court grant BMNA's motion to dismiss the state law claim for lack of subject matter jurisdiction? If so, why? If not, why not?

A. The motion should be granted because novel issues of state law predominate in Plaintiff's state law claim.

B. The motion should be granted because the facts underlying the state law claims are unrelated to the facts underlying the federal law claim and there is no independent basis of jurisdiction over that claim.

C. The motion should be denied because the federal and state law claims are so related that they form the same case or controversy.

D. The motion should be denied because the parties are diverse.

16. Paula believes that she was the victim of national origin discrimination when she was approved for a mortgage on discriminatory terms. She believes she was given a loan at a higher interest rate than she would have otherwise received but for illegal discrimination. She believes this higher interest rate is the result of her status as an Italian-American. Such act on the part of her bank is a violation of the federal Fair Housing Act. Paula's lawyer believes that this practice is also a violation of New York State's predatory lending law because of the excessive interest rate that was charged by the bank. Paula's attorney files a case in federal court alleging that the bank violated the federal Fair Housing Act by charging Paula the higher interest rate on discriminatory grounds. She seeks $200,000 in damages. Paula is a resident of New York. Boston Bank is incorporated in New York with its principal place of business in Boston, Massachusetts. Paula also seeks $100,000 in damages under the state predatory lending law for charging her an interest rate that violates that law's interest rate cap.

Could Paula's attorney add a state law claim based on the state predatory lending law to the federal action brought under the Fair Housing Act in federal court? If so, why? If not, why not?

A. Yes, there is supplemental jurisdiction over the state law claim because the federal and state law claims are logically related.

B. Yes, there is supplemental jurisdiction over the state law claim because the federal and state law claims arise from the same nucleus of operative facts.

C. No, there is no jurisdiction over the state law claim because the parties are not diverse, despite the fact that the Plaintiff satisfies the amount-in-controversy requirement.

D. No, there is no supplemental jurisdiction over the state law claim because the federal and state law claims do not arise from the same nucleus of operative facts.

17. Peter is a high-frequency bond trader who typically earns $1 million a year, even in down years for the economy as a whole. He sues his former employer, DK Industries, alleging that he was fired based on his national origin, a claim under federal law. He also alleges that his firing was wrongful, a tort under applicable state law that incorporates many of the same protections found in federal employment discrimination law. Peter is a resident of Nassau County, New York, who commutes daily to the office of DK Industries in Brooklyn, New York. DK is incorporated in Delaware, with its principal place of business in New York State. Peter alleges that he was discriminated against because he is from the Basque region of Northeastern Spain. Peter believes that his boss, Michael, whose family is originally from Madrid, Spain, is prejudiced against him because of his Basque origins and fired him based on this. Peter also alleges that Michael fired him based on complaints Peter raised with the Chief Executive Officer of the company, alleging that Michael and others were engaged in illegal practices that violated the Foreign Corrupt Practices Act (FCPA). Although the FCPA is a federal law, it does not offer any employment protections to him. Instead, he argues that the state's wrongful discharge law protects him from being fired for being a whistleblower, that is, for alerting the company to wrongdoing occurring within the company. Peter alleges that other individuals in the company also complained about the illegal conduct, but they were not fired. Peter believes, once again, that he was fired because of his Basque origins. Peter brings an action in federal court alleging violation of federal employment discrimination laws and state protections against wrongful discharge. He seeks $200,000 for the federal claim and $200,000 on the state claim. DK Industries, the defendant, brings a motion to dismiss the federal discrimination claim, arguing that federal non-discrimination laws protecting against national origin discrimination do not protect someone from a particular region of a country. DK Industries is successful and the federal claim is dismissed. DK Industries then brings a second motion to dismiss alleging only that there is no longer federal subject matter jurisdiction over Peter's state law claim because the federal claim has been dismissed. DK Industries does not challenge the merits of the claim, only whether the court has subject matter jurisdiction over it.

What statement is the most accurate in terms of how the court should treat the remaining state law claim?

A. The court must dismiss Peter's state law claim.

B. The court must retain jurisdiction over Peter's state law claim.

C. The court may dismiss Peter's state law claim.

D. The court may not retain jurisdiction over Peter's state law claim.

18. Paula believes that she was the victim of national origin discrimination when she was turned down for a mortgage, a violation of the federal Fair Housing Act. When her attorney researches the matter, she learns that it appears that Paula was also the victim of a breach of state privacy laws. Boston Bank, the bank from which she sought a mortgage, disclosed her credit score to several marketing companies. Those companies then used it to market products to Paula without her consent. The evidence related to the discrimination claim is revealed in internal emails between company personnel who say they did not want to lend to Paula because "she looks Italian." The evidence related to the privacy breach also comes from emails, but different emails, that is, from those between company personnel and employees of the marketing firms to which Boston Bank sold Paula's personal information. Paula's attorney files a case in federal court alleging violation of the federal Fair Housing Act. She seeks $200,000 in damages. Paula is a resident of New York. Boston Bank is incorporated in New York, with its principal place of business in Boston, Massachusetts. Paula also has a state law claim for breach of privacy and wants to seek $100,000 in damages under that claim.

Could Paula's attorney add a state law claim based on breach of privacy to the federal case brought under the Fair Housing Act in federal court? If so, why? If not, why not?

A. Yes, there is supplemental jurisdiction over the state law claim because the federal and state law claims are logically related.

B. Yes, there is supplemental jurisdiction over the state law claim because the federal and state law claims arise from the same nucleus of operative facts.

C. No, there is no supplemental jurisdiction over the state law claim because the federal and state law claims are not logically related.

D. No, there is no supplemental jurisdiction over the state law claim because the federal and state law claims do not arise from the same nucleus of operative facts.

19. Plaintiff suffers superficial physical injuries when the tire on his moped explodes while he is riding through the streets of the City of Albany, New York. He is taken to the hospital and a few small bandages are applied to his minor scrapes, which completely heal in less than a week. His Crespa Moped, which is mass-produced in Pine Plains, New York, is destroyed, but it can be easily replaced, and Plaintiff does replace it relatively soon after the accident. Plaintiff also has a car and is not inconvenienced in the least for the period in which he does not have a functioning moped, which is just a few days. The replacement cost of the moped is $3,000, which Plaintiff pays for out of his own savings. Plaintiff is a resident of Albany, New York, and a citizen of New York. Albany is located in the jurisdiction of the federal district court for the Northern District of New York. A manufacturing defect in the tire caused the accident. The manufacturer of the tire, Flint Tire, is located in Flint, Michigan, located in the jurisdiction of the federal district court for the Northern District of Michigan. After submitting to a physical examination from the Defendant's insurance company that reveals his physical injuries were slight, Plaintiff nevertheless sues the tire manufacturer, seeking $100,000 in damages for the injuries he sustained and the loss of his moped. He files suit based on state tort claims in the federal district court for the Northern District of Michigan. Flint Tire challenges the court's subject matter jurisdiction over the proceeding.

Will the court grant the motion to dismiss based on an alleged lack of subject matter jurisdiction? If so, why? If not, why not?

A. The motion will be denied because the parties are diverse and the allegations in Plaintiff's complaint satisfy the amount-in-controversy requirement.

B. The motion will be denied because the interstate nature of the dispute warrants the court's exercise of subject matter jurisdiction over the proceeding.

C. The motion will be granted because the federal court does not have jurisdiction over a home-state defendant under the court's diversity jurisdiction.

D. The motion will be granted because it is a legal certainty that the Plaintiff cannot satisfy the amount-in-controversy requirement.

2.4 "Mixed" Jurisdiction Questions

This section tests your understanding of the various bases of jurisdiction explored so far.

20. State University, a public university located in New York State, files a lawsuit in New York state court in Albany County, alleging that one of its vendors, DiDi Dee, the sole proprietor and owner of Dee's Donuts, has violated her contract with the University by driving around campus in the Dee's Donuts van with a placard, posted on both sides of the van, proclaiming that the University system should divest from investing in companies that do business with the government of the rogue nation of Catan, which Dee believes supports terrorism. State University states that the contract with Dee provides explicitly that Dee may not communicate any political statements in any advertising or through other means while Dee is present on campus. State University is seeking damages in the amount of $100,000 on a state contract claim. Dee will assert as a defense that State University, a public entity, cannot deprive her of her free speech rights in violation of the First and Fourteenth Amendments to the U.S. Constitution. State University is a governmental corporation incorporated in New York State, with its principal place of business in New York State. Dee is an individual who is a citizen of and resides in the State of New York. Dee seeks to remove the case from the state court in Albany County to the federal court for the Northern District of New York, the district that encompasses Albany County. State University will object to the removal and seek to have the federal court remand the matter to the state court.

Will the federal court remand the matter to state court? If so, why? If not, why not?

A. Yes, because Dee is a home state defendant and thus removal of the case to federal court in her home state is inappropriate.

B. Yes, because no basis for federal jurisdiction appears in the plaintiff's complaint.

C. No. Because the federal claims likely predominate over any state claims, the matter is appropriately before the federal court.

D. No, because the case involves critical questions related to important federal rights.

21.   Plaintiff files an action against Big Pharma, a pharmaceutical company that is incorporated in New York, with its corporate headquarters in Connecticut. Plaintiff is a citizen and resident of New Jersey. Plaintiff files a personal injury action against Defendant for allegedly negligent distribution of a medication that triggered a serious allergic reaction in Plaintiff, causing her considerable physical and psychiatric side effects. Plaintiff seeks over $1 million in damages, making several novel and creative claims based on several different state law theories of recovery, including products liability, personal injury, fraudulent labeling, and intentional tort. Plaintiff also interposes a federal claim based on a federal drug labeling law, saying that the labeling of the drug in terms of its side effects was negligent. On this federal claim, Plaintiff seeks $5,000 in damages, the statutory cap on damages under the relevant law. Plaintiff brings her action in federal court. Defendant will move to dismiss the state law claims, alleging that they predominate over the federal claim and the court should exercise its discretion to dismiss them.

Will Defendant succeed in dismissing Plaintiff's state law claims? If so, why? If not, why not?

A. Yes, because the state law claims are novel and predominate over the federal law claims due to the fact that Plaintiff's case seeks far more in damages under the state law theories of recovery and they are far more numerous than the solitary federal claim.

B. No, because there is an independent basis of jurisdiction over the state law claims, and the discretionary factors of supplemental jurisdiction should not be applied to dismiss those claims.

C. Yes, because the claims do not arise out of the same common nucleus of operative facts.

D. No, although the court has discretion to weigh several factors to determine whether to dismiss the state law claims, it would be fundamentally unfair to deny Plaintiff the opportunity to litigate all of her claims together.

22. Peter brings an action in federal court in the Southern District of New York, the district that encompasses Manhattan, against his employer under federal employment laws. Peter alleges that he was denied promotion on the basis of his national origin, a violation of federal anti-discrimination laws, in his work as a bond trader. He also interposes supplemental claims under state law alleging that the same alleged misconduct of the employer leads to liability under state anti-discrimination law. He seeks $200,000 in damages: $100,000 under the federal law claims and $100,000 under the state law claims. Peter is of Moroccan descent and is a Moroccan citizen who is residing lawfully and permanently in the United States. Peter resides in Brooklyn, New York. Defendant is Golden-Max, an investment bank. Golden-Max is incorporated in Delaware with its principal place of business in Manhattan, in New York State. Golden-Max moves to dismiss Peter's state law claims, alleging that the court does not have subject matter jurisdiction over those claims.

Will the court dismiss Peter's state law claims? If so, why? If not, why not?

A. Yes, because the parties are not diverse even though Peter is a Moroccan citizen.

B. Yes, because the claim does not arise out of the same common nucleus of operative facts as the federal claim.

C. No, because Peter can claim diversity jurisdiction over the state law claim because he is a Moroccan citizen.

D. No, because the claim arises under the same common nucleus of operative facts as the federal claims and the citizenship status of the parties is irrelevant.

23. Pauline makes a living playing the popular poker game "Texas Hold 'Em." She is very good at it and regularly brings in over $10 million in earnings annually by playing in nationally televised tournaments. Danny is an investigator for the New York Gambling Commission, a state agency that regulates gambling in New York State. Danny believes Pauline cheats, and he wants to report her to the New York State Office of the Attorney General for fraud. Danny is a resident and citizen of New York State. He tracks Pauline's every move, taps her cell phone, hacks her computer, and even enters her hotel room without a warrant while she is out gambling at several of New York State's gambling establishments in order to try to figure out how she is cheating. Pauline learns she is being tracked and that Danny has broken into her hotel room without a warrant. Pauline is a resident and citizen of California. Pauline brings an action in federal court in New York asserting one claim: that Danny violated the New York State Constitution when he entered her hotel room without a warrant, tapped her cell phone, and hacked her computer. She seeks $1 million in damages for violation of the New York State Constitution. Danny seeks to dismiss the case for lack of subject matter jurisdiction.

Will Danny succeed in dismissing the case for lack of subject matter jurisdiction? If so, why? If not, why not?

A. No, the basis for federal jurisdiction appears on the face of the well-pleaded complaint.

B. No, Pauline is suing Danny in a state in which there are sufficient minimum contacts to justify the exercise of jurisdiction over him in a federal court.

C. Yes, Pauline's claim raises novel and complex issues of state law and should be resolved by a state and not a federal court.

D. Yes, Danny is a resident and citizen of New York State, and thus the case cannot be heard in a federal court in his home state.

24. Plaintiff is a domestic worker who sues Defendant in federal court in New York, alleging employment discrimination in violation of federal law. Plaintiff is a resident and citizen of New York State, as is her employer, a prominent politician in the Albany, New York, area, who is also a resident and citizen of New York State. Plaintiff alleges that she was subject to ethnically charged epithets during the course of her work for her employer. She alleges that this created a hostile work environment in violation of federal law and caused her significant mental anguish. She seeks $30,000 on her federal claim. She also seeks to include two state law claims against the employer. First, she alleges that these same allegations give rise to a common law intentional tort because the conduct that created the hostile work environment was intentional, extreme, and outrageous, thus constituting sufficient basis under the law for such a claim. Second, she alleges that her employer failed to pay her according to state minimum wage laws. There is no allegation that the minimum wage claim is related to the facts that give rise to the allegations that the employer created a hostile work environment. She seeks an additional $10,000 in damages for each of these state claims, so that her case as a whole seeks $50,000 in damages. Because the state minimum wage law requires a wage higher than the federal minimum wage and the employer satisfied the federal minimum wage law but failed to satisfy the state minimum wage law, Plaintiff has not included any claims in her complaint based on the federal minimum wage law.

If Defendant seeks to dismiss both of the state law claims based on his argument that the federal court lacks subject mat-

ter jurisdiction over them, will the court dismiss either or both of those claims? If so, why? If not, why not?

A. The court will dismiss both of the state law claims because they do not satisfy the amount-in-controversy requirement.

B. The court will dismiss both of the state law claims because the parties are not diverse.

C. The court will dismiss only the minimum wage claim because it does not arise out of the same nucleus of operative facts as the federal claim.

D. The court will dismiss neither of the state law claims because the claims arise out of the same case or controversy as the federal claim.

25. Plaintiff commences an action in the federal court for the Southern District of New York, alleging violations of federal securities laws against two defendants, Able Corp. (Able) and Baker Corp. (Baker), two securities brokerage firms whose employees, Plaintiff alleges, made material and fraudulent misrepresentations with respect to the sale of a stock that Plaintiff purchased. Soon after Plaintiff purchased the stock on the advice of employees of Able and Baker, that stock became essentially worthless because the company issuing the stock went bankrupt. Plaintiff alleges Able and Baker's employees knew this was going to happen and engaged in the sale to Plaintiff of the stock in the company. Able and Baker held such stock in their own portfolios and were trying to sell it in an effort to cut their own future losses. (Assume that the brokerage firms are liable for the actions of their employees under applicable law.) Plaintiff is a resident of New York, residing in Manhattan, which is located within the jurisdiction of the federal court for the Southern District of New York. Able is incorporated in Delaware, with its principal place of business in New York State. Baker is also incorporated in New York, but with its principal place of business in New Jersey. The wealthy clients of both companies reside predominantly in Manhattan, and that is where these companies market their business almost exclusively. It is a result of this marketing effort that Plaintiff agrees to do business with both companies. Assume that all of the alleged illegal conduct took place in an in-person meeting that was held in the offices of Baker in Jersey City, New Jersey, at which representatives of both Able and Baker were present. During this meeting, em-

ployees of both companies tried, successfully, to convince Plaintiff to purchase the stock. Plaintiff seeks $200,000 in damages from his losses in the stock, which he can easily show if Defendants' conduct turns out to have violated the applicable law.

If Defendants seek to dismiss the case for lack of federal subject matter jurisdiction over the action, will the court grant the motion? If so, why? If not, why not?

A. The court will deny the motion because the basis for federal subject matter jurisdiction appears on the face of the complaint.

B. The court will grant the motion because there is not complete diversity between the parties.

C. The court will deny the motion because, although there is not complete diversity between the parties, the court can take into account only Defendants' respective principal places of business when considering the diversity of the parties.

D. The court will grant the motion because a substantial portion of the events giving rise to Plaintiff's claims occurred outside the forum state.

26. Plaintiff, a resident and citizen of Maryland, travels into Delaware every day, where she works as a pediatric neuroscience researcher at a research laboratory owned by a Maryland-based hospital, DuMont Children's Hospital (DCH). DCH is incorporated in Delaware, with its principal place of business in Baltimore, Maryland. Plaintiff is worried that the laboratory is not disposing of its medical waste in accordance with Delaware state law and complains to the environmental agency of the State of Delaware, the agency with authority over the proper disposal of medical waste. She is then fired. Under a state environmental law statute, Plaintiff has a cause of action for wrongful termination because she was fired under conditions that make her believe that the termination was the result of her reporting DCH to the state environmental agency for its failure to properly dispose of medical waste. Plaintiff was a highly paid researcher at DCH and sues for lost wages of more than $200,000. Her lawyer wants to sue DCH in federal court out of concern that DCH is a political powerhouse in Delaware, as the DuMont family has a long history of having political ties to elected officials in the state.

Can Plaintiff bring her action in federal court in Delaware? If so, why? If not, why not?

A. Yes, because Defendant DCH has its principal place of business in Maryland, and thus the parties are diverse.

B. Yes, because Defendant DCH is incorporated in Delaware, and thus the parties are diverse.

C. No, because Defendant DCH has its principal place of business in Maryland, and thus the parties are not diverse.

D. No, because Defendant DCH is incorporated in Delaware, where Plaintiff works and travels to every working day, the parties both have systematic and continuous contacts with the forum state, are at home in the state of Delaware as a result, and are not diverse from each other.

27.   Plaintiff is a winner of a beauty pageant, the Miss Galaxy Contest. Upon winning the contest, she enters into an employee-employer relationship with Miss Galaxy, Inc. (MGI), the company that runs the contest. Part of the employment contract involves Plaintiff's engaging in publicity events and other activities related to the pageant. Plaintiff is a lawful permanent resident residing in the United States who is also a native and current citizen of Mexico. She alleges that she was paid less than prior beauty pageant winners based on her ethnicity and national origin, which are both grounds for a claim under Title VII, a federal statute that bars discrimination in employment. She seeks $50,000 in damages, alleging that this amount represents the difference between what she was paid and what prior contest winners were paid, that is, what she would have been paid were it not for the discrimination she claims to have faced. MGI is incorporated in Delaware, with its principal place of business in New York. Plaintiff resides in Brooklyn, New York. Plaintiff files her action alleging violation of federal anti-discrimination law against MGI in the federal district court for the Eastern District of New York, where she resides. MGI will seek to challenge the subject matter jurisdiction of the federal court to hear Plaintiff's case but does not challenge venue.

Will the court grant the motion to dismiss for want of subject matter jurisdiction? If so, why? If not, why not?

A. The motion will be granted because Plaintiff cannot satisfy the amount-in-controversy requirement.

B. The motion will be denied because Plaintiff's federal claim gives the court subject matter jurisdiction.

C. The motion will be granted because Plaintiff's lawful permanent residence status renders her, for the purposes of the subject matter inquiry, a citizen of New York State, and thus the parties are not diverse.

D. The motion will be denied because Plaintiff's status as a foreign national renders the parties diverse for the purposes of determining the court's subject matter jurisdiction.

28.　Peter is an international artist who creates unique designs which involve likenesses of famous comic book heroes dressed in nineteenth-century garb. Marble Comics (Marble) believes that Peter has infringed on Marble's federal copyright covering its comic book characters and writes a cease-and-desist letter to Peter, threatening that it will bring a federal copyright infringement suit against Peter for his alleged improper use of Marble's characters which are covered by Marble's federal copyrights. Peter consults with an attorney and brings an action in federal court under federal copyright laws, asserting that his use of Marble's characters is "fair use" and lawful under federal law. He seeks an order from the court stating that his actions comply with federal law. Peter spends most of his time working out of his studio in Rome, Italy. Peter files a complaint in the federal court for the Southern District of New York where Marble has its headquarters. In the complaint, Peter alleges that he is a resident of Rome, Italy. He does not state if he is an Italian or a U.S. citizen, nor does he state that he has any residence other than Rome, Italy. Marble files a pre-answer motion to dismiss the action, arguing that the court lacks subject matter jurisdiction over Peter's case.

Should the court grant Marble's motion to dismiss? If so, why? If not, why not?

A. It should be granted. Peter has failed to state whether he is a citizen of Italy or the United States.

B. It should be granted. Peter fails to satisfy the amount-in-controversy requirement because he has not claimed any damages.

C. It should be denied. Peter's citizenship is irrelevant to the subject matter jurisdiction of the court.

D. It should be denied. Marble cannot raise lack of subject matter jurisdiction in a pre-answer motion to dismiss.

29.   Paula Parr sues DeLacroix Opticians in federal district court in Louisiana, alleging violation of federal civil rights statutes because the business, an eyeglass store in the French Quarter of New Orleans, is not wheelchair accessible. Paula is a resident of New Orleans, Louisiana, and DeLacroix is a corporation organized under the laws of Louisiana, with its principal place of business in New Orleans, Louisiana. The cost of making the business wheelchair accessible is relatively minimal: the entrance to the storefront is at sidewalk grade, but the wooden door, an original French Quarter wooden frame, is so narrow that it does not comply with the federal Americans with Disabilities Act (ADA). Since DeLacroix recently made some renovations to the store, it is obligated to ensure that it is fully wheelchair accessible under the ADA. The door can be modified for approximately $10,000. Parr's action will seek an injunction ordering DeLacroix to renovate the door to widen it to make it comply with the requirements of the ADA.

Does the federal district court have subject matter jurisdiction over the action by Parr against DeLacroix? If so, why? If not, why not?

A. Yes. There do not appear to be any impediments to federal subject matter jurisdiction under the facts given.

B. No. Both parties are from Louisiana, and thus there is not complete diversity between the parties.

C. Yes. Because the action seeks an injunction, the amount in controversy requirement is waived.

D. No. The action does not satisfy the amount-in-controversy requirement.

30. Plaintiff brings an action against her former employer alleging violations of federal employment discrimination law in the manner in which she was compensated when she worked for the employer. Plaintiff currently resides in Ravena, New York, located in Albany County. She was formerly employed as an attorney in a law firm in Bennington, Vermont. She used to commute to Bennington from her home in Ravena. Plaintiff seeks $75,000 in damages in her action against her former firm because she alleges she was improperly denied the year-end bonus male attorneys received. She alleges that the denial of the bonus was a violation of federal statutes that prohibit discrimination in the workplace. Plaintiff brings her action against the firm in federal district court for the District Court of Vermont. Defendant law firm files a motion to dismiss claiming the court does not have subject matter jurisdiction over the claim and that it should have been filed in state court. Defendant is a professional corporation that is incorporated in Vermont and has its principal place of business in Vermont.

Should the federal court dismiss the action for lack of subject matter jurisdiction? If so, why? If not, why not?

A. No. The basis for federal jurisdiction appears on the face of the well-pleaded complaint.

B. Yes. Even though the parties are diverse, the Plaintiff has not satisfied the amount-in-controversy requirement that would enable her to sue in federal court.

C. Yes. State courts have concurrent jurisdiction over this action, and thus the action should have been filed in state court at the outset given that De-fendant is at home in the courts of Vermont.

D. No. The parties are diverse and the Plaintiff satisfies the amount-in-controversy requirement.

31. Plaintiff brings an action against his former employer alleging violation of federal and state minimum wage laws. Most of Plaintiff's claims involve alleged violations of federal law. Plaintiff is a resident and citizen of New York State. Defendant is incorporated in Delaware, with its principal place of business in New York. Plaintiff seeks $150,000 on his federal claims. Plaintiff will also seek $1,000 on a relatively obscure state law, asserting that Plaintiff was required to wear a uniform at his place of employment and that uniform needed to be dry cleaned every week according to Defendant's policies. Plaintiff asserts that he was required to pay out of pocket for not just the uniform but also for the dry cleaning of it. Plaintiff alleges, correctly, that this is a violation of state law, and the damages sought on this claim amount to the costs for the purchase of the uniform and the dry cleaning of it over the course of the last two years. Defendant will move to dismiss the state law claim, alleging the court does not have subject matter jurisdiction over it.

Will the court grant Defendant's motion? If so, why? If not, why not?

A. Yes, because the federal law claims predominate over the lone and obscure state law claim.

B. No, because the Plaintiff's state law claim is not required to satisfy the amount-in-controversy requirement since the anchor claims are based on federal law.

C. Yes, because the state law claim does not arise from the same common nucleus of operative facts as the federal claims.

D. No, because the state law claim arises from the same common nucleus of operative facts as the federal claims.

2.5 Removal and Remand

Plaintiffs can choose a federal forum if there is subject matter jurisdiction for doing so, but if they do not, defendants are not without their own ability to transfer the case to federal court. There are some nuances to the defendant's power here and the plaintiff's ability to check it where appropriate, and this section explores these nuances.

32. Plaintiff and Defendant are both citizens of New York. Plaintiff files an action alleging that Defendant engaged in employment discrimination and claiming Defendant's failure to promote him was a violation of state anti-discrimination law. Plaintiff believes he was discriminated against because he used to receive unemployment benefits, and his employer believes that everyone should raise themselves up by their own bootstraps. Such an adverse employment decision on these grounds is a violation of state law prohibiting what is known as "source of income" discrimination, which is not a violation of federal law but is a violation of the applicable state law. Because the parties are not diverse, the Plaintiff brings an action in state court against his employer on this ground. During the discovery phase of the action, Plaintiff learns that it appears his failure to receive a promotion was also based on his sexual orientation. The statute of limitations on Plaintiff's being able to file a new action against his employer based on these newly discovered grounds has not expired. Plaintiff seeks to amend his complaint thirteen months after commencing his original action by adding a new claim based on discrimination against him because of his sexual orientation, which is a violation of federal law. Assume the state court has concurrent jurisdiction over that claim. The Defendant's counsel will not object to the amendment of the complaint itself, but within five days of receiving that amended complaint, Defendant will seek to remove the case to federal court. Plaintiff will object to that removal as untimely.

Will Defendant succeed in removing Plaintiff's case to federal court? If so, why? If not, why not?

A. Yes, because the new claim relates back to the prior claim.

B. Yes, because the basis for removal appears on the face of the amended complaint and the removal was timely.

C. No, because the removal request was made more than one year from the commencement of the action.

D No, because the state court has concurrent jurisdiction over the new claim.

33. Plaintiff, a resident and citizen of New Jersey, files an action in state court in New Jersey alleging that Defendant violated state labor laws when it failed to pay him in accordance with the state minimum wage law. Defendant's actions also violate federal law, but Plaintiff's attorney, in an effort to attempt to keep the case out of federal court, has chosen not to assert any federal claims in the complaint. Defendant is a multi-national corporation that is incorporated in Delaware, with its principal place of business in New Jersey. Plaintiff seeks $10,000 in damages on claims based on allegations that Defendant violated state law only. Without admitting liability, Defendant wishes to remove the case to federal court, arguing that had Plaintiff filed a well-pleaded complaint, Plaintiff would have also alleged violations of federal minimum wage laws. For this reason, Defendant will attempt to remove the case to federal court in New Jersey.

Will Defendant succeed in removing the case to federal court in New Jersey based on the argument that Plaintiff's complaint should have included federal claims? If so, why? If not, why not?

A. Yes, because Plaintiff should have interposed federal claims in addition to his state claims, and thus there is federal jurisdiction over the case and removal is proper.

B. Yes, because any federal claims would arise out of the same common nucleus of operative facts as the existing state law claims.

C. No, because the basis for federal jurisdiction does not appear on the face of Plaintiff's complaint and the Plaintiff is not required to assert any federal claims he might have in this case.

D. No, because Defendant wishes to assert a federal defense in the action and that is not a sufficient basis upon which a federal court would have subject matter jurisdiction over the action in the first instance.

34. Plaintiff files an action in federal court alleging that defendant engaged in trade practices that violated both federal antitrust laws and state-based anti-fraud protections. Plaintiff operates a gas station and is the franchisee of a large multi-national corporation. Plaintiff is incorporated in Delaware, with its principal place of business in New York. Defendant is also incorporated in Delaware, and has its principal place of business in New York as well. Plaintiff seeks $21 million in damages: $1 million for the federal claim and $20 million in damages based on the state claim. An analysis of the federal and state claims conducted by Defendant's counsel reveals that the federal law claim hinges on a few critical facts. At the same time, many of the facts alleged by Plaintiff as evidence that Defendant violated both federal and state law tend to provide evidence related only to Plaintiff's state law claim, although the two claims do arise out of the same basic series of acts and occurrences that give rise to both the state and federal claims. Once Defendant determines that the state law claim would appear to substantially predominate over the federal claim, it seeks to dismiss the state law claim.

If the court should find that the state law claim substantially predominates over the federal claim, which statement most accurately describes the parameters under which the court will operate with respect to the motion to dismiss the state claim?

A. The court has no choice and must grant the motion.

B. The court may dismiss the state law claim but is not required to do so.

C. The court has no choice and must deny the motion.

D. The court must grant the motion but only if it also dismisses the federal claim.

35.   A small group of plaintiffs brings a personal injury action against Defendant, a pharmaceutical company, alleging a medicine produced and sold by Defendant worsened their symptoms. The four plaintiffs each seek $100,000 in damages on state tort claims against Defendant, seeking a total of $400,000 in their action. Plaintiffs are all residents and citizens of California (the "California Plaintiffs"). The California Plaintiffs understand that Defendant is also being sued in state court in Nevada by residents of Nevada (the "Nevada Plaintiffs") for claims concerning the same medicine that the California Plaintiffs allege harmed them. For the convenience of their lawyers who are also based in Nevada as well as for the perceived convenience of Defendant, the California Plaintiffs file their claims based on California state law in state court in Nevada. Defendant markets and sells the medicine that is at the center of the two separate actions brought by the California and Nevada Plaintiffs, but there is no allegation that any California Plaintiff purchased or ingested the medicine in Nevada. There are also no allegations that Defendant marketed the medication from Nevada to the California Plaintiffs or even that the California Plaintiffs were marketed the medication when they were present in Nevada. Defendant is incorporated in Delaware, with its principal place of business in New York. Defendant has extensive contacts with the state of Nevada regarding the sale and distribution of the medication that is at the center of the California Plaintiffs' complaint. Defendant correctly alleges, however, that it has no contacts with the forum state of Nevada with respect to the California Plaintiffs themselves. Defendant does not challenge the Nevada court's personal jurisdiction over it in the case filed by the Nevada Plaintiffs. In its response to the California Plaintiffs' complaint, however, Defendant argues that the exercise of personal jurisdiction over it in a Nevada court in an action brought by the California Plaintiffs violates the Due Process Clause of the Fourteenth Amendment to the U.S. Constitution. Defendant also seeks to remove the case to federal court in Nevada.

Will Defendant's effort to remove the case filed by the California Plaintiffs in state court in Nevada to federal court succeed? If so, why? If not, why not?

A. Yes, because Defendant is raising a defense that arises under the U.S. Constitution.

B. No, because if a Nevada state court does not have personal jurisdiction over Defendant, neither will the federal court.

C. Yes, because the basis for federal jurisdiction appears on the face of the complaint.

D. No, because any claim that might give rise to federal subject matter jurisdiction over the action only appears as a defense.

36. Plaintiff is a resident of Albany, New York, who lives on a stream that feeds into the Hudson River. Upstream from Plaintiff's residence there is a quartz mine, operated by Quartz, Inc. (Quartz), that sometimes releases toxic chemicals into the stream. Plaintiff alleges that this affects the well on her property which is fed from the polluted stream and from which she draws much of her drinking water. She brings a tort action alleging that Quartz is creating a nuisance under state tort law by polluting the stream and her well. This, she alleges, has made her ill, has caused her significant pain and suffering, and has resulted in her having to miss many days of work. She seeks $80,000 in damages. Quartz is incorporated in the state of Delaware, with its principal place of business in New Jersey, although it has mines in several states, including New York, where the mine that allegedly pollutes Plaintiff's well is found. Quartz has operated that mine uninterrupted for the last thirty years. Plaintiff files her case in state court in New York. Quartz will allege as a defense in its answer that it is authorized to periodically release pollutants from its mining operations into the stream in accordance with a permit issued by the federal government under the Clean Water Act, a federal environmental law statute.

If Quartz seeks to remove Plaintiff's case to federal court, will the court honor the request? If so, why? If not, why not?

A. The removal request will be honored because the court has subject matter jurisdiction over the matter based on the nature of the Plaintiff's own claims.

B. The removal request will be denied and the matter remanded to the state court because the basis for federal jurisdiction does not appear on the face of the well-pleaded complaint.

C. The removal request will be denied and the matter remanded to the state court because Defendant is, for all intents and purposes, at home in the forum state, and thus the parties are not diverse.

D. The removal request will be honored because there is subject matter jurisdiction over the case due to the federal defense.

37. Plaintiff is seriously injured when, as a pedestrian, she is struck by a truck driven by Universal Parcel Delivery, Inc. (UPD). Plaintiff is a resident and citizen of Florida. UPD is organized under the laws of the State of Delaware, with its principal place of business in the State of Georgia. The accident occurred in Savannah, Georgia, where Plaintiff was visiting on a long weekend. She sues for $2 million in actual damages and $1 million in punitive damages, alleging the UPD driver was reckless. Because Plaintiff lives in Florida near the Georgia border, she brings her action in a state court in Georgia based on state tort law. Defendant interposes an answer and seeks to remove the case to federal court. Plaintiff's lawyer opposes the action and seeks to remand the matter to state court in Georgia.

Will Plaintiff be successful in remanding the action to state court? If so, why? If not, why not?

A. Yes. The Plaintiff's action is based exclusively on state law claims.

B. No. The Plaintiff satisfies the amount-in-controversy requirement and the parties are diverse.

C. Yes. Based on the defendant's citizenship in this situation, it cannot remove the case to federal court.

D. No. An out-of-state plaintiff cannot oppose a defendant's effort to remove a case to federal court when the defendant invokes the federal court's subject matter jurisdiction.

38. Assume that the State of New York has just passed new legislation that creates a civil remedy for individuals who are defrauded by any company offering pools for wagering in online fantasy sports, giving a cause of action to anyone in the United States affected by a company operating out of New York State that violates the law. An action is brought by a citizen of New Jersey in the state court of New York under this statute against SportsKings, which is incorporated in Delaware, with its principal place of business in New York. When the action is filed, SportsKings makes a timely request to remove the case from state court to the U.S. District Court for the Southern District of New York, which encompasses SportsKings' principal place of business and the location of the state court in which the case was first filed. The Plaintiff seeks to remand the case back to state court, arguing that the District Court does not have subject matter jurisdiction over the action. Plaintiff seeks $100,000 in damages.

Will Plaintiff's effort to remand the case back to state court succeed? If so, why? If not, why not?

A. Yes. The matter will be remanded to state court because the action is based entirely on state law.

B. No. The parties are diverse and Plaintiff satisfies the amount-in-controversy requirement.

C. No. The case involves important issues of the interstate application of the laws, invoking the federal court's subject matter jurisdiction.

D. Yes. Defendant cannot remove this case to federal court because of its state citizenship.

39.   Plaintiff brings a claim under federal fair housing legislation that bans discrimination in housing accommodations, alleging discrimination in mortgage lending based on race, a violation of federal law. Plaintiff alleges that he was seeking a mortgage for a weekend home in Sandwich, Massachusetts, and was denied a mortgage because he is Asian-American. He seeks $50,000 in damages, the amount he will have to pay on the higher-priced mortgage he entered into when his mortgage bank turned him down based on his race. Plaintiff is a resident and citizen of New York. Defendant is Hartford Mortgage Bank (HMB), which is incorporated in Delaware, with its principal place of business in Connecticut. Because there is not exclusive federal jurisdiction over the federal anti-discrimination claim, he files his action in state court in the State of New York, the site of the filing of Plaintiff's mortgage application with a local branch of HMB. After the action is filed in state court in New York, HMB seeks to remove it to federal court. Plaintiff opposes the request to remove and seeks to remand the case to state court.

Will HMB be successful in removing the case to federal court? If so, why? If not, why not?

A.   Defendant will succeed in removing the case to federal court. The federal court has subject matter jurisdiction over the proceeding through diversity jurisdiction.

B.   Defendant will not succeed in removing the case to federal court. An in-state plaintiff may prevent removal of a case to federal court.

C.   Defendant will succeed in removing the case to federal court. The basis for subject matter jurisdiction appears on the face of the well-pleaded complaint.

D.   Defendant will not succeed in removing the case to federal court. The action does not satisfy the amount-in-controversy requirement.

40.   Paula works as a waitress in a cocktail bar, in a restaurant owned by Dany, located in a trendy neighborhood in Manhattan. Dany is an internationally renowned French chef. He's also a hot-head and notorious for berating and harassing his workers. Dany is now a U.S. citizen who resides in Manhattan in New York City. Paula is a resident of Hoboken, New Jersey. Manhattan is located in the jurisdiction of the federal district court for the Southern District of New York. Hoboken is located in the jurisdiction of the federal district court for the District of New Jersey. Paula is the victim of some of Dany's abusive behavior, but with her he seems to engage in more sexually charged comments and makes inappropriate advances towards her while in the workplace. She brings an action based on federal law in state court in Manhattan, which has concurrent jurisdiction over the federal law claims. She seeks $100,000 in damages. Dany seeks to remove the case to federal court in Manhattan and files his request to do so in a timely fashion. Paula objects to the removal and files a request to remand the case to state court in a timely fashion.

What is the likely outcome of Paula's objection to the removal, and why?

A. The federal court will reject the remand request because the parties are diverse.

B. The federal court will reject the remand request because the basis for federal jurisdiction appears on the face of the well-pleaded complaint.

C. The federal court will remand the case to state court because Dany cannot remove the case to federal court.

D. The federal court will grant the remand request because the state court has concurrent jurisdiction over the claims and Paula's choice of forum should be respected.

41. Alan is an independent architect working under subcontract with an architectural design firm that is building a new building in downtown Albany, New York. The main offices of the firm, Capitol Construction (Capitol), are located in Albany. Capitol's principal place of business is in Albany, New York, as well. Capitol is incorporated in the State of Delaware. Alan resides in Great Barrington in Western Massachusetts. He does most of his work in his studio located in his residence in Massachusetts. He travels into Albany about once every other week for meetings and to deliver his architectural drawings as he completes them. He delivers his final plans due under the contract with Capitol. Alan invoices Capitol for final payment under the contract, which is $100,000. Capitol refuses to pay, alleging that Alan's drawings are not consistent with the specifications set forth in the contract. Alan sues Capitol in state court in Albany to enforce the contract with Capitol and receive payment he believes is due. His action raises claims under state law only and seeks $100,000 in damages. Capitol wishes to remove the case to federal court for the Northern District of New York in Albany and makes a timely removal request.

May Capitol remove Alan's case to federal court? If so, why? If not, why not?

A. Yes, Plaintiff has satisfied the amount-in-controversy requirement and the parties are diverse.

B. Yes, the basis for federal jurisdiction appears on the face of the well-pleaded complaint.

C. No, Defendant cannot remove the case to the federal court of New York because it is considered a citizen of the State of New York for jurisdictional purposes.

D. No, the basis for federal jurisdiction over the case does not appear on the face of Plaintiff's well-pleaded complaint.

42. SureWay, a local hardware store operating in Ballston Spa, New York, is a business incorporated in New York State, with its principal place of business in New York State. Recently, Home Repo, a company incorporated in Delaware, with its principal place of business in Riverhead, New York, became the sole distributor of PipeOtter, a wildly popular and effective device for purifying drinking water that many of SureWay's customers wish to purchase. Home Repo is both a retail hardware store, selling directly to customers, and a wholesale distributor of hardware products, selling to other hardware stores. After Home Repo purchases the rights to license and sell the popular PipeOtter device, the Ballston Spa Department of Public Health issues a warning that all residents of Ballston Spa should refrain from drinking the water supplied by the town because there is a threat that the water is significantly contaminated. All residents are instructed to drink bottled water or utilize a water purifying device or system. PipeOtter is on an approved list of such devices that enable residents to drink tap water once the device is installed over a faucet. When Home Repo learns of this warning issued to Ballston Spa residents, it dramatically increases the price it charges all hardware stores in the vicinity of Ballston Spa to purchase the PipeOtter device; this drives up the device's price in those area hardware stores, including at SureWay. SureWay brings a lawsuit in federal court seeking $1 million in damages, including a claim alleging that Home Repo's actions violate federal antitrust laws. SureWay also files a supplemental state law claim as part of its lawsuit, under state unfair trade practices laws, alleging that the same actions on the part of Home Repo that form the basis of the federal claim also give rise to this state law claim. It seeks an additional $1 million in damages on this claim. After extensive discovery, and on the eve of trial, Sureway and Home Repo settle the federal claim, which includes SureWay's consent to dismiss that claim, leaving only the state law claim for trial. Home Repo's lawyers now file a motion to dismiss both the federal claim and the remaining state law claim.

If Home Repo moves to dismiss both the federal claim and the remaining state law claim, which answer most accurately describes how the court should handle the motion?

A. The court must dismiss both the federal claim and the remaining state law claim.

B. The court should dismiss the federal claim and may dismiss the remaining state law claim.

C. The court cannot dismiss either the federal claim or the remaining state law claim because then it would be without subject matter jurisdiction over either claim.

D. The court must permit the case to proceed to trial in federal court on both the federal and state claims because it has allowed the parties to engage in extensive discovery and to dismiss either claim at this point would constitute a waste of judicial resources.

43. Plaintiff wishes to claim that her employer violated federal employment discrimination laws when she alleges that she was denied a promotion on the basis of her gender. In reviewing Plaintiff's employment records, Plaintiff's lawyer also believes that Plaintiff was not paid in accordance with applicable state employment laws governing the minimum wage. Plaintiff will not allege that her employer's failure to pay her in accordance with the state minimum wage law was due to her gender because she believes many other employees, men and women, were also the victims of this type of violation of law. Plaintiff is a resident and citizen of New York. Defendant is incorporated in Delaware, with its principal place of business in New York. Plaintiff's lawyer wishes to file Plaintiff's action in federal court, alleging violations of federal employment discrimination law and the state minimum wage law. The complaint seeks a total of $160,000 in damages: $80,000 on the federal claim and $80,000 on the state claim. Defendant will move to dismiss the state minimum wage claim from the federal action, alleging the court does not have subject matter jurisdiction over that claim.

Will defendant succeed in dismissing the state minimum wage claim? If so, why? If not, why not?

A. Yes, because the state claim does not arise out of the same common nucleus of operative facts as the federal claim.

B. No, because the state claim arises out of the same common nucleus of operative facts as the federal claim.

C. Yes, because the parties are diverse and plaintiff's claims exceed the amount-in-controversy requirement.

D. No, because the state law claim does not raise novel and complex issues of state law.

44. Plaintiff Pam works at the Hunter-Geffin paper supply company, in its branch office in Scranton, Pennsylvania. Plaintiff alleges that Dwight, in an effort to force Pam to leave the company so that she does not receive a promotion over him, has been engaging in abusive conduct directed at her. Pam alleges that, in an attempt to accomplish this goal, Dwight has left Pam threatening voice mail messages. In addition, Pam believes Dwight has recently begun to vandalize her car while it is in the company parking lot as a part of his intimidation campaign. Pam believes these actions are discriminatory in nature and, as such, are in violation of federal and state law. She brings an action under federal anti-discrimination statutes and includes in her complaint a state tort claim based on the damage to her car. She seeks $10,000 in damages on the federal claim and $5,000 on the state claim. Pam is a resident and citizen of New York who resides in Binghamton, New York, and commutes each day to Scranton. Dwight is a citizen and resident of Pennsylvania. Pam commences an action raising these claims in federal court in Pennsylvania. Dwight will move to dismiss the state law claim, arguing that the federal court has no subject matter jurisdiction over that claim.

Will Dwight succeed in dismissing Pam's state law claim? If so, why? If not, why not?

A. No, because the court has concurrent jurisdiction over the state law claim.

B. Yes, because Pam's claims, even when aggregated, fail to satisfy the amount-in-controversy requirement.

C. Yes, because the state law claim does not arise out of the same common nucleus of operative facts as the federal claim.

D. No, because the state law claim arises out of the same common nucleus of operative facts as the federal claim.

45. Plaintiff wishes to commence an action against New York Pizza alleging that New York Pizza has breached a contract to purchase a large supply of pizza boxes from Plaintiff. Plaintiff will sue New York Pizza based on state law theories of recovery. Plaintiff is a resident and citizen of New Jersey. New York Pizza is incorporated in Delaware. Its corporate headquarters, which houses its leadership and where all corporate decisions are made, is based in the State of New York. Despite its name, however, almost all of its pizza restaurants are located in New Jersey, and its main equipment and product supply warehouse is based in New Jersey as well. All of Plaintiff's interactions with New York Pizza personnel took place in its warehouse in Newark, New Jersey. Plaintiff brings an action in federal court in New Jersey seeking $100,000 in damages for claims under state law alleging breach of contract for New York Pizza's failure to honor the contract Plaintiff has with New York Pizza for the supply of pizza boxes. New York Pizza will move to dismiss the complaint, arguing that the federal court does not have subject matter jurisdiction over the action. Assume that the applicable long-arm statute is satisfied.

Will New York Pizza succeed in dismissing the complaint on the basis that the federal court lacks subject matter jurisdiction over the action? If so, why? If not, why not?

A. Yes, because New York Pizza has sufficient minimum contacts with the forum state such that the exercise of jurisdiction is consistent with traditional notions of fair play and substantial justice.

B. Yes, because New York Pizza is at home in the subject forum, and thus the parties are not diverse.

C. No, because the basis for federal jurisdiction appears on the face of the complaint.

D. No. Because an out-of-state defendant will face no home-state bias in favor of a plaintiff due to the fact that the action was filed in federal court, the matter cannot be dismissed for lack of subject matter jurisdiction.

46. Plaintiff, a resident and citizen of Vermont, wants to bring an action against her former employer, a nursing home, alleging she was terminated from her employment for alerting federal authorities that her employer was not adhering to a federal "mask mandate" imposed after the outbreak of a global pandemic. Federal law provides what are known as "whistleblower protections" for any nursing home employees who report violations of the federal health and safety guidelines related to the pandemic. The federal law also provides that state courts have concurrent jurisdiction with federal courts over actions asserting whistleblower rights under the law. Plaintiff commences her action under the federal law in state court in Albany County, New York, the location of the nursing home facility where she worked. That facility is run by Defendant, a company incorporated in Delaware, with its principal place of business in the City of Albany, New York. Plaintiff will seek $200,000 in damages under the federal law, an amount equivalent to Plaintiff's lost wages since she was terminated, allegedly for reporting her employer for violating federal workplace safety guidelines. Defendant will seek to remove the case to the U.S. District Court for the Northern District of New York, the district that encompasses the Defendant's principal place of business and where the state court in which the case was first filed is located. Plaintiff will seek to remand the case to that state court.

Will Plaintiff succeed in remanding the case to the state court in Albany County? If so, why? If not, why not?

A. No, because the basis for federal jurisdiction appears on the face of the complaint.

B. Yes, because the state court has concurrent jurisdiction over Plaintiff's claims.

C. Yes, because Defendant has its principal place of business in New York State.

D. No, because the parties are diverse and Plaintiff's claims exceed the amount-in-controversy requirement.

2.6 Formative Assessment Quiz

This section tests your developing knowledge of issues related to subject matter jurisdiction.

47. Plaintiff wishes to claim that her employer violated federal employment discrimination laws when she alleges that she was denied a promotion on the basis of her gender. In reviewing Plaintiff's employment records, Plaintiff's lawyer also believes that plaintiff was not paid in accordance with applicable state employment laws governing the minimum wage. Plaintiff will not allege that her employer's failure to pay her in accordance with the state minimum wage law was due to her gender because she believes many other employees, both men and women, were also the victims of this type of violation of law. Plaintiff is a resident and citizen of New York. Defendant is incorporated in Delaware, with its principal place of business in New York. Plaintiff's lawyer wishes to file Plaintiff's action in federal court, alleging violations of federal employment discrimination law and the state minimum wage law. The complaint seeks a total of $160,000 in damages: $80,000 on the federal claim and $80,000 on the state claim. Defendant will move to dismiss the state minimum wage claim from the federal action, alleging the court does not have subject matter jurisdiction over that claim.

Will Defendant succeed in dismissing the state minimum wage claim? If so, why? If not, why not?

A. Yes, because the state claim does not arise out of the same common nucleus of operative facts as the federal claim.

B. No, because the state claim arises out of the same common nucleus of operative facts as the federal claim.

C. Yes, because the parties are diverse and Plaintiff's claims exceed the amount-in-controversy requirement.

D. No, because the state law claim does not raise novel and complex issues of state law.

48. Plaintiff Pam works at the Hunter-Geffin paper supply company, in its branch office in Scranton, Pennsylvania. Plaintiff alleges that Dwight, in an effort to force Pam to leave the company so that she does not receive a promotion over him, has been engaging in abusive conduct directed at her. Pam alleges that, in an attempt to accomplish this goal, Dwight has left Pam threatening voice mail messages. Pam believes these actions are discriminatory in nature and, as such, are in violation of federal law.

One day while Pam is exiting the company parking lot, Dwight backs into Pam's car with his own. Pam believes this incident is nothing more than an unintentional accident, and she is unable to allege that that incident is part of Dwight's intimidation campaign. She brings an action under federal anti-discrimination statutes and includes in her complaint a state tort claim based on the damage to her car. She seeks $10,000 in damages on the federal claim and $5,000 on the state claim. Pam is a resident and citizen of New York who resides in Binghamton, New York, and commutes each day to Scranton. Dwight is a citizen and resident of Pennsylvania. She files her action with these claims in federal court in Pennsylvania. Dwight will move to dismiss the state law claim, arguing that the federal court has no subject matter jurisdiction over that claim.

Will Dwight succeed in dismissing Pam's state law claim? If so, why? If not, why not?

A. No, because the federal law claims predominate over the state law claim.

B. Yes, because Pam's claims, even when combined, fail to satisfy the amount-in-controversy requirement.

C. Yes, because the state law claim does not arise out of the same common nucleus of operative facts as the federal claim.

D. No, because the state law claim arises out of the same common nucleus of operative facts as the federal claim.

49. Plaintiff is incorporated in Delaware, with its principal place of business in Connecticut. Defendant is incorporated in New York, with its principal place of business in New York. Plaintiff wishes to file a lawsuit against Defendant, seeking $100,000 in damages under a single claim based on federal securities laws. Plaintiff wishes to commence the case in state court because there is concurrent jurisdiction over Plaintiff's claims in federal and state court. Plaintiff brings the action in state court in Albany County, where Defendant has its principal place of business. Defendant wishes to remove the case to federal court for the Northern District of New York, the district encompassing Albany County.

Will Defendant succeed in removing the case to federal court? If so, why? If not, why not?

A. No, even though the parties are diverse and the case satisfies the amount-in-controversy requirement.

B. Yes, because the basis for federal jurisdiction appears on the face of the complaint.

C. No, because an in-state defendant cannot remove a case to the federal court of its home state.

D. Yes, because Plaintiff will be at a disadvantage in state court in New York because Plaintiff would be considered an out-of-state party.

50. Plaintiff sues Big Corp. alleging state fraud claims and arguing that Big Corp. misrepresented the "clean energy" status of its delivery trucks. For years, Big Corp. has advertised that its delivery trucks emitted no greenhouse gasses, but this turns out to be false. Plaintiff sues Big Corp. under state law theories of recovery, seeking damages on behalf of the environment amounting to several hundred million dollars that will cover the cost of remediation measures, an amount that is not far-fetched given how much the Big Corp. trucks have polluted the environment over the years. Big Corp. is incorporated in the State of Delaware and has its corporate headquarters in the State of New York. Its global distribution center is located adjacent to the Newark Airport in the State of New Jersey.

Products from around the world that are distributed by Big Corp. are brought to Newark Airport by plane or to the Port of Newark by shipping vessel; Big Corp.'s trucks all commence their routes and travel throughout the United States from this distribution center in Newark, New Jersey. As a result, every trip a Big Corp. truck has taken over the last five years (five years being the period of time that has elapsed since the company first made claims about its supposedly environmentally friendly trucks) has originated from this center in New Jersey. Plaintiff is an environmental advocate and a citizen and resident of New York. Plaintiff seeks to file her complaint alleging state law theories of recovery under the laws of both New Jersey and New York in federal court in New Jersey. Plaintiff files the case in that court, alleging diversity of citizenship between Plaintiff and Big Corp., because Big Corp.'s main distribution center is located in New Jersey and because that is where the majority of actions giving rise to the liability in this case have occurred. Big Corp. will move to dismiss the case for lack of subject matter jurisdiction.

Will Big Corp. succeed in dismissing Plaintiff's action on the ground that the federal court does not have subject matter jurisdiction over the proceeding? If so, why? If not, why not?

A. Yes, because the parties are not diverse.

B. No, because Plaintiff's claims are diverse in that they are seeking claims under New Jersey and New York Law.

C. No, because Plaintiff's claims clearly exceed the amount-in-controversy requirement and the parties are diverse.

D. Yes, because Plaintiff's claims raise novel and complex questions of state law.

51.   Plaintiff believes she was illegally steered into a mortgage with unfavorable terms for discriminatory reasons by a local mortgage broker (Broker). She brings a claim under the federal Fair Housing Act alleging discrimination in mortgage lending, which is a violation of that law. She will seek $50,000 in damages on the claim. Broker asserts that if she is guilty of mortgage discrimination, Iron Bank, the bank that ultimately made the loan to Plaintiff, is jointly and severally liable with Broker for any damages a court might award Plaintiff. Plaintiff is a resident of New York, and Broker is a resident of Connecticut. Iron Bank is incorporated in Delaware, with its principal place of business in New York. Plaintiff files her action in federal court in New York under the Fair Housing Act, originally suing only Broker. Broker immediately moves to implead Iron Bank, alleging that if Broker is liable, then Iron Bank is liable to her for all or part of the claims against her. Once Iron Bank is joined in the action, Plaintiff seeks to interpose a new, affirmative claim against Iron Bank. This second claim, based on state law, alleges that due to the discriminatory treatment of Plaintiff, Iron Bank violated the state Unfair and Deceptive Practices Act that makes it illegal to wrongfully deny Plaintiff favorable terms in a mortgage. The claim arises from the same set of facts as the federal claim and is novel and creative, but Plaintiff's lawyer has a good-faith basis for bringing it. Plaintiff seeks $10,000 on the state law claim. Iron Bank moves to dismiss the state law claim, alleging that the court does not have subject matter jurisdiction over it.

Which of the following is an accurate statement regarding Iron Bank's motion?

A. The court must deny the motion because the state claim against Iron Bank arises out of the same nucleus of operative facts as Plaintiff's other claim and there is no other bar to the court's subject matter jurisdiction.

B. The court may deny the motion even though the claim is novel.

C. The court must grant the motion because the parties are not diverse and Plaintiff cannot satisfy the amount-in-controversy requirement.

D. The court must deny the motion because there is an independent basis for the court's asserting subject matter jurisdiction over the claim.

52.   Plaintiff, a resident and citizen of Vermont, wants to bring an action against her former employer, a nursing home, alleging she was terminated from her employment for alerting federal authorities that her employer was not adhering to a federal "mask mandate" imposed after the outbreak of a global pandemic. Federal law provides what are known as "whistleblower protections" for any nursing home employees who report violations of the federal health and safety guidelines in light of the pandemic. The federal law also provides that state courts have concurrent jurisdiction with federal courts over actions asserting whistleblower rights under the law. Plaintiff commences her action under the federal law in state court in Albany County, New York, the location of the nursing home facility where she worked. That facility is run by Defendant, a company incorporated in Delaware with its principal place of business in the City of Albany, New York. Plaintiff will seek $200,000 in damages under the federal law, an amount equivalent to Plaintiff's lost wages since she was terminated, allegedly for reporting her employer for violating federal workplace safety guidelines. Defendant will seek to remove the case to the U.S. District Court for the Northern District of New York, the district that encompasses the Defendant's principal place of business and where the state court in which the case was first filed is located. Plaintiff will seek to remand the case to that state court.

Will Plaintiff succeed in remanding the case to the state court in Albany County? If so, why? If not, why not?

A. No, because the basis for federal jurisdiction appears on the face of the complaint.

B. Yes, because the state court has concurrent jurisdiction over Plaintiff's claims.

C. Yes, because Defendant has its principal place of business in New York State.

D. No, because the parties are diverse and Plaintiff's claims exceed the amount-in-controversy requirement.

53.   Plaintiff is a resident of Albany, New York, who lives on a stream that feeds into the Hudson River. Upstream from Plaintiff's residence there is a quartz mine, operated by Quartz, Inc. (Quartz), that sometimes releases toxic chemicals into the stream. Plaintiff alleges that this affects the well on her property, which is fed from the polluted stream and from which she draws much of her drinking water. She brings a tort action alleging that Quartz is creating a nuisance under state tort law by polluting the stream and her well. This, she alleges, has made her ill, has caused her significant pain and suffering, and has resulted in her having to miss many days of work. She seeks $50,000 in damages. Quartz is incorporated in the State of Delaware, with its principal place of business in New Jersey, although it has mines in several states, including New York, where the mine that allegedly pollutes Plaintiff's well is found. Quartz has operated that mine uninterrupted for the last thirty years. Plaintiff files her case in state court in New York. In its answer, Quartz will allege as a defense that it is authorized to periodically release pollutants from its mining operations into the stream in accordance with a permit issued by the federal government under the Clean Water Act, a federal environmental law statute.

If Quartz seeks to remove Plaintiff's case to federal court based on the fact that the federal government has issued a permit for Quartz's actions, will the court honor the request, or will it remand the matter to the state court? In addition, what will be its reason or reasons for choosing one of these options?

A. The removal request will be denied and the matter remanded to the state court because the basis for federal jurisdiction does not appear on the face of the well-pleaded complaint.

B. The removal request will be denied and the matter remanded to the state court because Defendant is, for all intents and purposes, at home in the forum state, and thus the parties are not diverse.

C. The removal request will be honored because there is subject matter jurisdiction over the case due to the federal defense.

D. The removal request will be honored because the parties are diverse.

54. Plaintiff brings an action in state court in New York alleging financial fraud against New York Mortgage Bank (Mortgage Bank) based on state law claims. Plaintiff is a citizen of Connecticut, and his palatial home is located in Darien, Connecticut. Mortgage Bank is incorporated in Delaware, with its principal place of business in Albany, New York. Plaintiff, suing in state court, alleges that Mortgage Bank violated state law prohibitions related to financial transactions when it improperly sold him mortgage insurance associated with his mortgage. He explicitly stated during negotiations over the mortgage that he did not want mortgage insurance. Plaintiff's mortgage is quite large, over $10 million, and his monthly payments are roughly $15,000 per month. He claims that the terms related to the payment of mortgage insurance were inserted by bank representatives into the mortgage agreement documents after Plaintiff signed them. Plaintiff's accountant only noticed the mortgage insurance payments, which were noted in the fine print of Plaintiff's monthly statements and equal nearly $2,000 per month, several years after Plaintiff began paying the mortgage. Plaintiff brings a state fraud claim against Mortgage Bank, within the applicable statute of limitations, seeking $100,000 in damages. Plaintiff files suit in state court in Albany, New York, which is located within the jurisdiction of the U.S. District Court for the Northern District of New York, against Mortgage Bank.

If Mortgage Bank seeks to remove the case to federal district court in Connecticut, what will be the outcome of that request, and why?

A. The request will be granted because Mortgage Bank can remove the case to federal district court in Connecticut because it is not at home in that state.

B. The request will be denied because Defendant must remove the case, if appropriate, to the district court that embraces the state court where the action has been filed and Defendant cannot remove it to that district based on its own state citizenship status.

C. The request will be denied because there is no basis for federal subject matter jurisdiction over the action on the face of the well-pleaded complaint.

D. The request will be granted because the parties are diverse and the case satisfies the amount-in-controversy requirement for federal subject matter jurisdiction.

55. Plaintiff brings an action in federal district court in Florida alleging mortgage fraud against Delta Bank (Delta). Plaintiff is a citizen of Louisiana, and his home is located in New Orleans, Louisiana. Delta bank is incorporated in Delaware, with its principal place of business in Gainesville, Florida. Plaintiff alleges that Delta violated state unfair trade practices laws when it made certain disclosures with respect to his mortgage loan, and he sues Delta, seeking $100,000 in damages allowed under the applicable state statute. Plaintiff anticipates that Delta will argue that it complied with the federal Truth In Lending Act (TILA) when it made the disclosure. Plaintiff will argue that, despite the federal defense based on TILA, the state unfair trade practices law goes further than the federal law and mandates additional disclosures that Delta failed to follow when it entered into the mortgage agreement. Plaintiff believes, and states in his complaint, that the federal defense Delta will raise regarding TILA implicates important issues of federal law, even though TILA was not violated. Plaintiff wants the federal court to resolve the important federal questions while also ruling on Plaintiff's state unfair trade practices claim, which necessarily arises out of the same set of facts giving rise to the TILA defense. Delta files its answer in federal court alleging, among other things, that the court does not have subject matter jurisdiction over Plaintiff's case. Delta makes a motion to dismiss on that ground, and Plaintiff vigorously opposes it.

Should the court grant Delta's motion to dismiss? If so, why? If not, why not?

A. It should be denied. The federal question regarding TILA appears on the four corners of the complaint.

B. It should be granted. The federal question regarding TILA does not appear on the face of the well-pleaded complaint.

C. It should be granted. The parties are not diverse and the Plaintiff fails to meet the amount-in-controversy requirement.

D. It should be denied. The Plaintiff can establish federal jurisdiction over the action.

56. Plaintiff sues her employer under federal civil rights statutes, alleging unlawful discrimination in employment based on her gender. She claims she was the victim of a hostile work environment. The environment was such that co-workers made sexual advances and would routinely walk up behind Plaintiff and rub her shoulders, despite her repeated protests that she did not appreciate such treatment. No male co-workers were subject to this treatment. Allegations regarding this offensive touching are included in the allegations Plaintiff says created a hostile work environment based on gender. Plaintiff sues her employer in an action in federal court alleging violation of federal anti-discrimination laws. She also seeks to include a claim based on state tort law against her employer, alleging that the repeated, offensive touching constituted a separate tort under state law. Defendant employer is incorporated in New York, with its principal place of business in New York. Plaintiff is a resident and citizen of New York. Plaintiff, a successful bond trader, sues for $1.5 million in damages in total: $1 million under the federal claims, and $500,000 under the state law tort claim.

Can Plaintiff include the state law claim in her federal lawsuit in federal court?

A. No. The parties are not diverse.

B. Yes. The dispute with the employer giving rise to the state court action arises out of the same nucleus of operative facts as the federal claim.

C. Yes. The amount in controversy requirement is satisfied for all claims, which establishes subject matter jurisdiction.

D. No. The claims do not arise out of the same nucleus of operative facts.

57. Big Bank enters into a mortgage agreement with Harry, lending him money to purchase his home. Big Bank wants to bring a foreclosure case against Harry in state court under state contract law alleging that he has failed to pay his mortgage. He has not paid his mortgage for well over a year, and the outstanding principal on the mortgage is $200,000. Harry consults with an attorney and learns that Big Bank may have failed to follow the federal Truth in Lending Act (TILA) when it processed Harry's mortgage. Harry's attorney wants to submit a defense to the foreclosure action that TILA was violated when Harry entered into the mortgage agreement. Based on the particular violation of TILA alleged by Harry, Harry may be relieved of the obligation to pay his mortgage. Big Bank files a foreclosure action in state court in New York, a claim arising under state law. In this action, the bank seeks payment of the outstanding balance on the mortgage or Harry's surrender of his home, which is now worth $210,000. Harry's attorney plans to submit a defense to the foreclosure action under TILA. Big Bank is incorporated in the State of Delaware and has its principal place of business in New York. Harry is a resident of Rensselaer County, New York.

If Harry's attorney includes a defense in Harry's answer under the federal Truth in Lending Act, may Harry remove the case to federal court once that is done? If so, why? If not, why not?

A. Yes. The federal defense gives rise to federal subject matter jurisdiction.

B. No. The complaint does not contain any basis for federal jurisdiction.

C. No. Harry cannot remove this case to federal court because he is considered a citizen of New York for jurisdictional purposes.

D. Yes. Big Bank's state of incorporation is Delaware, meaning there is complete diversity between the parties and the case can be removed to federal court under diversity jurisdiction.

58. Dan is a famous wedding singer who lives in Hoboken, New Jersey, and takes the short trip into Manhattan, New York, for many of his musical gigs, which include playing weddings and corporate events. One of his steady jobs is playing at events hosted by Bertha Stuart Living (BSL), which organizes and caters events throughout the Tri-State Region (New York, New Jersey, and Connecticut). In fact, BSL has a contract with Dan through which he agrees to play at least 20 events a year for BSL, provided he complies with all reasonable expectations for his performances at those events. BSL is incorporated in Delaware, with its principal place of business in Connecticut. Dan doesn't like to travel to Connecticut because it is a hike to commute there from his home in New Jersey, but he books a gig hosted by BSL in Cos Cob, Connecticut, anyway. He performs at the wedding without incident at a lovely reception held on a Saturday. Soon after the Cos Cob wedding, he performs at another reception hosted by BSL at City Hall in Manhattan. It does not go well. Dan is intoxicated while performing and constantly fails to perform adequately. BSL informs Dan that his conduct has left the company no choice but to void the contract between them. BSL also wants to seek compensation from him for his performance at City Hall. Since Dan has other contracts with other contractors, he continues to work, albeit less often, and needs to accept any gigs that come his way. Once again, he is invited to perform in Connecticut, but this time in Danbury. As soon as he arrives in Danbury for the performance there, he receives a summons and complaint filed by BSL seeking compensation for the event at City Hall at which he was intoxicated. The case is filed in state court in Connecticut, with BSL seeking $10,000 under state law contract law theories. This amount represents Dan's compensation from BSL for his failed City Hall performance. Dan will seek to do two things in response to receiving the summons and complaint. He will seek to remove the case to federal court, and then he will ask either the state court or the federal court (depending on whether his removal is permitted) to dismiss the case for lack of personal jurisdiction over him.

What should be the outcome of Dan's request to remove the case to federal court and his motion to dismiss for lack of personal jurisdiction?

A. The request to remove should be rejected and the motion to dismiss denied.

B. The request to remove should be honored and the motion to dismiss granted.

C. The request to remove should be rejected and the motion to dismiss granted.

D. The request to remove should be honored and the motion to dismiss denied.

59. Paul works as a barista for a small coffee chain, MudCup, that operates sites in New York State and Connecticut. Paul works at the store in Albany, New York, which is located in the jurisdiction of the federal district court for the Northern District of New York. Paul alleges that MudCup has violated the federal Fair Labor Standards Act (FLSA), a federal law, by allegedly failing to pay him an hourly wage that complies with FLSA. Paul also alleges claims under state labor laws that govern overtime pay. As evidence to support both claims, Paul will submit his weekly time sheets to show the hours that he worked as well as his pay stubs to show his weekly pay. His claims go back several years, and because he was underpaid by so much, according to his reasonable calculations, he alleges $20,000 in damages for all of his claims. He files a suit in the federal district court for the Northern District of New York. MudCup is incorporated in Delaware, with its principal place of business in Albany, New York. Paul is a resident and citizen of Albany, New York. MudCup seeks to challenge the federal court's subject matter jurisdiction over the supplemental state law claim.

Should the court grant MudCup's motion to dismiss the state law claim for want of subject matter jurisdiction? If so, why? If not, why not?

A. The motion should be denied because Paul's state law claim arises under the same nucleus of operative facts as his federal law claim.

B. The motion should be granted because Paul's state law claim does not arise under the same nucleus of operative facts as his federal claims.

C. The motion should be granted because Paul has failed to satisfy the amount-in-controversy requirement to establish a basis for the court's jurisdiction.

D. The motion should be denied because Paul and MudCup are diverse, as MudCup's state of incorporation is different from Paul's state of citizenship.

Chapter 3

The *Erie* Doctrine, Claim Preclusion and Issue Preclusion, and Preliminary Relief

In this chapter, we will cover a few topics that tie together some of the things you have already learned but also prepare you for what is to come: the concept of joinder of claims and parties and then pleading. While this is a comparatively short chapter, the material can be somewhat challenging and is not always intuitive. This chapter tries to offer you some effective tools for working through problems in these areas and to prepare you for understanding and success in subsequent chapters.

3.1 The *Erie* Doctrine

1. Plaintiff brings an action based on diversity jurisdiction in federal court. The court has subject matter jurisdiction over the action. Plaintiff seeks damages for wrongful termination under state anti-discrimination laws but does not seek relief under similar federal laws because Plaintiff feels the remedies available under state law are superior to those under federal law. In addition, under federal law, a case of this nature would be tried by a jury, not the court, and Plaintiff believes a jury would be unsympathetic to her. Upon filing its answer, Defendant interposes a demand for a trial by jury.

Should the court honor Defendant's demand for a jury trial? If so, why? If not, why not?

A. Yes. Once Plaintiff chooses to file the case in federal court, the risk of judicial bias against Defendant is high,

and thus the matter must be heard by a jury.

B. No, the basis for a jury trial does not appear on the face of the well-pleaded complaint.

C. No, only a plaintiff can ask for a trial by jury.

D. Yes, because of the important federal interests at stake in respecting the right to a jury trial, the matter should be heard by a jury.

2.   Plaintiff brings an action based on diversity jurisdiction in federal court. The court has subject matter jurisdiction over the action. Plaintiff seeks damages for wrongful termination under state anti-discrimination laws but does not seek relief under similar federal laws because Plaintiff feels the remedies available under state law are superior to those under federal law. At the same time, under the relevant state law, a litigant is not permitted to file requests for admission during the discovery process in any case alleging such claims. Nevertheless, Plaintiff wishes to file requests for admission during the discovery process in the action in federal court.

Should the court permit Plaintiff to file requests for admission in her action in federal court? If so, why? If not, why not?

A. Yes, because responding to requests for admission will not be burdensome on Defendant.

B. Yes, because the federal rules provide for the use of requests for admission in the discovery phase of a civil case.

C. No, only a defendant can file requests for admission in a civil case in federal court.

D. No, because of the important state interests at stake in respecting the bar on the filing of requests for admission, the court should not permit the Plaintiff to file them in this action.

3.   A federal judge hearing a case based on the court's diversity jurisdiction is frustrated by conduct of one of the lawyers appearing before her. The lawyer is repeatedly rude and obnoxious to her, court personnel, litigants, and even the jury. He uses abusive language and evinces a deep contempt for everyone around him. His verbal abuse of a witness is the last straw for the judge. The judge issues several warnings to the lawyer to rein in his conduct. The most recent one seems only to infuriate the lawyer, and he goes on a tirade, insulting the judge even more. When she says, "You're out of order, Counselor," he barks back, "No, Judge, YOU'RE out of order," and storms out of the room, throwing some documents at opposing counsel. Following this behavior, the judge issues a written order directing the lawyer to "show cause" why she shouldn't issue an order issuing sanctions against him under her inherent authority as a federal judge. The lawyer chooses not to appear in court on the day directed in the order to show cause. After a hearing in which the lawyer does not appear, the court issues the lawyer a fine, to be paid to the court, citing her inherent authority to do so and setting forth in meticulous detail the facts of the lawyer's conduct in open court that, she says, justifies the issuance of the sanctions order. The judge writes in her order that she has reached the decision reluctantly but must do so to protect the integrity of the court and its processes. The court in question is the federal district court for the Northern District of New York. Assume that New York law explicitly prohibits a court from issuing a fine for lawyer misconduct in open court. There is no federal law or rule directly on point that would permit

the federal court to sanction the lawyer in this way, but you may assume that the inherent powers of the court as articulated in the Supreme Court's decision in *Chambers v. NASCO*, 501 U.S. 32 (1991), would permit it.

If, on appeal, the lawyer challenges the court's authority to issue this sanctions order under the doctrine announced by the Supreme Court in *Erie Railroad v. Tompkins*, 304 U.S. 64 (1938), what is the likely outcome?

A. The sanctions order will be overturned because it conflicts with a substantive rule under New York state law.

B. The sanctions order will be overturned because the interest of New York State in not permitting judges to issue sanctions orders for abusive conduct at trial is a legitimate state interest.

C. The sanctions order will be upheld on appeal because there is a federal rule directly on point that addresses the matter.

D. The sanctions order will be upheld on appeal because the federal interest in the integrity of the federal courts is significant.

3.2 Claim Preclusion and Issue Preclusion

This section covers the doctrines of claim preclusion and issue preclusion. Courts can use the former to determine that a party is barred from relitigating a claim that has already been resolved (or could have been resolved) in a prior action and the latter to determine that an issue is deemed to have been resolved in prior litigation.

4. Farmer Jane operates a farm in Colorado where she grows marijuana legally under state law. Federal officials have begun to explore bringing actions against marijuana growers in the state for violations of federal law. Federal government officials enter Jane's farm without a warrant and seize the marijuana on her property and destroy it. Jane brings a civil action in federal court for damages against the federal government for what she alleges was the harm she suffered when it raided her farm without a warrant in violation of the Fourth Amendment to the U.S. Constitution. She loses this action and brings a second civil action in federal court alleging that the raid which culminated in the government's seizure and destruction of her marijuana was a violation of the Fifth Amendment's protection against unlawful seizure of property without due process of law. The federal government moves to dismiss the second action based on the principle of claim preclusion.

Should the federal government move to dismiss the complaint based on its argument that Jane is precluded from raising the Fifth Amendment claim in the second action, will the motion be granted? If so, why? If not, why not?

A. The motion will be denied because Jane's claims do not arise from the same common core of operative facts.

B. The motion will be denied because the claims are not logically related.

C. The motion will be granted because Jane cannot establish the likelihood that she will suffer irreparable harm from the government's actions.

D. The motion will be granted because the claims arise from the same common core of operative facts.

5.   Dena is a former prosecutor accused of stealing money from a settlement fund created by Dena's former office. The fund was set up by a bank that Dena had prosecuted. Dena, upon joining a private firm, was asked to oversee the management of the fund. The purpose of the settlement fund was to compensate the bank's victims, and Dena was given control over the fund to distribute its proceeds to victims according to a formula agreed upon by the bank and the prosecutor's office. The political corruption unit of the U.S. Department of Justice (DOJ) brings a criminal action against Dena in federal court alleging she violated federal law when she purportedly raided this fund for personal gain, stealing money intended for victims. After a lengthy criminal trial, Dena is acquitted of all charges. Soon after Dena secures her acquittal, the victims of the bank's malfeasance sue Dena in a civil action in federal court under federal fraud and anti-corruption laws alleging she is responsible for the theft of money from the settlement fund, which is essentially the same allegation that was at the heart of the DOJ criminal complaint against Dena. Dena will move to dismiss the civil complaint brought by the bank's victims. She will allege that, due to her acquittal in the criminal case filed by the DOJ, the doctrines of both claim preclusion and issue preclusion will prevent the plaintiffs in the second action from arguing Dena is guilty of stealing from the settlement fund.

Upon which basis, if any, will Dena succeed in her motion for summary judgment: claim preclusion and/or issue preclusion?

A. On both claim preclusion and issue preclusion.

B. On neither claim preclusion nor issue preclusion.

C. On the basis of claim preclusion but not issue preclusion.

D. On the basis of issue preclusion but not claim preclusion.

6.   Plaintiff is evicted from her home in city-owned property by the local city's housing department. Representatives of the city showed up one day at Plaintiff's home and informed Plaintiff that she had one hour to gather her belongings and vacate the premises because, it was alleged, Plaintiff was operating an illegal gambling ring on the premises. The eviction was carried out in apparent violation of a local ordinance that requires all evictions to be carried out only after the tenant receives notice of the planned eviction and has an opportunity to contest the eviction in the local housing court. Plaintiff also asserts that the city's workers used physical force while conducting the eviction and Plaintiff was injured as a result of the physical removal from the space. Plaintiff files an action in state court alleging that the city's actions violated the local ordinance and that the city is liable under state law theories of recovery for the physical injuries Plaintiff sustained in the eviction. The court finds that the eviction did not violate the local ordinance regarding unlawful evictions because Plaintiff was operating an illegal gambling ring on the premises, and thus she is not covered by the law. The court also finds that Plaintiff sustained no physical injuries as a result of the eviction. Plaintiff commences a new action in federal court. This action alleges two claims. Claim 1 is an alleged violation of the U.S. Constitution's Due Process Clause for the city's carrying out the eviction without due process of law. Claim 2 alleges that Plaintiff's civil rights were violated because the city officials used physical force against her when removing her from the building. One of the factual allegations in Claim 2 is that these actions resulted in physical injuries.

Assume that the state court had concurrent jurisdiction over both of these claims and these contentions when it issued its prior ruling. In federal court, the city will file a motion to dismiss Plaintiff's federal claims alleging that Plaintiff is barred from filing many of these claims and interposing many of these factual allegations by the doctrines of claim preclusion and issue preclusion.

Which of the following is a true statement with respect to whether issue preclusion and/or claim preclusion applies to any or all of Plaintiff's claims and factual contentions?

A. Only Claim 1 can be dismissed under the doctrine of issue preclusion.

B. Based on the doctrine of issue preclusion, the Plaintiff will be barred from asserting that she suffered physical injuries in the eviction.

C. Neither the doctrine of claim preclusion nor that of issue preclusion will impact Plaintiff's ability to raise any of their claims or allegations in the federal action.

D. Only Claim 2 can be dismissed on the basis of the doctrine of claim preclusion.

3.3 Preliminary and Interim Relief

For a case to work its way through to resolution in any court system can take time, sometimes lots of time. While a case is pending, a party can experience significant harm and otherwise have to wait until the conclusion of the action to obtain any relief. The federal court system, through FRCP 65, provides several mechanisms through which a party can seek preliminary or interim relief during the pendency of the action, such as the temporary restraining order (TRO) or preliminary injunction, both of which are provided for in that rule. Their specific contours and the standard by which they are achieved are described below.

7. Lisa files an action in federal court seeking to enjoin the federal government from deporting her client, a refugee from Guatemala, who entered the country illegally but has since filed a claim for asylum. Over the objections of the government lawyers who appear on an emergency basis when Plaintiff's lawyer shows up in court seeking an immediate order stopping the deportation, the court grants Plaintiff a temporary restraining order for twenty-four hours, preventing the government from immediately deporting her client. The court orders lawyers for the government to show cause in court the next day why the court should not convert the temporary restraining order into a preliminary injunction. The government lawyers appear the next day and oppose the motion for a preliminary injunction. Without disputing Plaintiff's factual allegations, and despite admitting that (1) Plaintiff has shown irreparable harm should she be returned to her country, (2) the balancing of the equities is on her side, and (3) public interest favors the granting of the temporary restraining order, the government lawyers argue that Plaintiff still cannot establish that the deportation would be illegal, and thus the preliminary injunction should be denied.

Should the court grant the preliminary injunction? If so, why? If not, why not?

A. No, the government lawyers should have been given more notice in advance of the hearing on the preliminary injunction.

B. Yes, taking Plaintiffs' allegations in their entirety, the court should grant the preliminary injunction since the balancing of the factors tip in her favor, even if it is unclear whether the action is illegal.

C. No, not if Plaintiff has not established all of the elements that would warrant the grant of a preliminary injunction.

D. Yes, if the court found that there was no genuine dispute as to a material fact with respect to her application for a preliminary injunction.

8. Plaintiff is a professor in a private university. She brings a claim in federal court against her employer under federal employment discrimination laws after she reviews her pay stubs for the past five years and discovers that her pay raise in 2010 seems surprisingly low. She reviews the university's guidelines for pay raises and determines that her 2010 pay raise violated the guidelines. This, in turn, means that she has not received adequate raises each year since 2010, as subsequent raises were determined by her base salary for that year. The inappropriate raise in 2010 thus had a ripple effect, meaning every year her salary increase was based on an inappropriately low base salary and was therefore lower than it should have been. She alleges this treatment is different from the treatment male professors have received. She contends that, as a result, she was discriminated against under federal civil rights statutes when she was denied a proper salary in 2010 and every year thereafter when her pay was artificially and illegally lower than it should have been based on the 2010 error. Plaintiff's attorney has compiled an analysis of the amount of money Plaintiff should have been paid over the years had her 2010 salary, and all subsequent salaries, been accurately calculated. Plaintiff claims to have been underpaid $30,000 and has undisputed proof of this underpayment. Evidence her lawyer presents makes it clear that the university has violated federal civil rights statutes because no male professors were treated in this way. The university is a so-called "Ivy League" institution with a $4 billion endowment. Plaintiff's lawyer wants to bring a preliminary injunction at the early stages of the litigation because Plaintiff should not have to do without the money she is owed during the pendency of the action, given the likelihood that the university violated important federal civil rights statutes. Plaintiff moves for a preliminary injunction for Defendant to release the wages she alleges she should have been paid while the case is pending, but the motion is denied.

If Plaintiff's motion for a preliminary injunction seeking payment of the money owed her during the pendency of the action is denied, which is the most likely reason for the court's decision on the motion?

A. She failed to establish a likelihood of success on the merits.

B. She failed to establish a likelihood of irreparable harm in the absence of the injunction.

C. She failed to establish that the equities tipped in her favor.

D. She failed to prove that the public interest supported granting the motion.

9.   Plaintiffs are members of an environmental group, HudsonKeeper, that advocates for the cleanup of the Hudson River and its tributaries in the Capital Region of New York State. It is a not-for-profit organization incorporated in and having its principal place of business in New York State. TE is a local construction company that operates a cement and asphalt plant on the banks of the Hudson River. Plaintiffs allege that TE is violating federal law by polluting the Hudson River when it releases certain materials into the river that are byproducts of its production process. Plaintiffs file a civil suit in federal court seeking an injunction against the continued operation of the plant. Plaintiffs argue the following: First, TE's actions may violate several federal environmental statutes. Although these are novel claims, plaintiffs argue that they have established a plausible claim for relief. Second, the materials from the plant are causing irreparable physical harm to native species in the Hudson River habitat, including that several indigenous species may become extinct as a result of defendant's actions. Third, the benefits to the community of preserving the Hudson River habitat and native species outweigh the benefits of continuing operations at the plant. Fourth, the public interest will be served by shutting down the plant because of the great importance of preserving the habitat and native species.

If the court should reject Plaintiffs' motion for a preliminary injunction, what is the most likely basis for its doing so?

A. Plaintiffs failed to establish the merits of their claims according to the legal requirements for the issuance of an injunction.

B. Plaintiffs failed to establish that the harm to the environment justifies the issuance of an injunction.

C. Plaintiffs failed to show that the equities involved with the issuance of an injunction are in their favor.

D. Plaintiffs failed to show that the public interest is served by the issuance of an injunction.

10.   Plaintiffs are a number of environmental activists who wish to challenge actions that are planned by a local utility provider, UP. The utility is about to engage in a controlled release of waters from the Hudson River into a flood plain just above Troy, New York, on UP's land. The purpose for this release is to help prevent what is feared could be catastrophic flooding in the event of a storm surge. Plaintiffs allege that this controlled release will disgorge toxins into the groundwater, likely endangering the lives of hundreds of New York residents. The activists wish to commence an action in the federal court for the Northern District of New York under federal environmental laws and will seek a preliminary injunction to prevent the controlled flooding. The activists commence their action and file for a temporary restraining order (TRO) and preliminary injunction with their complaint. Plaintiffs' lawyer called UP's lawyer in advance of going to court to alert her that he was taking such action. He was unable to reach her and left a message on her voicemail regarding his intent to go to court to seek the TRO. Since the actions of UP were imminent and Plaintiffs' lawyer could not await a response from the UP lawyer, Plaintiffs' lawyer did not delay going to court to see if a lawyer for UP could attend the court hearing on Plaintiffs' request for a TRO. Plaintiffs' lawyer also did not afford UP an opportunity to reconsider its actions before filing the lawsuit and requesting this provisional remedy from the court. Affidavits from several of the Plaintiffs and an engineer credibly describe the imminent risk from UP's actions. Plaintiffs' lawyer certifies in the motion papers that he attempted to contact the attorney for UP in advance of seeking the emergency relief and sets forth in those papers the need for the court to take immediate action without the presence of a lawyer for UP. After the initial court hearing at which the TRO was granted without a lawyer for UP present, the court orders a hearing on Plaintiffs' request for a preliminary injunction and directs a lawyer for UP to be present at that hearing. A lawyer for UP appears at that preliminary injunction hearing and objects to Plaintiffs' lawyer having requested a TRO without the lawyer for UP present and without having afforded UP an opportunity to refrain from engaging in the controlled flooding voluntarily before Plaintiffs filed for the TRO. For these reasons, UP's lawyer will argue that the motion for preliminary injunction should be denied and the TRO vacated as if the court never issued it.

Will UP succeed in having the court deny the preliminary injunction and vacate the TRO on the grounds articulated by its lawyer? If so, why? If not, why not?

A. Yes. Plaintiffs were under an obligation to await a response from UP's lawyer in advance of filing the request for a TRO and preliminary injunction.

B. Yes. Plaintiffs cannot seek a TRO and preliminary injunction without affording Defendant an opportunity to refrain from the action it plans to take prior to the Plaintiffs' seeking provisional relief.

C. No. Although Plaintiffs were obligated to provide UP with an opportunity to correct the situation prior to seeking relief from the court, that requirement would be waived in this instance because of the threat to life from the UP's planned actions.

D. No. Plaintiffs were under no obligation to provide UP an opportunity to refrain from taking its planned actions and the advance notice they provided UP's lawyer of their intent to file for provisional relief was sufficient.

11. Plaintiff wishes to commence a legal action seeking to halt a program operated by a local manufacturer of rechargeable batteries that, Plaintiff alleges, results in the release of toxic substances into the air during the manufacturing process. Plaintiff wishes to move for a preliminary injunction halting the production of these batteries.

Which of the following is not one of the elements required to secure a preliminary injunction in federal court?

A. That members of the community are likely to suffer irreparable harm if the injunction is not granted.

B. That Plaintiff can show the balance of equities tips in favor of granting the injunction.

C. That Plaintiff can make out a plausible claim for the relief sought.

D. That the public interest favors the granting of the injunction.

12. Plaintiff's counsel brings an action in federal court, seeking both a temporary restraining order and a preliminary injunction to prevent Plaintiff's deportation on immigration enforcement grounds while the action to overturn the deportation order is litigated. Plaintiff, it is alleged, has a well-founded fear of persecution on her return to her native country of Ukraine. First, the TRO is granted against the U.S. government, which is the defendant. Next, the preliminary injunction is denied.

Which of these orders is appealable by the appropriate losing party if each request to file the appeal is made in a timely fashion?

A. The TRO but not the preliminary injunction.

B. The preliminary injunction but not the TRO.

C. Neither the TRO nor the preliminary injunction.

D. Both the TRO and the preliminary injunction.

3.4 Formative Assessment Quiz

Test your knowledge of these complicated areas of law with the following formative assessment quiz.

13. Plaintiffs are residents of a small apartment building that the City of Albany has determined is unsafe for human habitation and must be demolished. As a result, the current residents must be removed from the building. Plaintiffs allege that they will be rendered homeless should the City remove them from the building. Plaintiffs want to bring an emergency action against the City to halt the demolition or, in the alternative, to ensure that the City is able to find them suitable housing into which they can move so that they can avoid becoming homeless. Plaintiffs will argue that they have a constitutional right to remain in their homes based on the nature of their tenancies, which creates a property interest protected by the Fifth and Fourteenth amendments to the U.S. Constitution.

The City claims that the building is in imminent risk of collapse and, if it collapses, it could affect the other structures to which it is attached (it is a row house that shares a common wall on both sides of the building with the two immediately adjacent buildings). Plaintiffs can establish that they will suffer irreparable harm if the injunction is not granted, that the public interest is in their favor, and that the balancing of the equities also tips in their favor.

What is the final element Plaintiffs will have to satisfy if they are to succeed in convincing the court that it should issue a preliminary injunction to halt the City from taking the planned action?

A. The plausibility of their claims on the merits.

B. There is no genuine dispute as to a material fact with respect to their claim.

C. They have a likelihood of success on the merits of their claim.

D. Their arguments are more plausible than other potential alternative theories that provide a wholly legal basis for the City's actions.

14. A federal judge hearing a case based on the court's diversity jurisdiction is frustrated by the conduct of one of the lawyers appearing before her. During a conference when the judge is attempting to help the parties reach a potential settlement of the matter, the lawyer for the plaintiff repeatedly makes oral misstatements of the holdings of relevant case law, overstates the damages his client suffered, and presents fabricated evidence in an effort to get the other party to make a higher offer of settlement. The judge issues several warnings to the lawyer to rein in his conduct.

Following this behavior, the judge issues a written order sanctioning the conduct of the lawyer based on the court's inherent powers, because at least some of the lawyer's conduct was outside the scope of any relevant federal rule of procedure. The court in question is the federal district court for the Northern District of New York. Assume that New York law explicitly prohibits a court from issuing a fine against a lawyer simply for misconduct in open court.

Was the court's sanctioning of the lawyer based on its inherent powers appropriate or should it have followed state law?

A. The sanctions order is appropriate because the federal interest in the integrity of the federal courts is significant, overriding any contradictory state interest that might exist.

B. The sanctions order was inappropriate because it conflicts with a substantive rule under New York state law.

C. The sanctions order was inappropriate because the interest of New York State in not permitting judges to issue sanctions orders in such situations is a legitimate state interest.

D. The sanctions order is appropriate because the court reduced its decision to a written order.

15.   Defendant CityBus operates a low-cost bus service between Albany, New York, and Boston, Massachusetts. One day, during one of these trips between the two cities, a CityBus driver veers off the highway when the steering fails and several passengers are injured. CityBus is incorporated in Delaware, with its principal place of business in New York City. In one civil action filed in federal court against CityBus, a Massachusetts resident and citizen, Alix, who was on the bus, wins a judgment after a fully litigated jury trial finding that the bus was negligently maintained, which resulted in the injuries to Alix in that incident. A second passenger, Beta, also a Massachusetts citizen and resident, who was injured in the same incident, files a second civil action against CityBus in federal court as well. Beta seeks to use the adverse ruling against CityBus in Alix's case against the company to win a partial summary judgment motion on CityBus's liability for Beta's injuries in the same incident and for the same reason. Please assume that the federal court has subject matter jurisdiction over Beta's action and had it over Alix's as well.

If Beta moves for partial summary judgment, seeking to use the adverse ruling against CityBus in Alix's case to establish CityBus's liability in her own case, what is the theory or theories on which this partial summary judgment motion would be based?

A. Both claim preclusion and issue preclusion.

B. Claim preclusion only and not issue preclusion.

C. Issue preclusion only and not claim preclusion.

D. Neither claim preclusion nor issue preclusion.

Chapter 4

Joinder

This chapter will focus on the concept of joinder—when claims or even parties are added to a case. The development of the doctrine that governs the issue of joinder tracks some of the issues covered already, most notably personal jurisdiction and subject matter jurisdiction. There are even issues related to service of process and claim and issue preclusion. This chapter thus builds on much of the knowledge that you have already gathered so far. It expands your knowledge because it breaks new ground and strengthens your understanding of some of these other issues.

4.1 Joinder of Claims

The simplest issue in this chapter is that of joinder of claims by plaintiffs. This mechanism is found in FRCP 18, which is deceptively simple in that it provides that a party that is "asserting a claim, counterclaim, crossclaim, or third-party claim may join, as independent or alternative claims, as many claims as it has against an opposing party." The important thing to remember about this rule is that it does not confer any jurisdiction on the court to actually hear the claim. In other words, although Rule 18 permits a party to append a claim to another claim it has against a party, it does not confer any authority on the court to actually hear the claim. The rules related to subject matter jurisdiction covered in Chapter 3 still apply. Similarly, when we discuss the ability of a party to add additional parties to the case, the rules of not just subject matter jurisdiction but also personal jurisdiction are still relevant. Rule 20 itself (addressed in Section 4.3, *infra*) does not confer personal jurisdiction. Watch for these sorts of questions as you work through this material.

1. Plaintiff is fired from his employment at a law firm on what Plaintiff believes are baseless grounds meant to serve as a pretext for dismissing him based on his ethnicity. Plaintiff's family comes from one nation in the Balkans, and his immediate supervisor is from another Balkan country, one which has historically been at war with the nation of Plaintiff's descent. After his termination, Plaintiff begins to experience pains in his chest and difficulty breathing at times. He consults with a doctor and learns that he was likely exposed to some kind of toxin at his place of work. It will not cause permanent health consequences provided he stays away from his former place of employment and gives his lungs time to heal. Plaintiff consults with a personal injury lawyer, and the lawyer suggests he might have two claims: one for the termination because it appears to have been based on his ethnicity, which is

illegal under federal civil rights laws, and a second for a personal injury action for the unhealthy work environment. The lawyer says that the second case probably cannot be brought against the employer because of the worker's compensation system, but she suggests bringing a separate action against the building owner because it appears the source of the toxin is the building's heating and air conditioning system. An investigation reveals that Plaintiff is not alone in the company in experiencing these symptoms, so there is no suggestion that he was intentionally poisoned on account of his national origin. Plaintiff's lawyer plans to file the case against the employer in federal court, under federal civil rights laws, and against the building owner, under state tort law but under the court's diversity jurisdiction. Plaintiff satisfies the amount-in-controversy requirement in the personal injury action and the parties to that second action are diverse. Plaintiff, who is not a lawyer, wonders if it might be less expensive to file a single action in federal court against both the employer and the building owner, alleging violations of civil rights laws and unsafe conditions, respectively.

Can Plaintiff bring the claim against the employer under civil rights laws and against the building owner under state tort law in the same action? If so, why? If not, why not?

A. Yes. A plaintiff can file all claims that arise out of the same nucleus of operative facts in a single action even where the defendants are different under each claim.

B. Yes. A plaintiff may bring these logically related claims in a single action against two separate defendants.

C. No. The two claims are based on two different legal theories, against different parties, and involve different factual scenarios.

D. No. The civil rights statute is federal law and the personal injury claim is based on state law.

2. Plaintiff believes that she was fired from her employment at a restaurant based on her gender. After her termination, Plaintiff consults with a civil rights lawyer. After reviewing the case, the lawyer believes that Plaintiff might also have a claim under the state's minimum wage laws because Plaintiff's employer failed to follow appropriate overtime rules related to the work that Plaintiff performed. However, the analysis suggests that many of Plaintiff's co-workers, of different genders, experienced similar treatment, so it is unlikely Plaintiff can argue that the failure to follow the state law regarding overtime was based on Plaintiff's gender or any other protected status. Plaintiff's lawyer plans to file a single case against the employer in federal court, asserting violations of federal civil rights law and the state's minimum wage law. Plaintiff will sue for $100,000 under the federal claim and $10,000 under the state claim. Plaintiff and employer are residents of the same state.

Can Plaintiff include both claims in the action against the employer? If so, why? If not, why not?

A. Yes, because the claims arise out of the same nucleus of operative facts.

B. No, because the two claims are two different types of claims and are based on different bodies of law.

C. Yes, because a plaintiff can join any claims it has against another party in a single action.

D. No, a plaintiff may not bring these unrelated claims in a single action because there is no subject matter jurisdiction over the state claim.

4.2 Counterclaims and Cross-Claims

The first section dealt with claims added by plaintiffs under FRCP 18. Although Rule 18 provides that it also applies to counterclaims, at least nominally, it imposes additional requirements on the filing of counterclaims (claims against an adverse party) and cross-claims (claims filed between parties on the same "side"—that is, plaintiffs against plaintiffs and defendants against defendants). This section deals with FRCP 13, which governs counterclaims and cross-claims.

3.   Theon alleges that his uncle, Euron, swindled him out of $1 million of his inheritance from his recently deceased father, Balon. Euron is a local elected official in his home state of New Jersey. Theon speaks to representatives of the press to complain about the stolen funds, and several local papers write scathing stories about Euron's alleged theft of Theon's inheritance. Euron sues Theon, claiming that the allegations that Euron stole the funds from Theon's inheritance are defamatory, a claim that arises under state law, and seeking $1 million in damages. Euron brings an action in federal court in New Jersey, where Euron is a resident and citizen. Theon is a resident and citizen of New York. Theon attempts to interpose a counterclaim based on fraud, asserting that Euron misappropriated the funds from Theon's father's estate that were supposed to transfer to Theon upon his father's death, seeking $1 million in damages on state law theories of recovery. These allegations are the same ones that led Euron to bring the defamation suit in the first place.

Is Theon's counterclaim a compulsory or permissive counterclaim? If so, why? If not, why not?

A. The counterclaim is a compulsory counterclaim because Theon satisfies the amount-in-controversy requirement.

B. The counterclaim is a permissive counterclaim regardless of whether the amount-in-controversy is satisfied.

C. The counterclaim is a compulsory counterclaim because it is logically related to Euron's defamation claim.

D. The counterclaim is a permissive counterclaim because it is not logically related to Euron's defamation claim.

4. Plaintiff sues Defendant in federal court over alleged patent infringement under federal law. Plaintiff company is a corporation incorporated in Delaware, with its principal place of business in New York. Defendant is incorporated in New Jersey, with its principal place of business in New Jersey. The federal patent infringement actions seek $500,000 in damages. Defendant submits an answer with a counterclaim based on state contract law, also seeking $500,000 in damages. The claim is unrelated to Plaintiff's patent infringement claim.

Is Defendant required to interpose its counterclaim in this proceeding? If so, why? If not, why not?

A. Defendant must interpose its counterclaim because the parties are diverse and the amount-in-controversy requirement is met.

B. Defendant must interpose its counterclaim, otherwise it will be barred by the doctrine of claim preclusion if it fails to do so.

C. Defendant is not required to interpose its counterclaim despite the fact that the court has subject matter jurisdiction over the claim.

D. Defendant is not required to interpose its counterclaim because the court does not have subject matter jurisdiction over the claim.

5. Defendant, a commercial real estate developer, is sued by the Able Corporation (Able) in federal court in New Jersey over Defendant's alleged failure to make a newly constructed commercial building available for use by Able in the time frame contemplated in the lease between the parties. The lease was supposed to commence on January 1, 2015, but as of July 31, 2015, the space was not yet occupied by Able. Because Able alleges that the building was not available for its on the date set forth in the lease, Able did not pay rent on it for the months of January 2015 through July 2015. Able's action, based on state contract law, seeks damages under the terms of the lease in the nature of lost revenue that could have been earned by Able had one of its highly profitable specialty coffee shops been operating in the commercial space prepared for Able by Defendant starting on January 1, 2015, as contemplated by the lease. Able seeks $100,000 in damages, its assessment of its loss of net revenue as a result of the failure of Defendant to make the premises available for use on the lease date. Defendant's answer to the action claims that the commercial space was available for use but that Able chose not to occupy the premises because it was attempting to exact more concessions from Defendant in terms of the renovations to the interior of the space. Defendant argues that the premises were ready for Able's use on January 1, 2015, based on the interior design plans agreed to by both parties to the lease. Defendant asserts that Able refused to accept the renovations that were consistent with the plans and was trying to obtain more expensive renovations than those to which both sides had agreed in the lease. Defendant's answer

contains these factual arguments but also includes a counterclaim for Able's failure to pay rent for the months of January 2015 through July 2015. Plaintiff's and Defendant's claims both require an interpretation of the lease's renovations clause. If Defendant made all of the renovations under the lease agreement by the commencement date of the lease, as Defendant argues, Plaintiff was obligated to start paying under the lease. If Defendant failed to abide by the renovations clause, as Plaintiff argues, Plaintiff was under no obligation under the lease to start paying rent, and Defendant will be liable to Plaintiff for the damages they claim they suffered by not being able to move into the commercial space. The monthly rent was $20,000, meaning the damages sought by Defendant in its counterclaim amount to $140,000. Able's company is incorporated in New York, with its principal place of business in New York. Defendant is incorporated in Delaware, with its principal place of business in New Jersey.

Is Defendant's counterclaim a compulsory counterclaim? If so, why? If not, why not?

A. Defendant's counterclaim is compulsory because it is logically related to the action by Able.

B. Defendant's counterclaim is compulsory because there is an independent basis of jurisdiction over it.

C. Defendant's counterclaim is not compulsory because it is not logically related to the action by Able.

D. Defendant's counterclaim is not compulsory because there is not an independent basis of jurisdiction over it.

6.   Plaintiff is a small, independent department store located in downtown Albany, New York. It is incorporated in New York, with its principal place of business in Albany, New York, its only store location. Plaintiff brings an action under federal antitrust laws against Mall Mart (MM), a large multi-national corporation that is incorporated in Delaware, with its principal place of business in Arkansas. Plaintiff's action is filed in U.S. District Court for the Northern District of New York. Plaintiff alleges that MM has engaged in anti-competitive actions by reaching out to Plaintiff's wholesale suppliers and offering to pay them premium prices to drive Plaintiff out of business because it cannot afford to pay the suppliers the same prices as MM. MM is also in the wholesale distribution business, and Plaintiff has several supply contracts with MM. Long before the dispute arose between Plaintiff and MM, Plaintiff failed to pay MM under a supply contract the two had entered into several years before MM began taking the actions that form the basis for Plaintiff's complaint. Plaintiff's action seeks $5 million in damages. MM seeks to interpose a counterclaim against Plaintiff seeking $100,000 in damages for Plaintiff's failure to pay under the supply contract, an action based in state law.

Is Defendant's counterclaim a permissive or compulsory counterclaim, and is there a basis for federal subject matter jurisdiction over it?

A. It is a permissive counterclaim, and there is a basis for subject matter jurisdiction over it.

B. It is a compulsory counterclaim, and there is a basis for subject matter jurisdiction over it.

C. It is a permissive counterclaim, and there is no basis for subject matter jurisdiction over it.

D. It is a compulsory counterclaim, and there is no basis for subject matter jurisdiction over it.

7. Plaintiff is a car dealer that sells luxury limousines. Plaintiff sues Limo Inc. (Limo), a manufacturer of limousines, for failing to deliver several luxury stretch models for which Plaintiff claims it paid $500,000. Plaintiff is based in East Greenbush, New York, and incorporated in New York. Limo is based in Groton, Connecticut, and incorporated in Delaware. Plaintiff brings an action in federal district court for the District of Connecticut seeking delivery of the limousines—valued at $500,000—in accordance with the contract between Plaintiff and Limo. The claims raised by Plaintiff arise under New York State contract law. Limo wishes to file a counterclaim. It alleges that Plaintiff engaged in corporate espionage when it had one of its employees hack into Limo's computer system to steal Limo's trade secrets, a claim which arises under Connecticut law and which Plaintiff's leadership denies. Limo seeks $1,000,000 in damages against Plaintiff. It alleges that the hacker employed by Plaintiff obtained copies of plans showing how Limo constructs its limousines so that Plaintiff can start paying a foreign manufacturer to manufacture them at a much lower price.

Will the court permit Limo to join its counterclaim to the action brought by Plaintiff? If so, why? If not, why not?

A. Yes. Limo's counterclaim is compulsory in nature, so there is supplemental jurisdiction over Limo's counterclaim in the case filed by Plaintiff.

B. No. Plaintiff's claim and Limo's counterclaim are not logically related, so there can be no subject matter jurisdiction over Limo's counterclaim in the action filed by Plaintiff.

C. No. Even though Limo's counterclaim is logically related to Plaintiff's claim, there is no independent basis of jurisdiction over Limo's counterclaim in Plaintiff's action.

D. Yes. Limo's counterclaim is permissive in nature, yet there is an independent basis of jurisdiction for Limo to file the counterclaim to the Plaintiff's suit, so the court has subject matter jurisdiction to hear Limo's counterclaim.

8.   Plaintiff is a wholesale distributor of specialty food products in Connecticut. Plaintiff enters into a contract with Roma Oil (Roma), an importer of olive oil from Tuscany, Italy, to distribute Roma's olive oil through the network of restaurants and retail food stores to which Plaintiff sells its products. Through aggressive marketing, Plaintiff builds up a significant demand for Roma's products throughout the state. Roma then begins to reach out directly to Plaintiff's clients, saying it will import its oil directly to the restaurants and retail outlets that are in Plaintiff's network. Because Roma can sell directly to the retail customers, it can cut out "the middle man" and charge less than Plaintiff for Roma's products. In other words, after Plaintiff created a market for Roma's oil in Connecticut, Roma went directly to that market to sell its product. Unsurprisingly, Plaintiff's customers no longer wish to purchase Roma oil from Plaintiff because they can get it directly from Roma at a lower cost. In addition, because Plaintiff's arrangement with Roma is for Plaintiff to pay Roma in installments once it accepts a delivery of Roma oil at its warehouse, and Plaintiff's customers are no longer buying Roma oil from Plaintiff, Plaintiff has a large stock of Roma products it has not paid for and cannot sell except at a steep discount to help it compete with Roma. Plaintiff decides it must bring an action against Roma for anti-competitive behavior under federal antitrust laws. Plaintiff is incorporated in the State of Connecticut, with its principal place of business in that state. Roma is an Italian corporation that has minimal contact with the United States. It deals directly with its customers in the United States by telephone and ships its products to the

United States using FedEx. Once Plaintiff files its action in federal court against Roma seeking $200,000 in damages for the loss of business with its customers as a result of Roma's actions, Roma answers the complaint and attempts to interpose a counterclaim against Plaintiff for its failure to pay for the stock of Roma's olive oil that Plaintiff has in its warehouse. The large quantity of expensive olive oil held in Roma's warehouse is estimated to be valued at $80,000. The basis of Roma's claim is in contract, under state law theories.

Is Roma's counterclaim permissive or compulsory, and does the federal court have subject matter jurisdiction over that claim?

A. Roma's counterclaim is permissive, but the court does not have subject matter jurisdiction over it.

B. Roma's counterclaim is compulsory, but the court does not have subject matter jurisdiction over it.

C. Roma's counterclaim is compulsory, and the court has subject matter jurisdiction over it.

D. Roma's counterclaim is permissive, and the court has subject matter jurisdiction over it.

9. Plaintiff alleges that two defendants, Able and Brewer, were involved in a scheme to engage in tortious acts in restraint of trade in violation of federal law. Plaintiff runs a small beer retailer in Troy, New York, and is incorporated in New York, with its principal place of business in that state. Able is a regional distributor of Angry Brewer beer, a popular beer in the region, and operates out of Litchfield, Connecticut. Able is incorporated in Connecticut, with its principal place of business in that state. The Angry Brewer Brewery (Brewer) produces Angry Brewer from its brewery in Great Barrington, Massachusetts. Brewer is incorporated in Massachusetts, with its principal place of business in that state. Plaintiff sues Able and Brewer in federal court for the Northern District of New York under federal law barring anti-competitive behavior, seeking $500,000 in damages for what it describes as a price-fixing scheme in which Able and Brewer improperly colluded to inflate the cost of a number of different beers so that local beer sellers would purchase Angry Brewer's lager line of beer instead. Brewer produces mostly two lines of beers: Angry Brewer Lager and Angry Brewer Pale Ale, although the pale ale line is only distributed in limited runs, and Plaintiff never purchases it for sale in its store. Plaintiff commences its suit against Able and Brewer for their actions with respect to the lager line of beers. There are no allegations that either defendant is engaged in improper conduct with respect to the pale ale line. Once the action is commenced against both Able and Brewer, and within ten days of filing its answer, Brewer files a cross-claim against Able seeking $100,000 in damages for Able's failure to pay for a recent shipment of kegs of Brewer's Pale

Ale line of beers. This claim arises under state law. Able will move to dismiss the cross-claim for the court's alleged lack of subject matter jurisdiction over that claim.

Will Able succeed in dismissing Brewer's cross-claim against it? If so, why? If not, why not?

A. Yes, because Brewer's claim does not have an independent basis of jurisdiction.

B. No, because Brewer's claim arises out of the same series of transactions as Plaintiff's claim.

C. No, because Brewer's claim has an independent basis of jurisdiction.

D. Yes, because Brewer's claim does not arise out of the same series of transactions as Plaintiff's claim.

4.3 Joinder of Parties

This section addresses the operation of FRCP 20. Like FRCP 18, it is deceptively simple (and generous). When reading its relatively wide-ranging permission structure, recognize that FRCP 20 cannot, on its own, confer personal jurisdiction or subject matter jurisdiction over any claim and/or party, even where FRCP 20 might appear to do just that.

10.   Plaintiffs Able and Baker want to bring a joint action against their employer, Dag Auto Group (DAG). Plaintiffs allege that DAG has engaged in pay discrimination against both African American and Latino employees, paying them less than DAG's white employees. Able is African-American and Baker is Latino. Plaintiffs together file a single action against DAG under federal statutes prohibiting discrimination in employment and seek over $200,000 in damages. DAG argues that the cases should not be joined together and moves for an order for the cases to be filed and tried separately.

Have Plaintiffs correctly joined together in a single action? If so, why? If not, why not?

A. Yes, because their claims raise some common questions of law and fact.

B. Yes, because the claims of both Plaintiffs raise issues of workplace discrimination.

C. No, because their claims raise common issues of law but not of fact.

D. No, because their claims raise some common issues of law and fact, but not all issues of law and fact will be the same.

AB

11.   Graduate students at the University at Albany (UAlbany) have been registering voters to vote in the upcoming elections. The local representative to the New York State Assembly has represented the district for twenty years, and she fears an influx of young voters might tip the balance against her, in favor of an upstart candidate who is challenging her in the local Democratic primary. The Assemblywoman is a former member of the state police, and she has excellent relationships with local public safety officials, police and firefighters in particular. One day, when the UAlbany students are registering their fellow students to vote, a small group of burly men and women come by and start harassing the students, trying to intimidate them by chanting and yelling to drown out the students' efforts to attract their fellow students' attention to get them to come to their table to register. The chanting and threats certainly attract attention, but not the kind that the students want. Other students are made nervous by the commotion, and the effort to register voters comes to a standstill. A university security guard comes over, and the students ask her to break up the demonstration. She just smiles and says, "Everyone is entitled to free speech, you *and* them." The students fold up their table and pack up their belongings. They consult with an attorney who suggests they might bring an action because their First Amendment rights were violated by the thugs, who, it turns out, were local police and firefighters (all government employees). The lawyer says the students might also have an action against the university for the actions of its employee, the university security guard. The attorney suggests bringing an action against the

police, firefighters, and UAlbany, each as a co-defendant, alleging that the three co-defendants conspired to violate the students' First Amendment rights. She has heard rumors that the defendants had each been working together and planning this type of action for some time.

Which of the following factors should a court *not* consider when determining whether the students can join the police, firefighters, and UAlbany as co-defendants in the same action?

A. Whether the claims against the co-defendants give rise to joint liability.

B. Whether the co-defendants' actions raise a common question of fact.

C. Whether all of the actions by the co-defendants that gave rise to the alleged liability necessarily arose on the same day.

D. Whether the co-defendants' actions raise a common question of law.

12.   Plaintiff is injured in a car accident when he stops abruptly on the highway to avoid hitting a deer that had entered the road and a series of cars behind Plaintiff's car rear-end Plaintiff's car in succession. Plaintiff suffered extensive personal injuries, but it is difficult to ascertain which of the three drivers who struck Plaintiff's car was responsible for any particular injury. Plaintiff wants to commence a personal injury action in federal court in the Northern District of New York, the district which encompasses the site of the accident, which occurred on Highway 787, just west of Troy, New York. Plaintiff is a resident and citizen of New York. The three drivers that all struck Plaintiff are Able, Baker, and Charlie. Able is a citizen and resident of Vermont. Baker is a citizen and resident of Massachusetts. Both Able and Baker travel regularly within New York on business and it is for this reason that they are driving through the state at the time of the accident. Charlie is a resident and citizen of Colorado. The accident occurred while Charlie was driving through New York State with a final destination of Boston, Massachusetts. This is the first and only time Charlie has ever been in New York. Plaintiff seeks $2 million in his personal injury action, which raises state law claims, and wants to join all three defendants in the action, claiming they are jointly and severally liable for Plaintiff's injuries. Questions that will inevitably arise in the litigation are whether Defendants are responsible for Plaintiff's injuries and how to apportion the damages among the three Defendants based on their relative level of culpability for Plaintiff's injuries. Defendants will argue that joinder of the parties is improper, seeking dismissal of the action in its entirety; in the alternative, Defendants will move that the Plaintiff must file separate actions against each Defendant, or, at most, two Defendants in a single action.

Will the court permit the case to proceed against any or all Defendants?

A. The court will permit the case to proceed against all three Defendants.

B. The court will permit the case to proceed against Able and Baker only.

C. The court will permit the case to proceed against Able only but allow Able to seek to implead the other Defendants.

D. The court will not permit the case to proceed against more than one Defendant in a single case and will require that the Plaintiff refile three separate actions, one against each Defendant.

4.4 Impleader

This section deals with the complex issue of impleader—when a defendant seeks to bring in a third party. In the next section, we will explore what happens when additional parties are added to the case and they want to assert their own affirmative claims against the other parties already in the case. In this section, focus on the situations in which defendants can bring in new parties to the case.

13. Plaintiff sues Construction Co. (Construction) for defects in the commercial building it constructed on behalf of Plaintiff in New York State. It turns out that the laminate wood floors were improperly installed such that in warm, humid weather they expand and buckle. Construction claims that the problem is defects in the laminate flooring and not in the floor's installation. Defendants recognize that they are responsible for putting in defective flooring and might be partially liable to Plaintiff for any damages it suffered. Construction insists, however, that the supplier of the laminate floors, Floors Inc. (Floors), is liable to Construction for providing Construction with substandard flooring that expands in warmer, humid weather. The action that Plaintiff brings against Construction is filed in federal court in New York. Plaintiff is incorporated in New York, with its principal place of business in New York. Construction is incorporated in Connecticut, with its principal place of business in Connecticut. Floors is incorporated in Delaware, with its principal place of business in Connecticut. New York law provides that a party supplying construction materials, like flooring, is liable to the purchaser through the doctrine of indemnity should those supplies not function as intended. The flooring did not function as intended. Construction seeks to implead Floors.

Should the court permit Construction to implead Floors? If so, why? If not, why not.

A. Construction should be permitted to implead Floors because the claim against Floors arises out of the same nucleus of operative facts as Plaintiff's claim against Construction.

B. Construction should not be permitted to implead Floors because there is no diversity between Defendants.

C. Construction should not be permitted to implead Floors because the claim against Floors is based on Construction's arguing that Floors is responsible for Plaintiff's loss, not Construction.

D. Construction should be permitted to implead Floors because the claim against Floors is based on Construction's arguing that Floors must indemnify Construction for the defects in Floors's product.

14.   Plaintiff is a jewelry manufacturer located in Albany, New York. He routinely purchases raw materials for the jewelry he makes in the Diamond District in New York City. He purchases primarily from Mike's Metals (Mike's), which has a storefront on 44th Street in Manhattan but is based in Phoenix, Arizona, where it has its principal place of business. It is incorporated in the state of Florida. Mike's purchases many of its metals from a Chilean mining company, Chilax. Chilax has a representative with an office in Florida. Chilax routinely sends a truck from Florida to Manhattan with its metals for delivery to Mike's. These metals arrive by container shipment via sea to the port of Miami. One of Chilax's shipments is defective. When producing the platinum raw materials in Chilax's factory, the platinum ore was mixed with a lesser metal. According to U.S. regulatory standards, the combination of the additive means that the materials produced in this batch cannot be labeled and sold in the U.S. as platinum. Chilax always sells its products with a quality guarantee and agrees to indemnify any purchaser of its materials in the event it turns out that they do not fit U.S. standards for quality and purity. For years, Chilax has regularly sent its salespeople to the Diamond District in Manhattan to attempt to sell its materials and to alert vendors that Mike's is its distributor in the area. Plaintiff purchases a batch of the tainted platinum from Mike's. The batch in question did not meet U.S. regulatory standards' the batch was brittle and was not of sufficient purity to meet such standards. All contracts of sale for the purchase of the platinum and other metals between Plaintiff and Mike's are executed in Manhattan. All of Mike's

dealings with New York-based dealers occur out of the office in Manhattan, located in the Southern District of New York. Plaintiff pays $85,000 for the tainted shipment of platinum. After attempting to use the platinum in the manufacturing of wedding bands, Plaintiff immediately recognizes that there is something wrong with the materials and has them tested. He realizes that the platinum is not sufficiently pure and that he can no longer market the rings as platinum if they are manufactured with the tainted metal from this shipment. He brings an action against Mike's in federal court in the Southern District of New York for Mike's' alleged violation of the contract between Plaintiff and Mike's. Once Mike's is sued, it attempts to add Chilax as a defendant by means of a third-party complaint. Assume that Chilax is subject to personal jurisdiction in the Southern District of New York.

Can Mike's add Chilax as a third-party defendant? If so, why? If not, why not?

A. Yes. Since there are common questions of law and fact in the action against Mike's and Mike's' third-party complaint against Chilax, joinder of Chilax is appropriate.

B. No. Since Chilax has an office in Florida and Mike's' state of incorporation is Florida, joining Chilax will defeat complete diversity.

C. No. Chilax is not liable to Mike's for any part of the claim against it, so joinder of Chilax is not appropriate under federal law.

D. Yes. Since Chilax has agreed to indemnify Mike's in the event its products are not pure by U.S. standards, Chilax may properly be joined in this action.

15. Plaintiff brings an action alleging that she was injured while operating a crane to remove some damaged underground pipe. While working on the pipes, she inadvertently strikes a buried power line that was unmarked. She is burned and suffers serious injuries when the pierced power line sparks a fire. She cannot bring an action against her employer because of the protections of the worker's compensation system, which insulate her employer from suit but allow her to file an action against any other party who may have been responsible for her injuries. Instead of filing suit against her employer, she brings an action against the company that buried the lines, First Party Power (First Party). Plaintiff is a resident and citizen of New York State. She brings an action under state tort law theories against First Party in federal court in Albany, New York, in the Northern District of New York, where the incident took place, seeking $500,000 in damages. First Party is incorporated in Delaware, with its principal place of business in Massachusetts. First Party seeks to implead the company that supplied the insulation that was supposed to prevent the lines from catching fire if pierced, 3PD. 3PD is incorporated in Delaware, with its principal place of business in New York. First Party provides evidence from its contract with 3PD that 3PD agreed to indemnify First Party in the event its insulation failed to prevent the power lines from catching fire, which is what First Party alleges occurred here. First Party asserts that if it is liable to Plaintiff, 3PD should be liable to First Party for all of the claims against First Party. 3PD objects to being impleaded in the action and will challenge the subject matter jurisdiction of the court over First Party's claims against it, alleging that it is not diverse from either the Plaintiff or Defendant First Party. As a result, 3PD will assert that it cannot be brought into the action when the basis of the court's underlying jurisdiction is diversity.

Will 3PD succeed in its efforts to resist the impleader in this action? If so, why? If not, why not?

A. Yes. 3PD is not diverse from Plaintiff, and thus to include it in this action will defeat diversity.

B. No. First Party has articulated a legitimate basis for impleading 3PD, and any lack of diversity with regard to the parties is irrelevant to First Party's ability to implead 3PD.

C. Yes, because First Party has not established an appropriate basis by which it can implead 3PD in this action.

D. No. The court has subject matter jurisdiction over the third-party claim against 3PD because First Party and 3PD are diverse from one another due to the fact that their respective principal places of business are in different states.

16. Plaintiff is the victim of alleged medical malpractice. Plaintiff files suit against the doctor who implanted a device designed to monitor Plaintiff's blood glucose levels. Plaintiff suffers serious medical complications and significant and lasting physical injuries when the device fails to detect a severe depletion of these levels. Plaintiff brings an action against Doctor in federal court in New Jersey, seeking $1 million on a state tort claim. Plaintiff alleges Doctor negligently implanted the device. In her defense, Doctor alleges that she did nothing wrong; instead, she asserts that the device itself malfunctioned. As a result, Doctor will allege that the manufacturer of the device is responsible for the injuries Plaintiff suffered and thus that company is liable to Plaintiff, not Doctor. Once the action is commenced against Doctor, she will seek to implead Cyberdyne Systems (Cyberdyne), the manufacturer of the device. Plaintiff is a resident and citizen of Pennsylvania. Doctor is a resident and citizen of New Jersey. Cyberdyne is incorporated in Delaware, with its principal place of business in Philadelphia, Pennsylvania. Cyberdyne will move to dismiss the claims filed against it by Doctor, alleging that impleader is improper in this action.

Is Doctor's effort to implead Cyberdyne in this action proper? If so, why? If not, why not?

A. The effort to implead Cyberdyne is improper because the parties are not diverse.

B. The effort to implead Cyberdyne is improper because Doctor has not alleged an appropriate basis upon which to implead Cyberdyne.

C. The effort to implead Cyberdyne is proper because to include it in the action will not offend traditional notions of fair play and substantial justice.

D. The effort to implead Cyberdyne is proper because Doctor has articulated an appropriate basis upon which to implead it in the action.

17. Giant Burger (Giant) is a chain restaurant with many locations. Each restaurant is an independent franchise and contractor. Giant wants to bring an action against several owners of these restaurants ("the original owners") that operate in Wisconsin. The owners of these restaurants have sold their interests in their franchises to third parties ("the third-party owners") in alleged violation of the original owners' franchise agreements with Giant. Giant wishes to sue both the original owners and the third-party owners. Giant's attorney conducts research to learn the names and corporate addresses of the third-party owners. They bring an action against the original owners, alleging breach of the contracts between the original owners and Giant, and against the third-party owners, alleging trademark infringement because the third-party owners are operating Giant restaurants without the permission of Giant, an express violation of Giant's intellectual property rights. A central question in the case is whether, under the contracts between Giant and the original owners, such owners can sell the rights to operate the franchises without Giant's permission. Giant's attorneys commence the action in federal court in Wisconsin alleging both federal trademark violation and violations of their contracts under state law. The amount in controversy in the action exceeds $1 million. The defendants are sued jointly and severally. The defendants are all citizens of Wisconsin. Giant is a citizen of New York.

Can Giant join the federal and state claims in the same action in federal court? If so, why? If not, why not?

A. No. There is no federal subject matter jurisdiction over the state law claims.

B. No. Although there is a common question of fact in the federal and state law claims, there is no common question of law, and thus joinder is inappropriate.

C. Yes. The federal and state law claims arise from the same series of transactions, the defendants are sued jointly and severally, and the question of whether all of the defendants are in material breach of the contracts with Giant is a question common to all defendants.

D. Yes. The legal question of whether the original owners are in violation of their contract is a question common to both the federal and state law claims.

4.5 New Claims After Joinder

Probably the most difficult issues related to joinder arise when a new party is added to the case and that party wants to assert its own claims against another party, or when one of the other parties in the case wants to file new claims directly against that party. This section explores the ins and outs of these complex situations.

18. Plaintiff sells high-quality imported foods in the city of Hartford, Connecticut. Able is a distributor of similar food products, most of which are made by Baker, an out-of-state producer of premium foods. Plaintiff sues Able, arguing that Able violated federal antitrust practices when it conspired with Baker to engage in the price fixing of Baker's products in an effort to undermine Plaintiff's business. Plaintiff sues only Able in the action in federal court in Connecticut. Able seeks to join Baker in the action, alleging that if Able is liable to Plaintiff, Baker is contributorily liable as well. Baker believes that Able, on its own, engaged in the anti-competitive behavior. Baker alleges that Able told Baker that it needed to price Baker's products at the amount it was charging customers for such products to remain competitive with Plaintiff, Baker's main competitor in the state of Connecticut. This, Baker alleges, was a violation of the distribution agreement between Able and Baker, which requires Able to follow all applicable laws in pricing Baker's products for sale. Baker also asserts that Able failed to fully reimburse Baker for sales of products unrelated to the sales of products involved in the lawsuit with Plaintiff. Once impleaded, Baker wishes to interpose two counterclaims against Able based in state contract law. The first, Counterclaim 1, will allege that Able failed to follow its contract with Baker for the pricing of the products that Able dis-

tributes that are a part of the lawsuit with Plaintiff. The second, Counterclaim 2, will allege that Able failed to compensate Baker for the distribution of products unrelated to that lawsuit, in violation of a different contract between Able and Baker. Baker will seek a total of $200,000 on both claims, $100,000 for each. Plaintiff is incorporated in Connecticut, with its principal place of business in Connecticut. Able is incorporated in Delaware, with its principal place of business in Massachusetts. Baker is incorporated in Pennsylvania, with its principal place of business in Pennsylvania. Able will move to dismiss both Counterclaim 1 and Counterclaim 2 filed by Baker against it, alleging the court does not have subject matter jurisdiction to rule on the two counterclaims.

How will the court rule with respect to Able's motion to dismiss Baker's two counterclaims?

A. The court will grant the motion with respect to Counterclaim 1 but deny it with respect to Counterclaim 2.

B. The court will grant the motion with respect to Counterclaim 2 but deny it with respect to Counterclaim 1.

C. The court will grant the motion with respect to both claims.

D. The court will deny the motion with respect to both counterclaims.

19. Plaintiff suffers long-lasting effects from the negligent implantation of a pacemaker for his ailing heart and believes he is the victim of medical malpractice. HartGard, the manufacturer of the pacemaker, is incorporated in Delaware, with its principal place of business in Connecticut. The doctor who performed the surgery, Dina Doctoroff, resides in and is a citizen of New York. Plaintiff is also a citizen of New York. Plaintiff brings an action in federal court in New York against only HartGard, alleging state tort theories of recovery and seeking over $1 million in damages. HartGard alleges, correctly, that if it is found liable, Doctoroff should be liable to HartGard for all or part of the claim against it because the two are jointly and severally liable to Plaintiff. Accordingly, HartGard files a third-party complaint against Doctoroff. Doctoroff answers the third-party complaint filed by HartGard and interposes a counterclaim against Plaintiff alleging that Plaintiff never paid Doctoroff for the implantation of the pacemaker, a claim arising under state law, seeking damages of $100,000 against Plaintiff. Plaintiff will not seek to amend his complaint to add new affirmative claims against Doctoroff but will instead move to dismiss Doctoroff's counterclaim.

Will Plaintiff succeed in dismissing Doctoroff's counterclaim against him? If so, why? If not, why not?

A. Plaintiff will not succeed in dismissing the counterclaim because it is logically related to the underlying claims and there is no other bar to that claim.

B. Plaintiff will succeed in dismissing the counterclaim because it is not logically related to the underlying claim.

C. Plaintiff will succeed in dismissing the counterclaim because the parties are not diverse.

D. Plaintiff will not succeed in dismissing the counterclaim because there is an independent basis for the court to entertain that claim.

20. Plaintiff was injured at a construction site. She was operating a forklift when a large canister of chemicals broke loose from the forklift as she was lifting it up, falling on her. Both of her legs were broken when the protective cage in which she was sitting gave way under the weight of the canister. Plaintiff consults with an attorney whose investigation reveals that a design flaw in the forklift permitted the canister to break free and defects in the materials used in the protective cage caused it to collapse when the canister fell on it. Because Plaintiff cannot sue her employer, the attorney files suit against the manufacturer of the forklift in federal court in the Southern District of New York, alleging over $300,000 in damages and raising personal injury claims under state law. Manufacturer, in turn, impleads the supplier of the materials for the protective cage, alleging that the Manufacturer was protected by an indemnity clause in the contract for the materials it purchased from Supplier. That contract clause provides that if the materials sold by Supplier failed in any way, Supplier would indemnify Manufacturer by reimbursing it for any losses incurred, including losses that arise from a lawsuit stemming from defective products sold by Supplier to Manufacturer. Plaintiff is a resident of New Jersey. Manufacturer is incorporated in Delaware, with its principal place of business in New York. Supplier is incorporated in New York, with its principal place of business in New Jersey.

Assuming Manufacturer may join Supplier as a third-party defendant in this action, may Plaintiff file a new affirmative claim against Supplier for the defective materials in the forklift?

A. Yes. Plaintiff can file new affirmative claims against Supplier because once Supplier is added to the case, Plaintiff can file any related claims against any defendant, and the claims against Supplier would be related to the claims against Manufacturer.

B. Yes. Plaintiff can raise all claims against both defendants that arise out the same nucleus of operative facts.

C. No. Plaintiff may not assert claims against any new third-party defendants added by means of a third-party complaint filed by a defendant already in the case.

D. No. Plaintiff may not file claims against a non-diverse third-party defendant.

21. Plaintiff is injured in a car accident in which her car accelerated on its own and crashed into a lane divider, causing significant physical injuries to Plaintiff and her two passengers. Plaintiff brings an action in federal court based on diversity jurisdiction against the dealer of the car for selling her a defective product. Defendant Dealer impleads the manufacturer of the car, asserting that Manufacturer had warranted to Dealer that all of the vehicles sold to Dealer were fit for their intended use. The failure of the accelerator was certainly a breach of this warranty. Third-party Defendant Manufacturer seeks to bring a claim against third-party Plaintiff Dealer, arguing that Dealer had failed to pay for a shipment of cars that had recently been delivered to Dealer. Plaintiff's car was not one of the cars in this shipment for which Defendant Dealer was liable to Defendant Manufacturer. Dealer, Manufacturer, and Plaintiff are all from different states. All claims arise under state law and each satisfies the amount-in-controversy requirement independently.

Can Defendant Manufacturer file the counterclaim against Defendant Dealer in the context of Plaintiff's action against Defendant Dealer in which Defendant Manufacturer has been joined as a third-party defendant? If so, why? If not, why not?

A. Yes, because there is an independent basis of subject matter jurisdiction for Manufacturer's claim.

B. Yes. Because Manufacturer's counterclaim arises out of the same nucleus of operative facts as Plaintiff's claim against Dealer, the counterclaim may be filed in this action.

C. No. Because Manufacturer's counterclaim does not have an independent basis of jurisdiction, it cannot be filed in the context of Plaintiff's action against Dealer.

D. No. Because Manufacturer's claim against Dealer does not arise from the same nucleus of operative facts as Plaintiff's claims against Dealer and Dealer's claims against Manufacturer, it cannot be filed as a counterclaim in the context of Plaintiff's action against Dealer.

22. Pete is injured in a car accident that was the result of a defective ignition. The defect caused the car to stall in the middle of accelerating. Pete's car stalls and he spins out of control, hitting a tree on the side of the road. He is severely injured in the accident. Pete brings an action based in state law in federal court in New York, suing both the manufacturer of the car, Testa Motors (Testa), and the manufacturer of the part that he alleges was defective, Fine Parts (Fine). He seeks over $2 million in damages. Testa is incorporated in California and has its principal place of business in California. Fine is incorporated in Michigan, where it has its principal place of business. Pete is a resident of New York State. Fine wants to add a cross-claim against Testa alleging that it has not paid Fine for a large delivery of specialized radiators it had delivered to Testa. The radiators are not involved in any way in the malfunction of Pete's car that caused the accident. Fine alleges Testa owes it $100,000.

Can Fine add a cross-claim against Testa in this action? If so, why? If not, why not?

A. Yes, the claim arises out of the same transaction or occurrence as the claim by Pete against the defendants, and there is a basis for subject matter jurisdiction over that cross-claim.

B. Yes, although the claim does not arise out of the same transaction or occurrence as Pete's claim against the defendants, there is subject matter jurisdiction for the Fine claim against Testa.

C. No, the cross-claim does not arise out of the same transaction or occurrence as the claim filed by Pete against Testa and Fine, and thus Fine cannot file the cross-claim in this action.

D. No, although the cross-claim arises out of the same transaction or occurrence as Pete's claim, the court does not have subject matter jurisdiction over it.

23. Plaintiff, a welder, is injured in a work-related accident that occurs in a construction site in Troy, New York, when a scaffolding structure on which she is working collapses, causing her significant injuries. Plaintiff cannot sue her employer, but she can sue the company that manufactured the scaffold: Acme. Acme is incorporated in Delaware, with its principal place of business in Connecticut. Another company, Beta, assembled the scaffold. Beta is also incorporated in Delaware, but with its principal place of business in Connecticut. Plaintiff is a citizen and resident of New York. Plaintiff commences a personal injury action against Acme seeking $500,000 in damages in federal court on state law theories of recovery, alleging diversity jurisdiction. Acme seeks to implead Beta, alleging that if Acme is liable, Beta is liable to Acme for all or part of the claim against Acme because Beta warranted in its service contract with Acme that if the scaffolding is not properly assembled, Beta will reimburse Acme for any losses it suffers as a result. In turn, Beta will assert a counterclaim against Plaintiff alleging that it was actually Plaintiff's negligent welding that caused the scaffolding to collapse and that Plaintiff's negligence has caused harm to Beta's reputation, which, Beta asserts, has cost Beta $200,000 in business. Beta's claim is based on the tort of tortious interference with contract, which arises under state law. Upon Beta's asserting a counterclaim against Plaintiff, Plaintiff will now seek to raise a claim against Beta alleging that Beta's allegation that Plaintiff was responsible for the collapse of the scaffolding has damaged her reputation and she is unable to get work. Plaintiff alleges $100,000 in lost wages due to Beta's claim against her, which is also brought under state law theories of recovery. Both Beta's counterclaim against the Plaintiff and Plaintiff's claim against Beta arise out of the same nucleus of operative facts as the Plaintiff's main claims. Once Beta learns of Plaintiff's claim against it, Beta will seek to interpose a second counterclaim against Plaintiff alleging that Plaintiff was on another site where a scaffolding collapsed (although Plaintiff was not injured in that collapse). Beta asserts that Plaintiff's negligent welding there caused that collapse as well, and it seeks $200,000 in damages from Plaintiff under a state law theory of recovery.

Which of the following is an accurate statement regarding Beta's second counterclaim against Plaintiff?

A. Beta must assert the second counterclaim against Plaintiff.

B. Beta may assert the second counterclaim against Plaintiff.

C. Beta is unable to assert the second counterclaim against Plaintiff.

D. Beta will be barred in a subsequent suit by the doctrine of claim preclusion from raising the second counterclaim against Plaintiff if it fails to interpose it in this action.

24. Plaintiff brings an action alleging that she was injured while operating a crane to remove some damaged underground pipe. While working on the pipes, she inadvertently struck a buried power line that was unmarked. She is burned and suffers serious injuries when the pierced power line sparks a fire. She cannot bring an action against her employer because of the protections of the worker's compensation system, which insulate her employer from suit but allow her to file an action against any other party who may have been responsible for her injuries. Instead of filing suit against her employer, she brings an action against the company that buried the lines (PowerInc). Plaintiff is a resident and citizen of New York State. She brings an action against PowerInc in federal court in Albany, New York, in the Northern District of New York, under state tort law theories, seeking $500,000 in damages. PowerInc is incorporated in Delaware, with its principal place of business in Massachusetts. Early in the case, she is contacted by a marketing company, SterlingCooper, which is incorporated in Delaware and has its principal place of business in Boston, Massachusetts. An employee of SterlingCooper says he can assist Plaintiff in winning her case in the "court of public opinion," as he says. Over the objections of her lawyer, who wants to stick to a real court to try the case, Plaintiff signs a contract with SterlingCooper that says that the company will indemnify Plaintiff in the event any advice given to her by SterlingCooper about speaking to the press turns out to damage Plaintiff in any way. Plaintiff speaks to the press, saying just what the SterlingCooper team suggests she should say, criticizing PowerInc for her injuries.

PowerInc obtains leave from the court to file a counterclaim against Plaintiff for alleged defamation, a claim arising under state law, seeking $1 million in damages for the harm it claims it has suffered to its reputation. Because the defamation suit will necessarily involve questions of the legitimacy of Plaintiff's claims against PowerInc, Plaintiff does not contest PowerInc's ability to file the counterclaim against it. Instead, Plaintiff seeks to file a new complaint against SterlingCooper claiming that if she is liable for defamation, SterlingCooper is liable to her for all or part of the claim.

Will the court permit Plaintiff to file a third-party complaint against Sterling Cooper? If so, why? If not, why not?

A. The court will reject Plaintiff's effort to file a third-party complaint against SterlingCooper because a plaintiff cannot implead another party by means of a third-party complaint.

B. The court will reject Plaintiff's effort to file a third-party complaint against SterlingCooper because to do so would defeat diversity.

C. The court will permit Plaintiff to file a third-party complaint against SterlingCooper because Plaintiff has alleged a sufficient ground for doing so and the court has subject matter jurisdiction over the claim.

D. The court will permit Plaintiff to file a third-party complaint against SterlingCooper because if Plaintiff cannot join the company, she will be barred from bringing a subsequent claim against it based on the principle of claim preclusion.

4.6 Necessary and Indispensable Parties

This section addresses the application of FRCP 19. As you work through the problems, compare its operation to that of other rules such as FRCP 18 and 20.

25. Plaintiff Bobby Axelrod is a billionaire who alleges that he is the victim of legal malpractice. At his trial for white collar crime, he is represented by two lawyers, Able and Baker, two of the most highly regarded criminal defense lawyers in the country. Able and Baker are solo practitioners engaged in a joint defense of Axelrod. During the trial, they confer at every critical juncture but fail to object to the introduction of some fairly damaging evidence against Axelrod, and he is ultimately convicted. Axelrod brings a legal malpractice action against only Able because Axelrod despises him and thinks he is really at fault for Axelrod's conviction. Axelrod seeks $1 million in damages for the malpractice, alleging, credibly, that he will have to spend thirty days in jail and this amount reflects his lost income during that period. At the same time, Axelrod has a long-standing relationship with Baker and does not want to sue her. Axelrod resides in New Jersey, as does Baker. Able resides in Manhattan, New York, which is located within the jurisdiction of the federal court for the Southern District of New York. Plaintiff files his legal malpractice action under state law theories of recovery in federal court for the Southern District of New York. Able will allege that he and Baker are jointly and severally liable for the malpractice, if any occurred. Able moves to dismiss the case for the failure to join Baker in the action, whose presence, if included, would defeat the court's subject matter jurisdiction over the action.

Should the court grant Able's motion to dismiss? If so, why? If not, why not?

A. The motion should be granted because Baker is jointly and severally liable with Able for the malpractice claims and is a necessary party to the action.

B. The motion should be granted because Baker is jointly and severally liable with Able to Axelrod and is thus an indispensable party to the action.

C. The motion should be denied because Baker is neither a necessary nor an indispensable party to the action.

D. The motion should be denied because Baker is a necessary but not an indispensable party.

26. Plaintiff is rear-ended in a multi-car accident in Albany, New York. Plaintiff stops in time to brake for a light that is turning red. The drivers in the two cars behind her are both distracted because they are texting while driving (texting each other, in fact). Plaintiff's car is rear-ended by Aaron's car, the car immediately behind hers, and then Aaron's car is rear-ended by the car immediately behind his, driven by Brian. Aaron and Brian were both driving negligently when the accident occurred. Brian's negligence contributed to Aaron's negligence, and their combined negligence made Plaintiff's injuries more severe. Nevertheless, but for Aaron's negligence, Plaintiff would not have been injured, so Plaintiff brings an action against Aaron claiming he is responsible for all of her injuries, which is a correct interpretation of the governing law of the jurisdiction in which the accident takes place. Plaintiff is a citizen of New York. Aaron is a citizen of Connecticut. Brian is also a citizen of Connecticut. Plaintiff brings an action against Aaron in federal court in New York for all of her injuries that resulted from the accident. Plaintiff may do this because, she alleges, Aaron and Brian are jointly and severally liable for all of her injuries. Plaintiff seeks $200,000 in damages. Aaron argues that Brian is a necessary party to the action and that the case should be dismissed for Plaintiff's failure to join Brian as a defendant.

Should the court grant Aaron's motion? If so, why? If not, why not?

A. Aaron's motion should be granted. Aaron and Brian are joint tortfeasors, and thus both are necessary parties to the action.

B. Aaron's motion should be granted. Aaron and Brian contributed to Plaintiff's injuries, and thus complete relief cannot be awarded Plaintiff in the absence of Brian.

C. Aaron's motion should be denied. That Brian is a joint tortfeasor and is contributorily liable to Plaintiff does not make him a necessary party to the action.

D. Aaron's motion should be denied. Brian is not diverse with respect to the other defendant and thus cannot be made a party to the action.

27. Plaintiff is an employee who worked on an oil rig in the Persian Gulf. While working on the rig, an explosion threw her onto a platform two stories below where she had been working. Plaintiff was severely injured. Plaintiff worked directly for AzerCo, an Azerbaijani company with an office in Texas from which it recruited Plaintiff to work on the rig. AzerCo inspects oil rigs throughout the world, including in Iran. AzerCo, in turn, works for the National Iranian Oil Company (NOIC), which owned the rig. Legislation in Iran makes NOIC immune from civil suit in Iran, but Iran is not subject to personal jurisdiction in a U.S. court because it generally does not do business with the U.S. market due to the sanctions imposed by the global community on the Iranian oil industry. Plaintiff's employment is not covered by a worker's compensation scheme, so she brings suit in the United States against AzerCo for her personal injuries. AzerCo alleges that the fault was not in its own efforts on the rig but rather in the poor quality of the safety systems that NOIC had deployed on the rig. Azer-Co argues that NOIC is a necessary party in the litigation and moves to dismiss the case.

Assume the court agrees that NOIC is a necessary party in this action. Which of the following factors will the court consider in weighing how and whether to proceed without NOIC in the action?

A. Whether there is a genuine dispute as to a material fact whether the case should proceed without NOIC in the case.

B. The extent to which AzerCo will be prejudiced if the case proceeds without NOIC in the case.

C. Whether AzerCo will have an adequate remedy if the case is dismissed for non-joinder.

D. The burden that would be imposed on a local jury if asked to adjudicate a dispute that arose outside the United States.

28. Plaintiff is the victim of an investment scam in which a financial advisor and the founder of an internet startup convinced Plaintiff to invest $100 million in the founder's company. In addition, as part of the investment scheme, Plaintiff paid the financial advisor a "finder's fee" of $2 million for helping secure the opportunity for Plaintiff to invest in the founder's company. Plaintiff is a resident and citizen of California. Both the founder and the investment advisor are residents and citizens of New York. The entire investment transaction is carried out in New York. The founder has no direct contacts with the state of California. The financial advisor recruits many of their clients from California, including Plaintiff, and regularly advertises on local media there, which is how Plaintiff found out about the financial advisor's services. The investment scheme turned out to be completely fraudulent. Plaintiff commences a federal diversity action against the financial advisor in the state of California seeking $102 million in damages on state law claims. This represents the sum total of the Plaintiff's losses in the transaction. A law in California provides that a financial advisor can be liable for a portion of a fraudulent investment if it can be shown that the financial advisor knew or had reason to know that the investment was, in fact, fraudulent. The law does not provide for joint and several liability, however. Plaintiff's attorney understands that the founder is not subject to personal jurisdiction in California, and as a result, Plaintiff sues the financial advisor alone for the entire $102 million in damages in federal court in California. The financial advisor asserts, correctly, that she will be unduly prejudiced should she have to defend against the entirety of the Plaintiff's claims without the founder as a party to the action because a jury is likely to hold her more responsible for Plaintiff's $100 million loss than it otherwise would if the founder were also a defendant in the case. The financial advisor then seeks to dismiss the action for Plaintiff's failure to join the founder as a necessary party. The court agrees that the founder is a necessary party. At the court's request, however, Plaintiff agrees to withdraw all claims related to the financial advisor's potential liability for a portion of the $100 million investment itself in order that the case will only involve a claim against the financial advisor for the $2 million for the finder's fee the financial advisor charged with regard to the transaction.

Will the court grant the financial advisor's motion to dismiss based on Plaintiff's alleged failure to join a necessary party? If so, why? If not, why not?

A. The court will grant the motion because the founder cannot be joined in the action.

B. The court will deny the motion because the founder cannot be joined in the action.

C. The court will deny the motion because the founder is not an indispensable party to the action.

D. The court will grant the motion because the founder is an indispensable party to the action.

4.7 Service of Process Issues Related to Joinder

Generally speaking, the seemingly generous rules around joinder do not create subject matter jurisdiction and typically do not create personal jurisdiction where it otherwise might not exist. In many instances involving joinder, as in situations where a claim is logically related, there will often be sufficient contacts with the dispute to render the exercise of personal jurisdiction appropriate. There is one instance where a related rule, FRCP 4(k), does create personal jurisdiction in limited situations, as the questions in this section highlight.

29.   Plaintiff Bobby Axelrod is a billionaire who alleges that he is the victim of legal malpractice. At his trial for civil restitution for unlawful insider trading, he is represented by Able, the most highly regarded lawyer in the country for this sort of matter. The civil trial is held in federal court in Newark, New Jersey. At trial, it is alleged that Axelrod engaged in insider trading in that state. Axelrod is a resident and citizen of New Jersey. Able, a solo practitioner, is a resident and citizen of New York, with his office in New Jersey, and much of the trial preparation occurs in the New Jersey office. On the eve of trial, Able entered into a joint defense agreement with Baker, a lawyer in New Jersey who exclusively practices in New Jersey and whose expertise is jury selection in New Jersey. Baker has an office in her home, which is located twelve miles from the federal court's Southern District of New York courthouse located in Lower Manhattan, New York. All meetings and conversations involving Baker took place in New Jersey. Acting on Baker's advice at the trial, Able chooses not to ask the court to remove for cause or even to use a peremptory challenge over a particular juror who, it is obvious, is likely to be antagonistic toward Axelrod. Axelrod loses at trial and the juror who Able and Baker did not challenge ends up having a large role in

Axelrod's losing the case. Axelrod files a malpractice action against Able seeking $10 million in damages for the malpractice, which is the amount of damages awarded by the jury in the action. Axelrod files the action under state law theories of recovery in federal court for the Southern District of New York, the jurisdiction that encompasses Able's home. Able moves to join Baker in the action commenced by Axelrod as a third-party defendant. Able alleges that, should Able be found guilty of malpractice, Baker is liable to Able for all or part of the claim against him because Able and Baker are jointly and severally liable for any acts of malpractice involving Axelrod's trial. Baker is personally served with the third-party complaint in her home in New Jersey, which is located within the jurisdiction of the District Court for the District of New Jersey. Nevertheless, Baker challenges the Southern District of New York's ability to exercise personal jurisdiction over her because she alleges, correctly, that she has no contacts with New York State, having contracted only with Axelrod, and not Able, to serve as additional trial counsel in New Jersey and, as a result, provided all of her services to Axelrod in New Jersey. Assume the relevant long-arm statute is satisfied with respect to the assertion of personal jurisdiction over Baker in the action.

Can the court exercise personal jurisdiction over Baker if Baker does not have any contacts with the subject forum? If so, why? If not, why not?

A. Yes, because of Baker's proximity to the federal courthouse where the action was filed.

B. No, because of Baker's lack of contact with the subject forum, even though she was personally served with a copy of the summons and complaint at her home.

C. Yes, because Baker was personally served in her home.

D. No, because it was not reasonably foreseeable that Baker might be liable in an action in New York State for malpractice committed against a New Jersey client.

4.8 Formative Assessment Quiz

Test your knowledge of the material contained in this chapter through this formative quiz.

30. Plaintiff operates a car dealership and sells Hessla vehicles, a new generation of electric car. Plaintiff is an independent contractor who resides in and is a citizen of New York State. Hessla is a company incorporated in Michigan, with its principal place of business in Delaware. Plaintiff and Hessla have the following arrangement, consistent with the type of arrangement Hessla makes with all of its dealerships: Plaintiff pays a small fee to Hessla to sell Hessla vehicles, and Hessla maintains ownership over all of its vehicles, even those in Plaintiff's lot, until they are sold by Plaintiff. Plaintiff earns a $10,000 commission from Hessla for each sale of a luxury vehicle.

One Saturday, Plaintiff has a good day. She sells eight Hessla vehicles in a single day, a new personal record, and she is very pleased with her success. That night, however, a terrible storm passes through the Capital Region of New York, where Plaintiff's lot is located. The storm fells several trees, and two Hessla vehicles stored on Plaintiff's lot are destroyed; however, the vehicles destroyed are not the ones Plaintiff had just sold because Plaintiff had brought the vehicles she sold into the showroom prior to the storm. Hessla refuses to pay Plaintiff her $80,000 in commission for the Hessla vehicles she sold. Plaintiff brings an action in federal court for the Northern District of New York, the federal court encompassing Plaintiff's lot, seeking the $80,000 in unpaid commission under state contract law theories of recovery. In its answer, Hessla includes a counterclaim under state law for $200,000, the value of the two vehicles damaged in the storm. Hessla's counterclaim is based on a clause in the contract between Hessla and Plaintiff that says Plaintiff must use due care to protect the vehicles maintained on her lot from damage. Hessla alleges that Plaintiff did not uphold her contractual obligations because she failed to provide the requisite level of care with respect to the damaged vehicles. After Plaintiff receives the answer with the counterclaim, she wants to amend her complaint to implead Tate Farm Insurance (Tate Farm), the insurance company that insures her lot from damages. Plaintiff asserts, correctly, that subrogation covers the relationship between Tate Farm and Plaintiff, and if Plaintiff is liable to Hessla, Tate Farm is, in turn, liable to Plaintiff for any successful damage award Hessla should obtain on its counterclaim. Tate Farm is incorporated in Delaware, with its principal place of business in New York. Notwithstanding her effort to implead Tate Farm, Plaintiff makes a motion to dismiss Hessla's counterclaim. Hessla, not wanting to have to litigate against Tate Farm as well, moves to dismiss that portion of the amended complaint impleading Tate Farm into the case, alleging that the court does not have subject matter jurisdiction over the claim against Tate Farm.

How should the court deal with the two motions (Plaintiff's motion to dismiss the counterclaim and Hessla's motion to dismiss that portion of the amended complaint that seeks to implead Tate Farm)?

A. The court should grant the motion to dismiss that portion of the amended complaint that seeks to implead Tate Farm but not the motion to dismiss the counterclaim.

B. The court should deny both motions.

C. The court should grant both motions.

D. The court should grant the motion to dismiss the counterclaim, which would render the motion to dismiss that portion of the amended complaint that seeks to implead Tate Farm unnecessary and moot.

31. Plaintiff files an action against Defendant Able State University (Able) alleging that Able discriminated against her in her application to a university graduate program run by the state, in violation of the U.S. Constitution and federal statutory protections, and seeking $250,000 in damages. Able claims that it "outsourced" all of its admissions decisions to Baker Consulting (Baker). Able is a public corporation incorporated in Connecticut, with its principal place of business in Connecticut. Baker is a private, for-profit corporation incorporated in Delaware, with its principal place of business in New York. Plaintiff is a resident and citizen of New York. Within ten days of Able's filing its answer in the district court, it seeks to interpose a third-party complaint against Baker alleging, correctly, that in the contract through which Baker agreed to provide consulting services to Able in administering Able's admissions programs, Baker also agreed to indemnify Able for any losses it suffers for Baker's actions. Once Baker is joined in the action as a third-party defendant, Plaintiff seeks to interpose new affirmative claims against Baker alleging that Baker also violated federal laws prohibiting discrimination in higher education and seeking an additional $100,000 in damages. Baker makes a motion to dismiss the claim filed against it by Plaintiff, challenging the court's subject matter jurisdiction to entertain Plaintiff's claims against Baker.

Will Baker succeed in dismissing Plaintiff's claim against it? If so, why? If not, why not?

A. Yes. Baker will succeed because the parties are not diverse.

B. No. Plaintiff can interpose a new affirmative claim against Baker because that claim independently satisfies the amount-in-controversy requirement.

C. Yes. Plaintiff is barred from interposing new affirmative claims against Baker as long as Baker has not interposed any direct counterclaims against it.

D. No. Plaintiff can interpose a new affirmative claim against Baker despite the fact that the parties are not diverse.

32. Plaintiff is a citizen of Connecticut and his palatial home is located in Darien, Connecticut. Mortgage Bank is incorporated in Delaware, with its principal place of business in Albany, New York. Plaintiff believes Mortgage Bank violated federal law prohibitions related to financial transactions when it improperly sold him mortgage insurance associated with his mortgage. He explicitly stated during negotiations over the mortgage that he did not want mortgage insurance. Plaintiff's mortgage is quite large, over $2 million, and his monthly payments are roughly $15,000 per month. He claims that the terms related to the payment of mortgage insurance were inserted by bank representatives after Plaintiff signed the mortgage agreement documents. Plaintiff's accountant only noticed the mortgage insurance payments, which were noted in the fine print of Plaintiff's monthly statements and equal nearly $2,000 per month, several years after Plaintiff began paying the mortgage. After Plaintiff's accountant noticed the mortgage insurance charge, and three months before commencing any action against Mortgage Bank, Plaintiff stopped paying the mortgage insurance. Plaintiff brings a federal action in federal court in Albany, New York, alleging violations of fraud provisions in federal law against Mortgage Bank for improperly charging him for mortgage insurance, and seeking $100,000 in damages. Mortgage Bank seeks to interpose a counterclaim for Plaintiff's failure to make monthly mortgage insurance payments for the last three months, a claim that arises under state contract law, seeking $6,000 in damages.

If Mortgage Bank seeks to interpose a counterclaim for Plaintiff's failure to pay mortgage insurance, will the court permit Mortgage Bank to do so? If so, why? If not, why not?

A. Defendant will be able to interpose the counterclaim because it is logically related to Plaintiff's claims.

B. Defendant will be able to interpose the counterclaim because it arises out of the same nucleus of operative facts as Plaintiff's claims.

C. Defendant will not be able to interpose the counterclaim because the action was filed in its home state.

D. Defendant will not be able to interpose the counterclaim because it is below the amount-in-controversy requirement for such a claim.

33. Plaintiff alleges that he was a victim of a fraudulent investment scheme in which he was induced to invest in what he was told was pristine waterfront property in the Florida Keys. The problem with the property was that it contained several buried gas tanks that were generally not visible and not discoverable without conducting a full environmental investigation of the property in question. Plaintiff files a state fraud claim in federal court in Florida against both the real estate developer who sold him the property and the environmental consultant, hired by the developer, who had filed the fraudulent environmental report that failed to reveal the presence of the buried gas tanks. Plaintiff is a resident and citizen of New York State. The real estate developer ("Developer") is a corporation incorporated in Florida, with its principal place of business in Florida. The environmental consultant ("Consultant") is an individual and a resident and citizen of Georgia. Plaintiff's claim seeks $10 million in damages against both Developer and Consultant, whom Plaintiff claims are jointly and severally liable to him. These damages amount to the purchase price of the property in question, which Plaintiff alleges is now worthless given the presence of the buried oil tanks. Consultant wants to file two claims against his fellow defendant, Developer. The first, asserting state contract law claims, alleges that Consultant was never paid under the contract with Developer for the environmental report of Plaintiff's property that Consultant prepared. This claim seeks $100,000 in damages, which is what Developer had agreed to pay Consultant for the work performed on Plaintiff's property on behalf of Developer. The second claim seeks $10,000 for injuries Consultant alleges he sustained when working on property owned by Developer but not the property Plaintiff purchased from developer. Consultant's second claim arises under federal workplace safety statutes.

If Developer seeks to dismiss both of Consultant's claims against it, what is the likely outcome with respect to both claims?

A. The court will dismiss both claims.

B. The court will dismiss the contract claim but not the workplace safety claim.

C. The court will dismiss the workplace safety claim but not the contract claim.

D. The court will dismiss neither claim.

34. Paul is a car dealer who sells luxury limousines. Paul sues Limo, Inc. (Limo), a manufacturer of limousines, for failing to deliver several luxury stretch models for which Paul claims he paid $500,000. Paul's business is incorporated in New York, with its principal place of business in East Greenbush, New York, and Limo is incorporated in Delaware, with its principal place of business in Groton, Connecticut. Paul brings an action in federal district court for the District of Connecticut seeking delivery of the limousines—valued at $500,000—in accordance with the contract between Paul and Limo. Paul's claim arises under New York State contract law. Limo wishes to file a counterclaim, however. It alleges that Paul failed to satisfy his obligations under a separate contract for the delivery of ten electric bicycles, each valued at $5,000. Paul made the first payment of $20,000 under the contract, but failed to make the final payment of $30,000 which was due under the contract, for the bicycles. Limo seeks to file a counterclaim under Connecticut law that seeks payment under the contract for the remaining $30,000.

Will the court permit Limo to join its counterclaim to the action brought by Paul? If so, why? If not, why not?

A. Yes. Limo's counterclaim is compulsory in nature, so at a minimum, there is supplemental jurisdiction over Limo's counterclaim in the case filed by Paul.

B. No. Limo's counterclaim is permissive and there is not an independent basis of jurisdiction over it.

C. No. Even though Limo's counterclaim is compulsory in nature, there is no independent basis of jurisdiction over it.

D. Yes, even though Limo's counterclaim is permissive in nature, there is an independent basis of jurisdiction for Limo to file it.

35. Plaintiff is an employee who took part in a humanitarian mission to deliver food and medical supplies to North Korea. When the ship docked at a port in that country, an explosion near the supplies that were being unloaded threw Plaintiff roughly twenty feet across the dock where she was working, and she sustained severe injuries. Plaintiff worked directly for GreenFleece, a not-for-profit company based in Texas that engages in these types of humanitarian missions throughout the world. An investigation reveals that the North Korean military planted a bomb near the GreenFleece ship while it was in port, and it was that bomb that caused the explosion that injured Plaintiff. Plaintiff's employment is not covered by a worker's compensation scheme, so she brings suit in federal court in Texas against GreenFleece for the injuries she sustained on GreenFleece's ship. GreenFleece alleges that the fault was not in its own efforts but rather in the acts of the North Korean military. Plaintiff does not name North Korea as a party to her action because she believes they are effectively immune from suit and will not appear in the action. GreenFleece argues that North Korea is a necessary party in the litigation and moves to dismiss the case for the failure to join that nation as a party.

Assume the court agrees that North Korea is a necessary party in this action. Which of the following factors will the court consider in weighing how and whether to proceed without North Korea in the action?

A. Whether GreenFleece will have an adequate remedy if the case is dismissed for non-joinder.

B. The extent to which GreenFleece will be prejudiced if the case proceeds without North Korea in the case.

C. The burden that would be imposed on a local jury if it is asked to adjudicate a dispute that happened outside the United States.

D. Whether the trier of fact will be able to visit the scene of the accident.

36. Plaintiff Ned Stark enters into a mortgage agreement with Lannister Bank (Lannister). Stark pays the mortgage for several years. After some time passes, Stark decides he wants to build a second home, a weekend retreat, and enters into an agreement for a multi-million dollar construction loan to build a new home in the Catskills, in Upstate New York. He then discusses the terms of his original mortgage with several neighbors and learns that they all received mortgages on better terms from Lannister than those contained in his mortgage. He talks this over with the business manager at the bank who informs him that, under a previous administration at the bank, individuals like him—Serbian Americans—were routinely discriminated against because the bank president was Bosnian American. This is a violation of federal statutes that ban discrimination in mortgage lending. Stark immediately stops paying on his primary mortgage and defaults on the construction loan for the second home. Stark is a resident and citizen of New York. Lannister is incorporated in Delaware, with its principal place of business in Connecticut. Stark commences an action in federal court for the Southern District of New York, the district in which the negotiations over his mortgage took place, alleging violation of federal law and claiming $80,000 in damages—the difference between what he paid on his mortgage each month and what he believes his mortgage payments would have been if he were not subjected to discrimination. There is no allegation of discrimination with respect to the construction loan, and it is not made a part of Stark's case against the bank. Lannister will submit its answer to Stark's complaint, including a defense that there was no discrimination in the execution of the mortgage loan. This argument will serve first as a defense: if there was no discrimination, Stark's claim will fail. Moreover, without the discrimination, Stark would be liable to Lannister for any outstanding debt, and that outstanding debt could serve as the basis of a counterclaim by Lannister against Stark. In fact, Lannister, which insists that its borrowers always pay their debts, interposes not one, but two counterclaims in the action against Stark. The first counterclaim (Counterclaim I) is for non-payment of the first mortgage, seeking $40,000 (the amount outstanding on the mortgage when the case was filed). Under the terms of the second loan (the construction loan), the failure to make the monthly payments on that loan permits Lannister to recall the loan and demand all of the original proceeds (i.e., the original loan amount). Lannister's second counterclaim (Counterclaim II) seeks $2 million in damages. Both of Lannister's claims arise under state law. Stark moves to dismiss both counterclaims on the grounds that the court does not have subject matter jurisdiction over them.

How will the court rule with respect to Plaintiff's motion regarding Lannister's two counterclaims?

A. The court will deny the motion with respect to both Counterclaim I and Counterclaim II, and neither will be dismissed.

B. The court will dismiss Counterclaim I but deny the motion with respect to Counterclaim II.

C. The court will deny the motion with respect to Counterclaim I and grant the motion with respect to Counterclaim II.

D. The court will grant the motion with respect to both Counterclaim I and Counterclaim II, and both will be dismissed.

37.　Frank is a popular restaurateur in Jersey City, New Jersey. His company is incorporated in New Jersey, with its principal place of business in New Jersey. Frank purchases much of his produce from the farmer's market in Union Square in Manhattan, New York, specifically from The Farmer's Coop (Coop), a company that purchases produce from a number of farmers in lower Rockland and Dutchess Counties in New York State. One of the farms that sells produce to the Coop, Dan's Farm, sells a batch of beets to Coop that are infected with Listeria. In turn, Frank purchases these beets from Coop and then serves them at his restaurant, where two of his customers get sick from eating the infected beets. These patrons are residents of New York, and they file suit against Frank in federal court for the District of New Jersey in Newark, New Jersey, the district encompassing Frank's restaurant, alleging claims based on state law tort theories and seeking over $1 million in damages for the serious illness they incurred by ingesting the tainted beets. Coop is incorporated in New York, with its principal place of business in New York. Coop markets its produce throughout the Tri-State Region, which comprises New York, New Jersey, and Connecticut. Dan's Farm, incorporated in New York State, with its principal place of business in Rhinebeck, New York, in Dutchess County, only markets its produce to wholesalers in the New York market and has no ties to New Jersey. Frank seeks by means of a third-party complaint to join Coop and Dan's Farm, alleging that if Frank is liable, they are as well, based on the implead warranty under applicable state law that the produce sold and purchased by Frank will not cause injury to individuals who consume it. A person authorized to accept service upon Coop is served with a summons and complaint at Coop's principal place of business. Dan's Farm is located 95 miles from the Newark courthouse where the action is filed. A person authorized to accept service of process upon Dan's Farm is served at the farm with the third-party summons and complaint at the farm.

If Dan's Farm makes a motion to dismiss the third-party complaint filed against it, will the court grant the motion? If so, why? If not, why not?

A. The motion will be denied because the court has personal and subject matter jurisdiction over Dan's Farm.

B. The motion will be granted because joinder of Dan's Farm would defeat complete diversity.

C. The motion will be granted because the court does not have personal jurisdiction over Dan's Farm.

D. The motion will be denied because Dan's Farm cannot raise the issue of improper joinder in a motion to dismiss.

38. Giant Burger (Giant) is a chain restaurant with many locations. Each restaurant is an independent franchise and contractor. Giant wants to bring an action against several owners of these restaurants (the "original owners") that operate in Wisconsin. The original owners have sold their interests in their franchises to third parties (the "Third-Party owners") in alleged violation of the original owners' franchise agreements with Giant. Giant wishes to sue both the original owners and the third-party owners. Giant's attorney conducts research to learn the names and corporate addresses of the third-party owners. They bring an action against both the original owners and the third-party owners, alleging breach of the contracts between the original owners and Giant, and for trademark infringement because the third-party owners are operating Giant restaurants without the permission of Giant, an express violation of Giant's intellectual property rights. A central question in the case is whether, under the contracts between Giant and the original owners, such owners can sell the rights to operate the franchises without Giant's permission. Giant's attorneys commence the action in federal court in Wisconsin alleging both federal trademark violation and violations of their contracts under state law. The amount in controversy in the action exceeds $1 million. The defendants are sued jointly and severally. The defendants are all citizens of Wisconsin and Giant is a citizen of New York.

Can Giant join the federal and state claims in the same action in federal court? If so, why? If not, why not?

A. No. There is no federal subject matter jurisdiction over the state law claims.

B. No. Although there is a common question of fact in the federal and state law claims, there is no common question of law, and thus joinder is inappropriate.

C. Yes. The federal and state law claims arise from the same series of transactions, the defendants are sued jointly and severally, and the question of whether all of the defendants are in material breach of the contracts with Giant is a question common to all defendants.

D. Yes. The legal question of whether the original owners are in violation of their contract is a question common to both the federal and state law claims.

39. Plaintiff is injured in an automobile accident. The driver of the vehicle that struck the Plaintiff is uninsured. Plaintiff is a resident and citizen of New York. She brings an action against AMC, the manufacturer of the vehicle that struck Plaintiff, alleging that a design defect in the steering column of the vehicle caused the accident. Plaintiff seeks $1 million in damages on the state law claim and files her action in federal court in New York alleging diversity jurisdiction. AMC is incorporated in Delaware, with its principal place of business in New Jersey. The vehicle was manufactured in New York and sold by one of AMC's dealerships in New York. AMC seeks to implead Bard Autobody (Bard), the manufacturer of the steering column, arguing that if AMC is found liable for the injuries to Plaintiff, Bard is liable to AMC for all or part of the claims against it due to the fact that Bard agreed to indemnify AMC if one of Bard's columns malfunctioned and AMC is found liable as a result. Bard is also incorporated in Delaware, but with its principal place of business in New York. The steering column in question was manufactured in New York. Once Bard is joined in the action, Plaintiff seeks to amend her complaint to add a new tort claim based on state law against Bard directly. Bard will move to dismiss the third-party complaint filed by AMC and the claim filed against Bard by the Plaintiff, alleging the federal court can entertain neither the complaint nor Plaintiff's claim against Bard.

Will Bard succeed in dismissing the AMC complaint and Plaintiff's claim against Bard?

A. Bard will succeed in dismissing the claim brought by Plaintiff but not the third-party complaint filed by AMC.

B. Bard will succeed in dismissing the third-party complaint brought by AMC but not the claim brought by Plaintiff against Bard.

C. Bard will succeed in dismissing both the third-party complaint and Plaintiff's claim against Bard.

D. Bard will succeed in dismissing neither the third-party complaint nor Plaintiff's claim against Bard.

Chapter 5

Pleading

5.1 General Requirements

This chapter will expose you to the rules surrounding pleadings—what parties making both affirmative and defensive claims must do when asserting such claims. It will also address the boundaries of acceptable factual allegations and legal assertions.

1. Plaintiff is a high school teacher who claims that Defendant, the local school district, refused to promote him to an assistant principal position in violation of federal laws that prohibit discrimination in employment. Plaintiff will allege further that Defendant's agents/employees conspired to deny him his rights under the law, which is a separate violation of the law. Plaintiff alleges that the decision to not promote him occurred during a meeting of Defendant's employees, the school district superintendent and the school principal. It was at that meeting, Plaintiff alleges, that these individuals conspired to deny him the promotion he sought. Plaintiff states that the principal and superintendent must have discussed the decision to pass him over at that meeting because he was alerted by the principal of the decision to not promote him the day after that meeting. Plaintiff further alleges that the decision to deny him the promotion was based on his ethnicity, a protected class under federal law. Plaintiff believes that the superintendent and principal conspired to choose not to promote him because they are biased against him because he and they are all from different ethnic backgrounds. However, Plaintiff fails to state the ethnicities of the Defendants. Plaintiff offers no evidence of discrimination or of a conspiracy other than the fact that the superintendent and principal have ethnic backgrounds different from his and that they met together the day before he learned of the decision to give the promotion to another member of the high school faculty. Plaintiff files an action in federal court against the school district, the principal, and the school superintendent alleging violations of federal law that protects against discrimination in employment based on ethnicity and also charging Defendants with a conspiracy to deny him of his rights. Defendants will move to dismiss the case for failure to state a claim upon which relief can be granted.

What is the likely outcome of Defendants' motion to dismiss?

A. The court will grant the motion because Plaintiff's claims are not plausible as alleged.

B. The court will deny the motion because Plaintiff has made a showing that his claims are plausible.

C. The court will deny the motion because it must accept Plaintiff's allegations as true.

D. The court will grant the motion because Plaintiff has not shown that the court has personal jurisdiction over Defendants.

2. Plaintiff, a resident and citizen of Minnesota, entered into a mortgage agreement with West Fargo Bank (Bank), which is incorporated in Delaware, with its principal place of business in North Dakota. Plaintiff alleges that Bank is liable to her for fraud in the negotiation or execution of the mortgage under state law theories of recovery. She seeks $200,000 in damages and brings her claim in the U.S. District Court for the District of North Dakota. Plaintiff alleges that fraud occurred in two potential aspects of her mortgage. First, she alleges that she was fraudulently induced to enter into the mortgage when she received a statement about the terms of the mortgage while she was shopping for a mortgage online. She alleges that the terms of the mortgage communicated to her were inconsistent with the terms of the mortgage she ultimately signed. Second, and in the alternative, she argues that if the marketing of the mortgage was not fraudulent, then the way her mortgage interest was calculated was inconsistent with the plain language of the mortgage itself, constituting a separate act of fraud. She alleges these two alternative theories in her action against Bank. Bank moves to dismiss the state law claims against it for failure on the part of Plaintiff to state a claim for which relief can be granted.

When the court entertains Defendant's motion to dismiss the complaint, what standard should it primarily consider when ruling on the sufficiency of the pleadings?

A. Whether the pleadings raise a plausible claim for relief.

B. Whether the allegations are pled with particularity.

C. Whether Plaintiff has pled inconsistent theories.

D. Whether Plaintiff has identified a genuine dispute as to a material fact.

3. Plaintiff Prisoner brings an action in federal court under the Prison Litigation Reform Act (PLRA) for abuses he says he suffered at the hands of prison guards while incarcerated at the federal Metropolitan Detention Center in Brooklyn, New York. He alleges that the warden specifically ordered that the prison guards abuse him. In his complaint, he alleges that he was subject to abusive treatment just a few hours after an all-staff meeting was held at the prison. The prison guards who beat him were in attendance at this meeting. The complaint alleges further that the warden ordered the guards to abuse him after this all-staff meeting. Notes from the meeting, obtained through the federal Freedom of Information Act in anticipation of the Plaintiff's filing, reveal that the warden issued a direct order to the prison guards to attack Plaintiff. These notes are referenced in the complaint, and they are the basis for the allegations that the warden ordered the attack. The warden is named as a defendant in Plaintiff's action. While she certainly may be liable for so-called supervisor's liability for the abuse the Plaintiff suffered, she seeks to dismiss that portion of the complaint that alleges she directly ordered the abuse of the Plaintiff. The relevant portion of the complaint regarding the warden's instructions to the correctional staff reads as follows:

> At an all-staff meeting held on November 19, 2013, Warden issued several directives to correctional staff to "take out" Plaintiff. Notes from the meeting state that this phrase was uttered by Warden on several occasions throughout the meeting. On November 1, 2013, and November 3, 2013, Plaintiff had filed complaints

against Warden with federal officials, which, upon information and belief, gave Warden reason to intimidate and harass Plaintiff in order to exact his silence.

If the warden brings a pre-answer motion to dismiss for failure to state a claim in which she challenges those allegations of the complaint that state that she ordered the attack at the all-staff meeting, what is the likely outcome?

A. The motion will be denied; the allegations are sufficient to state a plausible claim for relief.

B. The motion will be granted; the allegations are not sufficient to state a plausible claim for relief.

C. The motion will be granted; the allegations are not conclusory and thus they are insufficient to state a claim upon which relief can be granted.

D. The motion will be denied; the warden cannot challenge the complaint for failure to state a claim upon which relief can be granted in a pre-answer motion to dismiss.

4. Assume that the U.S. Congress has just passed and the President has signed new legislation creating a civil remedy for individuals who were defrauded by any company offering pools for wagering in online fantasy sports. As a part of that legislation, an individual with a claim must file an action in federal court within six months of the incident which the claimant alleges constituted fraud. The six-month statute of limitations is identified as an affirmative defense to any action under the legislation. Litigation under this legislation has arisen, and defendants have begun to assert that any plaintiff wishing to file suit under the law must allege in the complaint that he or she has satisfied the six-month statute of limitations. In fact, in one case, a defendant, SportsKings, one of the fantasy wagering websites, has brought a motion to dismiss the action for Plaintiff's failure to allege that she filed the case within six months of the alleged fraud.

Should the court grant the motion for Plaintiff's failure to allege that she satisfied the statute of limitations when she filed her suit? If so, why? If not, why not?

A. Yes. The court should grant the motion because Plaintiff cannot make out a plausible claim for relief if she cannot establish that she satisfied the statute of limitations.

B. Yes. The court should grant the motion because Plaintiff has not satisfied a legislatively created condition for bringing her action.

C. No. The Plaintiff can make out a plausible claim for relief, and thus the motion should be denied.

D. No. The Plaintiff does not have to plead in the complaint that she satisfied the statute of limitations.

5. A federal statute governing the operation of federally subsidized residential rental property requires that a private landlord operating such property must follow certain guidelines prior to seeking to evict any tenant from that property. First, the landlord must provide any tenant it wants to evict with written notice of the grounds upon which that eviction will be based and that notice must be served on the tenant prior to any eviction action actually being commenced. Second, in any complaint in an eviction action, the landlord must both state that it complied with the notice requirement as well as set forth facts sufficient to establish that the landlord actually complied with that notice provision. Landlord intends to evict Tenant from the Landlord's federally subsidized rental housing to which the statute described above applies. Landlord complies with the requirement that it serve the pre-complaint notice on Tenant, but Landlord's lawyer neglects to include any language in the complaint in the eviction action describing the actions taken by the Landlord to comply with the notice requirement. The case is filed in federal court, and Tenant's lawyer moves to dismiss the action on the grounds that the complaint failed to set forth facts describing Landlord's efforts to serve the pre-complaint notice on Tenant.

Will Tenant's motion to dismiss succeed? If so, why?

A. No, because Landlord is not required to plead around an anticipated defense in its complaint.

B. Yes, because Landlord is attempting to deny Tenant her property without due process of law.

C. Yes, because Landlord was required to plead compliance with the pre-complaint notice requirement.

D. No, because Landlord actually complied with the pre-complaint notice requirement, which is all the statute requires.

5.2 Responding to the Complaint

The first section addressed the requirements of a party making an affirmative claim. This section covers the rules related to the different responses that the adverse party can make. Sometimes that response is an answer. An adverse party can also make a motion to dismiss the action. That motion can even be filed before the answer, as a pre-answer motion to dismiss. This section will address the procedures covering these different responsive maneuvers.

6.   Plaintiff is an inmate serving a sentence for bank robbery. In the robbery in which Plaintiff took part, a security guard was killed. The security guard was a retired corrections officer. Although Plaintiff just drove the getaway car during the robbery and did not play any role in the death of the security guard, Plaintiff alleges that he is subject to harassment by the correctional officers at the prison where he is currently incarcerated. Plaintiff alleges that his constitutional right to be free from unjust prison conditions has been violated. He brings a federal action against the prison in federal court, alleging violations of the federal Constitution. The suit also names the warden as a defendant for allegedly initiating the course of harassing conduct to which Plaintiff claims he is subjected. One of Plaintiff's allegations is that the warden conspired with the head of the corrections officers' union to subject Plaintiff to unconstitutional conditions. Plaintiff's complaint contains the following allegations:

1. Defendant warden and the president of the corrections officers' union conspired at a meeting held on April 1, 2016, to subject Plaintiff to harassing conduct in violation of Plaintiff's constitutional rights.

2. This action was taken due to the fact that a former corrections

officer and union member died in the course of the robbery that served as the basis of plaintiff's prison sentence.

The warden denies that she was in a meeting with the leader of the corrections officers' union on this date, telling her lawyer that at no time did she ever discuss taking retaliatory action against Plaintiff with anyone. Moreover, she adds that she was not even aware that the security guard killed in the robbery was a former corrections officer until she read that fact in the complaint after it was served upon her.

Given that the warden disputes the allegations contained in these paragraphs of the complaint, what is the proper response on the part of the warden to these allegations?

A. Move to dismiss the allegations for lack of subject matter jurisdiction.

B. Deny these allegations in the complaint when she files her answer.

C. Make a motion to dismiss the allegations because they are not sufficiently specific to raise a plausible claim for relief.

D. State in her answer that she does not have knowledge or information sufficient to form a belief about the truth of the allegations.

7. Plaintiff is involved in a car accident in New Mexico. The allegation is that a part on the Plaintiff's car, manufactured by Lodge Motors (Lodge), was defectively designed, causing the accident. It is also alleged that an engineering company, Striper Parts (Striper), designed and manufactured the allegedly defective part in San Francisco, California, where Striper is incorporated and has its principal offices. Plaintiff brings an action in the U.S. District Court for the District of New Mexico alleging that the design and manufacturing defects were the proximate cause of her injuries, but sues only Lodge, which is incorporated in Michigan, with its principal place of business in Michigan. Defendant Lodge wishes to file a pre-answer motion to dismiss the action.

Which of the following defenses will Defendant have waived if it fails to include it in this pre-answer motion to dismiss?

A. Improper venue.

B. Failure to state a claim upon which relief can be granted.

C. Lack of subject matter jurisdiction.

D. Failure to join a necessary party.

8. Plaintiff files an action against Defendant alleging that Defendant breached a contract between the parties. Plaintiff is a resident and citizen of New York. Defendant is a resident and citizen of Delaware. Plaintiff seeks $50,000 on a contract claim that arises under state law. Plaintiff files the case in the federal court for the Southern District of New York, where Plaintiff resides and where a substantial percentage of the acts giving rise to the alleged liability occurred. Defendant makes a pre-answer motion to dismiss based on the argument that Plaintiff failed to commence the action within the time frame set forth in the applicable statute of limitations. The motion is denied, and Defendant is given twenty days to file an answer. Defendant interposes an answer that includes the following defenses: that the court lacks subject matter jurisdiction, that venue is inappropriate in the Southern District of New York, and that Plaintiff has failed to set forth a claim upon which relief can be granted. Plaintiff will move to strike the answer, arguing that Defendant is barred from interposing these defenses because they were not submitted with the Defendant's original pre-answer motion to dismiss.

Has Defendant waived any or all of the new defenses it seeks to interpose through the answer? If so, which ones?

A. By failing to include them in Defendant's pre-answer motion to dismiss, Defendant has waived all of these defenses.

B. By failing to include them in Defendant's pre-answer motion to dismiss, Defendant has waived the right to object to subject matter jurisdiction and venue but not the defense based on

failure to state a claim upon which relief can be granted.

C. By failing to include it in Defendant's
pre-answer motion to dismiss, Defendant has waived the right to object to
venue but did not waive the defenses
based on an alleged lack of subject
matter jurisdiction and the purported
failure to state a claim upon which relief can be granted.

D. Defendant has not waived the ability
to interpose any of these defenses
even though Defendant failed to include them in Defendant's pre-answer
motion to dismiss.

9.   Plaintiff files an action against Kirin,
a company based in Japan that manufactures electronic vehicles. Plaintiff alleges
there was a design defect in the Kirin
vehicle Plaintiff purchased that led to
the car's autopilot function assuming
control of the car, leaving Plaintiff unable to regain control of the vehicle. The
autopilot function then led Plaintiff to
drive off the road, ultimately coming to
a stop only after hitting a telephone pole.
Given the effective safety mechanisms in
the vehicle, it is not clear at the time of
the incident whether Plaintiff sustained
physical injuries. Nevertheless, Plaintiff says that he wants to file a lawsuit to
highlight the risks associated with Kirin
vehicles. Plaintiff files an action in federal court in California, the site of the
accident, alleging diversity jurisdiction
and raising state law theories of recovery.
Plaintiff seeks $75,001 in damages. Kirin's
vehicles are not generally for sale in the
United States, and Plaintiff purchased his
Kirin vehicle in Canada, where they are
sold. Kirin does some direct business in
the United States, but only related to its
sale of motorcycles. Kirin has several motorcycle showrooms throughout California. Kirin is incorporated in Japan, with
its principal place of business in the city
of Osaka, Japan. Plaintiff commences the
action, and Plaintiff's counsel follows the
legal requirements for serving a foreign
corporation with a copy of the summons
and complaint at Kirin's headquarters in
Japan. Kirin files an answer in which its
only argument is that Plaintiff failed to
set forth a claim upon which relief could
be granted. The case proceeds through
discovery, and at Plaintiff's deposition,
Plaintiff admits that he essentially suffered
no physical injuries in the accident and,

as a result, has no damages claims against Kirin other than for $5,000 for repair of the vehicle damaged in the action. When this information comes out in discovery, Kirin's counsel immediately makes a motion to dismiss on two grounds: that the court has no subject matter jurisdiction over the action and that the court cannot exercise personal jurisdiction over Kirin. Plaintiff will object that Kirin waived its right to assert both of these as bases for a motion to dismiss since they were not included in Kirin's original answer.

By failing to raise the defenses of a lack of subject matter jurisdiction and personal jurisdiction in its answer, has Kirin waived the right to assert either or both defenses in a motion to dismiss at this stage in the litigation?

A. Kirin has waived the right to assert the defense related to an alleged lack of subject matter jurisdiction but not the defense related to an alleged lack of personal jurisdiction.

B. Kirin has waived the right to assert both defenses.

C. Kirin has not waived its right to assert these defenses.

D. Kirin waived its right to assert the defense based on an alleged lack of personal jurisdiction but not the defense based on an alleged lack of subject matter jurisdiction.

5.3 Rule 11

In addition to the requirement that pleadings be plausible, all parties (and their lawyers) must only make good faith legal and factual assertions as required under FRCP 11, as this section explores.

10. Larry is a personal injury lawyer. One afternoon, he is approached in his office by an individual who claims that he was the victim of medical malpractice. The prospective client informs Larry that he was injured while on vacation on Cape Cod, Massachusetts, and he suffered further injuries while being treated at Cape Cod Hospital on the island. As the deadline for the statute of limitations gets closer and closer, the lawyer does little about the case until there are just a few days left to bring the action. The lawyer pulls together a hastily prepared complaint alleging that his client was injured at the hospital with little factual support for the claims. He is able to obtain the medical records of the Plaintiff's stay at the hospital and is able to make out a plausible claim for relief, however. As he litigates the case, the lawyer engages in the following conduct: First, several of the factual contentions made in the complaint were made without a good faith basis and were interposed without reasonable investigation. Second, during a deposition, he is abusive toward one of the doctors who treated his patient, using foul language and at one point throwing a copy of a medical dictionary at the deponent. Third, he proceeds in bad faith in negotiations with the lawyers for the hospital: by changing his negotiation position repeatedly, acting erratically, making unreasonable and unwarranted demands, failing to prepare for the negotiations, and acting in an abusive manner toward the court-appointed mediator. Fourth, he includes baseless claims in a motion for summary judgment that he files without having conducted any research. The lawyers for the hospital cite all of these allegations in their motion seeking Rule 11 sanctions against the lawyer for the Plaintiff. Prior to filing the motion, they properly serve the lawyer with a copy of the motion and wait twenty-one days before they file it. During the twenty-one-day period, the lawyer insists that he will not retract any allegations, claims, or factual contentions, and he certainly will not withdraw his motion for summary judgment. At oral argument on the motion, the judge, correctly, points out that she can consider all of the facts set forth by the hospital's lawyers in considering what punishment to impose, if any, on Plaintiff's lawyer, but she does not think she can impose Rule 11 sanctions on the lawyer for all of the conduct cited in the hospital's brief.

Putting aside the issue of what information may be taken into account when considering the severity or type of sanction the judge might impose on the lawyer for any conduct she finds to have violated Rule 11, which of the following most accurately identifies all of the conduct of the lawyer that may serve as a basis for the imposition of sanctions solely under Rule 11 of the Federal Rules of Civil Procedure?

A. The baseless factual contentions contained in the complaint.

B. The filing of the summary judgment motion and the lawyer's behavior in the deposition of the doctor.

C. The filing of the summary judgment motion and the baseless factual contentions contained in the complaint.

D. The behavior in the deposition and his bad faith negotiations in the settlement negotiations.

11. Plaintiff believes she was illegally steered into a mortgage with unfavorable terms for discriminatory reasons by Defendant, a local mortgage broker. Plaintiff brings a claim under the federal Fair Housing Act, alleging discrimination in mortgage lending and asserting that the discrimination was based on Plaintiff's sexual orientation. Recent U.S. Supreme Court precedent has found that discrimination in employment contexts based on sexual orientation is a violation of federal law based on the plain language of the federal employment discrimination statute. Plaintiff's attorney argues, although this has not been tested in any court, that language identical to the critical language found in the federal employment discrimination statute that provided the basis upon which the Supreme Court extended that statute to cover sexual orientation discrimination is also contained in federal housing discrimination law. Based on this argument, Plaintiff contends that federal law covering discrimination in housing should similarly extend to protect against discrimination based on sexual orientation. At the outset of the litigation, Defendant makes a motion to dismiss for Plaintiff's alleged failure to state a claim upon which relief can be granted as well as a separate motion for sanctions under Rule 11 against Plaintiff's counsel, following the appropriate procedures for doing so. The trial court deferred action on the sanctions motion until after it could consider Defendant's motion to dismiss. The trial court finds for Defendant on the motion to dismiss, dismissing the claim of sexual-orientation-based mortgage discrimination. The court now plans to rule on the motion for sanctions.

Will the court grant Defendant's motion for sanctions with respect to Plaintiff's now-dismissed claim? If so, why? If not, why not?

A. Yes, because the mortgage discrimination claim was dismissed by the trial court.

B. No, because Plaintiff's counsel presented a creative argument in favor of the novel mortgage-discrimination claim.

C. Yes, because Plaintiff's counsel failed to make a good faith argument for the extension of existing law in support of the claim.

D. No, because Plaintiff's counsel made a good faith argument for the extension of existing law in support of the claim.

12.   During the course of a civil lawsuit in federal court, lawyer Larry, representing the plaintiff, engages in the following actions: During oral argument on a pre-answer motion to dismiss several of the plaintiff's claims, Larry makes statements that are utterly baseless; he makes no effort to support them with any nonfrivolous arguments for the reversal, modification, or extension of the law or for establishing new law. Despite Larry's opposition to the motion, the motion is granted and several of the plaintiff's claims are dismissed, but the case proceeds to the discovery phase on those claims that were not the subject of the dismissal motion. During a deposition of Larry's client, he repeatedly interrupts his client's testimony, saying things like, "That's crap, you don't mean that." He also turns to his adversary and says, "When are you going to ask a question that someone with more than an IQ of 60 might ask?" and, "This isn't Little League, chum, why don't you ask a big boy question?" After the close of discovery, the defendant moves for summary judgment. In Larry's written opposition to the motion for summary judgment, he clearly misrepresents the factual record and fails to make a nonfrivolous argument for a reversal, modification, or extension of existing law or for establishing new law. After prevailing on the motion for summary judgment, the lawyer for the defendant decides to move for Rule 11 sanctions against Larry.

Which statements and actions, if any, on the part of Larry, can form the basis of sanctions under Rule 11?

A. The statements made at oral argument, the statements made at the deposition, and the arguments contained in the papers opposing the motion for summary judgment all can serve as bases for sanctions under Rule 11.

B. The statements made at oral argument and the statements contained in the papers opposing summary judgment can serve as bases for sanctions under Rule 11.

C. The statements made in the papers opposing summary judgment alone can serve as a basis for sanctions under Rule 11.

D. None of these statements or submissions can serve as a basis for sanctions under Rule 11.

13.   Plaintiff appears in her lawyer's office and alleges that she fears that the town in which she lives is planning to seize her property through the process of eminent domain and is not planning on compensating her in violation of her due process rights, which is a constitutional claim based in both federal and state law of the state in which she resides. The lawyer researches the matter and learns that Plaintiff has been involved in protracted negotiations with the town and that the town has actually sent her a check for what it believes is the fair market value of the property. When the lawyer confronts Plaintiff about this, Plaintiff admits that the town has been negotiating in good faith and has sent her a check, but she is not happy with the amount of compensation she is being offered. She believes that if she were to file a suit alleging that the town was not planning on paying her reasonable compensation for her property, she might be able to exact a higher price for the property because of the bad press she believes the town will receive when she files the lawsuit. The lawyer agrees in the strategic value of filing a case and so files an action on behalf of Plaintiff in federal court that seeks an injunction and damages for what is alleged to be the town's failure to offer compensation for the seizure of Plaintiff's property through eminent domain. The complaint contains factual allegations that both Plaintiff and her lawyer know are baseless and have no support. It also contains legal claims that are not supported by a nonfrivolous argument for the reversal, modification, or extension of the law or for establishing new law. The town's attorney wishes to seek Rule 11 sanctions based on both the factual and legal contentions contained in the complaint.

Which acts of the plaintiff described above can give rise to a finding that the plaintiff violated Rule 11 in the filing of the complaint and is subject to sanctions through a properly filed motion under that Rule?

A. The factual contentions but not the legal contentions.

B. Both the factual and the legal contentions.

C. The legal contentions but not the factual contentions.

D. Neither contention.

14.   Paul walks into Linda's law office claiming that his business partner has swindled him out of the proceeds of the recent initial public offering (IPO) of their company which provides a platform for consumers to exchange gently worn shoes. Paul explains the situation, telling Linda that the sale of stock netted the company $100 million and that because of the profit-sharing agreement between Paul and his business partner, Danielle, he is supposed to retain 50% of those proceeds. Paul says Danielle has retained 90% of the proceeds and is maintaining those proceeds in a local bank. The statute of limitations is not close to expiring in Paul's potential action against Danielle, so Linda leaves Paul's file in her desk drawer, setting up a calendar reminder to start working on the case a few months before the statute of limitations is set to expire. After several months go by, but still before the date on which the statute of limitations will expire, Paul comes to Linda's office and states that he fears Danielle is going to expatriate the funds in the bank account to an off-shore bank that has no financial relationship with the United States. Once those funds are gone, Paul will never see them, even if he brings a suit and is victorious. Although Linda believes she has a few more weeks before Danielle goes ahead with her plan to expatriate the funds in the account (that is, send them to the offshore account), Linda immediately commences a lawsuit in federal court in the Southern District of Florida, where Danielle has deposited the money for the time being. The lawsuit alleges a violation of the agreement between Paul and Danielle on how they would divide the proceeds raised from their company's public offering. Paul is a citizen of the state of Georgia and Danielle is a citi-

zen of Florida, for subject matter jurisdiction purposes. The case arises under state contract theories and seeks $40 million in damages (the difference between what Paul received from the IPO and how much he believes he is owed). Once the action is commenced, Linda receives a motion under Rule 11 of the FRCP from Danielle's lawyer, which is served but not filed, showing proof that the binding agreement between Paul and Danielle only apportions 10% of the public offering proceeds to Paul, which is exactly how much Paul received of those proceeds. Linda has no good faith basis on which to doubt the legitimacy of the agreement Danielle's attorney has produced or the accuracy of Danielle's position regarding the propriety of the earlier payment to Paul. Paul is unable, when asked, to produce any documentation of his claims or provide any reason for Linda to believe the agreement Danielle's attorney has produced is not the actual agreement between the parties regarding the proper apportionment of the IPO proceeds.

What action, if any, is the most appropriate for Linda to take in response to her receipt of the Rule 11 motion?

A. She should ignore it. The motion has not been filed and thus is a nullity. Moreover, her inquiry was reasonable under the circumstances.

B. She should oppose the motion. It is possible that she could negotiate some sort of payment for her client just because of the threat of litigation, and she has an obligation to pursue her client's best interests.

C. She should withdraw the complaint because there is no good faith basis for the claims it contains.

D. She should make her own motion for Rule 11 sanctions against her opponent for inappropriately delaying the proceeding by the service of the Rule 11 motion as opposed to simply making a motion to dismiss or filing an answer refuting Paul's allegations.

15. Plaintiff's lawyer brings an action challenging the constitutionality of a regulation that, the lawyer alleges, violates the takings clause of the U.S. Constitution. The regulation in question was promulgated by the City of Albany and requires that no building that is zoned as residential may be used to host short-term rentals if the owner of the premises is not also present in the building when the guest is staying in the building. In other words, it bars owners from short-term rentals of their entire home (for example, when the owner might be away on vacation). This rule does not prevent owners from renting a portion of their homes when they are physically present, nor does it limit the use of the property in any other way that is consistent with the residential character of the building. Plaintiff, iHotel, an internet-based home-sharing platform, sues the City of Albany, challenging this regulation as an improper taking and alleging it diminishes the value of a property because it takes away a potential use: the opportunity for the owner to earn income while he or she is away from the home on vacation. The case is filed in federal court. iHotel's lawyer will argue, in good faith, that some U.S. Supreme Court precedent can be read to state that complete prohibition on any viable use of the property constitutes a taking, warranting compensation for the loss of that use. It is a novel argument, yet one that can be made from different aspects of existing Supreme Court precedent. The City, in response, argues that residential building owners within city limits affected by the new rule can still use any residential property for its intended use: a residence. The City moves to dismiss the action. After following the proper procedures for interposing a motion based on FRCP 11, the City also moves for sanctions, arguing that iHotel's claims are frivolous. The court hearing the case grants the City's motion to dismiss iHotel's action, holding that iHotel failed to state a claim upon which relief could be granted. The court concludes that the U.S. Supreme Court's rulings on the issue of takings hold that when a government entity does not prohibit all reasonable uses of a property, the action does not constitute a taking. According to the court, since the City's actions did not destroy all reasonable uses of the property, there was no taking, and iHotel's claims lack merit. The court is now considering the City's motion for sanctions against iHotel's lawyer under Rule 11.

Should the court grant the City's motion for Rule 11 sanctions? If so, why, if not, why not?

A. The court should grant the motion for Rule 11 sanctions because it dismissed iHotel's complaint as lacking merit.

B. The court should grant the motion because the plaintiff's lawyer did not conduct an inquiry reasonable under the circumstances prior to filing the action.

C. The court should deny the motion because the plaintiff's lawyer had a good faith basis for her arguments.

D. The court should deny the motion because plaintiff's lawyer did not file the action with malicious intent.

16. Plaintiff, a resident and citizen of Maryland, sues multiple Defendants over a personal injury action in federal court. Plaintiff argues that there is subject matter jurisdiction over the proceeding based on diversity jurisdiction. Plaintiff has alleged that Defendants are all incorporated in Delaware, each with its principal place of business in a different state: New York, New Jersey, and Connecticut, respectively (there are three separate defendants). Counsel for one of the Defendants wishes to make a motion to dismiss arguing that, because Defendants are all incorporated in Delaware, there is not complete diversity and the matter should be dismissed. Defendant bases its arguments on notes on Article III to the U.S. Constitution written by James Madison during the Constitutional Convention when the U.S. Constitution was drafted. Defendant's argument is novel and creative, based on a law review article from a well-respected law professor in a reputable law journal. The argument is advanced in good faith and is not frivolous. While these notes may shed some light on the original meaning of diversity jurisdiction under Article III, two centuries of case law interpreting the Constitution and the diversity jurisdiction statute would appear to undermine Defendant's argument. Nevertheless, Defendant moves to dismiss the action for lack of subject matter jurisdiction based on this argument. After affording Defendant's counsel a twenty-one-day opportunity to withdraw the motion to dismiss by serving a motion under Rule 11 of the Federal Rules of Civil Procedure upon that counsel without filing it, once Defendant refuses to withdraw the motion, Plaintiff's counsel goes forward and files the motion.

Will the court grant Plaintiff's motion for Rule 11 sanctions against Defendant's counsel for making the motion based on an alleged lack of subject matter jurisdiction?

A. Yes, because Plaintiff followed the appropriate procedure for filing a Rule 11 motion.

B. Yes, because of the weight of the arguments against Defendant's position.

C. No, because Plaintiff failed to notify the court in advance of serving the motion of Plaintiff's intent to make the motion.

D. No, because Defendant's counsel had a nonfrivolous argument in support of the grounds for the motion.

17.   Plaintiff appears in her lawyer's office and alleges that she fears that the town in which she lives is planning to seize her property through the process of eminent domain, and she is not satisfied with the amount of compensation they are offering her for her property. She knows the appraisal that was conducted of her property was legitimate, but she still says she believes she is entitled to more compensation for her property. She objects, correctly, that the process by which the town has proceeded against her is a violation of her due process rights. Plaintiff understands that the town will ultimately be successful and she will eventually lose her home because the town can just restart the process and follow the correct procedures for seizing the property. Nevertheless, she believes that if she were to file a suit challenging the process the town used, she could delay the process and perhaps exact greater compensation from the town for her property. Plaintiff's lawyer agrees in the strategic value of filing a case and files an action on behalf of the Plaintiff in federal court that seeks an injunction and damages for what is alleged to be the town's failure to follow the appropriate procedures for taking Plaintiff's property. The town's attorney wishes to seek Rule 11 sanctions against Plaintiff's lawyer because, the town attorney believes, Plaintiff does not have a legitimate basis for bringing the lawsuit and all she wants to do is delay the proceeding.

Regardless of the merits of the motion for Rule 11 sanctions, what steps is the lawyer for the town *not* required to follow in proceeding with its motion?

A. The town attorney must serve the motion for Rule 11 sanctions on Plaintiff's lawyer.

B. The motion must set forth the grounds upon which the motion is based.

C. The town attorney must set forth in its supporting materials on the motion the efforts it carried out to resolve the motion prior to actually filing the motion.

D. After serving the motion upon Plaintiff's lawyer, the town attorney must wait at least twenty-one days before filing the motion.

5.4 Amending Pleadings

During the course of a dispute, parties may seek to amend their pleadings. FRCP 15, explored in this section, covers this issue.

18. Plaintiff files a brief, simple complaint in federal court so as to ensure that she can file her action within the applicable statute of limitations. Defendant waives service of the summons when he receives a copy of the complaint by first-class mail. Plaintiff knows that she will want to file an amended complaint at some point. Defendant intends to file an answer to the action and will not file a pre-answer motion to dismiss. Plaintiff now wants to amend her complaint without seeking leave of the court or consent from Defendant for doing so. She has not already amended her complaint before.

Assuming Plaintiff wants to amend her complaint without seeking leave from the court or consent from Defendant, can she do so, and, if she can, what is the latest possible date by which she must amend her complaint without obtaining such leave and/or consent?

A. Now that Defendant plans to answer the complaint and will not file a pre-answer motion to dismiss, Plaintiff can no longer amend her complaint without seeking leave of court or consent from Defendant.

B. Plaintiff will have to file an amended complaint within twenty-one days of Defendant's serving its answer.

C. Plaintiff will have to file an amended complaint within 60 days of receiving Defendant's answer because Defendant waived service of the summons.

D. Plaintiff can amend her complaint at any point prior to the commencement of the discovery process because Defendant has not filed and will not file a pre-answer motion to dismiss.

19. Plaintiff asserts that Defendant, a social media company, engaged in anti-competitive behavior when Defendant allegedly conspired with other social media platforms to collectively agree to raise their advertising rates across these different social media platforms. Plaintiff brings a federal antitrust case against Defendant alleging this anti-competitive behavior. The case is filed in federal court in the Southern District of New York in December 2019. Plaintiff is a corporation incorporated in Delaware with its principal place of business in New York. Defendant is also incorporated in Delaware, but with its principal place of business in California. Defendant files its answer to the complaint, and a discovery schedule is set by the court at the first conference in the matter held in late February 2020. Soon thereafter, a global pandemic slows the course of discovery. During the discovery phase in the action, in early 2021, Plaintiff uncovers evidence in internal emails shared among Defendant's employees that appears to indicate that not only did Defendant conspire with other social media companies to set advertising rates for all of their business customers but that Defendant also worked with these other companies to specifically raise the price of advertising for Plaintiff alone. These emails establish not just Plaintiff's original claims about general anti-competitive actions but also that Defendant saw Plaintiff as an acquisition target; if Defendant could make the cost of doing business very high for Plaintiff, officials working for Defendant believed Plaintiff would be more willing to sell to Defendant at a lower acquisition price. The emails also show that Defendant saw the effort against Plaintiff as part of its overall anti-competitive efforts to maximize market share and profits more generally. Soon after sifting through this new evidence, in March 2021, Plaintiff moves to amend its complaint to add the new federal claims asserting that Defendant singled out Plaintiff for particularly onerous advertising rates. The statute of limitations for such claims expired in January of 2021, however. Defendant will oppose the motion to amend.

Will the court reject Plaintiff's effort to amend the complaint? If so, why? If not, why not?

A. No. The court will determine that the claims relate back to the original filing date of the complaint and permit Plaintiff to amend its complaint.

B. No. The court will determine that Defendant's motion is in bad faith and an effort merely to prevent Plaintiff from raising legitimate claims.

C. Yes. The claims are outside the statute of limitations, so amending the complaint to add the new claims would be futile.

D. Yes. Plaintiff is attempting to amend the complaint more than one year from the original filing date, and therefore, regardless of whether the claims relate back to the original filing, they cannot be added now.

20. Plaintiff, a resident and citizen of New York, operates a food truck that he parks illegally outside of several restaurants in downtown Albany, New York. Plaintiff is a sole proprietor operating and owning the truck in his personal capacity. After the local police department receives complaints from the restaurants that Plaintiff is disrupting and stealing their business, Plaintiff receives several warnings from local authorities that he must obtain a proper license from the local health department before operating his food truck and that once he obtains the license under local health and safety laws, he must then apply for a permit under local zoning laws from the parking authority to operate on city streets. Both permits will cost him thousands of dollars he does not have and will eat up profits from the food truck operations well into the future. Plaintiff decides to disregard the written warnings from the local authorities, which say that his truck will be confiscated if he does not apply for and obtain the required license and permit. One night, after Plaintiff is through operating the food truck, he parks it behind a locked chain-link fence in a lot he owns in an industrial area. The next morning, he goes to the lot and realizes that the padlock on the gate to the fenced-in area has been clipped and, more importantly, the truck is gone. Fearing that it was stolen, he calls the police, only to learn that the truck was impounded by the authorities for his flagrant violations of the health and safety and zoning laws. He commences an action in federal court alleging violations of his due process rights under federal constitutional principles. The City of Albany, Defendant, files an answer. Three months pass. Before discovery commences, Plaintiff wants to move to amend his complaint to add new claims alleging that the authorities trespassed on his property when they seized his truck, which constituted a violation of federal constitutional protections against unwarranted searches. Defendants argue, correctly, that the statute of limitations has run on the new set of claims, although it would have been satisfied had Plaintiff included those claims in the initial complaint. Defendant argues that the motion to amend should be denied and that Defendant will be prejudiced because it will have to change its entire trial strategy to defend against these new claims, and moreover, it will have to defend against claims that would otherwise be barred by the statute of limitations.

Should the court grant the motion to amend the complaint? If so, why? If not, why not?

A. Yes. Plaintiff can still amend his complaint once as of right, without the court's approval or Defendant's consent.

B. Yes. The second set of claims contained in the proposed amendment arises from the same basic transaction as the claims set forth in the initial complaint.

C. No. The second set of claims pursues clauses of the federal Constitution different from the first set of claims.

D. No. Defendant will be unduly prejudiced by the amendment, and thus it should be denied.

5.5 Formative Assessment Quiz

Test your knowledge of the issues surrounding pleadings with this formative assessment quiz.

21. Plaintiff is a resident and citizen of Tioga, Pennsylvania, who lives on a lake that is fed by the Cooperstown River that runs through New York, from Ithaca, New York, into Pennsylvania. Upstream from Plaintiff's residence, in New York, there is a quartz mine, operated by Quartz, Inc. (Quartz), that sometimes releases toxic chemicals into the Cooperstown River. Plaintiff alleges that these toxins affect the lake on which she lives and the well on her property that is fed from the polluted river and from which she draws much of her drinking water. She brings an action in federal court in Pennsylvania alleging that Quartz is violating state nuisance law. She seeks $200,000 in damages, which she can easily show. Plaintiff alleges Quartz's actions have made her ill, caused her significant pain and suffering, and resulted in her having to miss many days of work. Quartz is incorporated in the state of Delaware, with its principal place of business in Ithaca, New York. Quartz brings a pre-answer motion to dismiss alleging the Plaintiff has not set forth in her complaint a claim upon which relief can be granted. The court denies that motion, granting Quartz leave to file an answer within thirty days of notice of the denial of the motion. Quartz prepares to file an answer and wants to include the following defenses: that venue in Pennsylvania is improper and that the court lacks subject matter jurisdiction over the action.

Putting aside the potential merits of the defenses Quartz wishes to include in its answer, as a procedural matter, which, if any, of these defenses may Quartz interpose at this juncture in the case?

A. Quartz cannot interpose either defense at this juncture.

B. Quartz can interpose the defense based on an alleged lack of subject matter jurisdiction but cannot interpose the defense based on improper venue at this juncture.

C. Quartz can interpose the defense of improper venue but cannot interpose the defense based on an alleged lack of subject matter jurisdiction at this juncture.

D. Quartz can interpose both defenses at this juncture.

22. Larry is a personal injury lawyer who litigates mostly in state court in New York. Occasionally, a lawsuit he files will be removed to federal court because he is suing an out-of-state defendant. Sometimes he brings personal injury actions in federal court in the first instance when he gets a case involving a potentially large judgment against an out-of-state defendant. One afternoon, he is approached in his office by an individual who claims that he is the victim of medical malpractice. The prospective client informs Larry that he was injured while on vacation on Cape Cod, Massachusetts, and he suffered further injuries while being treated at Cape Cod Hospital on the island. Because the potential client presents with fairly extensive injuries, Larry believes this is the type of case and type of defendant he can sue in federal court; he puts the case on the bottom of his "pile" of cases, however, because he knows that the statute of limitations will not run for almost another year. The client calls Larry repeatedly for updates on the case, and all Larry says is "I'm working on it." As the deadline for the statute of limitations gets closer and closer, Larry does little about the case until there are just a few days left to bring the action. Larry pulls together a hastily prepared complaint alleging that his client was injured at the hospital with little factual support for the claims, mostly because Larry had neither sought nor obtained the medical records concerning the client's hospital stay, treatment, or injuries. After filing the complaint in federal court, which has jurisdiction based on the diversity of the parties, Larry receives a motion for sanctions under FRCP Rule 11 (which is served but not filed). He is informed that he has twenty-one days to withdraw the complaint; otherwise, the hospital's lawyers will seek sanctions against him for filing a frivolous complaint. As it turns out, the client's story is a complete fabrication. The hospital has no record that the client was ever a patient there, let alone that he was injured through any medical malpractice. Larry confronts his client, who just responds, "Oops, I guess they caught me." Larry's subsequent investigation of the matter establishes the position of the hospital: the client was never a patient of the hospital, and any injuries he sustained were the result of his own reckless behavior having nothing to do with the hospital. Larry does not think he did anything wrong, however. His only "crime," at least the one that he will admit, is that he trusted his client. Besides, the statute of limitations was about to run and he did not have time to thoroughly research the case. He believes he did what research he could under the time constraints and circumstances and does not believe the motion will be granted. He refuses to withdraw the complaint and urges the hospital's lawyers to go ahead and file the motion if they wish.

If the hospital goes ahead with filing the motion for sanctions, how should the court rule on the motion, and why?

A. It should deny the motion. Larry's inquiry into the facts underlying the client's case was reasonable under the circumstances.

B. It should grant the motion. Larry's inquiry into the facts underlying the client's case was not reasonable under the circumstances.

C. It should deny the motion. Larry had a good faith belief in the client's claim.

D. It should grant the motion. Larry failed to negotiate in good faith to resolve the motion during the twenty-one-day "safe harbor" period.

23.   Plaintiff brings an action alleging that her rights were violated by the local police department when several officers searched her home without a warrant. The police allege that they were engaged in the pursuit of a thief who had recently robbed a local bank. Plaintiff files for the damages incurred when the police ransacked her house while supposedly searching for the thief. Plaintiff believes the actions of the police were politically motivated. She had recently announced her candidacy for the local city council, making police accountability one of her main causes. As they were rummaging through her belongings, one officer was overheard saying, "This is what accountability looks like." Plaintiff files an action in the local federal district court seeking damages for the alleged violation of her federal constitutional rights against the local police department and the individual police officers who conducted what she describes as a raid on her home. Defendants will argue that they are protected by qualified immunity, which would require Plaintiff to show that the officers violated Plaintiff's clearly established rights under the law. Defendants will file a pre-answer motion to dismiss Plaintiff's action, arguing that in order to show that Plaintiff is entitled to relief, as required by Rule 8 of the Federal Rules of Civil Procedure, Plaintiff was required to plead sufficient facts showing that Defendants had violated clearly established rights in order to overcome their defense of qualified immunity.

Will Defendants succeed in their motion to dismiss Plaintiff's action for her failure to plead facts sufficient to overcome their defense of qualified immunity? If so, why? If not, why not?

A. The motion will be denied because Plaintiff has pled sufficient facts to make her claims plausible.

B. The motion will be granted because Plaintiff has not pled facts sufficient to overcome Defendants' defense of qualified immunity.

C. The motion will be granted because Plaintiff's claims are not plausible.

D. The motion will be denied because Plaintiff is not required to plead facts in anticipation of Defendants' defenses.

24.   Plaintiff brings an action in federal district court under state tort law in New Mexico seeking $200,000 in damages and alleging the design and manufacturing defects in a vehicle component were the proximate cause of her injuries. She sues only the car manufacturer, which is incorporated in and has its principal place of business in Michigan, and does not file against the manufacturer of the allegedly defective part. The car manufacturer wishes to file a pre-answer motion to dismiss the action, including a failure to join the necessary party (the manufacturer of the component).

Which of the following defenses will Defendant have waived if it fails to include it in this pre-answer motion to dismiss?

A. Failure to state a claim upon which relief can be granted.

B. Lack of subject matter jurisdiction.

C. Insufficient process.

D. Failure to join a necessary party.

25. Plaintiff alleges she has been discriminated against in her place of employment based on her race. She files an action in federal court, and Defendant files its answer. The parties engage in discovery, and Plaintiff's counsel uncovers evidence suggesting that Plaintiff was discriminated against based on her race and her nationality, both of which would violate federal anti-discrimination laws. Plaintiff's case centers around her employer's failure to promote her to a particular position that would have meant a higher salary and more public visibility and which would have improved her future career opportunities. The evidence that suggests that she was likely subject to both racial and national origin discrimination comes from a series of emails between her supervisors. In those emails, Plaintiff's supervisors use epithets in their communications about Plaintiff that are both racially charged and relate in a derogatory fashion to her national origin. These slurs completely infuse the communications between the supervisors as they consider whether to promote Plaintiff (and they ultimately decide not to do so). Plaintiff's action was filed in federal court for the Northern District of New York, the district in which she resides and Defendant has its principal place of business. Six months have passed since she first filed the case, and the parties have already engaged in extensive discovery. The statute of limitations on her potential nationality discrimination claims expired several weeks ago. Nevertheless, her lawyer moves to amend her complaint to add a claim based on national origin discrimination. Defendant will resist the effort and argue that Plaintiff cannot amend her complaint at this time to add a new claim based on national origin discrimination.

Will Plaintiff succeed in amending her complaint to add claims based on national origin discrimination?

A. Yes. Since the evidence of this discrimination was revealed in discovery obtained through her original case, she can amend her complaint to include the new claim despite the expiration of the statute of limitations.

B. Yes. Although the statute of limitations has run on her national origin discrimination claim, that new claim is sufficiently related to her original claim, which means she can use the original filing date of the complaint to satisfy the statute of limitations with respect to the new claim.

C. No. The statute of limitations has run on her national origin discrimination claim, and thus it is time barred.

D. No. The case has progressed past the pleading stage to the discovery phase, and it would be unduly prejudicial to and burdensome on Defendant and the court to allow Plaintiff to amend her complaint at this point in the litigation.

26. Plaintiffs are college students who work for an organization called the Sunset Movement, whose stated goal is to require all states within the United States to adhere to daylight saving time year-round in order to save energy. Recently, the U.S. Department of Transportation (DOT), the federal agency that sets the rules around daylight saving time, issued guidelines for all state governments; the guidelines provide that any state which sets daylight saving time year-round will be denied federal highway funding, a major source of federal aid for states. Plaintiffs file an action in federal court for the District of Columbia, where the DOT is based. They file their action under the federal Administrative Procedure Act, which requires that before filing an action against a federal agency, a Plaintiff must exhaust all administrative remedies prior to commencing an action challenging administrative agency action. This requirement has been treated as an affirmative defense under the law. Plaintiffs have not exhausted their administrative remedies because they failed to file an administrative proceeding before the DOT prior to filing their complaint. Lawyers for the DOT will file a pre-answer motion to dismiss under FRCP 12(b)(6) for the Plaintiffs' alleged failure to state a claim upon which relief can be granted. The DOT will base its motion on its argument that, under the Supreme Court's ruling in *Ashcroft v. Iqbal*, 556 U.S. 662 (2009), since the Plaintiffs have not alleged that they exhausted their administrative remedies, the claim is not plausible.

Will the court grant Defendant's motion to dismiss for Plaintiffs' failure to set forth a plausible claim in their complaint? If so, why? If not, why not?

A. The court will deny the motion because the argument that Plaintiffs failed to exhaust administrative remedies is an affirmative defense and such a defense cannot be raised on a motion to dismiss.

B. The court will deny the motion because the failure to exhaust administrative remedies is only an affirmative defense and there is no indication that it is described as a pleading requirement under the law.

C. The court will grant the motion because Plaintiffs cannot make out a plausible claim for relief if they cannot show they exhausted administrative remedies.

D. The court will grant the motion because the court has no subject matter jurisdiction over the proceeding if Plaintiffs have failed to exhaust administrative remedies.

27. Plaintiff sues Defendant in federal court under Title VII, federal legislation that prohibits discrimination in employment based on race, ethnicity, national origin, and gender. During the course of the litigation, the following occurs:

- Defendant's counsel interposes a defense based on the statute of limitations which he believes was valid at the time he filed the answer. During discovery, it is revealed that Plaintiff did file her action in a timely fashion. Defendant's counsel does not withdraw the defense and continues to assert it orally, in open court.

- Defendant's counsel instructs his client to destroy email evidence that might assist in Plaintiff's case, evidence that Plaintiff has sought in discovery as the litigation has unfolded.

- In a motion to dismiss filed by Defendant, Defendant's counsel asserts in his brief on the motion that a longstanding precedent of the Supreme Court directly supporting Plaintiff's claim is no longer good law, based on Defendant's counsel's good faith argument that more recent Supreme Court precedent has weakened the constitutional basis for the claim.

- In a mediation session between Plaintiff's counsel and Defendant's counsel, Defendant's counsel refers to Plaintiff in a derogatory way, demeaning her ethnicity.

- Plaintiff first serves a Rule 11 motion against Defendant's counsel on these four grounds and then waits the appropriate twenty-one days before filing it. Defendant's counsel believes he has done nothing wrong and says Plaintiff should go ahead and file her motion after the twenty-one-day waiting period passes, which she does.

Given the facts as presented, upon what grounds, if any, may the court issue a Rule 11 sanction against Defendant's counsel?

A. The court may issue a Rule 11 sanction for continuing to assert the defense based on the statute of limitations but on no other grounds.

B. The court may issue a Rule 11 sanction for the argument contained in the brief on the motion to dismiss but on no other grounds.

C. The court may issue a Rule 11 sanction for instructing the client to destroy evidence and his conduct at the mediation session but on no other grounds.

D. The court may not issue a Rule 11 sanction for any of the conduct described here.

28. Danco produces parts for wind turbines throughout the United States. It is incorporated in Delaware with its principal place of business in Pennsylvania. Danco has secured a large contract with TurbineNY, a large public-private partnership located in New York State that is creating a wind farm on the outskirts of the Adirondacks, in New York State. Since securing the contract, Danco has hired two employees who are independent contractors as technicians on site with TurbineNY in New York State. Those workers consult with TurbineNY as it sets up the wind farm, using Danco's turbines. The current plan is for the Danco contractors to consult with TurbineNY on site throughout the duration of the wind turbine project, which could last at least two years. However, the independent contractors' work is sporadic. They only work an average of ten hours each per week, though sometimes they might work on the turbines for as few as two hours a week, and other times as many as twenty hours per week.

Danco begins to fall on hard times; its investments in renewable energy are not paying off because of the drop in the price of fuel oil. Danco fails to pay the independent contractors it has hired to administer the TurbineNY contract. The independent contractors sue TurbineNY in federal court in New York for violations of the Federal Labor Standards Act (FLSA). They allege that when they were paid, their payment did not satisfy the federal minimum wage laws. Despite Plaintiffs' being considered independent contractors, they are covered under FLSA's protections as employees. Plaintiffs are all residents and citizens of New York State. Their suit seeks over $10,000 in damages,

$5,000 for each Plaintiff. After the suit is filed, Plaintiffs' attorney researches the applicable state labor law and determines that Danco's underpayment of Plaintiffs during the period covered by the federal lawsuit also violated state law. The statute of limitations for Plaintiffs' state law claims expired after Plaintiffs filed their action in federal court, however, and it is too late for Plaintiffs to amend their complaint as of right; they must seek the consent of Defendant or permission from the court to do so. Danco's attorney will not consent to an amendment of the complaint to add state law claims because, she asserts, the amendment would be futile because of the expiration of the statute of limitations. The case is in the early stages of discovery when Plaintiffs make a motion to amend their complaint to add the state law claims even though the statute of limitations has expired.

Should the court grant Plaintiffs' motion to amend their complaint to add the state law claims even though the statute of limitations has expired on those claims? If so, why? If not, why not?

A. Yes, the court should grant the motion to amend the pleadings because leave to amend should be freely given regardless of any prejudice that might impact Defendant by the filing after the expiration of the statute of limitations.

B. Yes, the court should grant the motion to amend the pleadings because they relate back to the claims set forth in the original complaint and it does not appear that Defendant will otherwise be prejudiced by the amendment.

C. No, the court should not grant the motion to amend the pleadings because Defendant will be prejudiced by the granting of the amendment.

D. No, the court should not grant the motion to amend the pleadings because to do so would be futile as the statute of limitations has already expired on the state law claims.

29.   Plaintiff is injured in a hit-and-run accident when what she believes is a brand-new Vintage Motors (Vintage) sedan side-swipes her as she is riding her bike down a suburban road, far from her home. She witnesses the car turn into a cul-de-sac after she is hit. When the police arrive at the scene of the accident, Plaintiff tells her story, and they take her in a squad car to the cul-de-sac where she saw the car that hit her turn after the incident. They drive past several homes in the squad car, and she sees a car matching the description of the car that hit her. Same make. Same model. Same year. Same color. Same everything, even a dent on the right-front fender where, she believes, the car struck her. The accident occurred in Hoosick Falls, where she was out riding her bike on a long excursion from her home across the Vermont border. She is a resident and citizen of Vermont. She files an action in federal court in the jurisdiction encompassing the accident asserting state law claims and alleging damages exceeding $200,000. Defendant is Dave, a citizen of New York, whose car she identified in her drive with the police down his street. Dave asserts that he was not driving the car that struck Plaintiff, that the damage to his car occurred when he recently clipped a deer, and that there are at least three other Vintage sedans in Dave's cul-de-sac, several of which have damage that could indicate they were responsible for Plaintiff's injuries instead.

What is the appropriate action for Dave to take in responding to the complaint?

A. Move to dismiss the complaint for failure to state a cause of action.

B. Move to dismiss the case for lack of subject matter jurisdiction.

C. File an answer denying the allegations against him.

D. File a third-party complaint impleading the other vintage sedan owners in the neighborhood, alleging that if he is liable to Plaintiff, so are these other drivers.

Chapter 6

Discovery

This chapter will explore issues related to discovery, the period before trial when parties exchange information about each other's claims and defenses. It will focus mostly on penalties for noncompliance in the discovery process (Part 6.3). Part 6.2, which covers the "tools of discovery" will be more straightforward and pose more pointed questions that track the rules covering those tools, FRCP 27 through 36. Those rules are relatively clear, which is why the questions related to those rules are far more pointed as compared to most of the other chapters in this guide.

6.1 Scope of Discovery

One of the most important parts of the trial process is the discovery phase. While it can help parties to focus their claims and defenses, it can also become a burden, miring the parties in onerous and wasteful forays into matters unrelated to the litigation. FRCP 26, which was amended in recent years, tries to calibrate the parties' need for information about an opposing party's claims and defenses with fairness to that party. This section explores the contours of FRCP 26.

1. **When considering whether to permit the parties to pursue particular issues in discovery, which of the following should a federal court NOT take into account?**

A. The amount in controversy in the action.

B. The relative plausibility of the claims and defenses.

C. The parties' resources.

D. Whether the expense of the proposed discovery outweighs its likely benefit.

2. Big Bank enters into a mortgage agreement with Harry, lending him money to purchase his home. Harry has not paid his mortgage for well over a year and the outstanding principal on the mortgage is $200,000. Big Bank has exerted a great deal of pressure on Harry to settle his balance with the bank, including sending harassing letters, making phone calls at his home at all hours of the day and night demanding payment, and informing Harry's employer that he is behind in his mortgage payments. Harry consults with an attorney and learns that Big Bank may be violating New York state law related to unfair debt collection practices, given the manner in which it has harassed Harry to get him to pay his mortgage. Under that

law, Harry is entitled to damages in the amount of the outstanding debt on the home and attorney's fees. Harry files an action in federal court under the state debt collection law seeking $200,000 in damages. Big Bank is incorporated in the State of Delaware, and has its principal place of business in South Dakota. Big Bank has seventeen branches in New York State and has had them in that state for over twenty years. Big Bank seeks, by way of counterclaim, to pursue its state-based contract claim for Harry's failure to pay his mortgage, which the court permits. Harry is a resident and citizen of Brooklyn, New York, where he has his domicile. During discovery, which proceeds under the Federal Rules of Civil Procedure that govern discovery in this action, Defendant's lawyer asks Plaintiff during his deposition whether he is in default on his student loans.

May Big Bank seek information about Harry's student loan debt in the action regarding his mortgage debt? If so, why? If not, why not?

A. Yes. The testimony regarding Harry's student debt repayment history is relevant to the proceeding.

B. Yes. Evidence of Harry's student loan debt repayment history is reasonably calculated to lead to the discovery of admissible evidence.

C. No. The evidence is irrelevant to the claims at issue in the case.

D. No. The evidence would be inadmissible at trial.

6.2 Tools of Discovery

This section will cover the different mechanisms for pursuing discovery. Once again, these questions are more straightforward than most questions in this guide because the rules covering these tools are also more straightforward than some of the concepts and rules explored so far.

3.   Plaintiff and Defendant have been locked in a contentious case that has involved a series of moves and counter-moves throughout the discovery process. Plaintiff is attempting to present her case and has run into some difficulty in doing so. Witness 1 was deposed in the action but has fallen ill and is unable to attend the hearing. Witness 2 is now outside the territorial United States, having been induced to travel by Defendant's counsel so that he would be unavailable for trial. Witness 3, who was already deposed in the action, has appeared to testify subject to a subpoena by Plaintiff's counsel to do so and has provided testimony that contradicts some of the testimony given in her deposition.

Which of the witnesses' prior testimony in their respective depositions, if any, may Plaintiff use in establishing her affirmative case?

A. None of the witnesses' deposition testimony.

B. All of the witnesses' deposition testimony.

C. Only Witness 1's deposition testimony.

D. Only Witness 2's and Witness 3's deposition testimony.

4.   **Which of the following is true with respect to the use of interrogatories during the course of discovery?**

A. A party may use them only to the extent no other mechanism of discovery can be used to obtain the information the party wishes to seek.

B. A party may only use interrogatories with leave of court.

C. A party may interpose or serve only twenty-five written interrogatories on an opposing party without that party's consent or leave of court.

D. A party receiving an interrogatory must provide the information sought through the interrogatory even if it seeks information beyond the scope of discovery in the action.

5.   Pedestrian is hit while in a crosswalk in Great Barrington, Massachusetts, where he had the right of way, by an uninsured driver from New York State. Pedestrian sues the driver in federal court in Massachusetts for his considerable injuries under state law theories of recovery, claiming both physical and mental injury from the incident. The damages for each class of injury exceed $100,000 on its own. Driver's counsel moves for an order from the court permitting its medical expert to conduct a physical and mental exam of the pedestrian. Upon receipt of the motion, Pedestrian's counsel withdraws the claims based on mental injury.

What is the status of the request that Pedestrian subject himself to the mental and physical examinations after Pedestrian has withdrawn the claims related to mental injury?

A. Pedestrian is under no obligation to subject himself to either examination as a breach of privacy.

B. Pedestrian is obligated to subject himself to the mental examination but not the physical examination.

C. Pedestrian is obligated to subject himself to the physical examination but not the mental examination.

D. Because Pedestrian initially filed claims for both physical and mental injury, he is required to subject himself to both types of examination.

6.   Defendant in a personal injury action filed in federal court based on diversity jurisdiction has received a request for admission from Plaintiff in the action. There are several items about which the opposing party has sought such admissions. Defendant is preparing a response and believes two of the requests for admission are inappropriate. One such request seeks information outside the appropriate scope of discovery. A second and different request covers a topic presently in dispute at trial.

May Defendant object to either or both of these two requests for admission based on the grounds identified above?

A. Defendant may object to the request which seeks items outside the scope of discovery but may not object to the request which raises a topic in dispute at trial.

B. Defendant may not object to a request which seeks items outside the scope of discovery but may object to the request which raises a topic in dispute at trial.

C. Defendant may object on both grounds.

D. Defendant may not object on either ground.

7. Plaintiff environmental group has filed an action against Defendant company for alleged release of toxic substances into a traversable waterway in the region, an alleged violation of federal law. Plaintiff's counsel serves a demand in discovery seeking the following: a request for all documents related to the substances maintained on Defendant's property that may have been a part of the release; documents related to all substances maintained on Defendant's properties anywhere in the United States; copies of internal emails related to the release; and an appointment to physically inspect Defendant's site from which the release is alleged to have emanated.

Which of these items may Plaintiff pursue through a discovery demand?

A. All of the items.

B. None of the items.

C. The demands for information related to the spill, the emails related to the spill, and the opportunity to conduct a physical inspection of the site, but not the documents related to other sites.

D. The demands for information related to the spill and the emails related to the spill, but not the documents related to other sites or the request for an opportunity to conduct a physical inspection of the site.

8. Peter plans to sue his former employer for alleged employment discrimination. Peter was formerly employed by an accounting firm that has recently entered into an agreement to merge with another company, and the principal of the firm that hired Peter is expected to retire upon the merger and relocate out of state upon retirement. Peter is concerned that it will be difficult for him to secure testimony from the principal once she retires because he does not know where the principal expects to move, and he fears she might relocate to a residence outside the United States. Peter's lawyer is unable to commence an action against the company before the expected merger and the time of the principal's expected retirement and relocation. Without commencing an action, Peter's attorney wants to depose the principal.

Is there a mechanism through which Peter's attorney can seek to take the deposition of the principal without commencing an action?

A. No, because in order to start the discovery process in federal court, a party must commence an action.

B. Yes, because there is subject matter jurisdiction in the federal court over Plaintiff's proposed action.

C. Yes. Due to the principal's expected relocation outside the United States, there is an apparent need for the defense attorney to take the principal's testimony in this action for which there would be subject matter jurisdiction.

D. No, because the rules only contemplate the use of written interrogatories to secure information from a potential opposing party before commencement of an action.

6.3 Motion Practice and Penalties Related to Discovery

While the tools of discovery are important throughout the discovery process, what is almost more important is what happens when those tools are abused or ignored. This section covers both the mechanisms for punishing those who might abuse the system in some way and the processes by which we enforce the use of the tools of discovery.

9.   Plaintiff is an environmental engineer who is terminated for complaining to government authorities that the oil refinery company for which she worked was violating federal law in disposing of waste products from the refinery process. She brings an action in federal court under a federal whistleblower statute that she says offers her a cause of action for wrongful termination. Plaintiff is immediately hired by an environmental non-profit group after she is fired and experiences no lost wages. She had actually been negotiating an employment contract before she was terminated at the refinery, and she was told by the non-profit, "We'll hire you the minute you leave the oil business." She is fired and then calls the non-profit. They ask her, "When can you start?" She says, "Today." They say, "Come on in." During the course of discovery in the case, Defendant seeks information related to the negotiations Plaintiff had with the non-profit while she was in the employment of the oil refinery. Defendant's lawyer argues that Defendant needs to know whether Plaintiff shared any of Defendant's trade secrets with the non-profit or whether there was any collusion with the non-profit in the ultimate decision to report the issue of the waste product release to the federal government. In response, Plaintiff's lawyer argues in good faith that this information is beyond the scope of Plaintiff's claims and is too burdensome to produce. Defendant first seeks to resolve the dispute without filing a motion, but Plaintiff's lawyer is not willing to turn over this information at this point in the case. Defendant then follows the proper procedure to obtain an order from the court compelling the discovery of this information. During oral argument on Defendant's motion, the judge hearing the motion expresses sympathy for Plaintiff's position and even says the arguments have considerable merit. The judge adds, however, that she is likely to rule in favor of Defendant because, she says, Defendant has the better argument as to why it should obtain the desired discovery, though the judge admits it is a close question. Upon hearing this from the court, Plaintiff's lawyer agrees to turn the information over to Defendant without the court's having to decide on the motion. After receiving the information from Plaintiff, Defendant makes a motion for an order directing Plaintiff to pay the costs and expenses associated with having to make the motion to compel in the first place.

What is the likely outcome of Defendant's motion for expenses associated with making the motion to compel discovery?

A.   Defendant will prevail on the request to have Plaintiff pay the costs associated with making the motion to compel discovery because Defendant ultimately prevailed on the motion when it obtained the information it was seeking, even if the court did not issue a formal ruling on the motion to compel.

B. Defendant will prevail on the request to have Plaintiff pay the costs associated with making the motion to compel discovery because Defendant followed the proper procedure for pursuing a motion to compel.

C. Defendant will not prevail on the request to have Plaintiff pay the costs associated with making the motion to compel discovery because the court never actually issued any order to compel, due to the fact that Plaintiff complied with the request without being forced to do so by the court.

D. Defendant will not prevail on the request to have Plaintiff pay the costs associated with making the motion to compel discovery because Plaintiff's position in opposing the order was substantially justified.

10.   Plaintiff sues Defendant in a personal injury action in federal district court for the Northern District of New York. The action is based on diversity of citizenship, and the amount-in-controversy requirement has been satisfied. Plaintiff has submitted several discovery demands seeking documents from Defendant which, Plaintiff asserts, will show that Defendant had failed to conduct proper maintenance of the parking lot where Plaintiff was seriously injured when she fell on a loose piece of asphalt. Plaintiff seeks maintenance records from Defendant, who refuses to turn them over. On a proper motion to compel the disclosure of the maintenance records, the court grants the motion, ordering Defendant to release the maintenance records to Plaintiff. Defendant refuses. Plaintiff moves for sanctions against Defendant under Rule 37 of the Federal Rules of Civil Procedure.

Which of the following sanctions is the court *not* likely to issue in this context?

A. Striking the answer as a whole.

B. Staying further proceedings until the order is obeyed.

C. Striking the complaint as a whole.

D. Treating the failure to obey the discovery order as contempt of court.

11.   Plaintiff has sued his former employer for discrimination, alleging that he was not promoted based on his ethnicity. This action is filed in federal court under federal civil rights statutes. During the course of discovery, Plaintiff is asked to reveal any instances in which he may have filed similar claims in other workplace settings. Plaintiff has never filed any such complaints before, but his attorney resists Defendant's efforts through discovery to obtain such information. Plaintiff's lawyer believes in good faith that the demands for such information are beyond the proper scope of discovery in this action because they are irrelevant to Plaintiff's claims. She responds to a wide range of Defendant's discovery requests but files an objection to the demand for information related to similar claims, arguing that it is outside the proper scope of discovery in this action. Defendant's lawyer contacts Plaintiff's lawyer to determine if the dispute over such evidence could be resolved. Standing on principle, Plaintiff's counsel does not tell Defendant's counsel that no such evidence exists, stands on her objections, and refuses to respond to that aspect of Defendant's demand for discovery. Defendant's counsel, after stating in her motion papers that she attempted to resolve the dispute over this aspect of her demand, moves for an order sanctioning Plaintiff for failure to respond to this discovery demand.

Should the court grant Defendant's motion for sanctions related to this demand? If so, why? If not, why not?

A. Yes. Even though Plaintiff's position is substantially justified in terms of the scope of discovery, the motion for sanctions should still be granted because Plaintiff's counsel knows that no evidence of prior complaints of discrimination exists, and she should have admitted as such.

B. No. Even though Defendant already sought to resolve the matter before filing the motion, Defendant must nevertheless first move for an order to compel discovery before moving for sanctions.

C. No. Plaintiff's position is substantially justified because Plaintiff's counsel believes in good faith that Plaintiff has no obligation to respond to such a demand.

D. Yes. Defendant, by attempting to resolve the matter before filing the motion, followed the proper procedure for filing such a motion, and Plaintiff's counsel was under an obligation to provide accurate information in response to the demand.

12.   Plaintiff and Defendant are in federal court in an action alleging violations of federal antitrust laws. Plaintiff's counsel has served upon Defendant's counsel a demand to have Defendant respond to a set of twenty-five interrogatories. Defendant has responded to most of them but has objected to seven, arguing that Plaintiff's counsel is asking for information protected by attorney-client privilege. Defendant has refused to respond to these seven interrogatories. Defendant has a good faith basis for interposing its objections to these outstanding interrogatories. Plaintiff's counsel sends an email to Defendant's counsel seeking to resolve the dispute. Defendant's counsel responds to the email, saying that the Defendant's position has not changed with respect to the outstanding interrogatories and continuing to raise the objections to them. Plaintiff then moves for an order to compel Defendant to respond to the seven outstanding interrogatories. The court rules on the motion, finding that although Defendant had a plausible basis for raising its objections to the interrogatories and was substantially justified in withholding its responses to them, Defendant must still answer all seven of the unanswered interrogatories. After receiving this favorable ruling, Plaintiff will make a second motion asking the court to order Defendant to pay the reasonable expenses Plaintiff incurred in making the original motion, including attorney's fees. Defendant will oppose this second motion.

Will the court order Defendant to pay the reasonable costs incurred by Plaintiff in making the motion to compel? If so, why? If not, why not?

A. Yes, because Plaintiff's counsel sought to resolve the dispute prior to making the motion.

B. No, because Defendant had a plausible basis for objecting to the outstanding interrogatories.

C. Yes, because Plaintiff prevailed on the original motion.

D. No, because the court found that Defendant was substantially justified in objecting to the outstanding interrogatories.

13. Plaintiff sues Defendants, several telecommunications companies, in federal court, alleging antitrust violations in their pricing strategies. Specifically, Plaintiff alleges that the companies conspired to fix the prices of broadband internet services in several communities. One of the pieces of evidence Plaintiff attempts to obtain from Defendants is a collection of emails between representatives of the different companies which were sent prior to the commencement of the action. Plaintiff believes these emails will show that these representatives conspired to fix prices. Plaintiff is able to obtain several months of emails between the parties that seem to hint that there are other communications in which price-fixing was discussed. Several critical months of emails are missing, however, and Defendants allege that the emails were destroyed in accordance with their routine file-destruction policies.

Which of the following issues is irrelevant as to whether the court should issue a directive to the jury that it must consider the missing evidence to be harmful to Defendants?

A. Whether the apparent destruction of the emails was carried out with a culpable state of mind.

B. Whether Plaintiff had knowledge of the potential destruction of evidence at a time when it could have been avoided.

C. Whether Defendants were under an obligation to preserve the emails from destruction.

D. Whether the evidence might have been relevant to and supportive of Plaintiff's claims.

6.4 Formative Assessment Quiz

Test your knowledge of the tools and processes of discovery in this relatively short formative assessment quiz.

14. Plaintiff is a low-wage worker seeking to claim rights under federal labor law for unpaid wages. She seeks $5,000 under her federal claims. Plaintiff is a legal permanent resident residing in Queens, New York. Defendant, her employer, is a restaurant also located in Queens, New York, and incorporated under New York law. It has its principal place of business in New York. Defendant seeks information from Plaintiff through discovery related to whether she has filed and paid federal personal income taxes. Plaintiff moves for a protective order to prevent Defendant from obtaining such information through discovery. Plaintiff's counsel first contacts Defendant's counsel to see if the matter can be resolved without having to seek the court's intervention through the issuance of a protective order. Those negotiations fail. Plaintiff's counsel makes a motion for a protective order.

Which of the following factors is the court *not* likely to take into account when determining whether to issue the protective order?

A. The amount in controversy in the case.

B. The immigration status of Plaintiff.

C. The party that is in possession of the information that is sought.

D. Whether the burden of producing the information outweighs its benefits to the case.

15. Plaintiff is suing her former employer over a dispute as to the grounds upon which she was fired from her job as a government official in the U.S. Department of State. Plaintiff believes she was terminated based on her gender in violation of federal statutory and constitutional law. During the course of discovery in the action, Plaintiff's lawyer learns of the existence of several files containing written transcripts of phone conversations between two of Plaintiff's superiors at the State Department. Plaintiff's lawyer learns that these transcripts reveal the existence of other email exchanges and documents that may be helpful to her in making out her case for discrimination. The government lawyers defending the State Department argue that the transcripts of the conversations that Plaintiff's lawyer wants to obtain contain hearsay evidence and thus will not be admissible at trial. Because they are inadmissible, the government lawyers argue, they are not obtainable through discovery. It will not be burdensome to produce the transcripts in question, however, and the scope of discovery with respect to these demands is proportional to what is at stake in the case. Nevertheless, the government lawyers assert that Plaintiff must have a compelling reason for seeking this discovery, and they do not believe such a showing has been made. Having failed to resolve the dispute as to whether they will turn over the transcripts of the conversations in question, the government lawyers move for a protective order alleging that

the hearsay nature of the information contained in the transcripts means that the transcripts are inadmissible and thus not subject to discovery; as a result, they allege, Defendant is entitled to a protective order to keep it from having to turn over such documents to Plaintiff's lawyer in discovery.

Will the government lawyers succeed in limiting Plaintiff's lawyer's access to the transcripts in the course of discovery in Plaintiff's case? If so, why? If not, why not?

A. Yes. Because the documents contain hearsay, they are inadmissible at trial, and thus they are not subject to discovery.

B. Yes. There is a presumption that hearsay evidence is not subject to discovery, and Plaintiff has offered no compelling reason for obtaining such evidence.

C. No. Given the nature of Plaintiff's claims, she is entitled to unlimited discovery from the government to ensure she can enforce important statutory and constitutional protections.

D. No. The fact that the documents sought contain hearsay is not grounds to withhold them in discovery, and no appropriate reason has been offered for issuing a protective order to prevent their disclosure.

16.   Plaintiff and Defendant are in federal court in an action alleging violations of federal antitrust laws. Plaintiff's counsel has served upon Defendant's counsel a demand for certain documents. Defendant's counsel believes in good faith that he can make out a plausible argument that Plaintiff's demand seeks documents that contain hearsay and are thus inadmissible in court. As a result, Defendant's counsel argues that it should not have to turn over such documents. Plaintiff's counsel sends an email to Defendant's counsel seeking to resolve the dispute. Defendant's counsel responds to the email, saying that Defendant will not turn over the documents and still asserting that the documents are inadmissible and thus not subject to discovery. Plaintiff then moves for an order to compel Defendant to respond to the document demands. The court rules on the motion, finding that Defendant's position with respect to these documents is baseless and that Defendant must respond to the demand for production of documents. After receiving this favorable ruling, Plaintiff makes a second motion asking the court to order Defendant to pay the reasonable expenses Plaintiff incurred in making the motion to compel, including attorney's fees. Defendant will oppose this motion.

Will the court order Defendant to pay the reasonable costs incurred by Plaintiff in making the motion to compel? If so, why? If not, why not?

A. Yes, because Defendant's counsel did not cooperate in resolving the dispute prior to Plaintiff's making the motion.

B. No, because Defendant had a plausible basis for objecting to the demand for the production of documents.

C. Yes, because Defendant's position was not substantially justified in objecting to the demand for the production of documents.

D. No, because the demand sought evidence inadmissible at trial.

Chapter 7

Summary Judgment, Trials, and Appeals

This chapter will start with the issue of summary judgment—the resolution of a case on the merits but without trial—and go through the trial process, including the pre-trial conference, jury trials, post-trial maneuvers, and appeals.

7.1 Summary Judgment and Other Resolutions Without Trial

FRCP 56 governs summary judgment—when a court determines that a party has established that the facts and the law on a particular claim or set of claims is ultimately uncontroverted sufficient to render full or partial judgment on behalf of that party. Since it is such a drastic remedy, the application of the rule is done relatively sparingly and generally disfavors the granting of relief. Still, it is a significant tool in the litigator's toolbox. When it appears, it can be applied to many situations, and parties will often seek summary judgment instead of risking the matter's coming to trial. This section covers this important motion.

1. Plaintiff sues Defendant for injuries sustained at a construction site. Plaintiff, an employee of the City of Memphis, Tennessee ("City"), alleges that she was operating a backhoe when it struck a power line maintained by Duke Power ("Duke"). Duke is responsible for maintaining the power lines for the city's power grid. Its maintenance obligations include posting notices in places where buried power lines can be found. Duke is incorporated in Delaware, with its principal place of business in North Carolina. Because of the worker's compensation system in North Carolina, Plaintiff cannot sue her employer, City, and instead sues Duke for failing to properly post and give notice of the location of its power lines. Both Plaintiff and Defendant wish to move for summary judgment on the issue of whether Duke had properly posted the location of its buried power lines at the time of the accident. Plaintiff submits her own affidavit saying that, based on her personal observations on the day of the accident, there were no postings regarding the location of the power lines at the site at which she was injured at the time of the accident. Defendant submits the affidavits of several high-level employees of Duke, those responsible for supervising the maintenance of the power lines and ensuring that the locations of all buried power lines are adequately posted. Each

affiant states that Duke complies with all of its obligations regarding the posting of buried power lines. They attest that the company has in place a regular inspection process through which all buried power lines are checked regularly to ensure there is proper signage identifying the location of the buried power lines. The affiants also state that they personally visited the site where Plaintiff was injured immediately after the incident occurred, and their inspection confirmed that the location of the buried power lines was adequately identified by proper signage.

What is the likely outcome of the two motions for partial summary judgment?

A. Defendant's motion will be granted and Plaintiff's motion will be denied.

B. Both motions will be denied.

C. Plaintiff's motion will be granted and Defendant's motion will be denied.

D. Both motions will be granted.

2.   Plaintiff brings an action in federal court alleging that he was discriminated against by his employer, a large residential real estate developer, on account of his race when he was turned down for a promotion under circumstances that suggest his claim has validity. Through discovery, Plaintiff has taken the depositions of several employees from Defendant company who all testify on personal knowledge that there is a racially charged atmosphere at the office, with many mid-level managers constantly making racially insensitive comments. In their depositions, these employees, speaking from personal knowledge, supply the dates of several unit-wide meetings at the company where some of this behavior took place. Despite this evidence, Defendant has moved for summary judgment on Plaintiff's racial discrimination claim. In support of the motion for summary judgment, Defendant's lawyers have produced affidavits of several senior-level managers. In those affidavits, senior company officials offer testimony based on personal knowledge that they do not permit any employees, let alone mid-level managers, to make racially charged jokes or comments at the office; that all managers receive training in implicit bias and racial stereotyping; and that several years ago, when it was learned that one mid-level manager had used a racial slur on social media, that employee was terminated.

Should the court grant Defendant's motion for summary judgment based on the affidavits of the senior-level officials at the company? If so, why? If not, why not?

A. No. The motion should be denied because Defendant has failed to show that there is no genuine dispute as to any material fact with respect to Plaintiff's claims.

B. Yes. The motion should be granted because Defendant has established that no racial discrimination occurs at the office.

C. Yes. The motion should be granted because Plaintiff has failed to establish that there is a genuine dispute as to any material fact with respect to his claim of racial discrimination.

D. No. The motion should be denied because Defendant's witnesses are not competent to submit the testimony in their affidavits.

3. Plaintiff prisoner brings an action under the federal Prison Litigation Reform Act (PLRA) alleging abuse at the hands of correctional officers at the prison at which she is serving out her sentence. Plaintiff drafts her own complaint because she is litigating the case pro se, that is, without an attorney. Under this prison's procedures, prisoners who wish to file actions in federal court must deliver a copy of the summons and complaint to the warden's office and then the complaint is mailed that day to the court, by overnight mail. There is no evidence that the warden's office failed to follow this procedure when it received Plaintiff's summons and complaint. There is a one-year statute of limitations under the PLRA, and an allegation that a plaintiff failed to satisfy the statute of limitations is an affirmative defense. At the conclusion of discovery, Defendants claim they have established that Plaintiff failed to file her action within the applicable statute of limitations.

If Defendants make a motion for summary judgment on its defense that Plaintiff failed to file her action within the applicable statute of limitations, what type of evidence will the court reject if Plaintiff submits it in an attempt to defeat the motion?

A. An affidavit from Plaintiff stating when she brought the summons and complaint to the warden's office for filing in federal court the next day.

B. The transcript from the deposition of the prison warden indicating the date he received a copy of the summons and complaint for filing.

C. An unsworn statement from another inmate stating when the Plaintiff told him she had delivered her complaint to the warden's office.

D. A sworn interrogatory response from Defendants stating the date on which the warden's office received a copy of the summons and complaint for filing with the federal court.

4.   Plaintiff files a suit based on diversity alleging that she was injured in her workplace, a construction site, when a steel beam being hoisted over her head fell on her and injured her shoulder. She does not sue her employer because she is barred from doing so, so she instead sues the company that operated the crane that was transporting the beam. She did not see the manner in which the beam was being transported, but three other witnesses did, or at least say they did. Two witnesses for the Defendant are security guards who were standing nearby when the accident occurred. They work for Plaintiff's employer. The third witness is an individual who was passing by the construction site when the beam was being transported and who claims to have been watching the process when the accident occurred. The security guards testify in their depositions that the crane operator appeared to be operating the crane in a careful manner. The third witness testifies at his deposition that the crane operator was distracted, looking at his cell phone and moving the beam at what appeared to be a very fast speed. Defendant's lawyers have uncovered what they say is evidence that the third eyewitness has paid penalties several times for cheating on his taxes. The third witness does not dispute the allegations about his tax penalties. There is no additional evidence related to the issue of the manner in which the crane was operated, and neither side will seek any more evidence on this point. Although discovery has not concluded generally, Defendant moves for summary judgment on the issue of the manner in which the crane was operating, alleging that the testimony of the security guards is sufficient to grant the motion because

the third witness's account with respect to this issue is not credible due to his history of tax evasion.

If Defendant moves for summary judgment on the issue of the manner in which the crane was operating, will it prevail on the motion? If so, why? If not, why not?

A. Defendant will prevail on the motion because, once the account of the third witness is disregarded, there is no evidence to oppose the motion for summary judgment and there will be no genuine dispute as to a material fact related to Plaintiff's claims.

B. Defendant will prevail on the motion because its evidence clearly outweighs Plaintiff's evidence.

C. Defendant will not prevail on the motion because it has failed to establish that there is no genuine dispute as to a material fact.

D. Defendant will not prevail on the motion because it failed to wait until the close of discovery to make its motion for summary judgment.

5.   UCar, a company based in San Francisco, California, operates a ride-hailing service in that city. In a case filed by the U.S. Department of Justice (DOJ) in federal court in San Francisco, UCar faces charges over discriminatory treatment of some residents of the city for its alleged failure to provide rides to people of certain ethnicities. The charges, if proven, would constitute a violation of federal civil rights statutes. The DOJ lawyers present testimony by way of affidavits from several individuals of certain ethnicities showing that, on specific dates and times, those individuals were turned down for rides from the service, whereas individuals of other ethnicities were not. UCar offers the affidavit of its director of training which alleges that all of its drivers are trained not to discriminate on the basis of ethnicity with respect to the riders those drivers serve. No other evidence on this issue is presented by either side during the course of discovery.

If, after the close of discovery, the DOJ moves for summary judgment on the question of whether UCar engages in illegal, discriminatory conduct, will the court grant the motion on this issue? If so, why? If not, why not?

A. The court will grant the motion because the DOJ has identified specific instances of illegal conduct and UCar has not offered evidence that specifically refutes that evidence.

B. The court will grant the motion because the DOJ's evidence is more plausible than UCar's evidence.

C. The court will deny the motion because the DOJ has not shown that there is no genuine dispute as to a material fact.

D. The court will deny the motion because the DOJ's evidence does not refute UCar's evidence.

6.   Plaintiff, a citizen and resident of New York, brings an action against a mortgage lender for alleged fraud in the sale of a mortgage. Plaintiff alleges that low-level, local bank officials worked collaboratively with a local housing appraiser to artificially inflate the value of the home Plaintiff wanted to purchase. Because of the inflated appraisal, Plaintiff agreed to purchase the home at a higher price than it was truly worth and took out a mortgage from the bank that was larger than she wanted. After a year, when interest rates began to drop, Plaintiff sought to refinance her home mortgage to get a better interest rate. But after the house is appraised at its true value, Plaintiff becomes unable to refinance her mortgage and must continue paying the higher interest rate. Plaintiff brings an action in federal court based on the court's diversity jurisdiction against the bank, which is incorporated in and has its principal place of business in Delaware, alleging that the bank's practices resulted in her being unable to refinance her mortgage, which means she will likely pay approximately $100,000 more over the life of her loan than she would have to pay if she had been able to refinance her mortgage. During the course of discovery, Plaintiff's lawyer uncovers email communications that show that the appraiser and the bank officials were involved in a broad, fraudulent scheme regarding several properties, including her own. To contest this evidence, the bank offers one witness for a deposition to discuss the bank's appraisal practices. This witness, Ken Carr, the director of training and quality control for the bank, testifies at his deposition that he trained all of the bank's mortgage officials on how to identify and avoid appraisal

fraud. He also testifies that he has conducted spot audits on many of the bank's mortgage transactions over the years and has never once identified any appraisal fraud through those audits. At the close of discovery, Defendant moves for summary judgment dismissing all of Plaintiff's claims, arguing that Carr's testimony negates any allegations of appraisal fraud in Plaintiff's mortgage transaction.

Should the court grant the bank's motion for summary judgment? If so, why? If not, why not?

A. Yes, because Carr's testimony negates Plaintiff's evidence related to appraisal fraud.

B. Yes, because Plaintiff has failed to establish a plausible claim for relief.

C. No, because no reasonable juror could rule for the bank.

D. No, because the bank has failed to establish that there is no genuine dispute as to a material fact related to Plaintiff's allegation of appraisal fraud.

7. Assume that in the mortgage fraud scheme described in Question 6, while the bank's motion for summary judgment is pending, Plaintiff learns that Ken Carr, the bank official who testified that the bank does not engage in appraisal fraud, has been found criminally liable for perjury in another case involving allegations of appraisal fraud in another state. Plaintiff now wants to move for partial summary judgment, arguing that this conviction should have an issue-preclusive effect, that is, Plaintiff should be able to prevail on her own motion for summary judgment because Carr's credibility has been completely undermined.

Will Carr's conviction have an issue-preclusive effect and provide Plaintiff with a basis for making a motion for summary judgment on her fraud claims as a result? If so, why? If not, why not?

A. Yes, because the standard for the finding of criminal perjury is higher than the standard applied in Plaintiff's civil case, and thus Plaintiff can use that conviction in the civil case.

B. No, because Plaintiff was not a party to the prior action and thus cannot use the Carr conviction in an offensive manner in her case.

C. No, because the conviction only relates to Carr's potential lack of credibility, which the court should not generally consider when ruling on a motion for summary judgment.

D. Yes, because the court can now treat Carr's deposition in Plaintiff's case as a nullity, and thus there is no evidence in the record to rebut Plaintiff's claims.

8.   Plaintiff has filed a case under the federal Truth in Lending Act (TILA) alleging that she did not receive the required notice under the law prior to her entering into a mortgage with Defendant Bank. Plaintiff has filed an action in federal court to rescind her mortgage. In her deposition taken by Bank's attorney and given under oath, Plaintiff alleges that she never received a copy of the required notice under TILA. Bank will move for summary judgment stating that Bank complied with the notice requirements of TILA. Bank's motion is supported by a sworn affidavit of someone who works for Bank who will allege on personal knowledge that it is always standard practice for employees of Bank to mail out all required TILA notices in accordance with the law. Based on these allegations, Bank will argue that the court should award summary judgment to Bank for Bank's alleged compliance with the TILA notice requirement.

Will the court grant Bank's motion for summary judgment? If so, why? If not, why not?

A. The court will grant the motion for summary judgment because Bank has established that there is no genuine dispute as to a material fact regarding Plaintiff's receipt of the notice required by the applicable law.

B. The court will deny the motion for summary judgment because there is a genuine dispute as to a material fact regarding whether Plaintiff received the notice required by law.

C. The court will grant the motion because Plaintiff is available at trial and her deposition testimony cannot be used to defeat the motion for summary judgment.

D. The court will deny the motion because Bank may not submit a mere affidavit in support of a motion for summary judgment.

7.2 Jury Trial Matters and Pre-Trial Maneuvers

This brief section will cover how to demand a jury trial, some basic aspects of jury trials in the federal system, and one question on pre-trial matters.

9. Plaintiff brings an action for breach of contract and trademark violation against a subcontractor Plaintiff hired who has not performed as required under that contract and has taken and used some of Plaintiff's trademarked materials in its business operations not related to Plaintiff's contract with the subcontractor. Plaintiff seeks $100,000 on the contract claim, additional damages for the trademark violation, and an injunction to prevent the subcontractor from further utilizing Plaintiff's trademark. The case is filed in federal court, and there is subject matter jurisdiction over all of these claims. When commencing its action, Plaintiff asserts a demand for a trial by jury on all of its claims and remedies. Subcontractor will object to the demand for a jury, preferring instead to have the entire matter adjudicated by a judge.

Can Plaintiff demand that a jury resolve any or all of its claims and order any or all of the remedies it has sought?

A. Once Defendant has objected to a trial by jury on any claims and/or remedies, the demand for trial by jury must be rejected with respect to all aspects of the case.

B. Plaintiff will be able to have its contract claim resolved by a jury, but its trademark claims and remedies must all be resolved by a judge.

C. Plaintiff will be able to have its contract claim and the damages portion of its trademark claim decided by a jury, but the request for an injunction must be adjudicated by the judge.

D. Because Plaintiff has made a timely demand for a trial by jury, all aspects of its case must be resolved by the jury only.

10. During the process of jury selection in a case involving alleged police brutality, members of the jury pool are answering questions related to the dispute. One such potential juror identifies herself as a retired police officer and admits that, as a police officer, she saw "some bad things happen." She also says, credibly, that she can be impartial in hearing the case as a juror. A second potential juror admits that he has been the target of profiling by his local police department and articulates that he is not certain he can be an impartial juror in the case. A third potential juror has a family member who is a police officer, but he also admits to having faced some petty criminal charges as a youth, all of which were dismissed without convictions. This individual states credibly that he does not feel any ill-will against or special favor toward either the police or someone who is an alleged victim of police brutality.

If counsel representing the defendant police department wants to remove any of these potential jurors from the jury pool, are there sufficient grounds for seeking to dismiss any or all of them for cause?

A. Counsel for the police department will be able to convince the court to strike all three potential jurors for cause.

B. Counsel for the police department will be able to convince the court to strike only the second potential juror for cause.

C. Counsel for the police department has no grounds to strike any of the potential jurors for cause.

D. Counsel for the police department has grounds to strike the second and third potential jurors for cause.

11. Plaintiff and Defendant appear at a final pre-trial conference in federal court. Throughout the course of the litigation, Plaintiff's lawyer has been exploring through discovery whether Plaintiff was subject to discrimination based on her gender. At the final pre-trial conference, the evidence as described by both parties addresses this issue. The court then issues an order that determines the manner and scope of the evidence that will be presented at trial. As the parties begin to conduct the trial, new evidence suggests Plaintiff was also potentially a victim of racial discrimination—something which Plaintiff had originally asked about during discovery. It turns out that, unbeknownst to Plaintiff, Defendant's counsel had withheld evidence specifically addressing this issue even though Plaintiff had sought it at discovery. Plaintiff's counsel asks that the final pre-trial order be amended to permit it to pursue a claim of racial discrimination as well. This claim had been a part of the initial complaint, but Plaintiff had effectively decided not to pursue it when it could not find any evidence of such discrimination, which has now surfaced at trial.

Should Plaintiff succeed in amending the final pre-trial order? If so, why? If not, why not?

A. Plaintiff should not succeed in having the court amend the pre-trial order because it had ample opportunity in discovery to pursue the claim of racial discrimination.

B. Plaintiff should succeed in having the court amend the pre-trial order because to do so would prevent a manifest injustice from occurring.

C. Plaintiff should succeed in having the court amend the pre-trial order so as to avoid the infliction of irreparable harm on her.

D. Plaintiff should not succeed in having the court amend the pre-trial order because the trial has already begun and Plaintiff has waived the right to pursue any additional claims.

7.3 Post-Trial Maneuvers

This section explores and explains the motions available to litigants to seek to either preclude a jury from reaching a verdict or to overturn a verdict after the jury has ruled against that party.

12. In a case heard before a jury, what is the applicable standard for a court's rendering judgment as a matter of law for a defendant on all of the plaintiff's claims after the close of the evidence in that trial?

A. That a reasonable jury would not have a legally sufficient evidentiary basis to find for the plaintiff on its claims.

B. That the plaintiff failed to nudge its factual assertions across the line from being merely conceivable to being plausible.

C. That there is no genuine dispute as to a material fact with respect to the plaintiff's claims.

D. If the court finds that any reason exists for which a new trial has previously been granted in an action at law in federal court.

13. Litigation between Plaintiff and Defendant over a claim for tortious interference with contract, litigated in federal court on the basis of the diversity of the parties, concludes. The jury reaches a verdict in favor of Plaintiff.

If Defendant wants to file a motion for judgment as a matter of law after the jury renders its verdict, what must Defendant have done before the jury rendered its verdict to make such a post-verdict motion?

A. Defendant must have attempted to meet and confer with Plaintiff to determine whether the matter could be settled.

B. Defendant must have served the motion for judgment as a matter of law on opposing counsel without filing it within twenty-eight days of the jury's verdict.

C. In its motion papers, Defendant has to certify that it attempted to resolve the matter without resort to making the motion.

D. Defendant has to have made a motion for judgment as a matter of law before the matter was submitted to the jury.

14. Plaintiff and Defendant are locked in an emotional trial in federal court in which Defendant is accused of engaging in housing discrimination against Plaintiff. Plaintiff alleges Defendant refused to rent him an apartment based on his ethnicity in violation of federal law. In a jury trial, Defendant moves for judgment as a matter of law at the close of the presentation of evidence by both sides and the judge denies it, saying she would like to see what the jury says after it completes its deliberations. The jury verdict is returned in favor of Plaintiff. Defendant files a renewed motion for judgment as a matter of law together with a motion for a new trial. The judge has reviewed the evidence presented by both sides in the case and, although she admits that it is a close call, believes Defendant probably should have won.

What motion, if any, should the court grant?

A. The motion for a new trial, but not for judgment as a matter of law.

B. The motion for judgment as a matter of law, but not for a new trial.

C. Both motions.

D. Neither motion.

7.4 Appeals

This section covers issues related to appeals, mainly how they interact with district court proceedings and orders.

15. Plaintiff files a case asserting that a group of defendants is engaged in price fixing in violation of federal antitrust laws. Plaintiff's complaint includes references to and excerpts from emails obtained from several former employees of a number of the defendants, and these references and excerpts appear to provide evidence that leaders of the defendant companies were, in fact, engaged in a price-fixing scheme. Defendants dispute this evidence, but the trial court, when ruling on Defendants' motion to dismiss for Plaintiff's alleged failure to state a claim, determines that the facts as alleged appear to establish a plausible claim for relief sufficient to withstand Defendants' motion to dismiss. Defendants wish to appeal the denial of the motion to dismiss directly to the appellate court without seeking the lower court's permission to do so.

Will Defendants succeed in seeking appellate review of the denial of their motion to dismiss? If so, why? If not, why not?

A. Yes, because the decision to deny a motion to dismiss is a final order warranting the direct appeal of it to the appellate court.

B. No, because the decision to deny a motion to dismiss is not a final order and thus a direct appeal of that decision to the appellate court is not permissible.

C. Yes, because Defendants will be irreparably harmed by having to face the discovery phase in the action if they are correct that the motion should be dismissed.

D. No, because Defendants can appeal any lower court orders in this action only after trial.

16. Plaintiff files an action against Dayboat Cruises (Dayboat), a company based in St. John, Canada. The company transports luxury cars by sea to ports throughout the Eastern Seaboard of Canada and the United States. Plaintiff enters into a contract with Dayboat to transport its luxury MyBock sedan, valued at $250,000, from Boston to Baltimore. The contract with Dayboat for such service provides that all disputes related to the ticket must be resolved in a court in St. John, Canada. Because of a shipping accident, Plaintiff's MyBock comes loose from its moorings, slides off the deck of the Dayboat vessel, and is lost at sea. Plaintiff brings an action in federal district court based on diversity jurisdiction (which the court has) in Boston, Massachusetts, seeking compensatory damages. Dayboat makes a motion to dismiss the case on *forum non conveniens* grounds, stating that the forum selection clause should be enforced and the action dismissed. The district court denies the motion, and Dayboat appeals that denial without seeking the approval of the district court to do so.

Will Defendant succeed in seeking appellate review of the denial of its motion to dismiss based on the forum selection clause? If so, why? If not, why not?

A. Yes. Denying the motion based on the forum selection clause effectively nullifies that clause, affording Defendant the right for immediate appeal.

B. No. The forum selection clause is unenforceable as unconscionable, so immediate appellate review is unavailable to the defendant.

C. Yes. The forum selection clause prohibits the district court from hearing the case, and thus immediate appellate review of the denial of the motion to dismiss is warranted.

D. No. The forum selection clause does not entitle Defendant to immunity from suit just to raise the right to have the suit decided elsewhere, and thus the decision denying Defendant's motion does not satisfy the final judgment rule.

17. Plaintiff files an action in federal court to halt certain police practices that Plaintiff argues violate the rights of certain members of the community due to their race. Plaintiff seeks an ex parte temporary restraining order (TRO) initially, and the court grants it. Upon issuing the TRO, the court establishes a schedule for Plaintiff's request for a preliminary injunction within eight days of the effective date of the TRO. At the conclusion of the hearing, the court dissolves the TRO and issues the preliminary injunction sought by Plaintiff. Defendant now seeks an immediate appeal of the TRO and the preliminary injunction.

May Defendant appeal the granting of the TRO and/or the preliminary injunction?

A. Defendant may appeal both orders.

B. Defendant may appeal the TRO because it was granted on an ex parte basis, but it cannot appeal the preliminary injunction because it was given a full and fair hearing to contest it.

C. Defendant may not appeal the TRO because there is no authority for an appellate court to review a TRO, but it can appeal the preliminary injunction.

D. Defendant cannot appeal either order.

18. During the pendency of litigation in federal court, a district court denies a motion to dismiss on a particular issue of law. Within days of its reaching that decision, an appellate court issues a subsequent decision which creates differences within appellate courts on the application of law upon which the district court based its ruling. Accordingly, the district court is asked to certify the decision on the motion for immediate and interlocutory appeal.

Should the district court certify the decision on the motion to dismiss for interlocutory appellate review? If so, why? If not, why not?

A. No, because the law upon which the court issued its ruling was not uncertain at the time of that ruling, and thus there is no basis upon which to certify the matter for interlocutory appeal.

B. Yes, because there appears to be substantial difference between appellate courts on the current state of the law upon which the decision on the motion to dismiss was based.

C. No, because a denial of a motion to dismiss is not a final judgment warranting interlocutory review.

D. Yes, because substantial rights of the litigants are at stake due to the denial of the motion to dismiss, and to continue to adjudicate the case without clarification from the appellate court will inflict irreparable harm on the litigants.

7.5 Formative Assessment Quiz

Take this brief formative assessment quiz to test your knowledge of this material.

19. During discovery in a case involving allegations of antitrust violations committed by coal-producing companies, evidence is uncovered that several officials from these coal companies conspired to raise prices during the winter months to garner more profits from homes heated by coal-fired power plants. There is some degree of conflicting testimony on this point, however. Several coal company officials admit during their depositions that conversations related to price increases were had; however, others flatly deny there was any such collusion. There is also contradictory documentary evidence; some of it seems to point to collusive, anti-competitive conduct, while other portions of it appear to undermine Plaintiffs' claims. Because Plaintiffs have several key company defendants admitting, under oath, that the coal companies conspired to fix prices, they wish to move for summary judgment on their claims.

Will Plaintiffs succeed in their motion for summary judgment? If so, why? If not, why not?

A. Yes. The admissions from the company witnesses are admissible and establish that there is no genuine dispute as to a material fact at the heart of Plaintiffs' claims.

B. No. The deposition testimony of the company witnesses is not admissible on a summary judgment motion because the witnesses are available to testify at trial.

C. No. Defendants have presented evidence in direct conflict with that presented by Plaintiffs, which establishes that there is a genuine dispute as to several material facts.

D. Yes. Plaintiffs have carried their burden of production and persuasion on their claims, and thus the motion should be granted.

20. Plaintiff brings an action alleging mortgage discrimination based on Plaintiff's race and gender. During the course of discovery, Plaintiff deposes an employee of Defendant Bank, who admits that the unit in which he worked routinely denied mortgage applications based on the prospective borrower's race. The employee reviews Plaintiff's file and states that in Plaintiff's case, the bank certainly denied the application based on Plaintiff's race. Plaintiff and Defendant are still in the process of seeking information related to the gender discrimination claim. Plaintiff believes she has enough evidence to move for summary judgment on the race discrimination claim. Plaintiff moves for partial summary judgment on that claim alone. Without coming forward with any evidence to refute the allegations of the employee, Defendant objects to the timing of the motion for summary judgment, alleging that discovery has not closed yet, and thus the motion is premature. For that reason, Defendant seeks denial of the motion.

Will the court deny Plaintiff's motion for summary judgment because it is premature, having been filed before the close of discovery? If so, why? If not, why not?

A. Yes, Defendant's request that the court deny the motion on the ground that it is premature will be granted because discovery has not yet closed and the court should let the discovery process run its course.

B. No, because despite the fact that discovery has not yet closed in this action, Defendant has not presented any arguments as to what additional information it needs to oppose the motion.

C. Yes, because Plaintiff cannot make a partial motion to dismiss addressing a single claim when it has other outstanding claims that are still going through the discovery process.

D. No, because Defendant has not identified a genuine dispute as to a material fact related to the grounds of the motion.

21. Plaintiff brings an action in federal district court against the warden of the prison where Plaintiff was incarcerated for alleged unconstitutional infringements on Plaintiff's rights. The warden will raise the defense of qualified immunity and seek to dismiss the case on that ground. The trial court rejects the defense and the motion to dismiss. The warden seeks an immediate appeal of the denial of the motion to dismiss without seeking approval from the district court to do so.

Will the warden be able to appeal the denial of the motion to dismiss based on qualified immunity directly to the appellate court without having to wait for the conclusion of the proceedings before the trial court? If so, why? If not, why not?

A. The defendant will succeed in appealing the denial of the motion to dismiss because of the important constitutional issues involved in the case and the appeal.

B. The defendant will not succeed in appealing the denial of the motion to dismiss because a denial of a motion to dismiss is not a final judgment which would warrant the immediate appeal.

C. The defendant will succeed in appealing the denial of the motion to dismiss because the defense on which it is based, if upheld on appeal, would insulate the defendant from the lawsuit entirely.

D. The defendant will not succeed in appealing the denial of the motion to dismiss because of the important constitutional issues raised in Plaintiff's complaint.

22. Plaintiff brings an action in federal court based on Defendant's alleged mortgage discrimination in violation of federal law. In its pre-answer motion to dismiss, Defendant successfully argues that Plaintiff's allegations in the complaint are not pled with sufficient particularity to render them plausible. Based on this motion, and on this ground, the court dismisses the action in its entirety without prejudice for Plaintiff's failure to state a claim upon which relief can be granted.

May Plaintiff appeal the granting of the motion to dismiss? If so, why? If not, why not?

A. No, because the granting of a pre-answer motion to dismiss is not a final judgment.

B. No, because the matter is only dismissed without prejudice.

C. Yes, because the court should not make plausibility determinations on a pre-answer motion to dismiss, meaning the appeal has substantial merit.

D. Yes, because the granting of a motion to dismiss constitutes a final judgment.

Chapter 8

Summative Exam

This summative exam tests your overall knowledge of the material contained in this guide. The answers that follow are somewhat shorter than the explanations in other chapters. If you still have questions after reading the explanations, you can go back to the relevant section of a prior chapter that covers the issues with which you are still struggling.

8.1 Summative Exam

1. Plaintiff is driving on highway I87 outside Albany, New York, when she slams on her brakes to avoid hitting a deer that has wandered into her lane. She is immediately rear-ended by Aaron, Brendan, and Carl. Albany, New York, is located within the jurisdiction of the federal district court for the Northern District of New York. Aaron is a resident and citizen of New Jersey. Brendan is a citizen of Great Britain but also a legal permanent resident of the United States who is domiciled in New York State, in Albany. Carl is a citizen of Germany visiting relatives outside of Buffalo (he was driving in a rental car up from New York City when the accident occurred). Plaintiff brings an action in federal court in Albany, the site of the accident, alleging claims under state tort law and seeking $500,000 in damages. Defendants jointly file a motion to dismiss for improper venue and for lack of subject matter jurisdiction.

Do any of the bases for Defendants' motion to dismiss have merit? If so, which one or ones?

A. Venue is improper in the chosen district, but there is subject matter jurisdiction over the action.

B. Venue is proper, but there is no subject matter jurisdiction over the claims against Brendan.

C. Venue is improper, and there is no subject matter jurisdiction over any of the claims.

D. Venue is proper and the court has subject matter jurisdiction.

2. Plaintiff is a pedestrian injured in a car accident in Toronto, Canada. She is struck by an autonomous vehicle operating on Toronto's new "smart city" grid, which the City created recently with the assistance of Lougle, a Silicon Valley startup. On the grid, autonomous vehicles operate through the receipt of remote signals, aided by surveillance cameras installed throughout the grid. The surveillance cameras are monitored mostly using artificial intelligence through a system of computers owned and operated by Lougle which are physically located in the Capital Region of New York State. Lougle is incorporated in Delaware, with its principal place of business in California. Plaintiff is a resident and citizen of New York State. Plaintiff brings an action in federal district court for the Northern District of New York, the district court that encompasses Lougle's artificial intelligence computer center consisting of three large quantum computers and a high-capacity server. Plaintiff alleges that the artificial intelligence system operated out of this center failed when it did not alert an autonomous vehicle that Plaintiff was planning to cross the street in a lawful manner, even though she was within the designated crosswalk and enjoyed the right of way. Plaintiff seeks $100,000 in damages under state tort theories of recovery. Lougle will appear and raise two defenses. It will make a motion to dismiss based on both defenses, but it alleges them in the alternative. First, it alleges that the court does not have subject matter jurisdiction over the action because, due to the artificial intelligence center's presence in the Capital Region, Lougle is "at home" in the State of New York. As a result, Lougle alleges, the court does not have subject matter jurisdiction over the proceeding because there is not complete diversity between the parties. Second, and in the alternative, Lougle argues that if the court does not find that it is at home in the state of New York, the case should be dismissed for lack of personal jurisdiction. Assume that New York's long-arm statute has been satisfied with respect to Lougle in this action.

Will the court grant either or both of Defendant's two motions? If so, why? If not, why not?

A. The court will deny both motions because Defendant cannot allege such alternative and inconsistent theories.

B. The court will deny the motion based on subject matter jurisdiction because the parties are diverse but grant the motion based on personal jurisdiction because of the defendant's lack of sufficient contacts with the forum.

C. The court will deny the motion based on lack of personal jurisdiction because of the defendant's systematic and continuous contact with the subject forum but will grant the motion based on a lack of subject matter jurisdiction because the parties are not diverse.

D. The court will deny both motions because it has subject matter jurisdiction due to the diversity between the parties and the defendant has contacts with the forum relevant to Plaintiff's injury.

3. Paul is a car dealer who sells luxury limousines. Paul sues Limo, Inc. (Limo), a manufacturer of limousines, for failing to deliver several luxury stretch models for which Paul claims he paid $500,000. Paul's business is incorporated in New York, with its principal place of business in East Greenbush, New York, and Limo is incorporated in Delaware, with its principal place of business in New Haven, Connecticut. Paul brings an action in federal district court for the Northern District of New York, the district which encompasses both East Greenbush and Albany. Paul's action claims that Limo is delaying delivery of the limousines because Limo is attempting to engage in an illegal restraint of trade, helping out one of Paul's competitors in an effort to drive Paul out of business. He brings this action under federal antitrust statutes, seeking actual and punitive damages, both of which are available under the federal provisions upon which the action is based. Limo wishes to file a counterclaim, however. It alleges that Paul failed to satisfy his obligations under a separate contract for the delivery of ten all-terrain vehicles (ATVs), each valued at $20,000. Paul made the first payment of $20,000 under the contract but failed to make the final payment of $180,000 which was due under the contract for the ATVs. Limo will attempt to file a counterclaim under state contract law that seeks payment under the contract for the remaining $180,000.

Will the court permit Limo to join its counterclaim to the action brought by Paul? If so, why? If not, why not?

A. Yes. Limo's counterclaim is compulsory in nature, so, at a minimum, there is supplemental jurisdiction over Limo's counterclaim in the case filed by Paul.

B. No. Limo's counterclaim is permissive and there is not an independent basis of jurisdiction over it.

C. Yes. Even though Limo's counterclaim is permissive in nature, there is an independent basis of jurisdiction for Limo to file it.

D. No. Even though Limo's counterclaim is compulsory in nature, there is no independent basis of jurisdiction over it.

4. Defendant enters into a contract with Burgers-Are-Us (BRUS) to open up a BRUS franchise in the state of Connecticut. The contract contains a clause that provides that New York law will govern the interpretation of the contract. It also contains a choice-of-forum clause stating that any dispute under the contract must be resolved in federal court in the Northern District of New York, the district that encompasses the BRUS headquarters. Defendant is a resident and citizen of Connecticut. BRUS is incorporated in Delaware, with its principal place of business in New York. Defendant traveled to the BRUS headquarters in Albany, New York, to negotiate and enter into the contract with BRUS. Defendant also attended classes on managing and operating a BRUS franchise in the BRUS training facility in Colonie, New York, and wires monthly payments under the franchise agreement to BRUS at its headquarters in New York. After one year of Defendant's operating the BRUS franchise, a dispute arises over the type of potatoes Defendant uses in its BRUS restaurant. BRUS argues that Defendant is using a lesser quality potato in violation of the franchise agreement between BRUS and Defendant, a violation which requires liquidated damages of $20,000 per month for each month in which the rogue potatoes are used. BRUS asserts that Defendant has been using these violative potatoes for the past six months. BRUS brings a claim in federal court in the Northern District of New York alleging state contract law theories of recovery. The BRUS complaint asserts claims under state contract law, seeking $120,000 in damages. Defendant will seek to dismiss the case on the grounds that the court has no personal jurisdiction over it and, in the alternative, seek a transfer to the federal court in Bridgeport, Connecticut, where Defendant's BRUS restaurant is located and where Defendant asserts all use of the allegedly violative potatoes occurred.

How will the court rule on the two parts of Defendant's motion?

A. The court will deny the motion to dismiss based on lack of personal jurisdiction but grant the motion to transfer the case to federal court in Bridgeport.

B. The court will grant the motion to dismiss but deny the motion to transfer venue because it is moot due to the fact that the complaint has been dismissed for lack of personal jurisdiction.

C. The court will grant the motion to transfer venue but defer decision on the question of whether to dismiss the action for want of personal jurisdiction to permit the court in Connecticut to consider that part of the motion.

D. The court will deny both parts of Defendant's motion.

5. Plaintiff, a citizen of Texas, is an employee who worked on an oil rig in the Persian Gulf. While working on the rig, an explosion threw her onto a platform two stories below where she had been working. Plaintiff was severely injured in the incident. Plaintiff worked directly for AzerCo, an Azerbaijani company with an office in Texas from which it recruited Plaintiff to work on the rig. AzerCo inspects oil rigs throughout the world, including in Iran. AzerCo, in turn, works for the National Iranian Oil Company (NIOC), which owned the rig. Legislation in Iran makes NIOC immune from civil suit in Iran, but Iran is not subject to personal jurisdiction in a U.S. court because it generally does not do business with the U.S. market due to the sanctions imposed by the global community on the Iranian oil industry. Plaintiff's employment is not covered by a worker's compensation scheme, so she brings suit in a federal district court in Texas against AzerCo for her personal injuries. AzerCo alleges that the fault was not in its own efforts on the rig but rather in the poor quality of the safety systems that NIOC had deployed on the rig. AzerCo argues that NIOC is a necessary party in the litigation and moves to dismiss the case.

Assume the court agrees that NIOC is a necessary party in this action. Which of the following factors will the court not consider in weighing how and whether to proceed without NIOC in the action?

A. Whether there is a genuine dispute as to a material fact whether the case should proceed without NIOC in the case.

B. The extent to which AzerCo will be prejudiced if the case proceeds without NIOC in the case.

C. Whether Plaintiff will have an adequate remedy if the case is dismissed for non-joinder.

D. Whether the court can shape the relief granted to AzerCo in a way that lessens any harm it may suffer by NIOC's absence.

6.   Plaintiff brings an action under the Prison Litigation Reform Act (PLRA) alleging that the warden of the prison in which she was incarcerated embarked on a scheme to deprive her of her civil rights. The basis of the scheme is that the warden colluded with members of the kitchen staff, also prisoners, to poison Plaintiff. The warden alleges that Plaintiff has failed to establish that she has brought her action within the relevant statute of limitations under the PLRA, and because Plaintiff has failed to allege that she has satisfied the statute of limitations, her claims are not plausible. The statute of limitations defense is an affirmative defense under the PLRA.

Will the warden succeed in dismissing Plaintiff's action based on his arguments that Plaintiff's claims are not plausible if the complaint fails to allege that the action was filed within the applicable statute of limitations? If so, why? If not, why not?

A. Yes. In order to show that Plaintiff is entitled to relief, she must raise facts that are not merely possible but plausible, and if she cannot show that she filed her action within the statute of limitations, she cannot set forth a plausible claim for relief.

B. Yes. Plaintiff always has the burden of establishing that the court has subject matter jurisdiction over the action, and if she cannot establish that she has satisfied the statute of limitations, she will fail to meet this burden.

C. No. Because the defense that Plaintiff has not complied with the applicable statute of limitations is an affirmative defense, Plaintiff is not expected to make any allegations regarding her compliance with the statute of limitations, let alone plausible ones.

D. No. The issue of whether the statute of limitations has been satisfied is only to be determined at trial.

7. Plaintiff brings an action against Defendant in federal court alleging securities fraud under federal anti-fraud statutes. Plaintiff alleges that Defendant made material misrepresentations regarding the purchase of stock in the initial public offering (IPO) of Noodle, an internet startup valued at over $1 billion (the "Noodle IPO"). Plaintiff claims that the representations made by Defendant in the Noodle IPO resulted in an inflation of the valuation of the stock, which dropped precipitously immediately after the IPO was issued, costing plaintiff millions of dollars. During the course of discovery in the action, Plaintiff seeks information well within the scope of discovery from Defendant concerning other material representations Defendant's employees made in other IPOs. During this time, Plaintiff's legal team reviews information on over thirty different IPOs handled by Defendant and finds that in the IPO for a company named Texla, Defendant's employees also made material misrepresentations and Plaintiff was also injured as a result of those misrepresentations. Other IPOs took place between Noodle's and Texla's IPOs, and those other IPOs were handled by Defendant and invested in by Plaintiff without any wrongdoing on the part of Defendant. The Noodle and Texla IPOs also involved different types of allegedly fraudulent statements. Furthermore, the Texla IPO occurred several years before the Noodle IPO that currently forms the basis of Plaintiff's case against Defendant. Indeed, if Plaintiff were to seek to amend her complaint to add a claim related to the Texla IPO, such a claim would be outside the statute of limitations for that new claim; in other words, the time period in which to file a claim regarding the Texla IPO had expired. Plaintiff nonetheless wants to seek to amend her complaint, alleging that a claim related to the Texla IPO "relates back" to the filing of the initial complaint. If Plaintiff can use the date of the filing of the original complaint as the date when the claim related to the Texla IPO was filed, that new claim would be filed within the statute of limitations and therefore timely.

If Defendant were to oppose the amendment based on its argument that the claim regarding the Texla IPO does not relate back to the date of the filing of the initial complaint, will the court allow the amendment and permit Plaintiff to assert the claim? If so, why? If not, why not?

A. The court will allow the amendment and the claim will relate back to the date of the filing of the initial complaint because the information about the claim surrounding the Texla IPO arose during the discovery phase of the original claim, and thus the two claims are logically related.

B. The court will allow the amendment and the claim will relate back to the date of the filing of the initial complaint because the claim about the Texla IPO arises out of the same transaction or series of transactions as the original complaint.

C. The court will not allow the amendment and the claim about the Texla IPO will not relate back to the date of the filling of the initial complaint because the Texla IPO is not logically related to the claims set forth in the initial complaint.

D. The court will not allow the amendment and the claim about the Texla

IPO will not relate back to the date of the filing of the initial complaint because the Texla IPO does not arise out of the same transaction or series of transactions as the original complaint.

8. Paula travels three days a week from Southern Vermont to Hudson, New York, where she has her sculpting studio. Hudson is located in the jurisdiction of the federal court for the Northern District of New York. Plaintiff takes this drive every week, rain or shine, and enjoys watching the changing seasons as she steers her truck through the winding back roads of Vermont, Massachusetts, and New York on her way to and from Hudson. She says she does not mind the drive because she is inspired by nature and often draws such inspiration from the vistas she sees on her drives. During one of these drives home from work on a Friday afternoon, she is rear-ended by Dan and suffers serious injuries. Dan was on his way to his weekend home in Massachusetts, which is located just across the border from New York, outside of Hudson. The accident ultimately occurs just outside the center of the City of Hudson but within city limits. Dan has no other contacts in the Northern District of New York apart from having his car serviced in Hudson, New York, and driving through there on the way to his weekend home, occasionally picking up take-out dinners as he drives through the city. In conversations with Dan's insurance company before the action is filed, Paula's lawyer learns that Dan's car was recently serviced at Steve's Auto Repair (Steve's) in Hudson, New York, and the insurance company claims it was Steve's failure to adequately service the brakes on Dan's car that caused the accident. When the complaint is filed, Paula's attorney names Steve's as a co-defendant in the action. Dan is a citizen of New Jersey, with his primary residence in Newark, New Jersey, which is located in the District Court for the District of New

Jersey. Steve's is incorporated in Delaware, with its principal place of business in Hudson, New York. Paula is a resident and citizen of Vermont. Paula sues Dan and Steve's in federal district court in the Northern District of New York, alleging state tort claims. She alleges over $200,000 in damages from the serious injuries she sustained in the accident.

If Dan files a motion challenging venue of the action in the Northern District of New York which Steve's joins, what is the best description of the status of venue in that district?

A. The motion will be granted because Dan is not subject to personal jurisdiction in the Northern District of New York.

B. The motion will be denied because a substantial portion of the events giving rise to the action occurred in that district.

C. The motion will be denied because Steve's is incorporated in Delaware.

D. The motion will be granted because Dan's place of residence is Newark, New Jersey.

9. Plaintiff has filed a case under the federal Truth in Lending Act (TILA) alleging that he did not receive the required notice under the law prior to entering into a mortgage with Defendant Bank. Plaintiff has filed an action in federal court to rescind his mortgage under TILA. In his deposition taken by Bank's attorney and given under oath, Plaintiff alleges that he never received a copy of the required notice under TILA. Bank will move for summary judgment stating that it complied with the notice requirements of TILA. Bank's motion is supported by a sworn affidavit of one of its employees, who alleges on personal knowledge that the employee personally served the required TILA notice upon Plaintiff at his home in accordance with the law. Based on these allegations, Bank argues that the court should award summary judgment to Bank for its alleged compliance with the TILA notice requirement.

Will the court grant Bank's motion for summary judgment? If so, why? If not, why not?

A. The court will grant the motion for summary judgment because Bank has established that there is no genuine dispute as to a material fact regarding Plaintiff's receipt of the notice required by the applicable law.

B. The court will grant the motion because Plaintiff is available at trial and his deposition testimony cannot be used to defeat the motion for summary judgment.

C. The court will deny the motion because Bank may not submit a mere affidavit in support of a motion for summary judgment.

D. The court will deny the motion for summary judgment because there is a genuine dispute as to a material fact regarding whether Plaintiff received the notice required by law.

10.   Plaintiff brings an action alleging that she was injured while operating a crane to remove some damaged underground pipe. While working on the pipes, she inadvertently strikes a buried power line that was unmarked. She is burned and suffers serious injuries when the pierced power line sparks a fire. She cannot bring an action against her employer because of the protections of the worker's compensation system. Instead, she brings an action against the company that buried the lines (PowerInc). Plaintiff is a resident and citizen of New York State. She brings an action against PowerInc in federal court in Albany, New York, in the Northern District of New York, under state tort law theories, seeking $500,000 in damages. PowerInc is incorporated in Delaware, with its principal place of business in Massachusetts. PowerInc seeks to implead the company that supplied the insulation that was supposed to prevent the lines from catching fire if pierced (SafeSeal). SafeSeal is also incorporated in Delaware, but its principal place of business is in New York. PowerInc provides evidence from its contract with SafeSeal that SafeSeal agreed to indemnify PowerInc in the event its insulation failed to prevent the power lines from catching fire. SafeSeal does not object to being joined as a third-party defendant to the action. As a result of the nature of the accident and Plaintiff's injuries, Defendants are joint and severally liable for Plaintiff's claims.

If Plaintiff attempts to bring new affirmative claims against SafeSeal once it is impleaded in the case, will it be able to do so? If so, why? If not, why not?

A. Plaintiff will not be able to bring new claims against SafeSeal because Safe-

Seal's principal place of business is New York.

B. Plaintiff will be able to bring the new claims against SafeSeal because Defendants are joint and severally liable for Plaintiff's injuries.

C. Plaintiff will not be able to bring new claims against SafeSeal because both Defendants are incorporated in Delaware.

D. Plaintiff will be able to bring new claims against SafeSeal because SafeSeal agreed to indemnify PowerInc for any harm it suffered as a result of any defective product SafeSeal supplied to PowerInc.

11. Plaintiff is a resident and citizen of Tioga, Pennsylvania, who lives on a lake that is fed by the Cooperstown River that runs through New York, from Ithaca, New York, into Pennsylvania. Upstream from Plaintiff's residence, in New York, there is a quartz mine, operated by Quartz, Inc. (Quartz), that sometimes releases toxic chemicals into the Cooperstown River. Plaintiff alleges that these toxins affect the lake on which she lives and the well on her property that is fed from the polluted river and from which she draws much of her drinking water. She brings an action in federal court in Pennsylvania alleging that Quartz is violating state nuisance law. She seeks $200,000 in damages, which she can easily show. Plaintiff alleges Quartz's actions have made her ill, caused her significant pain and suffering, and resulted in her having to miss many days of work. Quartz is incorporated in the state of Delaware, with its principal place of business in Ithaca, New York. Quartz brings a pre-answer motion to dismiss challenging the court's venue over the action. The court denies that motion, granting Quartz leave to file an answer within thirty days of notice of the denial of the motion. Quartz prepares to file an answer and wants to include the following defenses: that the complaint fails to state a claim upon which relief can be granted and that the court lacks subject matter jurisdiction over the action.

Putting aside the potential merits of the defenses Quartz wishes to include in its answer, as a procedural matter, which, if any, of these defenses may Quartz interpose at this juncture in the case?

A. Quartz cannot interpose either defense at this juncture in the proceeding.

B. Quartz can interpose the defense based on an alleged lack of subject matter jurisdiction but cannot interpose the defense based on the failure to state a claim upon which relief can be granted at this juncture in the proceeding.

C. Quartz can interpose the defense based on the failure to state a claim upon which relief can be granted but cannot interpose the defense based on an alleged lack of subject matter jurisdiction at this juncture in the proceeding.

D. Quartz can interpose both defenses at this juncture in the proceeding.

12. A party wishing to move for a preliminary injunction must meet all requirements of a four-prong test to obtain that preliminary injunction. According to U.S. Supreme Court precedent, as a part of that test, the moving party must establish the merit of her claim or claims.

Which of the following is the element of the preliminary injunction standard as it relates to the merits of the claim or claims?

A. That the moving party has established the plausibility of the merits of her claim or claims.

B. That the moving party has a probability of success on the merits.

C. That the moving party has established that there is no genuine issue of material fact in dispute with respect to the merits of the claim.

D. That the moving party has a likelihood of success on the merits.

13. Plaintiff sues Defendant in a personal injury action in federal district court for the Northern District of New York. The action is based on diversity of citizenship, and the amount-in-controversy requirement has been satisfied. Plaintiff has submitted several discovery demands seeking documents from Defendant which, Plaintiff asserts, will show that Defendant had failed to conduct proper maintenance of the parking lot where Plaintiff was seriously injured when she fell on a loose piece of asphalt. Plaintiff seeks maintenance records from Defendant, who refuses to turn them over. On a proper motion to compel the disclosure of the maintenance records and ruling that Defendant does not have any reasonable grounds for withholding such information, the court grants the motion, ordering Defendant to release the maintenance records to Plaintiff. Upon receiving the order, Defendant turns over the documents sought by Plaintiff. Plaintiff moves for sanctions against Defendant under Rule 37 of the Federal Rules of Civil Procedure.

Which of the following sanctions is the court likely to issue in this context?

A. Striking the answer as a whole.

B. Staying further proceedings in the action.

C. Awarding costs and attorney's fees to Plaintiff for the expenses related to making the motion to compel.

D. Treating the failure to obey the discovery order as contempt of court.

14. The ridesharing company Goober, incorporated in Delaware, with its principal place of business in California, is sued in federal court in Portland, Oregon, by a pedestrian who claims she was hit by a Goober car one evening on a quiet street in a suburb of Portland. She is a resident and citizen of the state of Oregon and seeks over $150,000 in damages under state law theories of recovery. The pedestrian claims that the last thing she saw before she was hit was a car coming from her left side. She could not make out a license plate or other distinguishing features other than the "Goober" insignia posted on the inside of the windshield on the passenger side of the vehicle. During her testimony, Goober's Chief Operating Officer introduces the company's data analytics report, which is linked to software that, she alleges, tracks all Goober drivers in real time when they are operating on the platform. The COO alleges that this report indicates there were no Goober vehicles in the vicinity of the accident when the accident is alleged to have occurred. Plaintiff will offer credible evidence that undermines Goober's position that its system for tracking its drivers is fully accurate. Plaintiff's evidence on this issue suggests that this system can only track a Goober driver in real time if the driver manually activates the tracking software each time he begins driving for the company, and many drivers either forget or choose not to activate the tracking system. It is thus possible, Plaintiff argues, that a Goober vehicle was responsible for the accident even though it may not have been actively tracked through the software at the time of the accident. Goober's data analytics report is admissible in court as a business record of Goober. Goober will move for summary judgment, arguing that its data analytics report establishes that a Goober vehicle could not have been responsible for the accident.

Will the court grant Goober's motion for summary judgment? If so, why? If not, why not?

A. No, because Plaintiff has raised a genuine dispute as to a material fact related to Plaintiff's claim.

B. No, because Plaintiff's testimony is eye-witness testimony and is thus superior to Goober's mere business record evidence.

C. Yes, because Plaintiff cannot establish a genuine dispute as to a material fact regarding her claim, that is, whether she was struck by a Goober vehicle.

D. Yes, because Goober has established that none of its vehicles was at the scene of the accident.

15. While driving from her home in New York to her vacation time-share in Florida, Paula is injured in a car accident in Virginia. She is rear-ended by a distracted driver, Dan, while at a stoplight. Her car was stationary at the time she was hit, and the other driver, who was texting at the time of the accident, did not realize the stoplight at the intersection had turned red. Paula, a resident of New York, commences a case in state court in New York against Dan, a resident of Virginia, alleging negligence under New York law and seeking $200,000 in damages. Dan is a salesman who sells parts for wind turbines throughout the United States. For the last year, irregularly but roughly just about every other month, Dan has been traveling to New York State on business, selling parts for turbines operating throughout Western New York State. He usually spends no more than a few hours in New York when he visits and rarely spends the night, choosing instead to fly in and out of the state on the same day. New York's long-arm statute reads in relevant part that an individual who "regularly conducts business in the state" is subject to personal jurisdiction for all harm caused to individuals in the state, whether that harm is caused in the state or outside of it.

Assume for the sake of this question that the trial court has found that Dan's conduct falls within the long-arm statute's definition of "regularly conduct[ing] business in the state." Dan is not served with service of process while he is present in the state, however. His lawyer wants to challenge the personal jurisdiction of the court over Dan.

If Dan's conduct does bring him within the reach of the long-arm statute, a court

determining whether the exercise of personal jurisdiction over Dan is consistent with the Due Process Clause of the U.S. Constitution is likely to find which of the following?

A. That the exercise of personal jurisdiction over Dan is consistent with the Due Process Clause because his conduct in the forum state is systematic and continuous.

B. That the exercise of personal jurisdiction over Dan is consistent with the Due Process Clause because his conduct in relation to the forum state is of such a nature that to exert jurisdiction over him will not offend traditional notions of fair play and substantial justice.

C. That the exercise of personal jurisdiction over Dan is inconsistent with the Due Process Clause because his connection to the forum state has not been systematic and continuous and is not connected to the dispute with Paula.

D. That the exercise of personal jurisdiction over Dan is inconsistent with the Due Process Clause because there is no federal subject matter jurisdiction over this state law claim.

16. Plaintiffs purchase plane tickets over the internet to travel on Eagle Flight Airlines (Eagle). Eagle is a subsidiary of American Airways (Airways). The trip has Plaintiffs flying out of New York City's John F. Kennedy (JFK) airport to Charles de Gaulle (CDG) airport in Paris, France, on an Eagle flight. Plaintiffs are U.S. citizens and residents and citizens of New York State. Eagle is incorporated in Delaware, with its principal place of business in New Jersey. Airways is incorporated in Illinois, with its principal place of business in Chicago, Illinois. The "fine print" in the terms of the contract that Plaintiffs accepted when they agreed to purchase the plane tickets included a choice-of-forum clause stating that all litigation between the parties to the contract related to the tickets should be decided in the federal district court for the Northern District of Illinois. Plaintiffs are injured as their plane flies over international waters when turbulence causes a drink cart to crash into them. They bring a state tort action in federal court in New York State for the Eastern District of New York (the site of JKF airport) seeking $1,000,000 compensation for their extensive injuries. They sue both Eagle, the subsidiary, and Airways, the parent company. Both Defendants seek to transfer venue to the federal court for the Northern District of Illinois. Airways has an airport hub in JFK, and 20% of its hundreds of flights pass through that airport on a daily basis. JFK airport is a major hub for Eagle, and 50% of its flights pass through or commence from that airport. Plaintiffs have no connection to the state of Illinois other than the choice-of-forum clause contained in the contract. Defendants interpose answers in the action in

which they challenge venue in the Eastern District of New York and make a joint motion to transfer venue to the Northern District of Illinois.

Should the court grant Defendants' request to transfer venue?

A. The motion should be granted. The choice-of-forum clause controls the venue determination in this action.

B. The motion should be granted. Defendant Airways is at home in the Chicago forum and that is the only forum where it is subject to jurisdiction.

C. The motion should be denied. The choice-of-forum clause should not determine the venue of the action, and venue is proper in Plaintiffs' chosen forum.

D. The motion should be denied. Airways is not subject to jurisdiction in the Eastern District of New York.

17.   Plaintiff Pauline was hired as general counsel to a bank operating in New York State. Pauline learns that the bank is engaging in some unlawful actions with respect to its mortgage practices. She reports the actions to the bank's Board of Directors, which takes no action to correct the unlawful behavior. She reviews her ethical obligations under New York State's Rules of Professional Conduct, the code of ethics governing lawyers operating in the state. Those Rules require Pauline to "report out" such legal breaches by her company if she comes to learn of their existence; she determines that this means she must report to federal banking regulators that the bank has engaged in unlawful conduct and its Board of Directors has done nothing to stop such conduct from continuing. Pauline prepares a memorandum detailing the bank's misconduct. She then sends a copy of this memorandum to federal banking authorities. After she sends the memorandum to federal authorities, the bank fires her. Pauline alleges that she was fired because she sent the memorandum to the federal authorities.

Pauline files a lawsuit against her former employer in federal court in New York. She brings a federal claim under a whistleblower statute that protects the employees of federally insured financial institutions who report certain types of bank misconduct to federal officials, which is precisely what Pauline did. Pauline's bank is a financial institution covered under the law and her actions fall within the law's protections. Pauline also alleges that because she was employed as an attorney, there is an implied contract under state law that she should follow the state's ethical rules when she acts in this capacity. She believes she was following those ethics rules when she reported the bank's misconduct to federal authorities. Assume that Paula's theory about her implied contract claim is well established under New York law. Pauline seeks $250,000 in damages under each claim. Pauline is a resident of New York State. The bank is incorporated in Delaware, with its principal place of business in New York State.

May the court exercise supplemental jurisdiction over Pauline's implied contract claim?

A. No. The claim is based in state law, and it does not arise out of the same case or controversy as the federal claim.

B. Yes. The court may exercise supplemental jurisdiction over the state law claim because it arises out of the same nucleus of operative facts as the federal claim.

C. No. The state law claim dominates the federal claim, and supplemental jurisdiction is not warranted.

D. Yes. The court may exercise supplemental jurisdiction over the state contract law claim because the contract claim raises novel issues of state law.

18.　Plaintiff alleges that Defendant failed to pay for the delivery of a classic MX Roadster automobile valued at $100,000. Plaintiff operates an MX dealership in Columbia County, New York. Plaintiff is incorporated in New York, with its principal place of business in New York. Defendant is a resident and citizen of Connecticut, residing in the town of Sharon in that state. Plaintiff alleges that pursuant to a written contract between it and Defendant, Plaintiff delivered the automobile in question upon the alleged wire transfer of funds from Defendant's bank account into Plaintiff's bank account. Once Plaintiff received confirmation of the payment, it delivered the automobile in question via flatbed truck to Defendant at his home. Upon review of the wire transfer by Plaintiff's bank following delivery of the car, Plaintiff learned that Defendant's wire transfer was fraudulent. Plaintiff sues Defendant in state court in New York based on a state contract law claim, seeking $100,000 in damages. Defendant seeks to remove the case to federal court in Connecticut.

Will Defendant succeed in removing the case to federal court in Connecticut? If so, why? If not, why not?

A. Yes, because the basis for federal jurisdiction appears on the face of the well-pleaded complaint.

B. No, because the basis for federal jurisdiction does not appear on the face of the well-pleaded complaint.

C. No, because the case can only be removed, if at all, to federal court in New York.

D. Yes, because Defendant would face out-of-state bias against if the case were removed to federal court in New York.

19.   Plaintiff is a professor at a private university. She reviews her pay stubs for the past five years and discovers that her pay raise in 2010 seems surprisingly low. She reviews the university's guidelines for pay raises and determines that her 2010 pay raise violated the guidelines. This, in turn, means that she has not received adequate raises each year since 2010, as subsequent raises were determined by her base salary for that year. The inappropriate raise in 2010 thus had a ripple effect, meaning every year her salary increase was based on an inappropriately low base salary and was therefore lower than it should have been. She alleges this treatment is different from the treatment male professors have received. She contends that, as a result, she was discriminated against under federal civil rights statutes when she was denied a proper salary in 2010 and every year thereafter when her pay was artificially and illegally lower than it should have been based on the 2010 error. Plaintiff's attorney has compiled an analysis of the amount of money Plaintiff should have been paid over the years had her 2010 salary been accurately calculated. Plaintiff claims to have been underpaid $30,000 and has undisputed proof of this underpayment. Evidence her lawyer presents makes it clear that the university has violated federal civil rights statutes because no male professors were treated in this way. The university is a so-called "Ivy League" institution with a $4 billion endowment. Plaintiff's lawyer wants to bring a preliminary injunction at the early stages of the litigation because Plaintiff should not have to do without the money she is owed during the pendency of the action given the likelihood that the university violated important federal civil rights statutes.

If Plaintiff moves for a preliminary injunction seeking payment of the money owed her, which is the most likely outcome of the motion, and why?

A. The motion will be granted because she has established, among the other elements of the preliminary injunction standard, that she is likely to prevail on the merits.

B. The motion will be granted because Plaintiff can establish at a minimum that she is likely to prevail on the merits and that the balance of the equities tips in her favor due to the fact that the university has a large endowment and can afford to pay the damages she seeks during the pendency of the action.

C. The motion will be denied because Plaintiff does not have a likelihood of success on the merits.

D. The motion will be denied because there is no evidence that Plaintiff will suffer irreparable harm in the absence of the injunction.

20. Plaintiff is injured in an accident at her place of employment, an automobile manufacturing plant in Detroit, Michigan. She is a citizen of Michigan. Plaintiff is injured when the steel-cutting machine she is using goes off track and slices her arm, causing considerable damage to her wrist tendons. It is unlikely that she can continue to work in the only job she has had for the last twenty years. She consults with a lawyer, and an investigation of the machine she was using reveals that the blade apparatus on the machine might have been poorly designed and potentially prone to such accidents. She also discovers that the machine may not have been properly maintained by the outside contractor that the manufacturer hired to service the machine. The machine was designed and manufactured by Acme Tool & Die (Acme) and serviced by Brown Machine Service (Brown). Acme is incorporated in Delaware, with its principal place of business in Cleveland, Ohio. Brown is incorporated in Ohio, with its principal place of business in Toledo, Ohio. Plaintiff brings an action in federal court in Michigan asserting state law claims against Acme and seeking $1 million in damages. Acme professes its innocence, claiming its machine was not defectively designed. Acme also files a third-party complaint that seeks to join Brown as a third-party defendant, asserting that if Plaintiff was in fact injured by the machine, it was Brown's fault for failing to properly maintain the machine. To justify its third-party claim against Brown, Acme alleges that in the service contract entered into between Acme and Brown, Brown agreed to indemnify Acme for any injuries that result from poor maintenance performed by Brown on the machines. Brown will seek dismissal of the third-party complaint against it.

If Brown moves to dismiss the third-party complaint against it, what is the likely outcome of the motion, and why will the court reach that outcome?

A. The motion to dismiss the third-party complaint will be denied because Brown agreed to indemnify Acme for any injuries caused by faulty maintenance on the machines.

B. The motion to dismiss the third-party complaint will be granted because Acme has not alleged a sufficient basis for impleading Brown.

C. The motion to dismiss the third-party complaint will be denied because the claim against Brown arises out of the same nucleus of operative facts as the claims against Acme and these claims are logically related to each other.

D. The motion to dismiss the third-party complaint will be granted because Acme and Brown are not diverse and any attempt to join Brown will defeat diversity.

21.   MexiChem is a chemical manufacturer that supplied defoliation chemicals to the government of Guatarica, a small, Central American country that used such chemicals in its effort to suppress a rebel uprising there in the early 2000s. Civilians who fled the war-torn country file a suit in federal district court in California against MexiChem for the distribution of chemicals that Plaintiffs allege MexiChem knew were being used essentially as chemical weapons. Victims exposed to the chemicals in Guatarica suffered severe illnesses, and the children of women exposed to the chemicals during pregnancy suffer from severe birth defects. Plaintiffs file a lawsuit in federal district court in California. They seek $100 Million in damages from MexiChem, alleging a variety of state and federal claims. MexiChem is incorporated in Mexico, with its principal place of business in Mexico City, Mexico. Plaintiffs, now lawful permanent residents residing in California, allege that the chemicals used by the Guatarican government were manufactured in a plant in New Mexico in the United States. Plaintiffs also allege that some of MexiChem's newer chemicals, although not the ones used in Guatarica to suppress the rebellion, have been used throughout California in the last twelve months and that MexiChem has marketed those chemicals in California in print media targeted toward farmers operating in the state. Prior to the release of these new products, MexiChem had neither targeted nor entered the California market to sell its products. MexiChem is a sprawling multi-national corporation with distributors throughout North and Central America: in Canada, the United States (specifically and solely in the states of New Mexico, Oregon, and Washington), Mexico, Belize, Nicaragua El Salvador, Guatarica, and Costa Rica. It does an equal amount of business in each of the countries listed above. Its overall sales in California are still just a fraction of its total sales, the equivalent of less than 2% of its net annual revenue. All of the sales of the chemicals to the Guatarican military took place in Mexico City, Mexico. Plaintiffs' counsel serves a copy of the summons and complaint on a representative of MexiChem in the MexiChem main office in Mexico City, Mexico, in accordance with Rule 4 of the Federal Rules of Civil Procedure. Assume that the California long-arm statute authorizes courts operating in the state to exercise personal jurisdiction to the full extent of the U.S. Constitution's Due Process Clause.

If MexiChem moves to dismiss the action alleging that the California court lacks personal jurisdiction over it, will the court grant the motion on this ground? If so, why? If not, why not?

A. The motion will be denied because MexiChem's contacts with the forum state are systematic and continuous such that it is at home in the forum state.

B. The motion will be denied because MexiChem has sufficient contacts with the forum state such that the exercise of personal jurisdiction over it is consistent with traditional notions of fair play and substantial justice and is reasonable under the circumstances.

C. The motion will be granted because MexiChem's contacts with the forum state are not related to the dispute between the parties and are not systematic and continuous to such a degree that it is at home in that state.

D. The motion will be granted for the sole reason that MexiChem was not served personally in the forum state.

22. Plaintiff brings an action in federal district court in Florida alleging mortgage fraud against Delta Bank (Delta). Plaintiff is a citizen of Florida, and her home is located in Fort Lauderdale in that state. Delta is incorporated in Delaware, with its principal place of business in Atlanta, Georgia. Plaintiff alleges that Delta violated federal law when it made certain disclosures with respect to her mortgage loan when the loan agreement was reached between the parties, and she sues Delta seeking $100,000 in damages allowed under the applicable statute. Delta wants to interpose a counterclaim against Plaintiff alleging that Plaintiff made fraudulent disclosures about her annual income when the mortgage agreement was consummated, a violation of state law. The counterclaim seeks $80,000, the maximum statutory damages allowed.

Can Delta interpose its counterclaim in this action?

A. No, because the claim does not satisfy the amount-in-controversy requirement.

B. Yes, because regardless of whether the claim is a compulsory or permissive counterclaim, there is an independent basis of jurisdiction for it.

C. No, because there is not an independent basis of jurisdiction for the claim.

D. Yes, because the aggregation of Plaintiff's and Defendant's claims satisfies the amount-in-controversy requirement.

23. Plaintiff, a real estate developer, sues Able in federal court over his failure to make timely payments on a loan. The complaint seeks $500,000 in damages and compensation for claims arising under state contract law. Plaintiff has developed a multi-unit residential condominium building in New Jersey. Plaintiff's business model includes lending money to prospective homeowners to purchase condominium units within the building. Plaintiff has a contract with Able for the purchase of one of the units in the building. The contract includes a loan for the purchase of the apartment. The contract also permits Able to lease out the space it purchased to tenants or sell it to other parties, but Able is still obligated to pay under his agreement with Plaintiff. Plaintiff alleges it has not received payment on the loan to Able for several months, forcing it to initiate an action against Able. Plaintiff has not received payments from Baker either. In his answer, Able admits that he has not paid on the loan but alleges that he passed on his obligations to Baker, a new homeowner who has assumed Able's liabilities to Plaintiff. Able is a resident and citizen of New Jersey. Baker is a resident and citizen of New York who has purchased the apartment in Plaintiff's condominium from Able to serve as a weekend getaway from her home in Manhattan, New York. Plaintiff is incorporated in New York, with its principal place of business in New York. Plaintiff brings a diversity suit in federal court in New Jersey against Able alleging state contract law claims and seeking $500,000 in damages. Able attaches to his answer the contract between Able and Baker in which Baker agrees to assume all liabilities under the Plaintiff-Able loan agree-

ment and agrees to indemnify Able in the event Baker fails to uphold her obligations under the contract. Defendant Able seeks by way of a third-party complaint to add Baker as a third-party defendant and asserts a claim against her alleging that Baker is liable to Able for all or part of Plaintiff's claim against him. Assume that the court has subject matter jurisdiction over Able's third-party complaint against Baker. Plaintiff seeks to amend its complaint to add affirmative claims against Baker, also seeking $500,000 in damages, and does so within five days of receiving Able's answer and third-party complaint. The amendment also occurs well within the statute of limitations period for the underlying claims.

Can Plaintiff file new affirmative claims against third-party Defendant Baker in this action?

A. Yes. The amendment occurs within the statute of limitations period and is otherwise timely.

B. No. The court does not have subject matter jurisdiction over any affirmative claim by Plaintiff against Baker.

C. No. The court does not have subject matter jurisdiction over Plaintiff's claims against either defendant.

D. Yes. The court has subject matter jurisdiction over Plaintiff's claims against Able *and* Baker.

24. Plaintiff is concerned that planned actions of the City of Albany, New York, along the Corning Preserve waterfront will disrupt the habitat of rare migratory waterfowl that frequent the area. Disrupting this habitat will place the continued existence of the species in danger. Plaintiff brings an action in the local federal court under the federal Endangered Species Act to halt the planned actions of the City. Plaintiff files her complaint, and before the City can answer or move to dismiss the action, Plaintiff moves for a preliminary injunction seeking to halt the planned actions of the City during the pendency of Plaintiff's lawsuit.

If Plaintiff were to move for a preliminary injunction, which of the following will the court not take into account when ruling on the motion?

A. The likelihood that the actions of the City will generate irreparable harm.

B. Whether Plaintiff can establish the likelihood of success on the merits of the claim.

C. Whether the granting of the injunction is in the public interest.

D. Whether Plaintiff can establish that there is no plausible dispute regarding the claim for relief.

25. Plaintiff commences a products liability action in federal court against Defendant claiming that Defendant's Nimbus 3000, the latest model of the storied Nimbus line of snowmobiles produced by Defendant, has a design defect that causes the engine to stall when the snowmobile accelerates up inclines. The case proceeds on state law theories of recovery and seeks $500,000 in damages. Plaintiff, an individual, is a resident and citizen of New York State. Defendant is a corporation incorporated in Delaware, with its principal place of business in Vermont. Plaintiff is injured when Defendant's snowmobile stalls in such a climb, throwing Plaintiff from the vehicle. The case is in the discovery phase of the litigation in federal court when Plaintiff's counsel learns that another vehicle produced by Defendant, an all-terrain vehicle (ATV), is also the subject of lawsuits filed against the company. Those suits allege that the ATV's emission system does not comply with federal air quality guidelines. The Nimbus 3000, has been in production for the five years prior to the injury sustained by Plaintiff. In discovery, Plaintiff seeks records of all complaints received by Defendant related to the stalling problem in the Nimbus 3000 since it was first introduced and any records related to the emissions system of Defendant's ATV. Defendant opposes these requests and, after unsuccessfully attempting to resolve the dispute in good faith, seeks a protective order from the court that would alleviate the obligation to respond to the demands related to these two classes of information, arguing that the demands are overly broad, irrelevant, and unduly burdensome.

Will Defendant succeed in obtaining a protective order related to these two

classes of documents—those related to the Nimbus 3000 and those related to the ATV's alleged emissions issues—relieving Defendant of the obligation to respond to the demands for them?

A. The court will issue a protective order covering both classes of information and will completely relieve Defendant of the obligation to respond to the requests.

B. The court will issue a protective order regarding the emissions information for the ATV but not with respect to the information regarding the Nimbus 3000.

C. The court will issue a protective order regarding the information related to the Nimbus 3000 but not with respect to the ATV's emissions records.

D. The court will deny the request for a protective order regarding both classes of information.

26. Plaintiff sues Defendant, a private company that operates a bus service between New York City and Boston. Plaintiff alleges she was injured on one of Defendant's buses as it travelled through Connecticut. Defendant is incorporated in Delaware, with its principal place of business in Delaware. Plaintiff also names as defendants in her action several individual members of Defendant's corporate board who sit on a board committee responsible for the safety of Defendant's buses ("the safety committee"). The individual defendants named in the suit are all residents and citizens of Connecticut. Plaintiff is a resident and citizen of Massachusetts. Plaintiff alleges that the individual board members on the safety committee had knowledge of the safety flaws in the bus on which she was riding when she was injured. She alleges that these flaws are the reason the bus veered off the highway, causing her extensive injuries. Plaintiff brings her action in Delaware state court alleging state tort claims and seeking $150,000 in damages. Plaintiff alleges the Delaware court has personal jurisdiction over the individual defendants who are members of the safety committee on the basis that they generally participate in quarterly meetings of the full board of directors of the corporation. These meetings take place in Delaware, but the safety committee members join the meeting by teleconference. According to the corporate defendant's charter and Delaware law, a board member who attends a board meeting, even if by teleconference, is considered "present" in the state. Plaintiff does not allege that the board meetings in which the individual defendants participated by telephone were related to the safety issues she claims caused her inju-

ries. Members of the board's safety committee, sued in their individual capacities by Plaintiff, only discussed safety issues at meetings of the board's safety committee, held in one of the corporate defendant's satellite offices located in New York City. The safety committee members participated in those meeting in person. The individual defendants have no other contacts with the State of Delaware. The corporate defendant does not object to the exercise of personal jurisdiction over it. The individual defendants will challenge the Delaware court's exercise of personal jurisdiction over them as a violation of the Due Process Clause of the U.S. Constitution.

Will the individual defendants succeed in challenging the Delaware court's exercise of personal jurisdiction over them? If so, why? If not, why not?

A. Yes. The individual defendants will succeed in challenging the Delaware court's exercise of personal jurisdiction over them because their contacts with the forum state are both limited and unrelated to the dispute.

B. Yes. The individual defendants will succeed in challenging the Delaware court's exercise of personal jurisdiction over them because Plaintiff's action does not satisfy the amount-in-controversy requirement.

C. No. The individual defendants will not succeed in challenging the Delaware court's exercise of personal jurisdiction over them because the court can exercise quasi in rem jurisdiction over them.

D. No. The individual defendants will not succeed in challenging the Delaware court's exercise of personal jurisdiction over them because they were present in the forum state according to Delaware law such that the exercise of jurisdiction over them will not offend traditional notions of fair play and substantial justice.

27. Mayor Cathey Meehan of the city of Oshkosh, Wisconsin, has surprised everyone in the crowded field of presidential candidates by rising to the top of the primary in her party in the Iowa Caucuses. One day while on the campaign trail, her campaign bus is side-swiped while driving through the outskirts of Sioux City, Iowa, by a pickup truck that is in the fleet of Sioux City Construction. Sioux City Construction is based in Sioux City, Iowa, which is located in the jurisdiction of the federal court for the Northern District of Iowa. Three of Meehan's campaign workers, all residents and citizens of Wisconsin, are injured in the accident. Meehan's Iowa office is located in the City of Des Moines, which is located in the jurisdiction of the Southern District of Iowa. All of the actions giving rise to liability in this action, if any, occurred in the Northern District of Iowa. Sioux City Construction operates only in Sioux City and does not market its services or provide those services outside the jurisdiction of the Northern District of Iowa. It is incorporated in Iowa, with its principal place of business in Iowa. Thinking it will be more convenient to bring their action in Des Moines where their office is located, the three injured campaign workers file their action in the federal court for the Southern District of Iowa, which encompasses Des Moines. They seek $1.2 million in damages, $400,000 each, under state law theories of recovery. Sioux City Construction will move to dismiss the action for want of personal jurisdiction and lack of subject matter jurisdiction; in the alternative, it will seek to transfer venue to the Northern District of Iowa.

How will the court rule with respect to the motions?

A. The court will deny the motions to dismiss for lack of personal jurisdiction and subject matter jurisdiction but grant the motion to transfer venue.

B. The court will dismiss the case by granting the motion challenging personal jurisdiction, which will render the other two motions moot.

C. The court will deny all three motions.

D. The court will dismiss the case by granting the motion challenging the court's subject matter jurisdiction, which will render the other two motions moot.

28. Plaintiff is a resident and citizen of Albany, New York, who lives on a stream that feeds into the Hudson River. Upstream from Plaintiff's residence there is a quartz mine, operated by Quartz, Inc. (Quartz), that sometimes releases toxic chemicals into the stream. Plaintiff alleges that this affects the well on her property, which is fed from the polluted stream and from which she draws much of her drinking water. She brings an action in state court in New York alleging that Quartz is violating federal environmental statutes, including the Clean Water Act, by polluting the stream and her well. There is concurrent state and federal jurisdiction over the statutes that form the basis of Plaintiff's complaint. Plaintiff alleges Defendant's actions have made her ill, caused her significant pain and suffering, and resulted in her missing many days of work. Plaintiff, a successful trial lawyer who has had trouble serving her clients and has lost several of them as a result, seeks $500,000 in damages. Quartz is incorporated in Delaware, with its principal place of business in Ithaca, New York. Quartz will seek to remove the case to federal court in the jurisdiction encompassing the state court where the action was filed.

If Quartz seeks to remove Plaintiff's case to federal court, will the effort be successful? If so, why? If not, why not?

A. The removal request will be unsuccessful because the state court has concurrent jurisdiction over the claim in the complaint.

B. The removal request will be unsuccessful because Defendant cannot remove the case to federal court in a state in which it has its principal place of business.

C. The removal request will be successful because the basis of jurisdiction appears on the face of the complaint.

D. The removal request will be successful because Plaintiff's claim satisfies the amount-in-controversy requirement.

29. Plaintiff is hit by a delivery truck while on a weekend vacation in Montreal, Canada. Plaintiff is a resident of Plattsburgh, New York, and a citizen of New York State. Defendant is a Canadian company, with its principal place of business in Canada. Defendant produces snowshoes and delivers its snowshoes throughout Canada and the northeast United States, including New York State. Plaintiff brings an action in federal court for the Northern District of New York seeking $200,000 in damages on state law theories of recovery for the personal injuries she suffered in the accident in Montreal. Defendant seeks to dismiss the case on *forum non conveniens* grounds, arguing that all of the sources of proof and witnesses are in Canada. Plaintiff opposes the motion, arguing that the court in Canada will not further substantive social policies important to the transnational scheme of highway safety because Canada does not recognize strict liability in automobile accidents, which makes Plaintiff's ability to prove Defendant's guilt much more difficult.

Will Plaintiff succeed in opposing the motion to dismiss on *forum non conveniens* grounds?

A. Yes, because the Canadian court does not recognize strict liability.

B. Yes, because dismissal on *forum non conveniens* grounds will not advance critical substantive social policies.

C. No, because Plaintiff has not shown that it will have no remedy in a Canadian court.

D. No, because Defendant is not subject to personal jurisdiction in New York.

30. Pauline makes a living playing the popular poker game "Texas Hold 'Em." She is very good at it and regularly brings in over $10 million in earnings annually by playing in nationally televised tournaments. Danny is an investigator for the New York Gambling Commission, a state agency that regulates gambling in New York State. Danny believes Pauline cheats, and he wants to report her to the New York State Office of the Attorney General for fraud. Danny is a resident and citizen of New York State. He tracks Pauline's every move, taps her cell phone, hacks her computer, and even enters her hotel room without a warrant while she is out gambling at several of New York State's gambling establishments in order to try to figure out how she is cheating. Pauline learns she is being tracked and that Danny has broken into her hotel room without a warrant. Pauline is a resident and citizen of California. Pauline brings an action in state court in New York alleging Danny violated her federal constitutional rights when he entered her hotel room without a warrant, tapped her cell phone, and hacked her computer. There is concurrent state and federal jurisdiction over Pauline's claims. She seeks $1 million in damages for violation of her constitutional rights. Danny seeks to remove the case to federal court, and Pauline opposes the effort.

Will Danny succeed in removing the case to federal court? If so, why? If not, why not?

A. No. The court will remand the case to state court because Danny is an agent of the state and not an employee of the federal government.

B. No. There is concurrent federal and state jurisdiction over this action and, because Danny is a resident and citizen of New York State, the matter cannot be removed to a federal court in his home state.

C. Yes. Pauline is suing Danny in a state in which there are sufficient minimum contacts to justify the exercise of jurisdiction over him in a federal court.

D. Yes. The basis for federal jurisdiction appears on the face of the well-pleaded complaint.

31. Plaintiff files an action against a manufacturer of durable medical equipment (Dura) alleging that a device inserted in his body to monitor his blood glucose levels was installed improperly. Plaintiff is a resident and citizen of Rhode Island. The operation in which the Dura device was installed in Plaintiff took place at Boston General Hospital (Boston General), and the operation was carried out by Doctor Qyburn (Qyburn). Plaintiff brings an action against Dura in federal district court in Massachusetts alleging state law theories of recovery and seeking over $2 million in damages. Dura is incorporated in Delaware, with its principal place of business in Massachusetts. Boston General is incorporated in Massachusetts, with its principal place of business in that state. Qyburn is a resident and citizen of Maine. Dura will seek to implead both Boston General and Qyburn, alleging that they are jointly and severally liable with Dura for Plaintiff's injuries, if any. Qyburn now wishes to interpose cross-claims based on state law against Boston General, seeking $100,000 on each claim. Qyburn asserts that Boston General failed to compensate Qyburn for the operation performed on Plaintiff in which the Dura device was installed (Cross-claim 1) as well as for the hospital's failure to pay for services performed by Qyburn that are unrelated to the operation performed on Plaintiff (Cross-claim 2). Boston General will seek to dismiss both cross-claims.

Which is an accurate statement with respect to Qyburn's two cross-claims?

A. Qyburn must assert Cross-claim 1 and may assert Cross-claim 2 provided there is an independent basis of subject matter jurisdiction for doing so.

B. Qyburn is permitted to raise Cross-claim 1 but is not required to do so; Qyburn is not permitted to interpose Cross-claim 2.

C. Qyburn is not permitted to interpose either cross-claim.

D. Qyburn must assert both cross-claims.

32. While driving from her home in New York to her vacation time-share in Florida, Paula is injured in a car accident in Virginia. She is rear-ended by a distracted driver, Dan, while at a stoplight. Her car was stationary at the time she was hit, and the other driver, a driver for Danco, Inc., who was texting at the time of the accident, did not realize the stoplight at the intersection had turned red. Paula, a resident of New York, commences a case in state court in New York against Danco. Danco is incorporated in Virginia, with its principal place of business in Virginia. The suit alleges negligence under New York law and seeks $200,000 in damages. Danco is a startup company that has just begun to provide consulting services to companies that operate wind turbines, and its goal is to expand the business throughout the United States. One year prior to the accident, Danco secured its first and only large contract with TurbineNY, a large public-private partnership located in New York State that is creating a wind farm on the outskirts of the Adirondacks, in New York State. Since securing the contract, Danco has stationed ten of its employees as technicians on site with TurbineNY in New York State. Danco employs just fifteen employees altogether, including the ten now stationed in New York. Those workers consult with TurbineNY as it sets up the wind farm using Danco's turbines. The current plan is for the Danco employees to consult with TurbineNY on site indefinitely throughout the life of the wind turbine project, which could last at least 20 years. New York's long-arms statute reads in relevant part that a corporation that "regularly conducts business in the state" is subject to personal jurisdiction for all harm

caused to individuals in the state, whether that harm is caused in the state or outside of it. Assume for the sake of this question that the trial court has found that Danco is responsible for the conduct of its driver in striking Paula and that Danco's conduct engaging with TurbineNY falls within the long-arm statute's definition of "regularly conduct[ing] business in the state." None of Danco's agents are served with service of process while present in the state, however. Danco's lawyer wants to challenge the personal jurisdiction of the court over Danco in the action commenced by Paula.

If Danco's conduct in New York State does bring it within the reach of the state's long-arm statute, a court determining whether the exercise of personal jurisdiction over Danco is consistent with the Due Process Clause of the U.S. Constitution is likely to find which of the following?

A. That the exercise of personal jurisdiction over Danco is consistent with the Due Process Clause because Danco's conduct and presence in the forum state is systematic and continuous such that it is essentially at home in the forum state, even though it is not connected to the controversy with Paula.

B. That the exercise of personal jurisdiction over Danco is consistent with the Due Process Clause because it is tied specifically to the conduct that caused injury to Paula.

C. That the exercise of personal jurisdiction over Danco is inconsistent with the Due Process Clause because its connection to the forum state has not been systematic and continuous and is not connected to the dispute with Paula.

D. That the exercise of personal jurisdiction over Danco is inconsistent with the Due Process Clause because there is no federal subject matter jurisdiction over this state law claim.

33. Plaintiff operates a car dealership selling Hessla vehicles, a new generation of electric car. Plaintiff is an independent contractor who resides in and is a citizen of New York State. Hessla is a company incorporated in Michigan, with its principal place of business in Delaware. Plaintiff and Hessla have an arrangement, consistent with the type of arrangement Hessla makes with all of its dealerships: Plaintiff pays a small fee to Hessla to sell Hessla vehicles, and Hessla maintains ownership over all of its vehicles, even those in Plaintiff's lot, until they are sold by Plaintiff. Plaintiff earns a $10,000 commission from Hessla for each sale of a luxury vehicle.

One Saturday, Plaintiff has a good day. She sells eight Hessla vehicles in a single day, a new personal record, and she is very pleased with her success. That night, however, a terrible storm passes through the Capital Region of New York, where Plaintiff's lot is located. The storm fells several trees, and the new Hessla vehicles that Plaintiff had just sold (although title had not yet transferred to the buyers) are in their path, resulting in significant damage to the vehicles. Hessla refuses to pay Plaintiff her commission of $80,000 on the sold Hessla vehicles, and Plaintiff brings an action in federal court for the Northern District of New York, the federal court encompassing Plaintiff's lot, seeking the $80,000 in commission under state contract law theories of recovery. When Hessla files its answer, it includes a defense that it should not have to pay Plaintiff her commission and brings a counterclaim under state law for $800,000, the cost of the vehicles damaged in the storm. Hessla's defense is based on a clause in the contract between Hessla and Plaintiff that says Plaintiff must use due care to protect the vehicles maintained on her lot from damage. According to the contract between Plaintiff and Hessla, any negligence on the part of Plaintiff in caring for these vehicles voids any commission Plaintiff might have earned on the sale of such vehicles. Hessla alleges that Plaintiff did not uphold her contractual obligations because she failed to provide the requisite level of care with respect to the damaged vehicles; thus, Hessla is not obligated to pay Plaintiff her commission. Moreover, Hessla's counterclaim is also based on this failure to exhibit the requisite level of care required under the contract; it alleges that this failure to uphold Plaintiff's obligations is what led directly to the damages to Hessla's vehicles being stored on Plaintiff's lot. When Plaintiff receives the answer with the counterclaim, she wants to amend her complaint to implead Tate Farm Insurance (Tate Farm), the insurance company that insures her lot from damages. Plaintiff correctly asserts that subrogation covers the relationship between Tate Farm and Plaintiff, and if Plaintiff is liable to Hessla, Tate Farm is, in turn, liable to Plaintiff for any successful damage claim Hessla should obtain on its counterclaim. Tate Farm is incorporated in Connecticut, with its principal place of business in Connecticut. Notwithstanding her effort to implead Tate Farm, Plaintiff makes a motion to dismiss Hessla's counterclaim, and Hessla, in turn, moves to dismiss that portion of the amended complaint impleading Tate Farm into the case.

Which of the two motions (Plaintiff's motion to dismiss the counterclaim and Hessla's motion to dismiss that portion of the amended complaint that seeks to

implead Tate Farm) will be successful, if either?

A. The motion to dismiss that portion of the amended complaint that seeks to implead Tate Farm will be successful but not the motion to dismiss the counterclaim.

B. The motion to dismiss that portion of the amended complaint that seeks to implead Tate Farm and the motion to dismiss the counterclaim will be successful.

C. The motion to dismiss the counterclaim will be successful but not the motion to dismiss that portion of the amended complaint that seeks to implead Tate Farm.

D. Neither the motion to dismiss that portion of the amended complaint that seeks to implead Tate Farm nor the motion to dismiss the counterclaim will be successful.

34.   Paula Parr sues DeLacroix Opticians in state court in Louisiana alleging violation of federal civil rights statutes. According to the complaint, the business, an eye-glasses store in the French Quarter of New Orleans, is not wheelchair accessible. Paula is a resident of New Orleans, Louisiana, and DeLacroix is a corporation organized under the laws of Louisiana, with its principal place of business in New Orleans, Louisiana. The cost of making the business wheelchair accessible is relatively minimal. The entrance to the storefront is at sidewalk grade, but the wooden door, an original French Quarter wooden frame, is so narrow that it does not comply with the federal Americans with Disabilities Act (ADA), a claim for which the state courts have concurrent jurisdiction. Since DeLacroix recently made some renovations to the store, it is obligated to be fully wheelchair accessible under the ADA. The door can be modified for approximately $10,000.

Can DeLacroix remove Plaintiff's action to federal court? If so, why? If not, why not?

A. No. Both parties are from Louisiana, and thus there is not complete diversity between the parties.

B. Yes. The federal claim appears on the face of the well-pleaded complaint.

C. Yes. A case brought by a home-state plaintiff in state court can always be removed to federal court to avoid potential parochial bias against the defendant.

D. No. The action does not satisfy the amount-in-controversy requirement.

35. Plaintiff, a resident and citizen of New York, wants to bring an action against her former employer alleging she was terminated from her employment for bringing to the attention of state authorities the fact that the employer, a nursing home, was not following proper state-mandated procedures for addressing the Covid-19 pandemic. A state law provides what are known as "whistleblower protections" for any nursing home employees who report violations of state health and safety guidelines in light of the pandemic. Plaintiff commences her action in state court in Albany County, New York, the location of the nursing home facility where she worked. That facility is run by Defendant, a company incorporated in Delaware, with its principal place of business in Massachusetts. Plaintiff will seek $200,000 in damages, an amount equivalent to Plaintiff's lost wages since she was terminated. Defendant will seek to remove the case to the Springfield Division of the District Court of Massachusetts in Western Massachusetts, the division that encompasses Defendant's principal place of business, alleging that the court has diversity jurisdiction over the action.

Will Defendant succeed in removing the case to the federal court in Massachusetts? If so, why? If not, why not?

A. No, because the basis for federal jurisdiction does not appear on the face of the complaint.

B. Yes, because the basis for federal jurisdiction appears on the face of the complaint.

C. No, because the matter can only be removed to the federal district that encompasses the state court where the action is currently pending.

D. Yes, because Defendant's principal place of business is in Massachusetts, and thus it is at home there for the purposes of subject matter jurisdiction and removal.

36. Able Corp. (Able) operates a franchise store of Baker King (Baker), a cookie company that specializes in serving college towns. When Able began operating as a franchise of Baker, it entered into a contract which provides that New York contract law would govern any disputes between Baker and any franchisee. Able is incorporated in Delaware, with its principal place of business in New Jersey. Baker is incorporated in New York, with its principal place of business in New York as well. Able has become concerned that, because of some malfeasance by members of Baker's leadership (it is alleged to have paid bribes to government health inspectors in New Jersey), the Baker King brand has been diminished, and fewer customers are patronizing Able's Baker King franchise in Newark, New Jersey, as a result. Able brings an action on state law grounds arguing that Baker King is in violation of its contract with Able because it has failed to ensure that the Baker brand is not diminished in any way during the course of the franchise contract between Baker and Able. Able also sues the Chief Executive Officer (CEO) of Baker, Chip Charlie (Charlie), for Charlie's outrageous behavior at a public event at a golf course in New Jersey, which Able argues has further diminished the Baker brand and constitutes tortious interference with contract, also a state law claim. Able brings its action in federal court in New Jersey, seeking $500,000 in damages on all claims against the defendants, Baker and Charlie. Baker has significant contacts with the state of New Jersey, and all of the interactions between Baker and Able occurred in New Jersey. Charlie is a resident and citizen of Connecticut. In addition to Charlie's bad behavior, Able alleges that the bulk of the action of Baker's leadership which amounted to corporate malfeasance of which Able complains also occurred in New Jersey. Upon commencement and filing of the action, Baker and Charlie will seek to transfer the case to the federal district court for the Southern District of New York, the district that encompasses Baker's principal place of business and Charlie's primary place of employment as CEO of Baker, claiming the choice of law clause determines venue in the action.

Will the defendants' motion to transfer venue to federal court in New York succeed? If so, why? If not, why not?

A. Yes, because the choice-of-law clause in the contract between Able and Baker requires that the matter be resolved in a New York court.

B. Yes, because the choice-of-law clause means a non-New York forum will be unfamiliar with the appropriate law to apply.

C. No, because the proper motion to make in response to a choice-of-law clause is a motion to dismiss based on *forum non conveniens* grounds, not a motion to transfer venue.

D. No, because the choice-of-law clause does not determine venue and there are other grounds upon which the court will find venue is appropriate in New Jersey.

37.   Plaintiff, a world-famous sculptor, wants to bring an action against Defendant for an alleged breach of a contract between the parties. Plaintiff alleges she was not paid for the delivery of a sculpture she made for Defendant's office in lower Manhattan, in New York City. Plaintiff's action seeks over $1 million in damages on a state contract claim. Plaintiff, an individual, is a resident and citizen of New York. Defendant, also an individual, is a resident and citizen of Connecticut, with her principal place of business in New York. Plaintiff wants to file her action in federal court in New York. The applicable New York statute governing the procedure of the action, were it filed in state court, authorizes service of the summons and complaint in Plaintiff's action by certified mail to Defendant's principal place of business. Plaintiff's lawyer follows this New York statute in carrying out service in the lawsuit upon defendant. Defendant will challenge the manner of service as inconsistent with the Federal Rules of Civil Procedure only, and will not challenge the constitutionality of the manner of service.

Was service on Defendant in the manner in which it was carried out in Plaintiff's federal action consistent with a manner of service authorized under the Federal Rules of Civil Procedure? If so, why? If not, why not?

A. No, the manner of service utilized by Plaintiff's counsel was not authorized under the Federal Rules of Civil Procedure because it does not expressly contemplate service by certified mail upon a person's principal place of business.

B. Yes, because the manner of service was consistent with the applicable state statute and thus authorized under the Federal Rules of Civil Procedure.

C. Yes, because service upon a defendant's principal place of business, even if by certified mail, is expressly permitted under the Federal Rules of Civil Procedure.

D. No, because service was not made upon an individual designated to accept service for the defendant.

38. Plaintiff works in a restaurant in New York City's swanky SoHo neighborhood. One day, a grease fire injures her as she is preparing the restaurant's signature dish: fried Snickers bars. Plaintiff cannot sue her employer under New York State's worker's compensation scheme but plans to sue FryOLator, the company that sold the restaurant the frying machine which caught on fire and caused Plaintiff's extensive injuries. Plaintiff is a resident of New Jersey. FryOLator is incorporated in New York State, with its principal place of business in New York City. FryOLator alleges the reason Plaintiff suffered injuries is because of a defective heating coil in the machine used in the restaurant at which Plaintiff worked. FryOLator admits that it installed the heating coils and is responsible for any injury that resulted from use of the FryOLator, but it alleges that the manufacturer of the coils, Coils-R-Us, is liable to it for any injuries resulting from the use of those coils pursuant to an express provision in the contract between FryOLator and Coils-R-Us. In that contract, Coils-R-Us agrees to indemnify FryOLator for all injuries that result from the use of its products. Coils-R-Us is located in Paramus, New Jersey, fifty miles from the courthouse in the Southern District of New York in Manhattan where Plaintiff files her action based on state law theories of recovery seeking $250,000 in damages. Coils-R-Us has no connection to New York, however. It markets its restaurant supply materials only in New Jersey. It is incorporated in New Jersey, with its principal place of business in New Jersey. The coils used in the fry machine that injured Plaintiff were sold from the Coils-R-Us retail store in Paramus. Within ten days of filing its answer to the complaint that names only FryOLator as a defendant, FryOLator's lawyer serves Coils-R-Us in its office in Paramus with a third-party complaint pursuant to Rule 14. Coils-R-Us moves to dismiss the third-party complaint for want of personal jurisdiction over it.

Will the motion by Coils-R-Us to dismiss the third-party complaint against it on personal jurisdiction grounds succeed? If so, why? If not, why not?

A. The motion will be granted because there is no specific jurisdiction over Coils-R-Us in this action.

B. The motion will be granted because there is neither specific nor general personal jurisdiction over Coils-R-Us in this action and it was not served personally in the district in which the action was commenced.

C. The motion will be denied because Coils-R-Us was served personally in its offices in Paramus, New Jersey.

D. The motion will be denied because Coils-R-Us is subject to personal jurisdiction in this action because of its proximity to the courthouse in which the action was filed.

39. Plaintiff and Defendant are in federal court in an action alleging violations of federal antitrust laws. Plaintiff's counsel serves upon Defendant's counsel a demand for certain documents. Defendant's counsel believes, in good faith, that it can make out a plausible argument that Plaintiff's demand seeks documents that contain hearsay and are thus inadmissible in court. As a result, Defendant's counsel argues that it should not have to turn over such documents. Plaintiff's counsel sends an email to Defendant's counsel seeking to resolve the dispute. Defendant's counsel responds to the email, saying that Defendant will not turn over the documents, still asserting that the documents are inadmissible and thus not subject to discovery. Plaintiff then moves for an order to compel Defendant to respond to the document demands. The court rules on the motion, finding that Defendant's position with respect to these documents is baseless and that Defendant must respond to the demand for production of documents. After receiving this favorable ruling, Plaintiff makes a second motion asking the court to order Defendant to pay reasonable expenses including attorney's fees which Plaintiff incurred in making the motion to compel. Defendant opposes this motion.

Will the court order Defendant to pay the reasonable costs incurred by Plaintiff in making the motion to compel? If so, why? If not, why not?

A. Yes, because Defendant's counsel did not cooperate in resolving the dispute prior to Plaintiff's making the motion.

B. No, because Defendant had a plausible basis for objecting to the demand for the production of documents.

C. Yes, because Defendant's position was not substantially justified in objecting to the demand for the production of documents.

D. No, because the demand sought evidence inadmissible at trial.

40. Plaintiff sues Defendants, several telecommunications companies, alleging antitrust violations in their pricing strategies. Specifically, Plaintiff alleges that the companies conspired to fix the prices of broadband internet services in several communities. One of the pieces of evidence Plaintiff attempts to obtain from Defendants is emails between representatives of the different companies which were sent prior to the commencement of the action. Plaintiff believes these emails will show that these representatives conspired to fix prices. Plaintiff is able to obtain several months of emails between the parties that seem to hint that there are other communications in which price-fixing was discussed. Several critical months of emails are missing, however, and Defendants allege that the emails were destroyed.

Which of the following issues is irrelevant as to whether the court should issue a directive to the jury to consider the missing evidence to be harmful to Defendants?

A. Whether Defendants will be harmed should the directive be granted.

B. Whether the apparent destruction of the emails was carried out with a culpable state of mind.

C. Whether Defendants were under an obligation to preserve the emails from destruction.

D. Whether the evidence is relevant to Plaintiff's claims.

41. Plaintiff brings an action in federal court to enjoin certain actions of the New York State Office of Temporary and Disability Assistance (OTDA), the state agency responsible for ensuring localities distribute welfare assistance to the state's indigent population. Plaintiff alleges that the manner in which OTDA distributes such benefits violates the Due Process Clause of the Fourteenth Amendment—that the system denies welfare beneficiaries property without due process of law because it cuts beneficiaries off from assistance without resort to a hearing before doing so. Plaintiff's action seeks a preliminary injunction to halt all welfare terminations during the pendency of the action.

If Plaintiff is going to move for a preliminary injunction, which of the following is *not* an element the court should take into account in ruling on the motion for a preliminary injunction?

A. The likelihood of Plaintiff's success on the merits of the action.

B. The likelihood of irreparable harm in the absence of the injunction.

C. Whether the equities tip in favor of Plaintiff.

D. Whether there exists a good faith basis for the reversal, extension, or modification of existing law in the issuance of the injunction.

42. Mary is involved in an automobile accident while on vacation in Italy. The accident involves Mary and a Dutch motorist who is also on vacation. Mary was driving a Volkswagen on lease from Italia Rentals. The Dutch motorist (Defendant Driver) was renting a French-made Renault from Roma Rentals. Both Italia and Roma are Italian companies. Mary alleges Defendant Driver was driving negligently when he swerved and hit her car on a dangerous stretch of road outside a Tuscan hill town. Defendant alleges that the steering column on the Renault was defective, which caused him to swerve, and that he was neither driving negligently nor unsafely on the dangerous stretch of road. Mary learns that Defendant is traveling to New York City where he regularly does business, and she commences an action in federal district court for the Southern District of New York seeking $500,000 in damages. She sues Defendant Driver and Renault. She serves Driver personally, and Renault receives the summons and complaint through an agent in New York who is authorized to accept service of process on behalf of Renault. The Dutch motorist's automobile involved in the accident was designed in France, assembled in Italy, and purchased in Italy by Roma Rentals. The cars involved in the accident have been impounded in Italy and are being maintained in their damaged state in a warehouse operated by the insurance company for Renault. Defendant Driver and Renault make a motion to dismiss the action based on *forum non conveniens* grounds.

When the court considers the motion, it should *not* take into account which of the following?

A. Whether a trier of fact in New York could view the scene of the accident.

B. The cost of obtaining testimony from witnesses to the accident who are willing to testify.

C. Whether there is a basis for the court to exercise subject matter jurisdiction over the action based on the diversity of the parties.

D. The burden on a New York jury in handling a matter that arose in Italy.

43. Plaintiff is a corporation incorporated in Delaware, with its principal place of business in Connecticut. Defendant is a corporation incorporated in New York, with its principal place of business in New York. Plaintiff wishes to file a lawsuit against Defendant seeking $100,000 in damages under a single claim based on federal securities laws. Plaintiff wishes to commence the case in state court because there is concurrent jurisdiction over Plaintiff's claims in federal and state court. Plaintiff brings the action in state court in Albany County, where Defendant has its principal place of business. Defendant wishes to remove the case to federal court for the Northern District of New York, the district encompassing Albany County.

Will Defendant succeed in removing the case to federal court? If so, why? If not, why not?

A. Yes, because the basis for federal jurisdiction appears on the face of the complaint.

B. No, even though the parties are diverse and the case satisfies the amount-in-controversy requirement.

C. No, because an in-state defendant cannot remove a case to the federal court of its home state.

D. Yes, because Plaintiff will be at a disadvantage in state court in New York because Plaintiff would be considered an out-of-state party.

44. Plaintiffs are several tourists who were injured in a bus crash in Rome, Italy. One of the main reasons for the crash is a defect in the design of the steering column in the bus. Because of the design flaw, substandard parts used in the manufacturing of the column gave way and caused the steering column to crack. As a result, the driver lost control of the steering on the vehicle. The bus involved in the accident was manufactured in Detroit, Michigan, by GM. Its steering column was manufactured by Japan Manufacturing (Japan) and contained parts purchased from Beijing Industries (Beijing). Beijing is a Chinese corporation, incorporated in and based in China, that supplies parts to companies throughout the world, including the United States. The bus was sold by GM to a company in Italy. GM is based in Detroit, where it is incorporated and where it has its principal place of business. Japan is a Japanese corporation, incorporated in Japan, with its principal place of business in Tokyo, and it has several large plants in Tennessee where it manufactures steering columns, including the column for the bus involved in the accident that injured Plaintiffs. Beijing is aware that its parts are used in steering columns manufactured in Tennessee by Japan, and it ships its parts directly to the Japan plants there, including the parts used in the steering column that failed in the accident that harmed Plaintiffs. Plaintiffs are residents of North Carolina. Plaintiffs bring an action against GM and Japan in federal court in Tennessee based on diversity jurisdiction alleging state law tort claims and seeking $10 million in damages. Japan claims it is jointly and severally liable with Beijing should the court find Japan responsible for the accident. It claims the parts supplied by Beijing were defective and that if Japan is liable to Plaintiffs, Beijing will be liable to Japan for all or part of those claims against it based on the clause in the contract between Japan and Beijing which provides that Beijing will indemnify Japan should any of Beijing's parts fail, as Japan claims occurred in the accident. Japan moves to dismiss the action against it for Plaintiffs' failure to join Beijing in federal court in Tennessee because, it alleges, Beijing is jointly and severally liable with Japan, making Beijing a necessary party in the action.

What is the likely outcome of Japan's motion to dismiss?

A. The court will grant the motion because it cannot obtain personal jurisdiction over Beijing.

B. The court will determine whether any of the parties will be prejudiced by Beijing's absence and whether it can issue complete relief to Plaintiffs without Beijing in the case before it decides to dismiss the case.

C. The court will grant the motion because Beijing is jointly and severally liable to Plaintiffs with Japan.

D. The court will deny the motion despite the fact that Beijing is jointly and severally liable to Plaintiffs with Japan.

Chapter 9

Answer Key

Chapter 1: Personal Jurisdiction

1.1 Specific Jurisdiction

1. B   2. B

1.2 General Jurisdiction

3. C   4. A   5. D

1.3 Other Issues Related to Personal Jurisdiction: Tag Jurisdiction, "Consent" Jurisdiction, and Long-Arm Statutes

6. C   7. C   8. D

1.4 Service of Process and Waiver of Service of Process

9. C   11. C   13. B   15. A

10. B   12. C   14. C   16. C

1.5 "Mixed" Questions

17. A   21. D   25. B   29. A

18. C   22. A   26. B   30. A

19. C   23. B   27. B

20. B   24. C   28. A

1.6 Venue

31. C   34. C   37. D   40. D

32. D   35. A   38. B   41. D

33. A   36. B   39. A

1.7 The Doctrine of Forum Non Conveniens

42. B   43. C   44. A   45. C

1.8 Formative Assessment Quiz

46. C	49. B	52. C	55. A
47. A	50. B	53. A	
48. C	51. A	54. C	

Chapter 2: Subject Matter Jurisdiction

2.1 Federal Question

1. B	2. D

2.2 Diversity Jurisdiction

3. D	5. A	7. B
4. B	6. D	8. C

2.3 Supplemental Jurisdiction

9. D	12. C	15. B	18. D
10. C	13. D	16. B	19. D
11. B	14. A	17. C	

2.4 "Mixed" Jurisdiction Questions

20. B	23. A	26. C	29. A
21. B	24. C	27. B	30. A
22. D	25. A	28. C	31. C

2.5 Removal and Remand

32. B	36. A	40. B	44. D
33. C	37. C	41. C	45. C
34. B	38. D	42. B	46. A
35. C	39. C	43. A	

2.6 Formative Assessment Quiz

47. A	51. B	55. D	59. A
48. C	52. A	56. B	
49. B	53. A	57. B	
50. A	54. B	58. A	

Chapter 3: The *Erie* Doctrine, Claim Preclusion and Issue Preclusion, and Preliminary Relief

3.1 The Erie Doctrine

1. D   2. B   3. D

3.2 Claim Preclusion and Issue Preclusion

4. D   5. B   6. B

3.3 Preliminary and Interim Relief

7. C   9. A   11. C
8. B   10. D   12. B

3.4 Formative Assessment Quiz

13. C   14. A   15. C

Chapter 4: Joinder

4.1 Joinder of Claims

1. C   2. D

4.2 Counterclaims and Cross-Claims

3. C   5. A   7. D   9. D
4. C   6. A   8. C

4.3 Joinder of Parties

10. A   11. C   12. A

4.4 Impleader

13. D   15. B   17. C
14. D   16. B

4.5 New Claims After Joinder

18. D   20. D   22. C   24. C
19. A   21. A   23. B

4.6 Necessary and Indispensable Parties

| 25. C | 26. C | 27. B | 28. C |

4.7 Service of Process Issues Related to Joinder

29. A

4.8 Formative Assessment Quiz

30. B	33. C	36. A	39. A
31. D	34. B	37. A	
32. A	35. B	38. C	

Chapter 5: Pleading

5.1 General Requirements

| 1. A | 3. A | 5. C |
| 2. B | 4. D | |

5.2 Responding to the Complaint

| 6. B | 7. A | 8. C | 9. D |

5.3 Rule 11

| 10. C | 12. C | 14. C | 16. D |
| 11. D | 13. A | 15. C | 17. C |

5.4 Amending Pleadings

| 18. B | 19. A | 20. B |

5.5 Formative Assessment Quiz

21. B	24. C	27. A
22. B	25. B	28. B
23. D	26. B	29. C

Chapter 6: Discovery

6.1 Scope of Discovery

1. B   2. C

6.2 Tools of Discovery

3. B   5. C   7. C
4. C   6. A   8. C

6.3 Motion Practice and Penalties Related to Discovery

9. D   11. B   13. B
10. C   12. D

6.4 Formative Assessment Quiz

14. B   15. D   16. C

Chapter 7: Summary Judgment, Trials, and Appeals

7.1 Summary Judgment and Other Resolutions Without Trial

1. B   3. C   5. A   7. C
2. A   4. C   6. D   8. B

7.2 Jury Trial Matters and Pre-Trial Maneuvers

9. C   10. C   11. B

7.3 Post-Trial Maneuvers

12. A   13. D   14. D

7.4 Appeals

15. B   17. C
16. D   18. B

7.5 Formative Assessment Quiz

19. C   20. B   21. C   22. D

Chapter 8: Summative Exam

1. B	12. D	23. B	34. B
2. D	13. C	24. D	35. C
3. C	14. A	25. B	36. D
4. D	15. C	26. A	37. B
5. A	16. A	27. A	38. D
6. C	17. B	28. C	39. C
7. D	18. C	29. C	40. A
8. B	19. D	30. D	41. D
9. D	20. B	31. B	42. C
10. A	21. C	32. A	43. A
11. D	22. B	33. D	44. D

Chapter 10

Answers and Explanations

Personal Jurisdiction

1.1 Specific Jurisdiction

1. B.   Defendant SPI purposefully availed itself of the market of the forum when it designed this drone specifically for the Texas market and directed its local distributor to sell it in that market. When a party takes actions that are likely to have some effects within a particular market or jurisdiction, and those particular actions cause harm within that jurisdiction, courts generally say that the exercise of jurisdiction over the party in that situation does not "offend traditional notions of fair play and substantial justice." *International Shoe v. Washington*, 326 U.S. 310, 316 (1945). In other words, if a party intentionally takes action that it knows could give rise to some liability in a particular forum, it is not unreasonable to expect that the party is going to face a lawsuit in that forum for that harm.

2. B.   This straightforward question asks about the Supreme Court's decision in *World-Wide Volkswagen v. Woodson*, 444 U.S. 286 (1980), ("*WWVW*"), a case that added a gloss to the Court's previous decision in *International Shoe*. In *WWVW*, the Court re-affirmed *International Shoe*'s emphasis on "purposeful availment"—the idea that one could find oneself subject to personal jurisdiction when one intended to take certain action within a particular forum that caused harm—but then added a new wrinkle: the Court determined that courts should also consider five additional issues, what it called "reasonableness factors." Those factors are (1) the burden on the defendant of litigating in the particular forum, (2) the forum state's interest in adjudicating the dispute, (3) the plaintiff's interest in obtaining convenient and effective relief, (4) the interstate judicial system's interest in obtaining the most efficient resolution of controversies, (5) and the shared interest of the several states in furthering fundamental substantive social policies. *WWVW*, 444 U.S. at 292. This question asks which of the factors listed among the possible answers is NOT one listed in *WWVW*. You will be asked to apply these factors to different factual scenarios in subsequent questions.

1.2 General Jurisdiction

3. C.   This question introduces a new concept: that of "general jurisdiction." Under the theory of general personal jurisdiction, a court can exercise power over a party in a jurisdiction where that party has such systematic and continuous connec-

tion to the forum such that it is considered to be "at home" in that forum. In other words, in a jurisdiction where a party has its home base, it is not unreasonable to expect that it must defend itself against any claims of liability, regardless of where that claim may have arisen. The Supreme Court originally had a somewhat expansive view of this concept, permitting the exercise of jurisdiction over a party wherever its connection to the forum was merely "systematic and continuous," but in subsequent years, it has added the following gloss: that systematic and continuous connection to the forum must render the party essentially at home in the forum. In many instances, although at times in dicta, it has said that a corporation is at home in the state where it is incorporated and has its principal place of business, and nowhere else. While the Court in recent years has had some opportunities to identify a corporation that is subject to general jurisdiction outside of its state of incorporation and principal place of business, it has yet to do so. Here, BM is incorporated in Delaware, with its principal place of business in New Jersey. It is likely that these are the only jurisdictions where a court could find BM truly "at home" under the Supreme Court's current jurisprudence regarding general jurisdiction and the facts of this case. The medications at the center of the lawsuit are only manufactured in Connecticut, it is true, and the company has had a factory there for several years, but those medications make up just 5% of the company's total global revenue. Those facts are not sufficient to render BM at home in Connecticut for the purposes of general jurisdiction and thus subjected to personal jurisdiction over this medication.

4. A.   Here, the long-standing presence of Panhandle in the forum state establishes personal jurisdiction under the general jurisdiction theory of personal jurisdiction. The Supreme Court has yet to identify a situation in which the exercise of general jurisdiction is authorized against a corporation that is not incorporated in a given state and does not have its principal place of business there; however, since Panhandle has been operating in the relevant state for decades and has spread out its branches fairly evenly throughout the states in which it does business, it is reasonable to assume a court would find general jurisdiction in this situation. In the case of *Daimler AG v. Bauman*, 571 U.S. 117 (2014), involving a multi-national automobile manufacturer having extensive contacts in the forum state but which were just a small fraction of its contacts throughout the world, the Court found that it was not reasonable to permit a court in California to exercise general jurisdiction over the manufacturer in that forum. Here, however, the actions of the defendant within the forum are a much larger share of its overall activities, and the activities in the forum state are systematic and continuous, meaning a court would likely find the application of general jurisdiction here appropriate. Answer "B" is incorrect because courts no longer look at personal jurisdiction on the basis of "quasi in rem" jurisdiction, the idea that a party could own some property in a jurisdiction even if it is unconnected to the dispute and that would give the court some basis upon which to exert personal jurisdiction over the party. In *Shaffer v. Heitner*, 433 U.S. 186 (1977), the

Supreme Court confirmed that the question of the exercise of personal jurisdiction should hinge on questions of due process and that courts should still conduct the "minimum contacts" analysis of the Due Process Clause of the U.S. Constitution even in cases in which the court might have exercised jurisdiction over a party based on such quasi in rem jurisdiction in the past.

5. D.   Although Defendant has extensive contacts with the forum state, the contacts are not related to the underlying dispute. Under the Supreme Court's prior decision in *Helicopteros Nacionales v. Hall*, 466 U.S. 408 (1984), the Court might have found that the contacts here warrant the exercise of general jurisdiction. Under more recent precedent, however, most notably *Goodyear Dunlop Tires Operations, S. A. v. Brown*, 564 U.S. 915 (2011), and *Daimler AG v. Bauman*, 571 U.S. 117 (2014), it is unlikely that a court could exercise general jurisdiction here.

1.3 Other Issues Related to Personal Jurisdiction: Tag Jurisdiction, "Consent" Jurisdiction, and Long-Arm Statutes

6. C.   Although Defendant's only contacts with the forum state are unrelated to the suit brought by Plaintiff, she was served personally while in the state of California. While Plaintiff's unilateral action of moving to California does not impact whether Defendant is subject to suit there, *Hanson v. Denckla*, 357 U.S. 235 (1958), under *Burnham v. Superior Court*, 495 U.S. 604 (1990), so-called "tag jurisdiction" enables the court in California to obtain personal jurisdiction over Defendant even when the visit to the state was unrelated to the litigation itself.

7. C.   In *Burnham v. Superior Court*, 495 U.S. 604 (1990), a divided Supreme Court found that the exercise of personal jurisdiction over a party that was served while physically located within the state where the court was located did not offend traditional notions of fair play and substantial justice and thus was consistent with the exercise of due process. The Court was divided over the basis for reaching this conclusion. One group of Justices found that since obtaining personal jurisdiction by personal service in the subject forum was a "traditional" form of securing jurisdiction, it thus should be recognized as a legitimate means of securing personal jurisdiction. The other group concluded that since an individual who is present in the forum is benefitting from the protection of the forum, that individual should also be subject to the court's jurisdiction.

8. D.   The court has specific jurisdiction over *neither* Tokyo nor Beijing in Tennessee because they do not satisfy the long-arm statute. Although due process would not be offended by the application of personal jurisdiction in this case, satisfaction of the long-arm statute comes before the due process analysis, making it irrelevant. State law can narrow the class of cases in which the courts in that state have jurisdiction over parties that come before those courts, and even a federal court located within that jurisdiction is bound by that same law. A state's

long-arm statute cannot, however, extend the power of the courts located within it to go beyond the reach of what the U.S. Constitution's Due Process Clause would permit.

1.4 Service of Process and Waiver of Service of Process

9. C.   FRCP 4 provides that the state's law for service of process is acceptable but not if it violates due process. Here, service to the P.O. Box, although acceptable under the state law (and thus a legitimate form of service under the Federal Rules of Civil Procedure), still needs to comport with the requirements of due process. Since the manner of service was not calculated to actually reach the defendant, it fails the requirements of due process. *See Mullane v. Central Hannover Bank & Trust Co.*, 339 U.S. 306 (1950).

10. B.   The manner of service utilized by Plaintiff's lawyer here is authorized by New York law. Rule 4(e)(1) incorporates the relevant state law in the state in which the federal court is located (or where the service is carried out) as an additional means of achieving service. Here, New York law authorizes this manner of service, and thus it is consistent with a manner of service authorized under the Federal Rules of Civil Procedure. Since the service was designed to actually reach the person, there are no issues related to whether this manner of service somehow denied the defendant due process. Furthermore, whether or not a defendant actually receives the summons and complaint is irrelevant if the manner of service is flawed. Here, however, the manner of service was not flawed and was expressly incorporated into Rule 4 as a legitimate means of effectuating service. As a result, it was not an inappropriate means of service.

11. C.   Manny's status as a live-in domestic worker satisfies Rule 4. Rule 4 provides that one can effectuate service by "leaving a copy of [the summons and complaint] at the individual's dwelling or usual place of abode with someone of suitable age and discretion who resides there." Manny resides at the usual place of abode. It does not require that the person is a family member of the party who is the object of the service.

12. C.   FRCP 4(e)(2)(B) provides that proper service can entail "leaving a copy of" the summons and complaint "*at the individual's dwelling or usual place* of abode *with someone of suitable age and discretion who resides there*" (emphasis added). Here, although the individual served may have been someone who does reside with the defendant, the service was not effectuated at the home and is therefore defective.

13. B.   Rule 4(e)(1) explicitly incorporates the state law for service of process of either the state in which the district court is located or the state where the defendant is served, and there is nothing suggesting this was not designed to effectuate service (that is, the means of delivery is not so risky so that it was not calculated to apprise the defendant of the action). At the same time, if the manner of ser-

vice was improper under the Federal Rules of Civil Procedure, the fact that Defendant actually received service would be irrelevant.

14. C. This question also deals with the constitutionality of a manner of service in accordance with the Due Process Clause, a question that requires application of the rule in *Mullane v. Central Hanover Bank*, 339 U.S. 306 (1950). Here, the manner of service, particularly the provision regarding rejected emails, was reasonably calculated to apprise the party of the pendency of the action and thus was consistent with due process.

15. A. Read FRCP 4(d). Everything but "A" is a consequence of failing to waive service. The defendant does not waive an objection based on personal jurisdiction if he waives (or does not waive) formal service and would still have to interpose an objection based on personal jurisdiction in his pre-answer motion to dismiss or answer.

16. C. Similar to the previous question, a defendant who does not waive formal service does not waive the right to object to venue. In fact, even a defendant who does waive service does not waive any potential objection to personal jurisdiction or venue. (FRCP 4(d)(5).) The other answers are all consistent with the types of punishment available when the defendant does not agree to waive formal service. Importantly, the question asked which punishment was not available when a defendant refuses to waive formal service of process.

1.5 "Mixed" Questions

17. A. Compare the facts here to those in *Bristol-Myers Squibb v. Superior Court of California*, 582 U.S. ___, 137 S. Ct. 1773 (2017). This is a specific jurisdiction question. Unlike the facts of *Bristol-Myers Squibb*, here, the injuries of the California Plaintiffs are connected to the defendant's actions in Nevada where the lawsuit was filed.

18. C. The statements made by Defendant that caused the alleged harm to Plaintiff occurred in New York, and thus there is a sufficient nexus between Defendant's conduct that gives rise to potential liability and the forum. If Defendant engaged in such conduct even on one visit to the state, and the conduct which occurred in the forum caused the alleged harm, there is sufficient connection between the dispute and the forum to vest a court in that state with personal jurisdiction over Defendant with respect to that suit. That Defendant was served personally in her home in Florida has no bearing on whether New York has personal jurisdiction over her.

19. C. The only state having a connection to Defendant's conduct which caused the incident is Vermont, under a specific jurisdiction theory of personal jurisdiction. Courts in Delaware and New Hampshire, which are, respectively, the state of incorporation and where defendant has its principal place of business, have personal jurisdiction over Defendant in this action, under a general jurisdiction

theory of personal jurisdiction. New Jersey is the home of Plaintiff, but there is no real connection between Defendant and that forum. Similarly, the other states that are listed as options have no real connection to the dispute. It is hard to argue that Defendant might be found to be "at home" in a state like Massachusetts, and, in all options other than "C", there is a state included in the answer where a court clearly does not have personal jurisdiction over the defendant.

20. B. This question tests your knowledge of general jurisdiction and its application to the problem. *See Bristol-Myers-Squibb v. Superior Court* 582 U.S. ___, 137 S. Ct. 1773 (2017). "Purposeful availment" must be specifically directed to the plaintiffs in a particular action; you cannot have general purposeful availment to anyone. The corporation is subject to general jurisdiction in the states in which it is incorporated and has its principal place of business.

21. D. Baja did not purposefully avail itself of the protections of the subject forum despite the fact that its products ended up in California and one of its products injured Plaintiff. *See McIntyre Machinery, Ltd. v. Nicastro*, 564 U.S. 873 (2011). There are also insufficient grounds upon which to establish that Baja's contacts with the subject forum are so systematic and continuous so as to render them at home in the subject forum. *Goodyear Dunlop Tires v. Brown*, 564 U.S. 915 (2011).

22. A. *See Bristol-Meyers-Squibb v. Superior Court*, 582 U.S. ___, 137 S. Ct. 1773 (2017). While there are extensive contacts between Defendant and the subject forum, such contacts are not related to the California Plaintiffs' injuries. Moreover, given the narrowing of general jurisdiction, these extensive contacts are still not consistent with the Court's rulings that have found that parties are exclusively subject to general jurisdiction only where they are incorporated or have their principal place of business.

23. B. Under a theory of specific jurisdiction, the interests of the several states in furthering substantive policies is one of the reasonableness factors a court should consider when assessing whether to exercise personal jurisdiction over a defendant. Answers "A" and "D" are not related to the personal jurisdiction question. Answer "C" relates to general, not specific, jurisdiction.

24. C. You should have started to develop the ability to discern whether there is specific or general jurisdiction in a particular case. Here, Hessla did not explicitly market this product to California and is not at home in the state. There is neither general nor specific public jurisdiction.

25. B. Even though they were sold in Mexico, the chemicals used by the Guatarican military were manufactured in New Mexico, and thus there is specific jurisdiction over the claims in that state. There is not specific jurisdiction over the claims in Washington State nor is there general jurisdiction there.

26. B. The court has specific jurisdiction over Dan. It does not have jurisdiction over GB because, like the car dealer in *World-Wide Volkswagen*, 444 U.S. 286 (1980),

although it is foreseeable that a car GB services could be involved in an accident in New York, New York is not GB's target market and GB does not avail itself of the protections of the jurisdiction such that it would be foreseeable that it would get haled into a New York court. Further, there is no general jurisdiction over GB because it is not at home in the forum state.

27. B. Despite Danco's protests, the act of failing to pay adequate wages in a forum state constitutes contact with the forum state. Since the lawsuit arises directly out of that contact with the forum state, there is personal jurisdiction over Danco in the forum state. *International Shoe v. Washington*, 326 U.S. 310 (1945).

28. A. This case follows that of *McIntyre v. Nicastro*, 564 U.S. 873 (2011), and is probably a close case at least with respect to Chinatown. It is not close regarding Bristol because of that company's lack of contact with New Jersey. With respect to Chinatown, it is unlikely that a court would find that the company has such a systematic and continuous presence in New Jersey that it is "at home" in the subject forum. Since the actions of Chinatown in New Jersey are unrelated to the plaintiff's injuries, there is not likely to be specific jurisdiction here.

29. A. This fact pattern is similar to *Hanson v. Denckla*, 357 U.S. 235 (1958). Plaintiff has moved to South Carolina and Barrister does not take affirmative steps to do business with her in her new location. In fact, its communication with Plaintiff is still through the New York post office. Although Barrister markets its products generally to the South Carolina market, this is a contract dispute and there is really no connection between the contract dispute itself and the South Carolina market but for Plaintiff's unilateral action to relocate to that state.

30. A. The effectuation of service of process on Darlene while she was physically present in the state of New York is sufficient grounds upon which to base the exercise of personal jurisdiction over Darlene. While it is certainly also likely that a court would find that there would be grounds for specific jurisdiction because Darlene hired Plaintiff to serve as counsel to settle the estate of Darlene's aunt in New York, you were given no answers that reflected personal jurisdiction on the grounds of specific jurisdiction.

1.6 Venue

31. C. Venue is generally governed by 28 U.S.C. §1391(b), which creates a hierarchy when considering the district in which venue is appropriate in the federal system. First, according to §1391(b)(1), venue is appropriate in any district in a state where all defendants are residents of the same state. Since (b)(1) is not available here (because Cam and Randi are not residents of Massachusetts), one must look to (b)(2) to determine if that might be an avenue through which one can establish venue. That subpart provides that venue is appropriate in "a judicial district in which a substantial part of the events or omissions giving rise to the claim occurred or a substantial part of property that is the subject of the

action is situated." It is clear that subsection (b)(2) can be applied to this situation because the accident occurred in Massachusetts. Assessment of venue under (b)(3) is not appropriate (which provides that venue is appropriate in any district in which a defendant is subject to personal jurisdiction), since (b)(2) provides a basis in this case for establishing venue.

32. D. *See* 28 U.S.C. §1391(c)(2). As in the previous question regarding a lawful permanent resident, in cases in which corporations are defendants, they are "deemed to reside" for the purposes of the venue determination in any district in which they are subject to personal jurisdiction. Because of Defendant's contacts with the forum, which are related to the injury, it is easy to find personal jurisdiction over Defendant in the relevant district.

33. A. For the purposes of venue in an action against an agent or officer of the United States (and the Attorney General qualifies), venue will lie in a range of districts (*see* 28 U.S.C. §1391(e)), including where a plaintiff resides, with one big caveat: Where Plaintiff is incorporated does not count in this context. What counts is where it has its principal place of business. *See* 28 U.S.C. §1391(c)(3).

34. C. The appropriate forum for venue purposes is where at least one of the defendants is subject to personal jurisdiction. The Eastern District of New York qualifies not only because the flight originated from JFK but also because of both airlines' extensive contacts with JFK (and an argument certainly could be made that both defendants are subject to personal jurisdiction in the forum). The choice of *law* clause is irrelevant. If it were a choice of *forum* clause, the outcome might be different. 28 U.S.C. §1391(b)(3).

35. A. *See* 28 U.S.C. §1391(b)(2). The events in this action all took place in the Northern District of California.

36. B. 28 U.S.C. §1391(c)(3). Courts are directed to disregard the presence of the foreign corporation for the purposes of venue determination. Sioux City is a corporation, and thus it is deemed to reside for venue purposes in the district where it would be subject to personal jurisdiction if that district were a separate state. §1391(d). Finally, a motion to transfer venue does not require the consent of all defendants; it only requires an effort to remove a case to federal court. §1446(b)(1). Consent of all parties could justify a transfer of venue but does not apply to bar transfer if transfer is otherwise appropriate.

37. D. Venue is appropriate in the chosen forum because the bulk of the actions and omissions occurred there, meaning §1391(b)(2) applies. Section 1391(b)(1) cannot apply because the defendants are not all residents of the same state. The foreign defendant's presence does not establish venue in any district because there are also domestic defendants, and venue with respect to them must be assessed first. *See* §1391(c)(3).

38. B. In a venue determination regarding a corporation operating within a state with multiple districts, we treat each venue almost as if it were its own state, conduct-

ing the same sort of "minimum contacts" analysis that we would for a personal jurisdiction inquiry. Here, the defendant only has contacts in the Eastern District. Is there personal jurisdiction over the defendant in the Western District? Yes. But this question asks about venue, and in accordance with 28 U.S.C. §§1391(c) and (d), in a state with more than one district, like Washington, the defendant is deemed to reside in the district with which it has the *most* contacts.

39. A. *See* 28 U.S.C. §1391(d).

40. D. The forum selection clause is considered consent by the Plaintiff to venue in the Middle District of Georgia, and thus the motion will be granted. You have been given no facts to suggest that there was any fraud in the execution of the contract which might warrant the court's refusal to honor the choice-of-forum provision.

41. D. 28 U.S.C. §1391(c)(3) provides that even if venue appears appropriate with respect to foreign defendants (irrespective of any personal jurisdiction issues), one must still conduct a separate venue determination with respect to the domestic defendant or defendants. Section 1391(c)(3) might suggest that venue is appropriate because foreign defendants are in the case, but nevertheless, the presence of a foreign defendant in the case "shall be disregarded in determining where the action may be brought with respect to other defendants." §1391(c)(3). The court is likely to grant the motion as a result.

1.7 The Doctrine of *Forum Non Conveniens*

42. B. *See Piper Aircraft Co. v. Reyno*, 454 U.S. 235, 241 n.6 (1981), for a list of what are considered the "public" and "private factors" the court should take into account when ruling on a *forum non conveniens* motion. The private interests include the "'relative ease of access to sources of proof; availability of compulsory process for attendance of unwilling, and the cost of obtaining attendance of willing, witnesses; possibility of view of premises, if view would be appropriate to the action; and all other practical problems that make trial of a case easy, expeditious and inexpensive'" (quoting *Gulf Oil v. Gilbert*, 330 U.S. 501, at 508 (1947)). The public factors include "the administrative difficulties flowing from court congestion"; the "local interest in having localized controversies decided at home"; the interest in having the trial of a diversity case in a forum that is at home with the law that must govern the action; the avoidance of unnecessary problems in conflict of laws, or in the application of foreign law; and the unfairness of burdening citizens in an unrelated forum with jury duty. *Id.* at 330 U.S. at 509. Here, answer "B" is one of the public factors that a court should consider. Answers "A" and "D" relate to personal jurisdiction and not *forum non conveniens*. Also, according to the Court in *Piper Aircraft*, unless the plaintiff's potential remedies in an alternative forum are essentially foreclosed, a court should not take into account the prospect that those remedies might be merely

diminished or less robust in any alternative forum; thus, the wording in answer "C" makes this option incorrect as well.

43. C. Unlike in *Piper Aircraft v. Reyno*, 454 U.S. 235 (1981), the remedies available in the Guyamalan court are likely unavailable to the plaintiffs because of the danger of bringing the action in that country, warranting denial of the application for dismissal based on *forum non conveniens* grounds. *See Guidi v. Inter-Continental Hotels Corp.*, 224 F.3d 142 (2d Cir. 2000).

44. A. This is similar to the Court's ruling in *Piper Aircraft v. Reyno*, 454 U.S. 235 (1981). Here, the question asks which of the answers represents something the court should *not* consider. Since the cap on damages is not a complete elimination of any meaningful remedy, "A" is the answer that best reflects what the court may not consider.

45. C. Although there are *some* factors weighing against dismissal based on *forum non conveniens* grounds, there are still enough weighing in favor of dismissal that the appellate court will not find that the trial court abused its discretion in granting the motion. In order for such a motion to be successful, the court weighs the different factors; it does not require that all of the factors point in one direction.

1.8 Formative Assessment Quiz

46. C. Defendant's only contacts with the forum state are unrelated to the suit brought by Plaintiff. Furthermore, they are sporadic and have lasted only several months so that she cannot qualify for general jurisdiction. Defendant was not served in the State of California, and Plaintiff's unilateral action of moving to California does not impact whether Defendant is subject to suit there (*Hanson v. Denckla*, 357 U.S. 235 (1958)). A long-arm statute cannot grant a court more authority over parties than the Due Process Clause would permit. It can be narrower, however, and limit a court subject to it from exercising the full authority the Due Process Clause might otherwise allow.

47. A. The issue identified in answer "A" relates to a choice-of-law clause in a contract between the parties. That fact carries no weight in the choice of the appropriate forum, that is, in the venue determination, which is the crux of the question. While it certainly is possible that answer "C" could be relevant as to whether the court even has jurisdiction in the first place, that is not the issue on which the question is focused. Moreover, the fact pattern provides that the court in Arkansas does, in fact, have jurisdiction over the defendant.

48. C. It would appear that BM has purposefully availed itself of all four jurisdictions through its actions within those jurisdictions in relation to the harm caused by Plarex generally. However, there are no allegations connecting the Ohio Plaintiffs to the actions of BM in Pennsylvania, and, thus, the Ohio Plaintiffs would not likely be able to obtain personal jurisdiction over BM in a Pennsylvania

court even though BM might be subject to jurisdiction in that state for an action pursued by people who *did* have an explicit connection to the distribution of the medication in that state (like, for example, the Pennsylvania plaintiffs). *See Bristol-Meyers Squibb*, 582 U.S. ___, 137 S. Ct. 1773 (2017).

49. B.   Here, Pottery has no real connection to Michigan. That a customer of Pottery mailed a product to Michigan does not change the situation. The unilateral acts of a customer (especially one that is one step removed from the actual plaintiff), cannot alter the personal jurisdiction calculus for Pottery. (*Compare McGee v. International Life Ins. Co.*, 355 U.S. 220 (1957), with *Hanson v. Denckla*, 357 U.S. 235 (1958).) Had the owner of Pottery asked the customer to tell her friend in Michigan to "spread the word" about Pottery, it still would not constitute the requisite "purposeful availment" necessary on the part of the defendant itself to connect Pottery to a Michigan forum for this dispute. Pottery is "at home" in the forum of Vermont because that is where it has its principal place of business. There is no barrier to Vermont's serving as the forum because Pottery is an "in-state" defendant. That issue is only relevant to a question related to removal. If this diversity case were filed in state court in Vermont, Pottery would not be able to remove it to federal court as an in-state defendant, but that is not the issue here. The plaintiff here can choose to file the case in federal court in Vermont if she wants to. However, the question is really asking about personal jurisdiction, and any court in the state of Vermont would clearly have personal jurisdiction over Pottery.

50. B.   The case cannot be removed or transferred directly to the federal court in New York from the California state court. First, there is no mechanism that would permit a state court to remove a case from a state court to a federal court in another state. Second, there is no mechanism for transferring a case from a state court system to a federal court. The defendants must first seek to remove the case to a federal court where the state court is located, and then seek transfer to the federal court in New York. See, for example, the procedural steps taken in *Piper Aircraft v. Reyno*, 454 U.S. 235 (1981). A motion for dismissal based on *forum non conveniens* grounds will not accomplish what the defendants appear to want: adjudication of the dispute in the Northern District of New York. Even if such a motion were granted, it would only accomplish dismissal of the action, not adjudication of the dispute in the Northern District of New York.

51. A.   A forum selection clause would normally control such a situation. *See Atlantic Marine Construction v. United States Dist. Court*, 571 U.S. 49 (2013). Whether or not the court can exercise personal jurisdiction over a party is not directly relevant to the *forum non conveniens* inquiry (*Piper Aircraft*, 454 U.S. 235 (1981)), and several of the possible answers relate to facts relevant primarily to personal jurisdiction, not *forum non conveniens*. It might be a separate defense that the court does not have personal jurisdiction, but it is not a factor under *Piper Aircraft*. In addition, as we know from *Piper Aircraft*, a somewhat less fa-

vorable remedy in another jurisdiction is not grounds for dismissal on *forum non conveniens* grounds.

52. C. The facts regarding contacts with the proposed forum are such that they are not connected to the underlying dispute nor are they so systematic and continuous that they give rise to the exercise of jurisdiction. *See Goodyear Dunlop Tires v. Brown*, 564 U.S. 915 (2011), and *Daimler AG v. Bauman*, 571 U.S. 117 (2014).

53. A. *See Piper Aircraft v. Reyno*, 454 U.S. 235 (1981); *Gonzalez v. Chrysler Corp.*, 301 F.3d 377 (5th Cir. 2002). The less favorable remedy available in Peru as a result of the statutory cap on damages is not a complete bar to any remedy in Peru, and the court should not have considered it in the *forum non conveniens* determination.

54. C. Iceland did not purposefully avail itself of the subject forum with respect to the sale of the specific battery involved in the incident in which Plaintiff was injured. *See McIntyre v. Nicastro*, 564 U.S. 873 (2011); *Bristol-Myers Squibb v. Superior Court of California*, 582 U.S. ___, 137 S. Ct. 1773 (2017). The other contacts are not sufficient to generate general jurisdiction. *Goodyear Dunlop Tires Operations, S. A. v. Brown*, 564 U.S. 915 (2011); *Daimler AG v. Bauman*, 571 U.S. 117 (2014). You were given no facts about the manner of service, and the answer related to that jurisdiction states that there was no jurisdiction, "but only because" Iceland wasn't properly served there. Tag jurisdiction is not the only potential basis of personal jurisdiction.

55. A. There is personal jurisdiction over SolarCo in New York State, even if venue should be changed to the Western District of New York. Venue is appropriate in the Northern District of New York, but the choice-of-forum clause determines that venue should be transferred to the Western District of New York, consistent with the holding in the *Atlantic Marine* case. Accordingly, the motion to transfer venue will be granted, but the motion for dismissal related to an alleged lack of personal jurisdiction will be denied.

Subject Matter Jurisdiction

2.1 Federal Question

1. B. In *Louisville & Nashville Railroad v. Mottley*, 211 U.S. 149 (1908), the Supreme Court adopted a test that has come to be known as the "well-pleaded complaint" rule. Under that rule, a case gives rise to federal jurisdiction if the basis for that jurisdiction appears on the face of the well-pleaded complaint. That is, the plaintiff's assertion of its claims in a well-pleaded complaint will give rise to federal jurisdiction if the basis for federal jurisdiction is clear from that pleading. But one of the issues that arose in *Mottley* was whether a plaintiff could anticipate a potential defense of the defendant and, if that defense were based on federal law, whether it could create federal jurisdiction. The Court ruled that

a plaintiff cannot anticipate a defendant's potential defense, nor can it create a federal question by articulating what it anticipates the defendant might raise as a defense under federal law. If no issue of federal law appears in the plaintiff's affirmative claims, a plaintiff cannot establish federal jurisdiction in the district court by arguing the defendant might raise some federal defense. While there might be grounds for the Supreme Court to have final say over the federal defense once it makes its way through a state court system, the district court will not have original jurisdiction—the ability to hear the case in the first instance—if the plaintiff merely asserts that the defendant might present some defense under federal law in its response to the plaintiff's case. Here, because the plaintiff only alleges that the defendant might assert a defense under federal law, and has not asserted an independent basis for federal jurisdiction in his complaint, there is no grounds for jurisdiction under 28 U.S.C. §1331.

2. D.   The basis for federal jurisdiction appears on the face of the well-pleaded complaint, and thus there is a basis for federal jurisdiction. *Louisville & Nashville Railroad v. Mottley*, 211 U.S. 149 (1908). The fact that there is not exclusive jurisdiction over this type of claim simply means that the plaintiff can file his complaint raising such a claim in federal or state court but is not required to file it in state court first, or at all. There is no amount-in-controversy requirement in an action raising a federal question such as this. The amount-in-controversy requirement only applies in diversity actions.

2.2 Diversity Jurisdiction

3. D.   This question tests your knowledge of diversity jurisdiction, the power of the federal court to hear cases where the parties are "diverse," that is, from different states or from a state and different nations. See 28 U.S.C. §1332 for a full list of the types of "diversity" the statute recognizes. Under diversity jurisdiction, there are a number of requirements in addition to simple diversity of the parties. First, there must be complete diversity: there can be no non-diverse parties opposing each other. In other words, if one of the plaintiffs in a suit is from New York and one of the defendants is as well, there is not complete diversity. There is also an "amount-in-controversy" requirement in the statute that requires that a case based on diversity must involve a claim that "exceeds" $75,000, so that it must seek at least $75,001 in order to warrant the court's exercise of jurisdiction over the matter. Finally, when dealing with a corporation, the company's "citizenship" for diversity purposes is its state of incorporation and where it has its principal place of business. For the Supreme Court, the principal place of business is where the leadership of the corporation sits, what is known as the "nerve-center test" from the Court's decision in *Hertz Corp. v. Friend*, 559 U.S. 77 (2010). In this case, under the now-rejected "muscle test," the defendant might have been able to say it was a "citizen" of New Jersey because the bulk of its operations took place in that state, but under the nerve-center test, the de-

fendant is considered a citizen of New York because that is where the corporate headquarters are located. It is also considered a citizen of Delaware, the state where it is incorporated. There is thus diversity because the "dual citizenship" for the defendant (New York/Delaware) is different from plaintiff's (New Jersey). Although the case raises only questions of state law, there is subject matter jurisdiction because the parties are diverse and the claims satisfy the amount-in-controversy requirement.

4. B.   PowerInc and the Plaintiff are both citizens of New York State, and thus there is not complete diversity between the parties. The court will dismiss the case as against PowerInc, but the claim against SafeSeal will proceed.

5. A.   Here, the plaintiff's claim is based on TILA, a federal statute, and thus there is federal question jurisdiction. There is no diversity requirement in a federal question case and there is no amount-in-controversy requirement if the basis of subject matter jurisdiction is federal question.

6. D.   Here, there are two problems with establishing diversity jurisdiction. First, under 28 U.S.C. §1332(a)(2), a lawful permanent resident residing in the same state as an adverse party is not considered diverse from that adverse party. Second, the plaintiff has not alleged that his damages *exceed* $75,000. Generally, courts will accept a plaintiff's allegation regarding the value of the plaintiff's claim unless it appears to a "legal certainty" that the plaintiff cannot establish that the amount-in-controversy requirement is satisfied. Here, the plaintiff does not even allege that he satisfies the amount-in-controversy requirement.

7. B.   Here, Plaintiff has not established that there is subject matter jurisdiction because he has not identified a basis for diversity jurisdiction. There is no basis under diversity jurisdiction for a lawsuit between someone "residing" in a foreign country and a U.S. citizen. If Plaintiff can establish that he is still a resident and citizen of a state different from Defendant's for diversity purposes, Plaintiff could refile the case. The case will thus be dismissed without prejudice for Plaintiff to return to court if he can present allegations that establish the court's jurisdiction. *See Redner v. Sanders*, 2000 WL 1161080 (S.D.N.Y. Aug. 16, 2000).

8. C.   There is complete diversity between the parties and the plaintiff satisfies the amount-in-controversy requirement.

2.3 Supplemental Jurisdiction

9. D.   Under 28 U.S.C. §1367, a federal court can exercise supplemental jurisdiction over a case that arises under the same "nucleus of operative facts" as a related federal claim. Here, there is subject matter jurisdiction over both of the federal claims. Since the state claim is connected to one of the federal claims, that is sufficient for a court to exercise supplemental jurisdiction over the related state claim. The claim does not need to arise out of the same nucleus of operative facts of *all* of the federal claims. Furthermore, if there is supplemental jurisdic-

tion over the state claim, there is no amount-in-controversy requirement imposed over this claim, just as there is no amount-in-controversy requirement for federal claims generally.

10. C. The grounds for supplemental jurisdiction exist—the state law claim arises from the same nucleus of operative facts—and thus there is subject matter jurisdiction under 28 U.S.C. §1367. There is no diversity or amount-in-controversy requirement.

11. B. Under 28 U.S.C. §1367(c), even where a case appears to satisfy the grounds for the court's exercise of supplemental jurisdiction, the court can still exercise its discretion to decline such jurisdiction over the state law claim if it "raises a novel or complex issue of state law"; if it "substantially predominates over the claim or claims over which the district court has original jurisdiction"; if the court has "dismissed all claims over which it has original jurisdiction"; or if "in exceptional circumstances, there are other compelling reasons for declining jurisdiction." Here, the state claim relates to a new state right that has not been tested in court before and thus raises novel issues of state law.

12. C. The claims are virtually identical, they arise out of the same facts (the termination), and the state law claim is "well-established." There is supplemental jurisdiction over the claim and no basis for the court to reject the claim on discretionary grounds.

13. D. The federal and state claims do not arise out of the same nucleus of operative facts. Under 28 U.S.C. §1367, amount in controversy is irrelevant.

14. A. The facts behind the federal and state claims are identical. Both claims arise out of the same nucleus of operative facts (i.e., Defendant's gender-based discrimination against Plaintiff), and thus there is supplemental jurisdiction over the state law claim. That the parties are not diverse is irrelevant because the anchor claim is a federal claim and the 28 U.S.C. §1367(b) bar does not apply.

15. B. The state law claim does not satisfy the requirements of 28 U.S.C. §1367 in that the additional claim does not arise out of the same nucleus of operative facts as the anchor federal claim. The federal claim goes to lost wages after termination based on discrimination; the state claim goes to unpaid wages while she was employed, under a different legal theory. There is no argument that the decision to not pay wages under the contract was motivated by discriminatory animus. Furthermore, even though the parties are diverse, the amount-in-controversy requirement is not met (even *if* the plaintiff could aggregate the claims). Thus, there is no independent basis of jurisdiction over the supplemental claim.

16. B. The federal and state claims arise under the same nucleus of operative facts.

17. C. Here, the question requires that you understand how subpart (c) to 28 U.S.C. §1367 works. The "anchor" federal claims have been dismissed, and all that is left is the state law claim. As a result, the federal court is well within its rights to dismiss the remaining state law claim but is not required to do so. Subpart (c)

provides the court with discretion to dismiss a remaining state law claim when the federal claims have been dismissed, but such dismissal is not required.

18. D. This question tests both your knowledge of the standard for assessing supplemental jurisdiction—that a state law claim arises under the same nucleus of operative facts as a federal law claim already in the case—as well as your ability to apply it. Here, there state law claim does not arise under the same nucleus of operative facts. Answer "C" is wrong because it provides the wrong standard.

19. D. It is clear that Plaintiff cannot establish an amount in damages that satisfies the amount-in-controversy requirement. Answer "D" supplies the legal standard for when one can challenge a plaintiff's allegations regarding damages to undermine their effort to meet the amount-in-controversy requirement.

2.4 "Mixed" Jurisdiction Questions

20. B. The plaintiff's complaint is strictly based on state law and the parties are not diverse. The defendant's potential federal defenses cannot manufacture a federal question for the purposes of removal, and thus the matter will be remanded to the state court. The case may ultimately make it to a federal court (the Supreme Court), but only on appeal from the highest court in the state in which the court is located. In cannot be filed in a federal district court initially on the basis of a federal defense only. Removal is not available to a defendant in such a situation, and when a defendant attempts to effectuate a removal, the appropriate remedy is for the district court to remand the matter to the state court where it originated.

21. B. There is an independent basis of jurisdiction over Plaintiff's state law claims (diversity), and the discretionary factors of 28 U.S.C. §1367(c) are inapplicable. Those discretionary factors only apply to claims where the basis of subject matter jurisdiction is supplemental jurisdiction only.

22. D. The state law claims arise out of the same nucleus of operative facts as the federal claims. The fact that Peter is a lawful permanent resident of the same state as the defendant is irrelevant as to whether the court has subject matter jurisdiction over the supplemental state law claim.

23. A. The federal court would have diversity jurisdiction over this case. Answer "B" relates to personal, and not subject matter, jurisdiction. Answer "C" pulls in matters related to supplemental jurisdiction under 28 U.S.C. §1367. Plaintiff's claim stands on its own, being filed directly under 28 U.S.C. §1332. The provisions and limitations available under 28 U.S.C. §1367(c) are thus inapplicable. Answer "D" relates to matters that might implicate questions of removal but not subject matter jurisdiction. If the case were originally filed in state court, Defendant would not be able to remove it because he is from the state in which the case was filed. That it originates in federal court is not grounds for dismissal.

24. C. There are no allegations that the alleged minimum wage violations arise out of the same nucleus of operative facts as the anchor federal claim, and thus 28 U.S.C. §1367 does not give the court jurisdiction over the minimum wage claim. At the same time, the intentional tort claim does arise out of the same nucleus of operative facts as the federal claim, meaning there is supplemental jurisdiction over it. There is no amount-in-controversy requirement under §1367, nor does it matter that the parties are not diverse. Subsection 1367(b) does not pose a problem here because Plaintiff's anchor claim is one based on federal question jurisdiction, and thus §1367(b) does not apply (moreover, Plaintiff is not seeking to add a non-diverse party to the case, which is what the §1367(b) bar is really about).

25. A. There is no impediment to subject matter jurisdiction, which is the basis of Defendants' motion. The case arises under federal securities law, which means there is jurisdiction under 28 U.S.C. §1331. Any questions related to the diversity of the parties are irrelevant. Any issue related to where the events arise—which might pertain to a venue or personal jurisdiction challenge—are irrelevant to the question of subject matter jurisdiction.

26. C. Here, the question is whether the parties are diverse; since Plaintiff is a citizen of Maryland as is Defendant, they are not. Whether they are "at home in the forum" is irrelevant in a subject matter jurisdiction inquiry as that is the standard used to determine whether personal jurisdiction can be obtained over a person or entity based on a theory of general jurisdiction. This is a question that many readers will answer incorrectly, likely because of an inability to keep personal jurisdiction and subject matter jurisdiction issues separate.

27. B. Plaintiff's status as a lawful permanent resident is irrelevant. This is a federal claim, and for subject matter jurisdiction purposes, that status does not affect the subject matter jurisdiction of the court. It can affect diversity jurisdiction and venue, but it does not impact subject matter jurisdiction based on 28 U.S.C. §1331. Once again, remember to identify the issue at the core of the question and make sure you are only looking at issues relevant to that core.

28. C. Unlike *Redner v. Sanders*, 2000 WL 1161080 (S.D.N.Y. Aug. 16, 2000), this is *not* a diversity action. The citizenship of the plaintiff is irrelevant. Federal jurisdiction is predicated on the federal copyright claim. 28 U.S.C. §1331.

29. A. The claim arises under federal law, and thus there is jurisdiction under 28 U.S.C. §1331. There is no diversity requirement and there is no amount-in-controversy requirement. In a diversity case seeking an injunction, the court will attempt to "value" the injunction—that is, it will ask what it is worth to the plaintiff and what it will cost the defendant to comply—in assessing whether the case satisfies the amount-in-controversy requirement. But here, there is no such requirement because it is a federal question case and not a diversity case.

30. A. This is a federal action, arising under 28 U.S.C. §1331. There is no amount-in-controversy requirement. That requirement only applies to claims brought under

28 U.S.C. §1332 (diversity jurisdiction). That the parties are diverse and the state court of Vermont might have concurrent jurisdiction does not undermine the federal court's exercise of jurisdiction in this action.

31. C. This question tests your understanding of the grounds for establishing supplemental jurisdiction generally and your understanding of the discretionary grounds for denying subject matter jurisdiction over a supplemental state law claim under 28 U.S.C. §1367(c). Here, it is apparent that the state law claim does not really arise under the same common nucleus of operative facts as the federal claims. Second, that the federal law might "predominate" over the state law claim in terms of the value of the federal claims when compared to the state law claim does not matter in the supplemental jurisdiction analysis. If the state law claim or claims predominated over the federal law claims, that would give the court grounds to deny supplemental jurisdiction under the discretionary factors of §1367(c). The reverse is not true, however: a court cannot deny (or even grant) supplemental jurisdiction because the federal law claims appear to predominate over any state law claims.

2.5 Removal and Remand

32. B. There are two issues to consider in this question. First, as with federal jurisdiction generally, the grounds for removal of a case from state to federal court must appear on the face of the well-pleaded complaint, as it does here, and that basis is a federal question. The second issue has to do with timing of the removal. 28 U.S.C. §1446(c) provides that where the basis of removal is diversity jurisdiction, the matter cannot be removed more than one year from the initial filing, even if the basis for removal does appear on the face of the amended complaint. Here, although the original case was based on state law, the basis for removal is §1331, the federal anti-discrimination claim. Therefore, the one-year bar does not apply. The statute only requires that the defendant must seek to remove the action within 30 days of receiving the pleading where the basis for removal appears; here, that would be the amended complaint which contains the federal discrimination claim. The basis for removal is §1331, not §1332, and the defendant can remove the case whenever the basis for federal subject matter jurisdiction appears in the pleadings. Just because the state court might have concurrent jurisdiction over the claim does not mean the case cannot be removed.

33. C. Plaintiff is free to choose to assert only state claims, even if the reason for doing so is to keep the case out of federal court. There is no risk here that this is really a federal claim where federal jurisdiction is exclusive (e.g., a patent challenge); Plaintiff is not attempting to mask the claims as a state claim in an effort to evade that exclusive federal jurisdiction. Here, Defendant is not asserting a defense; rather, it is an argument over Plaintiff's affirmative claims.

34. B. See the discretionary factors set forth in 28 U.S.C. §1367(c). Even if the court finds that the state law claim predominates over the federal claim, it is permitted

to retain jurisdiction over the state law claim. It is not obligated to dismiss the state law claim.

35. C. While there is a great deal of information about personal jurisdiction in this case, the question asks whether the matter could be removed by Defendant to federal court. The basis for the federal jurisdiction is simple: diversity. The parties are diverse (and completely diverse at that) and they satisfy the amount-in-controversy requirement. There *is* a federal defense, but that does not prevent removal here, where the basis for federal subject matter jurisdiction appears on the face of the California Plaintiffs' complaint.

36. A. Based on the face of the well-pleaded complaint, the removal request will be honored. There is diversity jurisdiction and the claims satisfy the amount-in-controversy requirement. At the same time, the federal defense does not create a federal question for the purposes of subject matter jurisdiction, and thus "C" is incorrect.

37. C. Removal in this instance is barred even where the basis for federal jurisdiction (in this case, diversity jurisdiction) appears on the face of the complaint. The bar to removal in this case—that a home-state defendant cannot remove a case to federal court when the basis of jurisdiction is diversity jurisdiction—appears in 28 U.S.C. §1441(b)(2). If one of the purposes of diversity jurisdiction is to ensure that an out-of-state defendant faces no bias in the courts of another state, then there is no reason to permit removal of a diversity case where the defendant is from the state in which the case is filed. If the plaintiff is willing to risk facing out-of-state bias by filing a diversity case in state court in the defendant's home state, the removal statute bars the defendant in such a situation from removing the case; the plaintiff can thus circumvent having to resolve a diversity case in a federal district court by filing such a case in the home state of the defendant.

38. D. This question addresses the issue of remand, the plaintiff's check on a faulty removal executed by an opposing party. When a defendant removes a case to federal court, it is a ministerial act requiring no review of the application by the state court; the clerk of the state court simply sends the case to the local federal court. Once that case is removed to federal court, the plaintiff who believes the removal is not warranted then asks the federal court to remand the matter back to state court because, the plaintiff alleges, the removal was improper. There can be many reasons why a removal is improper, the most likely being that there simply are no grounds for removal, that is, there is no federal subject matter jurisdiction over the case. Here in this diversity case, the removal was flawed because the defendant is an in-state defendant, and thus removal is inappropriate. 28 U.S.C. §1441(b)(2).

39. C. Review 28 U.S.C. §1441 and *Louisville & Nashville Railroad v Mottley*, 211 U.S. 149 (1908). A legitimate basis for removal appears on the complaint and there is federal question jurisdiction (even though jurisdiction over the relevant claim is not exclusive); thus, removal is appropriate.

40. B. If this were a diversity case, the in-state defendant could not remove it because of their New York residence. Here, it is a federal question case and there is no such bar to removal in such a case.

41. C. This question tests your ability to combine your knowledge of the "citizenship" of corporations with the application of the removal statute. Here, since the defendant is considered a citizen of New York, the bar prohibiting in-state defendants from removing a case based on diversity still applies.

42. B. Under 28 U.S.C. §1367(c), the court should dismiss the federal claim at the parties' request after it has been settled and can choose to dismiss the remaining state law claim but has the discretion to continue to hear it. While most courts would likely dismiss this claim, the judge here may think it makes more sense to retain jurisdiction since the case has gone through discovery and is on the eve of trial, and the permissive nature of §1367(c) gives her the option to do so. It is rare for a court to do so, but the court certainly has the option to proceed in this way. Answer "B" says that the court "may" dismiss the state law claim. This is the correct standard. The court can also choose not to do so. If Home Repo were not a citizen of New York, there would be separate diversity jurisdiction over the state law claim, but that is not the case.

43. A. Plaintiff's wage-and-hour claim is unrelated to her federal discrimination claim. As a result, it does not enjoy supplemental jurisdiction. Moreover, there is not diversity between the parties. Even though the amount-in-controversy requirement is satisfied, Plaintiff and Defendant are both "citizens" of New York for diversity purposes, and thus they are not diverse, defeating diversity jurisdiction.

44. D. Dwight's vandalizing of Pam's car is all a part of the same intimidation campaign and thus it arises out of the same common nucleus of operative facts as the federal discrimination claim. As such, there is supplemental jurisdiction under 28 U.S.C. §1367 over the state claim and the amount-in-controversy requirement of the 28 U.S.C. §1332 does not apply. You were not asked about the 28 U.S.C. §1367(c) discretionary factors, so, that was not an issue.

45. C. The parties are diverse and the claims satisfy the amount-in-controversy requirement. The facts surrounding New York Pizza's extensive contacts with the forum state are relevant to potential issues of personal jurisdiction and not subject matter jurisdiction. In *Hertz Corp. v. Friend*, 559 U.S. 77 (2010), the Supreme Court dispensed with the "muscle test" as a basis for determining "citizenship" for diversity jurisdiction purposes. The question of bias against an out-of-state defendant is only an issue when dealing with matters in which removal is sought, which is not at issue here.

46. A. Although there is concurrent jurisdiction, there is still federal jurisdiction in the federal court.

2.6 Formative Assessment Quiz

47. A. Plaintiff's wage-and-hour claim is unrelated to her federal discrimination claim. As a result, it does not enjoy supplemental jurisdiction. Moreover, there is not diversity between the parties, so even though the amount-in-controversy requirement is satisfied, the plaintiff and defendant are both "citizens" of New York for diversity purposes and thus are not diverse, defeating diversity jurisdiction.

48. C. The accident between Pam and Dwight does not appear to be part of the intimidation campaign, and thus it does not arise out of the same common nucleus of operative facts as the federal discrimination claim. As such, there is no supplemental jurisdiction under 28 U.S.C. §1367 over the state claim. If there were, the amount-in-controversy requirement of the 28 U.S.C. §1332 would not apply. You were not asked about the §1367(c) discretionary factors, so that was not an issue.

49. B. The case can be removed to federal court because the basis of the removal is federal question. There is no "in-state-defendant" bar to removing the case in that instance. That bar only applies to cases in which the basis of federal jurisdiction is diversity.

50. A. This question once again tests your knowledge of corporate "citizenship," discussed in Section 3.2, *supra*. As in *Hertz Corp.*, 559 U.S. 77 (2010), the defendant's state of citizenship is the state in which it is incorporated and where it has its principal place of business. The fact that defendant operates its main distribution center in Newark, New Jersey, does not override its citizenship for the purposes of diversity jurisdiction in New York and Delaware. It doesn't matter if a defendant corporation has a significant number of operations in a state if its corporate headquarters are not there. Those significant operations will not alter the corporation's principal place of business if its corporate headquarters are not in the state with those extensive operations. It might have some bearing on personal jurisdiction if those operations are connected in some way to the liability at issue in a particular case. But personal jurisdiction was not at issue in this problem. When trying to assess diversity jurisdiction, the "citizenship" of the corporation is strictly where it is incorporated and where it has its principal place of business, i.e., its corporate headquarters. The extensive Newark operations do not alter the fact that the company's principal place of business is in New York. As a result, the parties are not diverse, meaning there is no subject matter jurisdiction in a federal court over this matter.

51. B. The claim arises out of the same nucleus of operative facts as the Fair Housing Act claim, and there is thus supplemental jurisdiction under §1367. At the same time, the court may decline jurisdiction, but is not required to, under §1367(c) because the claim is novel. There is no §1367(b) bar because the initial claim is not based in diversity.

52. A. Although there is concurrent jurisdiction, there is still federal jurisdiction in the federal court.

53. A. Based on the face of the well-pleaded complaint, the removal request will be rejected and the matter remanded because the case, based on diversity jurisdiction, does not satisfy the amount-in-controversy requirement. The federal defense does not create a federal question for the purposes of subject matter jurisdiction.

54. B. There are two problems with Mortgage Bank's request to remove the action. First, the request can only be made to the district court "embracing" the action: here, the Northern District of New York. 28 §U.S.C. 1441(a). Second, a defendant cannot remove a diversity case filed in state court in its home state. 28 U.S.C. §1441(b)(2). A defendant cannot seek to avoid the application of §1441(b)(2) by seeking to remove the case to a district court outside of its home state.

55. D. There is jurisdiction under 28 U.S.C. §1332 because the parties are diverse and the amount-in-controversy requirement is satisfied. The federal question is relevant only to any defense on the part of the defendant to the jurisdictional issue, however, and bears no relation to the jurisdictional question.

56. B. The acts of the employer that form the basis of the federal claim also form the basis of the state law claim, and thus they arise under the same nucleus of operative facts. As a result, there is supplemental jurisdiction over the state law claim in addition to the federal question jurisdiction over the federal claim.

57. B. Although there may be a defense based on TILA, a federal statute, that alone does not give rise to federal jurisdiction in the district court. There is no diversity because of the bank's dual citizenship—New York and Delaware—and one of these is the same as Plaintiff's state of residence and citizenship.

58. A. There is no basis for federal jurisdiction because, although the parties are diverse, the amount-in-controversy requirement is not satisfied. At the same time, the state court has personal jurisdiction over the defendant because he was served with process in the forum state.

59. A. The claims arise out of the same nucleus of operative facts, and with a supplemental state law claim that is anchored to a federal claim, the diversity of the parties is irrelevant. It can come into play in a setting with multiple parties, but we will get into that problem when we discuss joinder of parties. Similarly, since there is an anchor federal claim, there is no need to satisfy the amount-in-controversy requirement of 28 U.S.C. §1332.

The *Erie* Doctrine,
Claim Preclusion and Issue Preclusion,
and Preliminary Relief

3.1 The *Erie* Doctrine

1. D.   The *Erie* doctrine, named for the case in which it was first adopted by the Supreme Court, *Erie Railroad v. Tompkins*, 304 U.S. 64 (1938), attempts to give guidance to federal courts as to how they should handle diversity cases and cases involving state law claims based on supplemental jurisdiction. As you know, when it comes to substantive law, a federal court can and will entertain and consider many issues of state law, but only when it has a basis in subject matter jurisdiction for doing so. When there is a basis for a federal court to hear a case, even one involving state law, as you have learned, the plaintiff can choose to file its case in federal court, or, in many instances, a defendant can choose to remove a case from state court to federal court. In such instances, the question then becomes what *procedural* law to apply. The Court in *Erie* articulated the standard that, pursuant to the federal Rules of Decision Act, 28 U.S.C. §1652, a federal court should consider the substantive state law claims according to the law of the state or states the parties invoke. The Court also went on to say that the federal court should apply the federal procedural rules to adjudicate that case. *Erie* doctrine problems generally involve drawing a line between what is substantive and what is procedural. Making matters more complicated, the Court has not articulated a clear test for determining when a question is governed by substantive or procedural law. The easiest type of *Erie* problem arises in situations where the Court has already spoken—that is, when it has already ruled that a particular situation is either procedural (and the applicable federal approach governs) or it is substantive (and the court should follow what state law says). In this question, pursuant to the interpretation of the *Erie* doctrine in *Byrd v. Blue Ridge Rural Electric Cooperative*, 356 U.S. 525 (1968), we have one of those situations. Since the matter would have to be tried by a jury, the Court's ruling in *Byrd* dictates that this case should be resolved according to the federal procedural rule. From this and other case law, it is possible to develop an approach to resolving questions where the Court has not yet ruled. We explore this in the following questions.

2. B.   Pursuant to the interpretation of the *Erie* doctrine in *Hanna v. Plumer*, 380 U.S. 460 (1965), where a federal rule of procedure directly addresses a particular practice, the federal court should follow that rule. Here, FRCP 36 expressly provides for requests for admission during the discovery process, and thus Plaintiff will be allowed to file such requests despite the conflicting state law.

3. D.   Dicta in the Supreme Court's decision in *Semtek International v. Lockheed Martin*, 531 U.S. 497 (2001), suggests that when a federal court is faced with such a

threat to the integrity of its proceedings, there is a significant enough federal interest to override the fact that there is a state law that might address the dispute yet no equivalent federal rule that governs the situation. This leads to an approach that could be considered the "*Erie* three-step." (1) Is there a federal rule of procedure that directly governs the situation? If yes, then that should control. (2) If there is no federal rule that addresses the situation, is there a rule that the court can follow from state law? (And *Erie* problems usually identify a relevant state law. That's what makes them an *Erie* problem in the first place.) (3) If there *is* a relevant state law but no clear federal rule, is there nevertheless an overriding federal interest that should still trump the state law, warranting an application of a federal procedural intervention? We saw this in *Byrd*, with the federal constitutional interest in trial by jury, as well as in *Semtek*, where the Court posed essentially the fact pattern presented in this question. Thus, where there is this overriding federal interest, even in the face of a weighty state interest, the federal approach should still govern the dispute.

3.2 Claim Preclusion and Issue Preclusion

4. D.   Generally speaking, when a party seeks to bar another party from raising a claim in an action that, it is alleged, could have been raised in a prior dispute between the parties, they are seeking to bar that party through the doctrine of claim preclusion. In order to establish that such a bar should apply, the party seeking to utilize this doctrine has to show that the claim that could have been raised in the prior action arises out of the same common core of operative facts as the dispute in the prior action, that the parties were the same, and that the adverse party failed to raise the claim in that prior action. When those conditions are met, the party against whom the bar is sought will be prevented from raising a claim in a new lawsuit, even when that party did not raise the claim in the prior lawsuit. Here, the plaintiff's different claims arose from the same operative facts as the plaintiff's first suit. Since she did not raise these claims in that suit, she cannot raise them in a subsequent suit based on the same critical facts.

5. B.   You have already learned the standard for establishing claim preclusion. In a situation where a party is seeking to invoke the doctrine of issue preclusion, however, the analysis is different. A party can raise issue preclusion to bar subsequent relitigation of a particular question, when an issue of law or fact is actually litigated and resolved through a valid final judgment, where the party against whom the issue preclusion is sought had a full and fair opportunity to litigate the question, and the determination on that question is essential to the judgment. Here, the standard in the civil trial is lower: preponderance of the evidence as opposed to beyond a reasonable doubt. Just because the DOJ was unable to show in the criminal trial that Dena stole money from the settlement fund under that higher standard does not mean that plaintiffs will not be able

to satisfy the lower standard in the subsequent civil action. Since the requirements for neither claim preclusion nor issue preclusion are met, Dena is unable to rely on either to thwart the plaintiffs' action against her.

6. B.   While claim preclusion would likely bar both claims, the fact that several potential answers ("A" and "D") say "only" those individual claims might be barred means that Answer "B" is the only truly correct statement.

3.3 Preliminary and Interim Relief

7. C.   Plaintiff does not meet *all* of the elements for a preliminary injunction, which are that the moving party has a likelihood of success, that it will suffer irreparable harm without the injunction, that the balance of the equities in the case favor the granting of the injunction, and that the public interest will be served by the injunction. The moving party has to establish each of these elements. The failure to establish even one warrants denial of the request for the injunction. *See Winter v. NRDC*, 555 U.S. 7 (2008).

8. B.   The harm she suffered—the loss of income—is not irreparable harm, standing on its own, which means the motion would be dismissed on this ground because every element of the preliminary injunction standard must be met in order for the court to issue one.

9. A.   The standard for the issuance of an injunction requires a likelihood of success on the merits, not merely that the claim is plausible. Plausibility is the standard for pleading a claim, not for establishing a right to the issuance of an injunction. The most likely reason the motion will be denied is the weak allegations on the merits.

10. D.   There is no obligation to afford an opposing party an opportunity to cure a problem prior to seeking interim/preliminary remedies. Rule 65 requires advance notice of the intent to file but not that the opposing party actually has to have representation at the TRO hearing.

11. C.   This is not an element of the preliminary injunction standard. The standard regarding the merits is that the movant must show a likelihood of success on the merits. That is different from asserting a plausible claim (which is the current standard under FRCP 8 that will be addressed in Chapter 6).

12. B.   The denial of a preliminary injunction is appealable but a TRO is not. 28 U.S.C. §1292.

3.4 Formative Assessment Quiz

13. C.   Again, see *Winter v. NRDC*, 555 U.S. 7 (2008).

14. A.   Once again, the opinion in *Semtek* suggests precisely this scenario and states that the federal interest would outweigh the state's in this setting, meaning the order will stand.

15. C.   Beta was not a party to Alix's action and thus cannot use claim preclusion in her motion for partial summary judgment. However, issue preclusion is appropriate, even if Beta was not a party to the prior action.

Joinder

4.1 Joinder of Claims

1. C.   While it is entirely possible that the plaintiff can file separate actions against the employer and the building owner and both could be filed in federal court (the first under federal question and the second under diversity jurisdiction), the two cases cannot be filed together. Under FRCP 18, unrelated claims *can* be filed against a single party (provided there is already personal jurisdiction over the party and that there is subject matter jurisdiction over all claims). Here, however, the parties against which the plaintiff wants to file his action are not the same, which means the Federal Rules of Civil Procedure is unavailable to the plaintiff to file them in the same action. If the claims were against the same party, even though unrelated, the plaintiff could file them in one action, provided the federal court had subject matter jurisdiction over all of them.

2. D.   While it might seem that under FRCP 18 the plaintiff could join these two unrelated claims, there is no basis for subject matter jurisdiction over the state claim. The court clearly has jurisdiction over the federal claim. The question is whether it can also retain jurisdiction over the state claim. Since it does not arise out of the same nucleus of operative facts—there are no facts linking the state claim to the federal claim—there is no supplemental jurisdiction over the claim. Since neither federal question nor diversity jurisdiction is available to the plaintiff, she must rely on supplemental jurisdiction, which is not available either. This shows how the seemingly generous grant of FRCP 18 is deceptive: there is still a need to have a basis for subject matter jurisdiction for any claim that FRCP 18 would permit a party to add.

4.2 Counterclaims and Cross-Claims

3. C.   This question introduces you to FRCP 13, which sets forth the mechanisms by which a defendant can interpose a counterclaim. FRCP 13(a) describes what are called "compulsory" counterclaims, and 13(b) identifies "permissive" counterclaims. This distinction is critical, but the terms used can be deceiving. When a counterclaim is considered compulsory, as its name suggests, the defendant must assert it against the plaintiff; otherwise, the defendant will be barred from raising it in subsequent litigation by the doctrine of claim preclusion (*see* Chapter 3). But there is another implication of the counterclaim's being considered compulsory in nature: there is almost always going to be subject matter jurisdiction over the claim, so the defendant will have the capacity to interpose that compulsory claim once it is identified as such. The reason for that is baked into the very meaning

of a compulsory counterclaim. While there are several different standards under which courts have determined whether counterclaims are permitted under FRCP 13, the most commonly applied standard was articulated by the court in *Plant v. Blazer Financial Services*, 598 F.2d 1357 (5th Cir. 1979). There, the court found that claims that are logically related to claims by the plaintiff should be designated as compulsory counterclaims. While there may be an independent basis for federal jurisdiction over a particular counterclaim (for example, if it raises a federal question), there is no need for it to have such an independent basis of jurisdiction if it qualifies as a compulsory counterclaim. If it is, in fact, compulsory because it is logically related to the plaintiff's claim, then there will certainly be, at a minimum, subject matter jurisdiction in federal court through supplemental jurisdiction. A permissive counterclaim, in contrast, does not have to be raised by the defendant if the defendant does not want to raise it. At the same time, if the defendant does, it does not enjoy the same near guarantee that there will be subject matter jurisdiction. The fact that the counterclaim is considered permissive does not mean there is "permission" to bring the claim. If a defendant wants to interpose a counterclaim that is not logically related to a claim filed against it by a plaintiff, then the defendant will need to have an independent basis for doing so. But if it does not interpose this type of counterclaim, it will not be barred by the doctrine of claim preclusion from filing it in a subsequent action. Here, since the counterclaim is logically related to plaintiff's claim, it is compulsory and the defendant can interpose it.

4. C.   The key issue here is baked into the question. It asks whether the defendant is required to interpose the counterclaim, which is another way of asking whether it is a compulsory counterclaim under FRCP 13(a). Here, the claim is permissive because it is not related to the plaintiff's claim. But the defendant can interpose the claim if it so chooses because there is subject matter jurisdiction over it. It is not required to do so, however, because of the permissive nature of the claim.

5. A.   Plaintiff's obligations to pay rent for the premises and whether it was free to demand more renovations of the premises hinge on the interpretation of the renovations clause of the lease. As a result, the affirmative claim and the counterclaim are logically related, and thus the counterclaim is a compulsory counterclaim under FRCP 13(a).

6. A.   This is a permissive counterclaim because the allegations are unrelated to Plaintiff's affirmative antitrust claims and thus are not logically related to the Plaintiff's case. Nevertheless, there *is* subject matter jurisdiction over the permissive claim because there is diversity jurisdiction over the counterclaim; the parties are diverse and that, standing alone, satisfies the amount-in-controversy requirement.

7. D.   Although the counterclaim is permissive because it is not related to the plaintiff's claims, there is subject matter jurisdiction over it because the case is based on diversity and the amount-in-controversy requirement is satisfied.

8. C.   First, the counterclaim is compulsory. Plaintiff's argument is that it has this extra stock and cannot pay for it as a result of Roma's anti-competitive behavior. The counterclaim—that Plaintiff has not paid Roma for this stock—is thus directly tied to the basis of Plaintiff's affirmative claim against Roma. Furthermore, because the counterclaim is logically related to Plaintiff's affirmative claim, it arises out of the same nucleus of operative facts, and thus there is, at a minimum, §1367 supplemental jurisdiction. There is likely an independent basis of jurisdiction for it as well, as the claim arises under state law, the parties are diverse under §1332, and the claim exceeds the amount-in-controversy requirement. But that independent basis is unnecessary because the counterclaim is logically related to the Plaintiff's anchor claim.

9. D.   This question addresses the issue of how to treat claims between two defendants. When claims are asserted against parties on the same side of the "v," those claims are considered cross-claims. As such, they are governed by Rule 13(g), which uses the same language as 13(a) with respect to compulsory counterclaims only. This might qualify as a permissive counterclaim if it were in a separate case against Able because there *is* an independent basis of jurisdiction (it qualifies for diversity jurisdiction). However, even if a cross-claim in this situation had an independent basis of jurisdiction, it would need to be logically related to the Plaintiff's original claims—and this claim is not logically related to the underlying claim of the Plaintiff and thus cannot be interposed, even if there is a basis for the court to exercise subject matter jurisdiction over it.

4.3 Joinder of Parties

10. A. Under Rule 20, plaintiffs can be joined in a single action if their claims arise out of the same transaction or occurrence or series of transactions or occurrences and there is *at least one* question of law *or* fact common to all plaintiffs. The claims do appear to arise out of the same series of transactions—the employer's discriminatory practices—and raise the same question about whether the employer has violated civil rights laws in its treatment of the plaintiffs. Answer "A" most accurately reflects the applicable standard for the joinder of the plaintiffs in one action.

11. C. Similar to the issue related to the joinder of plaintiffs, when considering whether defendants can be joined in a single action, the claims against them must be "asserted against them jointly, severally, or in the alternative"; those claims must arise out of the same transaction/series of transactions; and "any question of law or fact" that is "common to all defendants" must exist with respect to the claims. Accordingly, answer "C" reflects an issue that the court should not consider.

12. A. The parties are properly joined under Rule 20 as they are jointly and severally liable and there are common questions of fact related to the three defendants.

4.4 Impleader

13. D. Construction has correctly identified Floors as being subject to indemnity to Construction for the inadequate flooring materials. As such, there is a basis under Rule 14 to implead Floors. The key to impleader is that the party the defendant wants to bring into the case must be liable to the *defendant* for all or part of the claim asserted against it. Generally speaking, there are four bases upon which a defendant can satisfy the requirement of Rule 14. The first of these is that a third party has warranted to the third-party plaintiff (this is the name the Rule gives to refer to the defendant that is seeking to bring in a new third party, which the rule refers to as the third-party defendant) that the product that the third-party defendant sold to the third-party plaintiff failed, and it was that failure that caused the harm which the original plaintiff suffered. Similarly, the second category is indemnity: where the third-party defendant agreed to indemnify the third-party plaintiff if the product it sold to the third-party plaintiff caused the harm that is the subject of the plaintiff's case. The third ground is that the third-party defendant must contribute to the harm the plaintiff suffered due to joint and several liability. The fourth is that the relationship between the third-party plaintiff and third-party defendant be one of subrogation, where, for example, the third-party defendant has agreed to insure the third-party plaintiff for the harm it is alleged to have caused the plaintiff. Here, the contractual relationship between Construction and Floors is one in which Floors has agreed to indemnify Construction, and thus impleader is an appropriate mechanism by which Construction can bring Floors into the case.

14. D. Since the contractual relationship between Chilax and Mike's includes an indemnification clause, FRCP 14 will permit the impleader of Chilax in this action.

15. B. The provisions of 28 U.S.C. §1367(b) typically operate as a bar to prevent a plaintiff from asserting claims against new parties joined in a case if the basis of jurisdiction over the case is diversity and the new party is not diverse from the plaintiff. It does *not* apply to a defendant's effort to implead a new third-party defendant, however, even when that new third-party defendant is not diverse to the original defendant. The same is not true, however, for Plaintiff's effort to file new affirmative claims against 3PD. Plaintiff and 3PD are not diverse. When such is the case, the §1367(b) bar applies to prevent Plaintiff from filing new affirmative claims against the non-diverse, impleaded third-party defendant. It does not affect a defendant's ability to join a non-diverse third-party defendant, and that third-party defendant can be from the same state as plaintiff *or* defendant. In addition, here, First Party has properly identified a basis—indemnity— upon which it can implead 3PD under Rule 14.

16. B. Alleging Cyberdyne is responsible for Plaintiff's injuries as opposed to Doctor is not an appropriate vehicle for impleader under Rule 14. Rule 14 only allows a defendant to join a third party when that party is responsible to the defendant

for all or part of the claim against it. A defendant seeking to implead a third party cannot assert that the third party is wholly responsible for the claims against the defendant. For this question, you were not asked about issues related to personal jurisdiction.

17. C. This answer properly articulates the standard under FRCP 20 related to the joinder of defendants, which is satisfied in this fact pattern.

4.5 New Claims After Joinder

18. D. The court will deny the motion with respect to both claims. This question asks you to address the ability of an impleaded party to assert counterclaims against the party that brought it into the case. In this scenario, there are compulsory and permissive claims as in a normal counterclaim situation, and Rule 14 treats these counterclaims in the same way that Rule 13 does. Here, the first claim is mandatory and a compulsory counterclaim because it arises out the same nucleus of operative facts as the underlying claim. There is thus, at a minimum, supplemental jurisdiction (but there is also diversity jurisdiction, as will be shown in a moment). Although the second claim is permissive under Rule 14(a)(2)(B) and thus filed under 13(b), there is an independent basis of jurisdiction for that claim: diversity. The parties are diverse and the claim exceeds the amount-in-controversy requirement.

19. A. This question addresses the issue of when and whether a third-party defendant can assert affirmative claims against a plaintiff. Rule 14(a)(2)(D) provides that such a party "may also assert against the plaintiff any claim arising out of the transaction or occurrence that is the subject matter of the plaintiff's claim against the third-party plaintiff." This provision is doing several things at the same time. First, the third-party defendant is allowed to assert what otherwise would be considered the equivalent of a "compulsory" counterclaim in the sense that, if this party were a traditional defendant, it would be a claim that is logically connected to the plaintiff's original claim. Second, unlike that type of counterclaim, the third-party defendant is not obligated to raise it if it does not wish to in this action. In other words, it will not be barred by the doctrine of claim preclusion from raising it in a subsequent case. Another thing to note: here, the claim would otherwise be barred because of the requirement of complete diversity if it were an affirmative claim raised by a plaintiff against a defendant. But if one reviews the requirement of 28 U.S.C. §1367(b), which bars such claims in a case based on diversity, it does not act as a bar on third-party defendants filing related counterclaims. It is important to note also that, in a case in which the plaintiff has not asserted new claims against the third-party defendant (assuming it can), the third-party defendant cannot assert unrelated claims against the plaintiff, even if there is an independent basis for doing so.

20. D. Here, we see the operation of the 28 U.S.C. §1367(b) bar to prevent plaintiff from filing new affirmative claims against the non-diverse third-party defen-

dant in a case where the basis of subject matter jurisdiction is diversity jurisdiction. In a case where the basis of subject matter jurisdiction of the underlying case is federal question jurisdiction, the §1367(b) bar does not apply.

21. A. Here, FRCP 14(a)(2)(B) permits a third-party defendant to assert the equivalent of a permissive counterclaim under FRCP 13(b) against a third-party plaintiff. Here, the claim is not logically related to the underlying claims, but, since there is an independent basis of subject matter jurisdiction for asserting it (diversity jurisdiction), the third-party defendant may do so.

22. C. Since Fine is a traditional defendant, it cannot file a cross-claim against another traditional defendant when that cross-claim is not logically related to the underlying claims. Had Fine been impleaded through Rule 14 by Testa, there would have been greater latitude for Fine to file a claim against Testa under the same grounds as Rule 13(b) would permit. Here, since Fine and Testa are both original defendants, Fine cannot file an unrelated claim against Testa.

23. B. Beta is entitled to file claims against Plaintiff that arise out of the subject matter of the underlying claims (FRCP 13(a)(2)(D)). Once Plaintiff interposes a new affirmative claim against Beta, which it can do, Beta may then file unrelated counterclaims against Plaintiff (provided there is subject matter jurisdiction for doing so). But the failure to do so does not preclude Beta from filing such otherwise unrelated claims in a subsequent suit. *See* FRCP 14(a)(3).

24. C. Rule 14 permits plaintiffs to bring in a third-party defendant in the same manner that a defendant can do so, that is, when that plaintiff faces a counterclaim against it and a third party might be liable to the plaintiff for all or part of the claim.

4.6 Necessary and Indispensable Parties

25. C. Even though Baker might be subject to impleader because she is responsible for contributing to the damages, if assessed, against Able, that does not make her a necessary party. If Baker is not a necessary party, she cannot be an indispensable party either. FRCP 19 asks three critical questions: First, is the party a necessary party? Second, if so, is there some barrier to the party's being joined? If there is no barrier to its being joined, then the so-called necessary party should be joined in the action. If there *is* a barrier to its being joined, then the FRCP 19 analysis asks a third question: is there some way to lessen any prejudice that might befall those parties in the action and the party that cannot be joined if the case proceeds without that party? If the case can proceed in some fashion without prejudice to the parties (both inside and outside the suit), then that missing party is not what is called an "indispensable party" and the case can move forward. If there is no way to proceed without that party in a way that does not cause undue prejudice to those parties in the case and outside of it, then that missing party *is* an indispensable party and the case must be dismissed.

26. C. That a party is a joint tortfeasor with a defendant already in the case does not make that party a necessary party to the action. Although the defendant in this case could certainly implead the absent party, that does not mean the case presents a situation where that absent party is a necessary party under FRCP 19.

27. B. FRCP 19(b) lists the factors the court can weigh to determine if a case should proceed without the absent party. Subpart (b)(4) provides that the court should consider if "the plaintiff would have an adequate remedy if the action were dismissed for nonjoinder." Here, AzerCo is not a plaintiff but a defendant. While under subpart (b)(1), the court can consider whether a judgment rendered in the missing party's absence "might prejudice that person or the existing parties," only (b)(4) looks at adequate remedies, and there, only for the plaintiff.

28. C. Under Rule 19(b), the court is able to shape the relief to narrow the prejudice to the plaintiff and the financial advisor in light of the founder's absence; thus, the founder is not an indispensable party.

4.7 Service of Process Issues Related to Joinder

29. A. Rule 4(k)(1)(B) extends the reach of personal jurisdiction when a party is added by virtue of FRCP 14 or 19 and is "served within a judicial district of the United States and not more than 100 miles from where the summons was issued." In a situation where such a party is added and can be served within that 100-mile radius of the courthouse where the case is filed, Rule 4 permits the exercise of personal jurisdiction over that party even if the party does not have any contacts with the forum.

4.8 Formative Assessment Quiz

30. B. Neither the counterclaim nor that portion of the amended complaint that seeks to implead Tate Farm will be dismissed. The counterclaim can exceed the amount sought in the underlying claim (Rule 13(c)) *and* Plaintiff appears to have provided adequate grounds to implead Tate Farm, which it can do (Rule 14(b)). Even though Plaintiff and Tate Farm are not diverse, the diversity rules do not apply to a plaintiff attempting to implead a third party under Rule 14. Plaintiff could not, however, file new affirmative claims against Tate. The counterclaim is clearly permissive, it is true, but all that means is that Hessla must have an independent basis for filing it, and it does: diversity.

31. D. All of the claims here arise under federal law, and thus §1367(b) does not apply to bar Plaintiff's claims.

32. A. The counterclaim can be filed because it is logically related to the anchor claims. Plaintiff asserts the mortgage insurance charge was fraudulent, and defendant seeks payment on that charge. The validity of the charge will be litigated with respect to both claims, and thus they are logically related. The home state of the defendant is not an issue because the case is based on federal law.

33. C. Even though there appears to be an independent basis of federal subject matter jurisdiction for the workplace safety claim, because it is not logically related to the plaintiff's initial claim against the defendants (it is thus a "permissive" cross-claim between two defendants, which is not allowed), the consultant cannot file that claim against the developer in this action. It *can* file the first claim (the contract claim), however, because it is logically related to plaintiff's anchor claim.

34. B. *See* FRCP 13. Defendant's claim is a permissive counterclaim because it is not related to the underlying affirmative claim of the Plaintiff; since there is no independent basis of subject matter jurisdiction for that claim, Defendant cannot interpose it. 28 U.S.C. §1332.

35. B. *See* Rule 19(b)(1).

36. A. The first counterclaim would appear to be a compulsory counterclaim, and thus there is subject matter jurisdiction over it. With the second counterclaim, there is an independent basis of jurisdiction for it. It satisfies 28 U.S.C. §1332. It is likely a permissive counterclaim, but, since there is an independent basis of jurisdiction for it, Lannister can file it as well.

37. A. See Rule 4(k)(1)(B), which extends the reach of the court in Newark to those parties that are within 100 miles of the courthouse, as Dan's Farm is, according to the facts given.

38. C. FRCP 20 provides that defendants may be joined in a single action if "(A) any right to relief is asserted against them jointly, severally, or in the alternative with respect to or arising out of the same transaction, occurrence, or series of transactions or occurrences; and (B) any question of law or fact common to all defendants will arise in the action." Here, all of these requirements are satisfied.

39. A. Plaintiff and Bard are not diverse, and thus the claims filed against Bard by Plaintiff will be dismissed. AMC has alleged a proper ground for impleading Bard, however, and those claims can proceed even if Bard is not diverse from AMC because they are both incorporated in Delaware. The diversity requirement of §1367(b) only applies to claims raised by plaintiffs.

Pleading

5.1 General Requirements

1. A. The Supreme Court's decisions in *Bell Atlantic v. Twombly*, 550 U.S. 544 (2007), and *Ashcroft v. Iqbal*, 556 U.S. 662 (2009), now require that a claim under FRPC 8 must include facts set forth with sufficient particularity to make the claim plausible.

2. B. Given that Plaintiff has alleged that Bank has engaged in fraud, FRCP 9(b) requires that she allege her claims with greater particularity than is expected under FRCP 8. While an argument can be made that Rule 8(a)(2) and the plausi-

bility standard found to lie within it still apply, the heightened pleading standard in Rule 9(b) would be the most appropriate standard to apply in this case. "C" is incorrect because a litigant *can* plead inconsistent theories. "D" is incorrect because it is the Rule 56 standard and not the Rule 12 standard.

3. A. Again, under *Twombly*, 550 U.S. 544 (2007), and *Iqbal*, 556 U.S. 662 (2009), the allegations in the complaint must be alleged with sufficient particularity to render the claims plausible. Here, the plaintiff did not simply allege without any factual specificity that the defendant ordered violence against the plaintiff.

4. D. According to the Supreme Court's ruling in *Jones v. Bock*, 549 U.S. 199 (2007), a party making an affirmative claim does not have to add arguments to its pleading in anticipation of a potential affirmative defense.

5. C. This is the reverse of *Jones v. Bock*, 549 U.S. 199 (2007). Here, unlike in that case, it *is* a pleading requirement under the statute that the landlord allege facts sufficient to establish that it has complied with pre-complaint notice to the tenant.

5.2 Responding to the Complaint

6. B. The warden disputes these allegations. Still, they are sufficient as alleged to satisfy Rule 8(a) because they are specific enough, even if the warden disputes them, to nudge the claim from the conceivable to the plausible. The proper response to such allegations is simply to deny them in the defendant's answer. They cannot form the basis of a motion to dismiss for failure to state a claim because of their apparent plausibility.

7. A. According to FRCP 12(h)(1), a defendant must assert in its initial response to the complaint (whether in an answer or a pre-answer motion to dismiss) the following defenses: lack of personal jurisdiction, improper venue, insufficient process, or insufficient service of process. If the defendant fails to interpose one of these defenses in that initial response, then the defendant has waived that defense and will not be able to raise it at a later time in the action.

8. C. Read FRCP 12(h). Venue is waived, but the other two defenses may be added in an answer, even if they were not raised in the initial pre-answer motion to dismiss.

9. D. See Rule 12(h). Defendant has waived the defense of personal jurisdiction but not subject matter jurisdiction.

5.3 Rule 11

10. C. Only baseless factual and legal contentions contained in pleadings, motions, and other writings submitted in the course of litigation are covered by Rule 11. Since answer "C" includes both the summary judgment motion and the allegations in the complaint, it is the correct answer. Inappropriate actions in discovery are covered by other rules, as explored in Chapter 6.

11. D. Plaintiff has a good-faith basis for the first claim. "Creative" is not the standard for a Rule 11 motion. Just because the claim was dismissed does not mean it was frivolous.

12. C. Only the arguments contained in the papers opposing summary judgment will subject Larry to Rule 11 sanctions in this problem.

13. A. Rule 11 provides that a party represented by counsel cannot be found to have violated Rule 11 for filing baseless legal claims. Such penalties are only reserved for lawyers.

14. C. The complaint appears to have been filed without an "inquiry reasonable under the circumstances" as required by FRCP 11. The first thing Linda should have done is ask to see the agreement between Paul and Danielle, which would have shown that Danielle had complied with it in apportioning the proceeds of the public offering. Moreover, once it appears clear that Paul has no claim, Linda must withdraw the action, even if she thinks it might have some settlement value, because it is simply baseless.

15. C. The claim, though novel, certainly had a good-faith basis for making new law or for extending prior precedent, which means it satisfies the Rule 11 standard. The fact that the case merely "lacked merit," as the court held, is not enough to grant the motion for sanctions.

16. D. This problem both addresses the relevant standard under FRCP 11 and describes the "safe harbor" procedure embedded in that Rule. A party that wishes to file a motion for sanctions under FRCP 11 must serve, but not file, the motion and give the non-moving party twenty-one days from service of the motion to withdraw whatever the moving party alleges is frivolous. If the non-moving party refuses to withdraw the allegedly frivolous matter, then the moving party is free to file the motion. At the same time, although the argument the non-moving party is making does not have much support, there is a good faith basis for making it, and thus it is not frivolous.

17. C. This is not a requirement under Rule 11.

5.4 Amending Pleadings

18. B. *See* FRCP 15(a)(1). This rule provides for an initial amendment "as of right," provided that the amended pleading is served within twenty-one days of its being served (if there has not been a responsive pleading). If a responsive pleading is required, then the as-of-right amendment must be served within twenty-one days of receiving that responsive pleading.

19. A. This question deals with the issue of "relation back," that is, when a party wishes to amend its pleading to include a claim for which the statute of limitations has already expired. When the new claim arises out of the same nucleus of operative facts as the original claim, the party seeking that amendment can inter-

pose that claim even if the statute of limitations has otherwise expired on it, provided that the *original* claim was filed within the applicable statute of limitations. Here, the actions specifically targeting Plaintiff are part of an overarching, anti-competitive scheme, a single nucleus of operative facts.

20. B.   The proposed amendments arise out of the same transaction as the claims contained in the original complaint, and thus those allegations "relate back" to the original complaint, meaning they are not barred by the statute of limitations. Defendant has suffered no prejudice in reality because discovery has not even commenced at the time of the motion to amend.

5.5 Formative Assessment Quiz

21. B.   Only the defense based on subject matter jurisdiction may be interposed at this juncture. The defense based on improper venue was waived when Quartz failed to include it in its pre-answer motion to dismiss. FRCP 12(h)(1)(A) and (B). The defense based on subject matter jurisdiction can be raised at any time. FRCP 12(h)(3).

22. B.   Review FRCP 11. Plaintiff's counsel had ample time to research the case but chose not to do so. Such an inquiry was not reasonable under the circumstances and thus is a violation of FRCP 11.

23. D.   Under *Jones v. Bock*, 549 U.S. 199 (2007), Plaintiff is not required to allege facts sufficient to overcome an anticipated defense of Defendant.

24. C.   *See* Rule 12(h)(1).

25. B.   *See* FRCP 15. The "relation back" doctrine would permit Plaintiff to amend her claims here because they appear to arise out of the same transactions—the decisions to not promote her—as her original claims.

26. B.   Review *Jones v. Bock*, 549 U.S. 199 (2007). The plaintiff does not have to anticipate and plead around an affirmative defense that has not yet been interposed in the action.

27. A.   In accordance with Rule 11(b), continuing to maintain the defense constitutes "later advocating," even if only done orally. The written component of Defendant's actions, the answer, is still involved in the action. Just because the "later advocating" is done orally does not take the action out of the application of Rule 11, because what is at issue is the defective answer.

28. B.   Review FRCP 15. The claims can relate back because they satisfy the requirement of Rule 15, that is, they arise "out of the conduct, transaction, or occurrence set out—or attempted to be set out—in the original pleading."

29. C.   Dave should simply file an answer denying he was responsible for the accident. If the factual allegations in the complaint are plausible, it is difficult to do anything other than simply submit an answer in which the defendant denies the allegations.

Discovery:
Answer and Explanations

6.1 Scope of Discovery

1. B. FRCP 26(b)(1) allows discovery of "nonprivileged matter that is relevant to any party's claim or defense and proportional to the needs of the case." It is designed to ensure the parties are able to obtain information about their opponents' claims and defenses without making discovery overly burdensome given the scope, size, and value of the case. When considering this proportionality, the court should consider "the importance of the issues at stake in the action, the amount in controversy, the parties' relative access to relevant information, the parties' resources, the importance of the discovery in resolving the issues, and whether the burden or expense of the proposed discovery outweighs its likely benefit." Furthermore, "[i]nformation within this scope of discovery need not be admissible in evidence to be discoverable." Although the term "amount in controversy" is familiar from other contexts, it is also relevant here.

2. C. The bank's claim is about Harry's mortgage debt, not about any student loan debt he may have. Whether or not Harry is current on his student loan debt is not relevant to whether he owes money on his mortgage, and thus it is outside the proper scope of discovery. For a discussion of the relevance of discovery requests, see *Steffan v. Cheney*, 920 F.2d 74 (D.C. Cir. 1990).

6.2 Tools of Discovery

3. B. Under Rule 32, there are grounds to use the prior deposition testimony of all of these witnesses, even in Plaintiff's presentation of its affirmative case.

4. C. FRCP 33 governs the use of interrogatories in discovery and only Answer "C" is consistent with that rule.

5. C. FRCP 35 covers "mental and physical examinations" but only permits them to take place on good cause and when a party "whose mental or physical condition ... is in controversy." Here, the physical condition of the plaintiff was at issue, but once the claim of mental anguish was withdrawn, it was no longer "in controversy" and thus could not be the subject of this examination.

6. A. FRCP 36 provides that requests for admission are still subject to FRCP 26 regarding the scope of discovery, but according to FRCP 36(a)(5), a party may not object "solely on the ground that the request presents a genuine issue for trial."

7. C. FRCP 34 covers this situation and is also limited to seeking information otherwise covered by Rule 26's limit on the scope of discovery. Here, all of the items except the records related to substances held on other sites operated by the defendant would be within the proper scope of discovery and contemplated within the mechanisms available through FRCP 34.

8. C.   Rule 27 provides for this sort of deposition for the reasons set forth in Answer "C". While Answer "B" is partially correct—any deposition used in this context must be in relation to a case that could be filed in federal court—the extraordinary remedy of a pre-complaint deposition is only available when there is a need to do so.

6.3 Motion Practice and Penalties Related to Discovery

9. D.   A party opposing a motion to compel after being ordered by the court to respond to a discovery demand will be expected to compensate the moving party for the expenses involved in having made the motion, which can include an award of attorney's fees, unless the non-moving party's position was "substantially justified," as the party's position was here. *See* FRCP 37(a)(5)(A)(ii).

10. C.   FRCP 37 provides a range of potential punishments for a non-conforming party, including striking a pleading in its entirety as well as several other similar punishments, including the other items described in this question. Here, however, the defendant is the recalcitrant party, which means there would be no reason to strike the *complaint*, that is, the plaintiff's pleading.

11. B.   The structure of Rule 37 requires that before one can move for a motion for sanctions, one must first move for an order compelling discovery. Here, Defendant went straight for an order for sanctions without pursuing the intermediate step.

12. D.   Once again, under Rule 37(a)(5)(A), the standard against which the non-moving party's conduct will be judged is whether the position is "substantially justified," and not whether the non-moving party merely has a "plausible basis" for that objection.

13. B.   This question tests your knowledge of the subject of "spoliation": when a party destroys or otherwise impairs an opposing party's access to materials in discovery. When a party destroys evidence, if the case is being heard before a jury, the court can direct the jury that it must consider the missing evidence to have been harmful to the party that destroyed it when that party had an obligation to preserve it and destroyed it knowingly. If the evidence is destroyed without such intent, the court could issue a directive to the jury that it may consider the evidence to have been harmful to the destroying party, but it is not required to do so. Here, the correct answer (meaning the answer that is "wrong" in the sense that it is irrelevant to the determination as to whether to direct the jury to consider the evidence harmful) is "B".

6.4 Formative Assessment Quiz

14. B. The immigration status of Plaintiff is irrelevant to the question of whether she should have to divulge the information on her taxes. *See* Rule 26(b)(1) and 26(c). All of the other information is relevant to this inquiry.

15. D. FRCP 26(b)(1) provides that matters sought through discovery "need not be admissible in evidence to be discoverable."

16. C. As in the previous question, although the non-moving party may have an argument as to why it did not want to comply with the discovery order, the court ruled that the position was baseless, which is another way of saying that it was not substantially justified. And if the position was not substantially justified, the court may order costs and attorney's fees. *See* FRCP 37(a)(5)(A)(ii).

Summary Judgment, Trials, and Appeals

7.1 Summary Judgment and Other Resolutions Without Trial

1. B. The standard in FRCP 56 for a grant of summary judgment is that there must be no genuine dispute as to a material fact. Whether there was proper posting of the warning signs is clearly a material fact that goes to the defendant's potential liability. Since the plaintiff's and defendant's witnesses have presented different eye-witness accounts regarding whether the area was properly posted, there is a genuine dispute as to that material fact. Resolving the matter, which is potentially one of credibility, is properly performed by the trier of fact and is not to be carried out at the summary judgment phase of the dispute.

2. A. As in the previous question, here there is a genuine dispute as to a material fact regarding whether the employees were subjected to inappropriate treatment. Senior-level officials simply testifying that they conduct proper trainings and issue appropriate warnings does not overcome the specific allegations contained in the plaintiff's evidence.

3. C. FRCP 56(c)(2) provides that "[a] party may object that the material cited to support or dispute a fact cannot be presented in a form that would be admissible in evidence." FRCP 56(c)(4) provides that supporting statements must be "made on personal knowledge, set out facts that are admissible in evidence, and show that the affiant ... is competent to testify on the matters stated." Here, the other inmate's statement is not a sworn statement and likely contains hearsay, which would be inadmissible at trial. For these flaws, it could not be utilized by the non-moving party to establish a genuine issue of material fact in dispute.

4. C. Defendant is trying to challenge the credibility of the third witness, which is more appropriately done at trial. There is still a genuine dispute as to a material fact—what caused the beam to fall. There is nothing that says that a party must

wait until the close of discovery to move for summary judgment, but if the nonmoving party asserts that it needs more time to pursue discovery on the issue that forms the basis of the summary judgment motion, the court can decide to grant more time or deny the motion. FRCP 56(d). Here, the fact pattern provides that all of the facts on the issue of the crane's operation are in evidence and neither party will seek more. As a result, a motion for summary judgment on this point is not premature.

5. A.   The specific evidence of illegal conduct has not been specifically refuted by UCar's evidence, and thus summary judgment *is* appropriate here. *See Bias v. Advantage Int'l, Inc.*, 905 F.2d 1558 (D.C. Cir. 1990).

6. D.   Carr's testimony does not speak directly to the allegations made by the plaintiff. Indeed, with a little more factual detail regarding Carr's allegations and whether he reviewed Plaintiff's transaction in particular, it is possible that Plaintiff might even be able to make a motion for summary judgment going the other way, as in *Bias v. Advantage International*, 905 F.2d 1558 (D.C. Cir. 1990). *See also Tolan v. Cotton*, 572 U.S. 650 (2014).

7. C.   Issues of credibility should not be determined at the summary judgment phase, and thus, even with this evidence, there are still genuine disputes as to material facts related to the matters in question.

8. B.   The allegations in the deposition are more than sufficient to defeat Bank's motion for summary judgment, which is based on general arguments rather than specific facts that would show that the TILA notices were in fact sent. There is thus at least a dispute as to the material facts regarding whether the notices were in fact sent. What is more, it is possible that, on this record, the court could rule for Plaintiff on summary judgment because Defendant's general statements are not specifically directed to whether the Bank ever mailed the required notices specifically to the Plaintiff. Rule 56 (c)(1)(A) makes it clear that deposition testimony is acceptable to support or oppose a motion for summary judgment.

7.2 Jury Trial Matters and Pre-Trial Maneuvers

9. C.   Traditionally, under the Seventh Amendment to the U.S. Constitution, the types of cases determined by a jury at the time of the ratification of the Constitution have continued to be heard by a jury, and those types heard by a judge at that time have continued to be handled by that trier of fact. When a new statutory right is established, Congress can also provide for whether the case can be heard by a judge or jury. In cases where it is not clear, it is appropriate to analogize the type of case to the type of claim in existence at the time of the ratification of the Constitution to determine whether it should be heard by a judge or jury (provided a timely demand for jury has been made—a plaintiff's demand for a jury must be asserted in the complaint, while a defendant's must be demanded in its answer). Here, since the contract claim and the damages component of the trademark claim are claims traditionally heard by the jury, the plaintiff will have

those matters decided by a jury. Since the injunction sought under the trademark claim is the type of remedy issued by a court of equity—where a judge alone would preside—it will not be heard by the jury.

10. C. The court must determine whether there is a ground to dismiss any of these potential jurors for cause under FCRP 47. Such cause would exist if any potential juror's impartiality related to the subject matter of the proceeding or the parties could reasonably be questioned. Here, it appears that the second potential juror's impartiality could reasonably be questioned. The other two credibly state that they can be impartial in this action. It is certainly possible that either of the other two potential jurors could be stricken by the defense counsel using one of its three peremptory challenges provided for under 28 U.S.C. §1870. But having the court dismiss these potential jurors without counsel's having to use one of its limited peremptory challenges is unlikely here, given the potential jurors' *credible* responses regarding their impartiality. If a court does not believe those responses, it can always dismiss those potential jurors for cause.

11. B. FRCP 16(e) provides that a court can amend a final pre-trial order in order to prevent "manifest injustice." Here, in addition to potentially issuing sanctions on the defendant for withholding evidence from the plaintiff, the court will also amend the pre-trial order to permit the plaintiff to assert her claims related to racial discrimination in the action.

7.3 Post-Trial Maneuvers

12. A. *See* Rule 50. All of the other standards are for different motions.

13. D. Rule 50 provides explicitly that in order to make a motion for judgment as a matter of law after the jury has rendered its verdict, the party seeking such motion must have made the same motion prior to its being submitted to the jury, which it can renew after the verdict comes down (assuming it goes against that party).

14. D. Neither motion should prevail because the evidence is a "close call." The standard for neither motion has been met, not even the standard for a new trial, which requires that the verdict is against the "great weight of the evidence."

7.4 Appeals

15. B. According to the final judgment rule, appellate courts have jurisdiction over appeals from all final decisions of the district courts of the United States, where a "final decision" is one that "ends the litigation on the merits and leaves nothing for the court to but execute the judgment." 28 U.S.C. §1291. *See also Caitlin v. United States*, 324 U.S. 229 (1945). While there are some exceptions to this rule, addressed in the following questions, the straightforward application of the final judgment rule in this instance means the denial of a motion to dismiss is not appealable at this stage in the litigation. At the conclusion of the matter, after

final judgment is rendered, the losing party can appeal not just that final order but also the failure to dismiss the action.

16. D. In *Lauro Lines v. Chasser*, 490 U.S. 495 (1989), on facts similar to the fact pattern here, the Court found that the rejection of a motion based on a forum selection clause is not "effectively unreviewable" such that in order to vindicate the interest without its being completely destroyed, immediate appeal is warranted. The right embodied in the forum selection clause, the Court ruled, does not exempt the litigant from facing adjudication. Rather, the application of the forum selection clause goes to the merits of the action, and the initial court can consider it as such and resolve the case in its entirety. Once there is a final judgment, the appellate court can, once again, review all prior orders, including the order related to the forum selection clause.

17. C. Orders "granting, continuing, modifying, refusing or dissolving injunctions, or refusing to dissolve or modify injunctions," are appealable under 28 U.S.C. §1292(a)(1). TROs are not appealable.

18. B. The grounds for interlocutory appeals of otherwise non-final orders are governed by 28 U.S.C. §1292(b). One of the bases found in that statute includes where a potential interlocutory appeal would involve a controlling question of law and there is a substantial difference of opinion as to the application of that law.

7.5 Formative Assessment Quiz

19. C. The fact that the different officials offer different versions of the facts creates a genuine dispute as to material facts. While it might be easier for Plaintiffs to prove their case by a preponderance of the evidence if they have several of these officials testifying against the interest of the defendant group and in support of Plaintiff's version of events, the consideration of these conflicting versions of events is most appropriately handled by the trier of fact and is not a question that should be resolved at the summary judgment stage.

20. B. FRCP 56(d) provides a basis upon which the court can deny or delay a motion for summary judgment if a party shows for "specified reasons" that "it cannot present facts essential to justify its opposition." Here, the fact that discovery has not yet closed and the possibility that there are new areas of discovery that the defendant needs to explore to gather the facts necessary to oppose the motion could establish the grounds necessary to delay or even deny the motion. At the same time, the defendant has not specified what information it needs to oppose the motion; if it fails to do so, the remedy of delay or denial under this provision of the rule is unavailable to the defendant.

21. C. According to the Supreme Court's decision in *Mitchell v. Forsyth*, 472 U.S. 511 (1985), the denial of a motion to dismiss based on qualified immunity is subject to immediate appeal (if the defendant wants to pursue it), because the point of

immunity would be undermined if the defendant were forced to stand trial at all and await the ability to appeal until the matter had concluded. This is different from the outcome in *Lauro Lines v. Chasser*, 490 U.S. 495 (1989), where the Court ruled that the denial of a motion to dismiss based on the existence of a forum selection clause was not subject to this sort of immediate appeal.

22. D. Since the motion to dismiss disposes of the action, the plaintiff may appeal the granting of the motion to dismiss. Such an order constitutes a final judgment for the purposes of appellate jurisdiction.

Summative Exam

1. B. Venue is proper because a substantial part of the acts in the lawsuit occurred in the district, but there is no subject matter jurisdiction over the claims against Brendan because Plaintiff and Brendan are not diverse. Brendan's lawful permanent residence status means he is treated like a New York citizen for the purposes of diversity. 28 U.S.C. §1332(a)(2).

2. D. Both motions should be denied. Lougle is not "at home" in the district for purposes of determining whether there is subject matter jurisdiction; that is a concept out of personal jurisdiction, not subject matter jurisdiction (i.e., it relates to the theory of general personal jurisdiction). Section 1332 states that a corporation for diversity purposes is a citizen of the state in which it is incorporated and where it has its principal place of business. Moreover, there is specific jurisdiction with respect to Plaintiff's action against Lougle in the Northern District of New York because the action that gave rise to the liability—the malfunctioning of the artificial intelligence—occurred in the State of New York.

3. C. Limo's counterclaim is unrelated to Paul's affirmative claims filed against Limo, and thus the only way for Limo to proceed with this FRCP 13(b) permissive counterclaim is if there is an independent basis for doing so. Here such an independent basis of jurisdiction exists because the claim arises under state law, there is diversity between the parties, and the amount-in-controversy requirement is met.

4. D. There are sufficient ties to the jurisdiction and the forum selection clause seals the deal.

5. A. *See* Rule 19. Answer "A" relates to the summary judgment standard and not FRCP 19. All of the other answers contain issues the court should take into account when determining whether to proceed without NOIC in the case.

6. C. Like in *Jones v. Bock*, 549 U.S. 199 (2007), and *Louisville & Nashville Railroad v. Mottley*, 211 U.S. 149 (1908), the plaintiff is under no obligation to "plead around" an anticipated affirmative defense.

7. D. The Texla IPO is a separate transaction from the Noodle IPO. There is no allegation that this type of activity is a pattern or practice. *See* FRCP 15(c).

8. B. The defendants are not from the same state, so 28 U.S.C. §1391(b)(1) is not an option, but subpart (b)(2) is because a substantial portion of the events—the accident and the failure to correctly fix the brakes—occurred in the Northern District.

9. D. There is a genuine dispute as to a material fact regarding whether Plaintiff was properly served. This has to be resolved at trial.

10. A. Plaintiff cannot interpose these new affirmative claims against a newly added non-diverse third-party defendant. Review 28 U.S.C. §1367(b).

11. D. FRCP 12(h)(1)(A) and (B) do not require that a Rule 12(b)(6) motion be interposed with a pre-answer motion to dismiss. The defense based on subject matter jurisdiction can be raised at any time. FRCP 12(h)(3).

12. D. Review *Winter v. NRDC*, 555 U.S. 7 (2008).

13. C. All answers except Answer "C" are inappropriate punishments for the court to issue if the non-moving party ultimately complies with the order. At the same time, the court can impose the costs of the moving party's having to make the motion to compel, even where the non-moving party ultimately complies after directed to do so.

14. A. Plaintiff has raised credible concerns about the accuracy of the Goober tracking system, which creates a genuine dispute as to a material fact and means Goober's motion for summary judgment must be denied.

15. C. Since the defendant's contacts with the state where the action was filed are not connected to the injury that formed the basis of the action, and his connections to that state are not systematic and continuous such that he is at home in that state, there are insufficient grounds for a court to exercise personal jurisdiction over that individual in the forum state in a manner that is consistent with the Due Process Clause of the U.S. Constitution.

16. A. The court here will enforce the choice-of-forum clause and transfer the case to the Northern District of Illinois. *See Atlantic Marine Construction*, 571 U.S. 49 (2013).

17. B. Here, the federal and state law claims arise under the same nucleus of operative facts, and thus there is supplemental jurisdiction over the state law claim pursuant to 28 U.S.C. §1367. The fact that the parties are not diverse is irrelevant if the basis for subject matter jurisdiction of the original claim is federal question jurisdiction.

18. C. *See* 28 U.S.C. §1446(a). If a case can be removed, it can only be removed to federal court where the case is pending. Here, the case was filed in New York. Defendant could conceivably remove the case to federal court in New York, but not Connecticut.

19. D. A claim for money damages cannot constitute irreparable harm. And if a party cannot make out all four elements of the preliminary injunction standard, such an injunction will not be issued.

20. B. *See* FRCP 14. Impleader is not to be used to excuse one's liability by claiming another party is at fault.

21. C. The contacts with the forum state are not related to the dispute; the chemicals used in Guatarica were not sold, marketed, or used in California. Taking into account MexiChem's contacts relative to its other contacts throughout the world, MexiChem would not be considered at home in the forum state (see *Bristol-Meyers* for the specific jurisdiction analysis and *Daimler* for the general jurisdiction analysis).

22. B. The key issues are whether the counterclaim is "logically related" to Plaintiff's original claim. This is actually a close question; courts could go either way. Both claims—Plaintiff's claim that the bank's disclosures in the mortgage transaction were faulty and the bank's claim that Plaintiff's own disclosures in that same transaction were also flawed—do arise out of the mortgage transaction. But it is entirely possible that a court might say the two allegedly faulty disclosures are completely independent of each other. Regardless, the counterclaim would appear properly within the federal court's diversity jurisdiction because Plaintiff and Defendant are diverse (using both Delta's state of incorporation and principal place of business) and Delta can meet the amount-in-controversy requirement. So, regardless of whether it is compulsory or permissive, there is an independent basis of jurisdiction over the case, and thus Answer "B" is the right answer.

23. B. Here we see the application of the bar contained in 28 U.S.C. §1367(b). In an action based on diversity jurisdiction, as this is, a plaintiff cannot interpose a new affirmative claim against a non-diverse third-party defendant.

24. D. The plausibility of the claim is tested at the motion to dismiss phase.

25. B. The request for documents related to similar incidents regarding the Nimbus 3000, even going back five years, is not inappropriate or overly burdensome. The request for the ATV materials is completely unrelated to the plaintiff's claims, and thus the court will grant a protective order regarding those items alone.

26. A. Although the individual defendants are considered "present" for the purposes of Delaware law, that does not create the type of contacts sufficient to provide the court with personal jurisdiction under either specific or general jurisdiction theories. Any contacts the individual defendants had with the dispute arose in New York, not Delaware.

27. A. While the defendant is subject to personal jurisdiction in Iowa generally and there is subject matter jurisdiction over the claims based on diversity, when it comes to venue, §1391(d) states that "[f]or purposes of venue under this chapter, in a State which has more than one judicial district and in which a defendant that is a corporation is subject to personal jurisdiction at the time an action is commenced, such corporation shall be deemed to reside in any district in that State within which its contacts would be sufficient to subject it to personal ju-

risdiction if that district were a separate State and, if there is no such district, the corporation shall be deemed to reside in the district within which it has the most significant contacts." 28 U.S.C. §1391(d). Here, the defendant only has contacts with the Northern District of Iowa and thus is deemed to reside, for venue purposes, in the Northern District of Iowa.

28. C. Based on the face of the well-pleaded complaint, the removal request will be successful. This is a case based on the plaintiff's federal claims contained in her complaint. Diversity and amount-in-controversy are irrelevant. Furthermore, the home-state status of the defendant is also irrelevant in a case arising under federal law.

29. C. *See Piper Aircraft v. Reyno*, 454 U.S. 235 (1981). The possibility of less-favorable remedies in the foreign forum is not sufficient grounds for dismissal on *forum non conveniens* grounds.

30. D. Although there may be concurrent federal and state jurisdiction over the action, if the defendant wishes the case to be heard in federal court, he can remove it because the basis for jurisdiction is 28 U.S.C. §1331, *not* diversity (§1332). In a §1331 case, the home state of the defendant is irrelevant.

31. B. The third-party defendant may assert related cross-claims (though they are not required to) but is not permitted to assert unrelated cross-claims, and the second claim is unrelated to the underlying claims at the center of the action. *See* FRCP 14(a)(2)(B) and 13(g).

32. A. Here, the bulk of Danco's services are now being provided in New York. It is fair to say that Danco is "at home" in the forum state due to its systematic and continuous connection to the forum state.

33. D. Neither the counterclaim nor that portion of the amended complaint that seeks to implead Tate Farm will be dismissed. The counterclaim can exceed the amount sought in the underlying claim (FRCP 13(c)) *and* Plaintiff appears to have provided adequate grounds to implead Tate Farm, which it can do (FRCP 14(b)). Although an argument could be made that the claim is permissive, Hessla would argue that the claims are connected, and rightly so. They both involve alleged negligence. Negligent protection of the vehicles would void the commission, which is at the heart of Plaintiff's own claim (because it is central to Defendant's defense to it), and the court would have to rule on that alleged negligence to determine both Plaintiff's affirmative claim and Defendant's defense. That negligence is also at the heart of Defendant's counterclaim. All of these claims are thus logically related. Regardless, however, even if the counterclaim is permissive, Hessla could interpose it because it has an independent basis of jurisdiction: diversity.

34. B. Review 28 U.S.C. §1331 and §1441. The case alleges violations of federal law. There are no "in-state" or "out-of-state" considerations with removal based on federal question.

35. C. A defendant seeking to remove a case to federal court can only remove it to the federal court that encompasses the state court where the case was filed. *See* 28 U.S.C. §1446(a). There are other mechanisms for seeking to transfer the case to another federal district after removal, but the removal itself can only occur directly to the local district.

36. D. Unlike in *Atlantic Marine Construction*, 571 U.S. 49 (2013), where the court enforced a choice-of-forum clause to identify a location where venue was appropriate (as explored in Chapter 1, *supra*), here the issue is simply a choice-of-law clause which, standing alone, is not grounds to warrant a transfer of venue.

37. B. Rule 4(e)(1) expressly authorizes a party to utilize state procedure in effectuating service. Here, the defendant was served in accordance with the applicable state statute authorizing service in the manner used by Plaintiff's counsel. There was no challenge to the constitutionality of the service. Even so, were it challenged on constitutional grounds, such a challenge would likely fail because service by certified mail to a known business address, when authorized by state law (and incorporated by the FRCP), would likely pass constitutional muster as "reasonably calculated" to apprise the party of the pendency of the action, pursuant to *Mullane v. Central Hanover Bank*, 339 U.S. 306 (1950).

38. D. *See* FRCP 4(k)(B). Coils-R-Us was served within 100 miles of the courthouse and was a party joined pursuant to FRCP 14.

39. C. The defendant's argument is not substantially justified. The court even calls it baseless. Having a subjective, good faith basis is not sufficient to overcome the obligation to pay costs.

40. A. This answer is not something the court should consider when determining the appropriate penalty for spoliation.

41. D. The material set forth in Answer "D" refers to the standard under Rule 11, not for the granting of a preliminary injunction.

42. C. While a court always has to determine whether it has subject matter jurisdiction over a particular case or controversy, that determination generally does not bear on the decision whether to dismiss an action based on *forum non conveniens* grounds.

43. A. The case can be removed to federal court because the basis of the removal is federal question. There is no "in-state-defendant" bar to removing the case in that instance. That bar only applies to cases in which the basis of federal jurisdiction is diversity. *See* 28 U.S.C. §1442(b)(2).

44. D. Just because a party is subject to joinder under Rule 14, as is the case here, does not mean it is a necessary party under Rule 19. Beijing is subject to personal jurisdiction, and the court would say that the burden is on Japan to use Rule 14, which it may do, to implead Beijing in this case if Japan wants Beijing to be a part of the action.

Index of Authorities

Constitutional Provisions

Statutes

Federal Rules of Civil Procedure (FRCP)

Index